G.I. G-MEN

Books by
STEPHEN HARDING

The Last Battle:
When U.S. and German Soldiers Joined Forces in the Waning Hours of World War II in Europe

Last to Die:
A Defeated Empire, a Forgotten Mission, and the Last American Killed in World War II

The Castaway's War:
One Man's Battle Against Imperial Japan

Dawn of Infamy:
A Sunken Ship, a Vanished Crew, and the Final Mystery of Pearl Harbor

Escape from Paris:
A True Story of Love and Resistance in Wartime France

G.I. G-Men:
The Untold Story of the FBI's Search for American Traitors, Collaborators, and Spies in World War II Europe

G.I. G-MEN

The Untold Story of the FBI's Search for American Traitors, Collaborators, and Spies in World War II Europe

Stephen Harding

CITADEL PRESS
Kensington Publishing Corp.
kensingtonbooks.com

CITADEL PRESS BOOKS are published by

Kensington Publishing Corp.
900 Third Avenue
New York, NY 10022

All Kensington titles, imprints, and distributed lines are available at special quantity discounts for bulk purchases for sales promotions, premiums, fund-raising, educational, or institutional use. Special book excerpts or customized printings can also be created to fit specific needs. For details, write or phone the office of the Kensington sales manager: Kensington Publishing Corp., 900 Third Avenue, New York, NY 10022, attn Sales Department; phone 1-800-221-2647.

CITADEL PRESS and the Citadel logo are Reg. U.S. Pat. & TM Off.

10 9 8 7 6 5 4 3 2 1

First Citadel hardcover printing: March 2026

Printed in the United States of America

ISBN: 978-0-8065-4413-7

ISBN: 978-0-8065-4415-1 (e-book)

The authorized representative in the EU for product safety and compliance
is eucomply OU, Parnu mnt 139b-14, Apt 123,
Tallinn, Berlin 11317; hello@eucompliancepartner.com

As always, for Mari

A nation can survive its fools, and even the ambitious. But it cannot survive treason from within. An enemy at the gates is less formidable, for he is known and carries his banner openly.

But the traitor moves amongst those within the gate freely, his sly whispers rustling through all the alleys, heard in the very halls of government itself.

—Marcus Tullius Cicero

Contents

Prologue

JUST BEFORE NOON ON SEPTEMBER 30, 1944, a twin-engine C-47 Skytrain cargo aircraft of the U.S. Army Air Forces' 27th Air Transport Group descended through an early fall rainstorm toward Le Bourget airport, nine miles northeast of Paris. The plane's two-hour flight from London's Hendon airdrome had been uneventful, save for two uncomfortably close bursts of antiaircraft fire loosed by jittery Allied gunners as the aircraft crossed the French coast near Dieppe.

The historic Le Bourget—where Charles Lindbergh received a tumultuous welcome on the conclusion of his transatlantic flight seventeen years earlier—had been heavily bombed by the Allies since falling under German control in 1940. Retaken by elements of the French 2nd Armored Division in late August 1944, the field was hurriedly put back into operation by U.S. Army engineers. Within days of its recapture Le Bourget had become a vital hub for the USAAF Air Transport Command European Division's cargo and passenger flights between Britain and newly liberated areas of France. Though still extensively damaged, the field's iconic art deco terminal was soon nearly as busy as it had been before the 1939 outbreak of war.

On this damp September day, the newly arrived C-47 taxied to the main ramp, a vast area of concrete already crammed with other aircraft taking on or disgorging people and materiel. Even before the transport's propellors stopped turning, crew members opened the seven-foot-wide two-section door that took up much of the Skytrain's left side aft of the wing, and ground personnel backed a six-wheeled 2.5-ton truck up to the opening. As troops began off-loading the aircraft's cargo—cases of rations, medical equipment, and boxes of blood plasma bound for forward field hospitals and aid stations—a dozen passengers began disembarking via a narrow metal ladder placed against the forward section of the open side door.

The new arrivals included a group of civilian reporters, who clambered into the covered rear cargo area of a Dodge quarter-ton weapons carrier for the ride to the terminal, and several senior officers. As the latter were being whisked off in two military sedans, the C-47's last two passengers descended the ladder. Both were wearing standard U.S. Army field uniforms, complete with web belts, puttees, and steel helmets. A sharp-eyed observer, however, would have noted several oddities about the men's attire. First, while the right collar of each man's shirt bore a major's gold oak leaf, their left collars were devoid of the standard insignia denoting their service branch affiliation. Moreover, the men's field jackets had no unit patch, and the duffel bags tossed down to them from the Skytrain lacked the usual stenciled name and serial number. Strangest of all, each man's web belt carried a decidedly nonmilitary holster—rather than the usual large brown leather version meant to accommodate the standard Army-issue M1911 .45-caliber automatic pistol, the men wore smaller "fast-draw" holsters bearing Smith & Wesson Model 10 .38-caliber revolvers.

Someone noting these odd details might initially have assumed the two men were rear-area staff officers unused to field duty, or perhaps academics hastily called into military service as part of the "Monuments Men"—the Allies' specialist organization then currently combing newly liberated areas of Europe for artworks and cultural items looted by the Nazis.[1] A closer look would have quickly dispelled either notion, however. Both men appeared to be in their late 20s, were obviously too physically fit to be desk-bound staff officers or bookish art experts, and both seemed to be carefully observing the activity on the busy arrivals ramp as though trying to fix in his mind the position of every aircraft, vehicle, and group of workers. So, an observer might have mused that perhaps the two men were military intelligence officers, or even members of the hush-hush Office of Strategic Services.

While the latter possibilities were close to the mark, the reality of the men's identities and their reason for traveling to newly liberated Paris would likely have surprised even the most observant and intuitive onlooker. For despite their apparel the two men—Frederick Ayer Jr. and Donald L. Daughters—were not soldiers. They were, in fact, special agents of the Federal Bureau of Investigation and had traveled to France on the express orders of the agency's legendary director, J. Edgar Hoover. Though monumental battles were still raging between Allied and German forces in Holland, Belgium, eastern France, northern Italy, and along Germany's western frontier, the two G-men had been dispatched to Europe to begin what Hoover believed to be an essential part of the "end phase" of the war in Europe.[2]

Ayer (pronounced "Air") and Daughters were to lead what Hoover referred to as the Army Liaison Unit, a group that would eventually comprise twenty-one special agents and support personnel drawn from throughout the Bureau. Given courtesy officer ranks and embedded with advancing American forces, the FBI men were each fluent in at least one European language, and most had either lived or traveled extensively on the Continent. As outlined to Ayer by Hoover himself, the ALU's mission was straightforward. The agents would work with U.S. and Allied military counterintelligence organizations and the newly reestablished civilian police forces of the liberated nations to locate and investigate American citizens who had spent the war in Axis-occupied Europe and were suspected of having collaborated with the Nazis or Italian Fascists. Should the agents' investigations substantiate the charges, the persons in question would be returned to the United States to stand trial for treason.

WHILE FRED AYER AND DON DAUGHTERS WERE CERTAIN the ALU's mission in Europe would not be as straightforward as Hoover apparently believed, on the day of their arrival at Le Bourget, neither agent had an inkling of just how challenging the task would turn out to be. Over the following months, their suspects would come to include the associates, relatives, and even lovers of senior U.S. political or military figures, including an erstwhile confidant of former president Theodore Roosevelt and a millionaire philanthropist's wife who'd spent the war literally sleeping with the enemy. Ayer and his men would find themselves under constant pressure to look the other way when it came to the possible wartime misdeeds of well-connected "persons of interest" lucky enough to have highly placed and influential friends.

Nor would interference in their investigations be the only challenge encountered by the G.I. G-men. Embedded with advancing Army units, the agents in Europe would be routinely exposed to hazards unknown to their gangster-fighting brethren in Chicago or New York—artillery bombardment, air attack, ambush, minefields, and possible capture by the enemy. And, finally, Ayer and his agents would find themselves attempting to do their jobs in the ever-changing and often dangerous shadowland of post-liberation Europe, a world inhabited by stay-behind agents of the nearly defeated Axis powers and the minions of a wartime ally that was quickly morphing into a postwar adversary—the Soviet Union.

Despite these myriad challenges, Ayer and his agents would work relentlessly to "get their man" (or woman)—the suspected American traitors seeking to avoid judgment for their acts; and the German spies, diplomats, and propagandists who recruited and "ran" the Yankee traitors. The ALU story would unfold across the landscapes of World War II on the Western Front—from Sicily and mainland Italy, to Normandy, to liberated Paris, to crumbling but still defiant and immensely dangerous Nazi Germany.

The story of the G.I. G-men is a tale of war and crime, treason and retribution. It is also a timely illustration of fascism's continuing allure—and the lengths to which some of our fellow citizens have always been willing to go to aid in the subversion of American democracy.

CHAPTER 1

Hoover Casts a Net

On a swelteringly hot and humid August afternoon in 1943, J. Edgar Hoover sat in the back of a black Chrysler Crown Imperial limousine as it drove from his Justice Department office at 950 Pennsylvania Avenue toward the White House. The fabled director of the Federal Bureau of Investigation had an appointment to see President Franklin Delano Roosevelt on a subject very close to Hoover's heart. With the war in Europe apparently turning increasingly in the Allies' favor, he wanted Roosevelt to give the Bureau permission to begin planning a campaign to be conducted in the nations soon to be liberated from Axis occupation and, in time, in defeated Italy and Germany as well. The effort, which Hoover intended to be undertaken by a group he referred to as the Army Liaison Unit, would send FBI agents after U.S. citizens who had remained in Axis-held territory and committed treason by willingly collaborating with Fascist Italy and Nazi Germany.

After being ushered into the Oval Office, the FBI director had hardly begun his presentation when Roosevelt stopped him with a peremptory wave of his ivory cigarette holder. The search for American traitors in the newly liberated countries of Europe, the president said, was rightly the prerogative of the U.S. military—specifically the intelligence units of the Army and the Office of Strategic Services (OSS). Chagrined as Hoover was by Roosevelt's abrupt announcement, it was the president's apparent belief that the vaunted FBI could be outdone by soldiers trained in tactical battlefield intelligence that particularly irritated the FBI director. Even more galling was Roosevelt's reference to an organization Hoover believed to comprise amateurs and dilettantes—and which he thought likely to be heavily penetrated by Communists—the OSS.

Hoover's antipathy toward the organization whose initials some Washington insiders archly suggested should more accurately stand for "Oh So Social"—because many of its members were Ivy League graduates or scions of upper-crust families—dated to Roosevelt's July 1941 establishment of the Office of the Coordinator of Information (COI). Headed by World War I Medal of Honor recipient and Roosevelt friend William J. Donovan, COI was intended to become the nation's single, centralized agency overseeing intelligence gathering, overseas counterintelligence operations, and should the United States enter World War II, covert operations against the Axis powers. Hoover and his military counterparts in the Office of Naval Intelligence (ONI) and the Army's Military Intelligence Division (MID, but usually referred to as G-2) had seen COI as a direct threat to the power and importance of their respective agencies and vigorously opposed "Wild Bill" Donovan's efforts to get his new agency up and running.[1] That opposition only intensified following COI's reorganization in the summer of 1942, when as the renamed OSS, it effectively became America's primary intelligence and covert operations organization—with Donovan still at its head.

It was a deep personal dislike for Donovan and suspicions about the breadth and depth of OSS's announced operational responsibilities—which included counterintelligence activities both on and off the battlefield—that had initially prompted Hoover to seek Roosevelt's authorization to dispatch Bureau agents to Europe.[2] Now, sitting in the stifling Oval Office, attempting to change the president's mind, Hoover laid out what he considered to be the two best reasons why the FBI was the only choice to form and operate the Army Liaison Unit. First, no arm of the U.S. government had more experience in the investigation and apprehension of foreign spies and their American collaborators, and second, the Bureau already had a division that had been working overseas since before Pearl Harbor—a covert operation in Latin American and the Caribbean that the president himself had authorized.

FROM THE VERY START OF HIS TENURE as head of the Bureau of Investigation's General Intelligence Division in 1919, J. Edgar Hoover had been best known by the American public for his war against organized crime. His agents' seemingly relentless pursuit of gangsters and the wild shootouts in which those pursuits often culminated were frequently front-page news across the country. Yet behind the scenes, Hoover doggedly—some would say obsessively—concentrated the agency's domestic counterintelligence operations on rooting out foreign radicals (almost exclusively Communists) and their American "fellow travelers."[3] That arguably myopic focus had continued following Hoover's 1924 appointment as the Bureau of

Investigation's acting head, though by the time the agency was renamed the FBI in 1935, its director's preoccupation with Communists had necessarily widened to include the growing domestic threat presented by the American adherents of another foreign totalitarian ideology—Nazism.

Following Adolf Hitler's 1933 appointment as Germany's chancellor, his government had launched a concerted campaign to gain followers both in neighboring European nations and in the United States, the primary objective being to undermine any political or military opposition to the Third Reich's expansionist plans. That effort had enjoyed considerable success among members of America's German and Austrian immigrant communities, as well as with homegrown anti-Semites, white supremacists, and reactionary opponents of Roosevelt's New Deal policies. Dozens of pro-Nazi organizations had sprung up across the country—often making common cause with the pro-Fascist groups that had prospered following Benito Mussolini's rise to power in Italy—and by February 1939, the German-American Bund was able to draw 22,000 people to an openly Nazi gathering at New York City's Madison Square Garden.[4] In a preview of what would in our own times become known as "extreme right-wing talk radio," before America's entry into World War II, the Detroit-based Roman Catholic priest and anti-Semitic populist Father Charles Coughlin's pro-Fascist, anti-Roosevelt rhetoric reached some 30 million U.S. listeners a week. Nor was sympathy for Hitler limited to private organizations and individuals; Nazi propagandists had even cultivated sympathizers within the halls of the United States Congress.[5]

While the seeds of pro-Nazi sentiment had certainly been sown in America by agents sent from Germany itself, the vast majority of the antidemocratic work planned and carried out by the Bund and similar organizations in New York, Chicago, Los Angeles, and scores of smaller cities across the country was undertaken by native-born or naturalized American citizens. As early as August 1936, Roosevelt—alarmed by what appeared to be increasingly widespread public support for Hitler's antidemocratic, anti-Semitic, and racist ideology—confidentially ordered Hoover to begin quietly investigating Communism and Fascism, which the president considered to be the two greatest threats to both world peace and domestic tranquility.[6] Hoover had, of course, already been relentlessly delving into the work of American Communists and their Russian masters for some two decades. He was therefore able to quickly turn the same investigative techniques against Nazi intelligence and influence agents working in the United States, and against the American citizens and organizations that worked to advance the beliefs and goals of German and

Italian fascism here at home. Over the next few years, the FBI was spectacularly successful on both fronts: By mid-1942, the Bureau had rolled up every significant German spy ring in the country and—aided by the intense surge of patriotism that followed Japan's December 7, 1941, attack on Pearl Harbor and America's subsequent entry into World War II—had penetrated and neutralized the homegrown pro-Fascist movement.[7]

Hoover had always loathed the idea of U.S. citizens "betting against America," and his experiences battling subversion by both Communists and Fascists before and after Pearl Harbor only strengthened his hatred for seditionists (citizens who conspire to fight against or overthrow the legitimate government by force during peacetime) and traitors (citizens who "give aid and comfort" to an enemy power during wartime). The FBI had effectively suppressed the various domestic pro-Axis conspiracies and organizations relatively soon after America's entry into the war and was continuing its hunt for traitors within the Continental United States.

But Hoover wasn't satisfied. As he explained to Roosevelt at the White House that hot August day in 1943, America's postwar healing, recovery, and indeed, its national security, would depend on the apprehension, trial, and conviction of the men and women who had sold out their nation by spending the war in occupied Europe and willingly, even enthusiastically, doing the Axis's bidding. And, Hoover added, the best organization for that important task was the same one that, almost exactly three years earlier, Roosevelt had authorized to work covertly in Central and South America—the FBI's Special Intelligence Service, or SIS.

THAT THE SIS EXISTED AT ALL within the larger FBI resulted from the fact that when war broke out in Europe in September 1939, the United States did not have a single, centralized intelligence service. Most foreign intelligence gathering at that time was done by the Navy's ONI and the Army's G-2, and to a lesser extent by the State Department. ONI focused its efforts on Asia and the Pacific, G-2 concentrated on Central and South America and Western Europe, and State handled diplomatic security. While each organization also undertook counterintelligence operations to a certain extent, none were manned or resourced to the level necessary to thwart the very real threat of German, Italian, and Japanese subversion and espionage activities in the Western Hemisphere outside the Continental United States.

The Roosevelt administration's concerns about Axis clandestine operations south of the U.S. border with Mexico had increased dramatically following Germany's May 10, 1940, invasion of France, Belgium, the Netherlands, and Luxembourg.[8] The possibility that the newly conquered nations' embassies, consulates, and business concerns in Latin America and the Caribbean would now become hotbeds of Nazi intrigue so concerned Hoover that just days after the German onslaught, he approached Assistant Secretary of State for Latin American Affairs Adolf A. Berle Jr.—a longtime friend and adviser of Roosevelt's and chairman of the State Department's Interdepartmental Committee on Intelligence and Security—with a proposal the veteran diplomat considered both innovative and, in terms of interagency relations, potentially incendiary.[9]

The crux of FBI director's proposal, and the element Berle feared would meet immediate and vociferous opposition from the heads of ONI and G-2, was that the organization Hoover proposed to call the Special Intelligence Service would in effect be the United States' first civilian agency dealing with foreign intelligence.[10] The assistant secretary of state for Latin American Affairs understood that the Navy and Army would both see the SIS's creation as a direct threat not only to their own overseas intelligence operations but also to their congressional funding streams. And Berle was correct—both ONI director Rear Admiral Walter S. Anderson and G-2 head Brigadier General Sherman Miles were initially incensed when told of Hoover's proposal. Their outrage cooled, however, when Berle informed them that Roosevelt was in favor of the FBI taking the lead south of the border.

Over the course of two Interdepartmental Intelligence conferences, held on May 31 and June 3, Hoover, Anderson, and Miles hashed out their differences and eventually reached a general agreement that the FBI would establish the SIS to gather secret information throughout Latin America and the Caribbean. Additional discussions followed, and in mid-June, Berle told Edward A. Tamm—Hoover's assistant director—that the president had verbally consented to the SIS's creation. That was followed on June 24 by a memorandum to Anderson, Miles, and Hoover in which Berle confirmed that Roosevelt had issued a binding presidential directive authorizing the establishment of the SIS and its responsibility for "foreign intelligence work in the Western Hemisphere on the request of the State Department."[11] The directive acknowledged that ONI would continue to focus on Asia and the Pacific, and that G-2 would concentrate on Western Europe and retain sole responsibility for Panama and its strategically vital canal. Those straightforward geographic delineations notwithstanding, the memorandum also included a statement that would ultimately prove vital to Hoover's argument for SIS operations in newly liberated Europe. Of the activities in Latin America, the directive said that they "should not supersede any existing work now being done and that the FBI might be called in by the State Department on special assignments outside the American Hemisphere under special circumstances."[12]

The presidential directive gave Hoover the green light for the establishment of the SIS, and knowing that there would inevitably be further interagency squabbling, he lost no time in getting the new FBI division up and running.[13] Hoover tapped Assistant Director Percy E. "Sam" Foxworth to head the new organization, with special agent in charge of the Richmond, Virginia, field division John E. Lawler as his deputy. The two men were tasked with getting at least forty special agents into the field in Latin America as soon as possible, with their primary mission being "the obtaining of data relating to the activities, identities, and the operations of individuals and corporations throughout the Western Hemisphere who were acting in a manner detrimental to the best interests of the United States in connection with the war then being waged in Europe or otherwise."[14] Because the State Department was exceedingly leery of having FBI personnel tasked with conducting intelligence-gathering operations working out of U.S. embassies and consulates, the deployed SIS agents were to operate entirely undercover, pretending to be representatives of American companies seeking foreign trade possibilities. Several of the nation's preeminent corporations secretly agreed to provide cover for the FBI men, so long as the agents' activities did not in any way embarrass their "host" companies or adversely affect the firms' businesses in the target countries.[15] As it happened, the first handful of men tapped for SIS work received precious little actual training pertaining to their "legends" (false background stories), primarily because the cover companies were loath to spend the necessary time or money to educate individuals who would not actually be making any sales.

To buttress the clandestine operations in Latin America, in August 1940, Foxworth received Hoover's approval to establish the fictitious Importers and Exporters Service Company in Room 4332 of the sixty-six-story RCA Building at 30 Rockefeller Plaza in New York City. The bogus company was supposedly engaged in providing information on import and export opportunities in Latin America to various clients (who were also fictitious). It quickly became apparent, however, that the creation of the phony business had consequences the FBI had not foreseen. Within days of its name first being listed on the directory in the RCA Building's cavernous ground-floor lobby, the Importers and Exporters Service Company began receiving a steady stream of salesmen, brokers, advertisers, and would-be entrepreneurs interested in doing actual business in Latin America. The few FBI employees who manned the office were there primarily to help agents establish their legends with the American corporations that had agreed to "sponsor" deployed SIS personnel and were of course unable to provide meaningful answers to the visitors' detailed questions. Moving the faux firm twelve floors down, to Room 3144, did nothing to stem the tide of walk-in business seekers, given that the RCA Building's unwitting maintenance staff helpfully added the company's new location to the lobby directory. Hoover and Foxworth ultimately determined that the Importers and Exporters Service Company was more of a "nuisance and detriment than an advantage" to SIS operations, and the fictitious firm was shut down in June 1941.[16]

Unfortunately for the fledgling SIS, the 30 Rockefeller Plaza office debacle was not an isolated incident. In his haste to dispatch the first agents to Latin America, Foxworth made decisions—some of them based on Hoover's direct guidance—that initially hindered the very work the deployed agents were meant to perform.

Among the most consequential of those decisions involved what would seem to have been two obvious and essential skills.

The first of these concerned the soon-to-be-deployed agent's understanding of just what sort of information he was expected to acquire and how he was to go about ferreting it out. As one of the first men tapped for SIS work later recalled, in the Bureau's haste to get him and his companions into the field as quickly as possible, they received no specific training in intelligence collection. Their predeparture instructions, the man said, "were not too specific. Pick up whatever you hear and let us know."[17]

Picking up useful information would, of course, depend to a large extent on the individual agent's knowledge of the country to which he would be assigned and the ability to fluently speak its language. An understanding of a target nation's history, culture, and politics and the ability to communicate with people at all levels of the country's society—from the man in the street to members of law enforcement and the military, to those in the highest echelons of business and government—has always been a necessary prerequisite for successful covert intelligence operations, especially by agents working alone. Yet, as the SIS's own official history dryly put it:

> The volume of intelligence information from each agent was in the beginning and for some time thereafter quite small and of little real value. The agents were, of course, more or less completely unfamiliar with the countries in which they were trying to operate and usually very deficient with regard to the use of the language thereof. The chance of worthwhile accomplishment in the way of local orientation and the establishment of worthwhile informants and sources of information naturally required considerable time. Meanwhile, of course, the agent, who is usually alone in the particular country to which he had been assigned, was possessed of a very poor pretext for clandestine operations and the widening of his circle of acquaintances.[18]

While the language situation eventually improved through the addition of mandatory instruction in Spanish and Brazilian Portuguese by native speakers, the first SIS agents sent south of the border were definitely hindered by their linguistic deficiencies.[19]

Another SIS policy that hampered the organization's initial operational effectiveness grew out of Hoover's belief that it would be neither possible nor feasible for men working undercover to be accompanied by their wives. This led to the recruitment of younger, unmarried men, who senior FBI officials also assumed would be better able to adapt to covert operations in foreign countries than would older agents accustomed to straightforward domestic field work. While the younger men might arguably have been more flexible in their approach to the uncertainties of clandestine work, they also often lacked the maturity, investigative experience, and technical savvy possessed by their older counterparts.

One decidedly nontechnical aspect of initial SIS operations in Latin America pertained to the way deployed agents communicated with headquarters. While the quickest way to receive instructions and pass back intelligence information they'd managed to collect would have been by secure radio, that method was denied to the agents because the State Department did not want the transmitters in its embassies or consulates used for the transmission of "intelligence data" (a somewhat disingenuous stance, given that State's own small diplomatic security service and U.S. military attachés routinely used embassy radios to pass exactly that type of information). Nor would the American corporations that provided cover for the SIS men allow their company radios to be used for the transmission of messages that might reveal the firms' cooperation with the FBI. The second-best way to swiftly transmit information, by international cable, was also denied to the SIS men. While the simple cipher developed for their use, known as the X Code, would have been adequate for the agents' purposes, most Latin American governments required that codes used over their communications facilities be registered and approved. Naturally, that was an unacceptable demand in that it would have exposed the X Code's existence and likely allowed it to be broken by foreign intelligence services.[20]

Given these restrictions regarding radio and cable traffic, the FBI opted for a distinctly low-tech method by which the SIS men in Latin America could pass on the information they'd gathered. The Bureau's Technical Laboratory developed various secret inks and a substitution cypher known as the XY code the agents could use when composing written reports. Before departing Washington for his foreign assignment, each man was assigned a specific post office box in New York City, to which he would mail his information. It was a far from satisfactory system, of course, in that it could take weeks for the agent's report to arrive in the United States. The postal systems in certain Central and South American nations were notoriously inefficient and, if that were not bad enough, international mail throughout Latin America was routinely delayed because letters were intercepted and read by a host of foreign intelligence services, including those of both Germany and Great Britain.[21]

Despite its initial teething problems, the SIS continued to slowly expand its operations. The first seven agents had been sent out in September 1940 to Peru, Uruguay, Brazil, Argentina, Venezuela, Cuba, and Mexico. On January 1, 1941, there were fourteen Bureau employees either stationed or traveling in Latin America. By July 1, that number had increased to twenty-six, and the FBI was formulating plans to have no fewer than 250 agents active throughout Central and South America and the Caribbean by November 1942.[22] Following the Japanese attack on Pearl Harbor and America's subsequent entry into World War II, however, the Bureau quickly upped the desired number of SIS agents to 500, with that goal to be reached "as soon as possible."[23]

As the SIS geared up for wartime operations, the rapid increase in personnel was matched by significant improvements to the organization's training and operational techniques. Even before Pearl Harbor the perfunctory predeployment training provided to the initial agents had been replaced by a formal five-week period of instruction that included regular lectures covering a range of topics. These included:

> The purpose and organization of the SIS division, the method of obtaining passports and visas, the problems of working undercover, living conditions in Latin America, the types of information desired and how to obtain it, the make up of the minority groups in Latin America . . . the handling of confidential informants, how to recognize a radio transmitter, how to recognize codes and letters that had been tampered with, the mistakes made by German agents in the region which caused their arrest and conviction, the method of reviewing Bureau files on SIS matters, and the manner of writing reports while on SIS assignment. In addition, there was given a discussion concerning the submission of expense vouchers and the problems relating to transportation between the United States and Latin America.[24]

The adoption of a formalized, country-specific training syllabus for SIS agents was complimented by significantly improved foreign-language instruction. In May 1941, a special agent fluent in Spanish began teaching nightly two-hour classes five days a week at the Washington, D.C., field office. The elementary class lasted the same five weeks as the daytime country-specific training, with advanced instruction taking place from the end of the first course until the time of the agent's actual deployment. Since fewer agents were required to know Brazilian Portuguese, instruction in that language was first conducted at the Berlitz language school in Washington before being taken over by an FBI agent who was a fluent speaker. The number of weeks allocated to both Spanish and Portuguese continued to evolve throughout the duration of the SIS program.[25]

With country-specific training and language instruction completed, each SIS agent underwent a final period of preparation before being deployed. First, the individual met with the SIS program supervisor for the country to which the agent was being assigned. This was followed by a brief stay in New York, during which time the SIS special agent in charge briefed the man on the cover company for which he would supposedly be working. The agent would then usually spend a week or two in the city where that company was located, being trained by the firm in the basics of its specific industry and details of its overseas operations.[26]

The incremental improvements in SIS training and language instruction were matched by technological enhancements. Since requiring agents to send back their reports via less-than-secure international mail had proven so woefully inadequate a way to gather timely, actionable intelligence, the FBI eventually opted to construct its own overseas radio infrastructure: By the end of 1942, the Bureau had established stations in Bogotá, ; Santiago; Quito; Rio de Janeiro; Havana; Lima; and Montevideo, with an additional six stations added over the following year.[27]

As the SIS program expanded and more agents were dispatched, it became all too obvious to Hoover and Frank Holloman (who had become SIS director in the summer of 1941) that there needed to be a lead agent in each nation in which SIS was at work. This individual, as Hoover and Holloman saw it, would essentially perform the same role as the special agents in charge of the Bureau's domestic field offices: providing supervisory oversight for the agents working in a particular country and ensuring that higher-level leaders (in this case, consuls general and ambassadors) were kept informed of useful intelligence the field agents had gathered. The Bureau's initial overtures to the State Department were rejected out of hand, but with the timely assistance of Assistant Secretary of State Berle, by November 1942, resident Bureau representatives were stationed in several consulates general and all U.S. embassies in Latin America, except those in Honduras and Panama. The FBI agents worked under diplomatic cover and enjoyed diplomatic immunity, and, with the State Department's grudging agreement, bore the official title of "legal attaché"—except in Mexico and Haiti, where they were called "civil attachés" in deference to the continued opposition of U.S. diplomats in those countries to the presence of FBI personnel. In order not to further ruffle the feathers of ONI and G-2, Hoover directed that the "legats," as they were known in Bureau parlance, should maintain close contact with the Army and Navy military attachés in each country. In order to ensure equally effective communications with Washington, the legats were provided with a cypher that was far more secure than the previous code.[28]

By the time of Hoover's August 1943 meeting with Roosevelt, the rapid personnel expansion and myriad operational improvements the SIS had undergone just before and following America's entry into World War II had transformed the organization. From being a small group of young and relatively inexperienced agents plucked from domestic law-enforcement roles and thrown almost arbitrarily into foreign intelligence work—in most cases without sufficient language skills, local knowledge, or sufficient Bureau support—the SIS had morphed into a highly competent agency of some 580 people spread across seventeen Latin American nations. In less than four years, its agents had managed to neutralize nearly every Axis intelligence organization operating south of the U.S. border, in the process, identifying spies, saboteurs, and smugglers; locating and shutting down clandestine radio stations; and helping the host countries improve their own counterintelligence and law-enforcement agencies.[29]

WHILE HOOVER TOOK PAINS TO EXPLAIN the SIS's capabilities and successes to Roosevelt during the Oval Office meeting regarding the proposed Army Liaison Unit, the director further buttressed his position by pointing out that several FBI agents had already been at work in the Old World.

The first of these, Hoover told the president, were four Bureau men who had been "loaned" to the State Department in 1940, before the creation of SIS, to undertake special courier work in Spain, Portugal, the Balkans, Central Europe, and Russia. Traveling unarmed but carrying diplomatic passports, these men—who included Zurich-based, French-speaking Special Agent Horton R. Telford, a future legat at the U.S. embassy in liberated Paris—carried highly classified documents among American embassies while dodging such local unpleasantries as the German blitz against England and the Greco-Italian War. These special courier assignments continued until late 1941 when the agents returned to the United States and were absorbed into the SIS program.[30]

SIS sent its first agent to Europe in mid-October of 1942, Hoover said, dispatching the man to Moscow in response to a special request by U.S. Army Chief of Staff General George C. Marshall. The Soviet Union had begun receiving American military aid on a "cash and carry" basis soon after German troops invaded on June 22, 1941, and five months later, Moscow was declared eligible for full participation in the no-cost Lend-Lease program. Billions of dollars' worth of military hardware—mainly armored vehicles, jeeps, trucks, and aircraft—as well as food and petroleum products immediately began pouring into the country. It quickly became apparent to many in Washington that some individuals in the notoriously corrupt Stalin regime were siphoning off significant amounts of the noncombat aid to be sold for personal profit. Since the U.S. Army was in large part responsible for operating the program under War Department auspices, Marshall had asked Hoover for an agent to assist the Army personnel who were conducting an investigation based out of the U.S. embassy. The Bureau agent had done so until his return to Washington in June 1943.[31]

Just three months following the dispatch of the man to Moscow, Hoover told Roosevelt, on January 2, 1943, three Bureau agents had been seconded to the State Department to investigate possible security breaches in the code rooms of the U.S. embassies in London, Madrid, and Stockholm. All three facilities handled highly classified material that if compromised, could severely damage the Allied war effort and adversely affect America's delicate relationships with neutral Sweden and fascist Spain.[32] Fears that the code rooms might be susceptible to penetration by a foreign intelligence service were well founded. In May 1940, Tyler Kent, a State Department cypher clerk who had been suspected of colluding with Soviet intelligence during his previous assignment at the U.S. embassy in Moscow, was arrested by Britain's MI5 counterintelligence service for stealing what was later determined to be more than one thousand classified documents from the London embassy's code room. Then U.S. ambassador to Britain Joseph P. Kennedy Sr. waived Kent's diplomatic immunity, which allowed the clerk to be tried by the British in secret for violations of the United Kingdom's Official Secrets Act. Convicted and sentenced to eleven years in prison, Kent was exactly the sort of insider threat the three FBI agents were sent to Europe to help prevent.

The last example Hoover gave Roosevelt of FBI agents who had already been sent across the Atlantic had to do with an investigation requested by then Major General Dwight D. Eisenhower, the supreme commander of Allied forces in North Africa. In early January 1943, Eisenhower had asked for FBI assistance in investigating Charles Bedaux, a French-born American millionaire suspected of collaborating with the Nazis. Bedaux had stayed in Paris following France's 1940 capitulation, and he and his wife were known to have been on friendly terms with various German officials in both occupied France and Vichy. In late 1942, Bedaux and his adult son had traveled from Paris to Algeria on business, and soon after their arrival in Algiers, they were arrested by Free French police on suspicion of collaboration with the Germans. Because he was a naturalized American citizen, the elder Bedaux was handed over to representatives of the OSS's X-2 counterintelligence division. Eisenhower felt that Bedaux's interrogation would best be handled by the FBI, and Hoover dispatched former SIS director Percy Foxworth and Special Agent Harold Haberfeld to Algiers. Unfortunately, both men were among the thirty-three people killed when their U.S. Army Air Forces C-54 transport plane crashed in Dutch Guiana (modern Surinam) while en route to Natal, Brazil, the jumping-off point for the southern Atlantic crossing to Africa. The deaths of Foxworth and Haberfeld did not derail the FBI's investigation of Bedaux, Hoover assured Roosevelt, because two additional agents were quickly dispatched to handle the case.[33]

Hoover's exhaustive presentation to Roosevelt about why the SIS was the best organization to form the Army Liaison Unit was ultimately convincing, for the president subsequently authorized revisions to the original delineation agreements among the FBI, ONI, and G-2 that specified the geographical areas in which each agency would operate. The Army's initial reaction to the alteration of those agreements was understandably the most negative, given that Western Europe had been G-2's sole preserve since America's entry into the war. However, G-2 head Sherman Miles was ultimately convinced to give up his opposition when reminded that Roosevelt's original directive authorizing the SIS's creation had stated that the FBI "might be called in by the State Department on special assignments outside the American Hemisphere under special circumstances." Since Adolf Berle was in favor of the SIS operating in newly liberated Europe, Miles reluctantly agreed to the extension of SIS activities there. During further discussions, Miles and Hoover agreed that because the Continent was still an active war zone, the SIS agents sent there on investigative missions would do so under Army cover—they'd wear Army uniforms, hold courtesy officer ranks, carry weapons, and work as closely as possible with Army intelligence and counterintelligence units in theater. Indeed, it's widely assumed that Miles and Hoover jointly agreed that SIS men sent to Europe would operate under the Army Liaison Unit designation.

With the plan blessed by Roosevelt and the kinks between the FBI and G-2 ironed out, Hoover wasted no time in setting things in motion. But even as the search began for qualified agents—each of whom would have to already be fluent in at least one of the major European languages—the director turned to the one man who would prove vital to the project's successful implementation, Special Agent Arthur McCaslin Thurston, the FBI's man in London.

CHAPTER 2

Our Man in London

ON A DAMP AND DREARY EVENING in mid-November 1942, American diplomat Robert D. Coe stood on an arrivals platform at London's St Pancras Station, his heavy Scottish tweed overcoat pulled tightly around him to ward off the chill. The forty-year-old second secretary at the U.S. embassy had been informed just hours earlier of the imminent appearance in the British capital of an FBI special agent personally dispatched by J. Edgar Hoover. The man, one Arthur Thurston, had crossed the Atlantic by air aboard Pan American's *Yankee Clipper* flying boat—via the Azores, Lisbon, and Foynes, Ireland. He'd then flown aboard a smaller aircraft to Prestwick, Scotland, and was even then London-bound on a fast train from Glasgow.[1]

Coe had been tasked to welcome the agent because the diplomat's duties included, among other things, supervision of the embassy's physical security and liaison with Britain's law-enforcement and intelligence agencies. While he did not know the exact reason for Thurston's visit to London, Coe knew that in 1940, several FBI men had spent two months in Britain studying the operational techniques of both MI5 (the country's domestic security service) and MI6 (its foreign intelligence service).[2] Assuming that Thurston was likely on some sort of similar fact-finding mission, the diplomat intended to bundle the FBI agent into a waiting car and convey him to Claridge's. Less than 200 yards directly west of the American Embassy complex on Grosvenor Square, the iconic hotel on Mayfair's Brook Street often served as the temporary home of visiting U.S. officials.

Having never met Thurston, Coe had written the agent's name on a small placard and was holding it up in the direction of passengers disembarking from the newly arrived Glasgow train. If the diplomat had imagined Hoover's emissary to be the sort of G-man popularized in the gangster films that had poured from American movie studios throughout the 1930s—stocky, grizzled, and taciturn, wearing an ill-fitting suit and a crumpled fedora—he would have been more than a little surprised by the appearance of the man who walked up to him in response to the placard. At 6 feet, 3 inches, and 205 pounds, twenty-eight-year-old Art Thurston did not look anything like the stereotypical cinematic FBI agent. Well dressed, boyishly handsome, and possessed of any easy grin and outgoing manner, Thurston probably seemed more like an affable and particularly fit stockbroker than someone who pursued enemy spies or desperate outlaws.

Yet the FBI agent had indeed spent time in the crime-fighting trenches. Born in Colorado, Thurston had graduated from Indiana University in 1938 with a degree in business administration. He joined the FBI two years later, and after initial training, he was posted first to Charlotte, North Carolina, and then to San Francisco. There, he led the counterintelligence probe into the activities of Rudolf Huebner, the German consul general in the city, who was attempting to sexually seduce soldiers from the Presidio Army base and Fort Mason in order to obtain classified information for transmission to Berlin. Thurston's successful investigation—which led to Huebner's expulsion from the United States and the courts-martial of several G.I.s—won him a transfer to the Bureau's National Defense Division in Washington. There he worked closely with both ONI and G-2, in the process, establishing relationships with key officers he would later encounter in Europe. In January 1942, Thurston transferred to the SIS office in New York, where his primary task was to convince various U.S. corporations to provide business cover for SIS men being sent to Latin America and the Caribbean.

Hoover's order to send Thurston to London was certainly a nod to the relatively young agent's counterintelligence training and his experience dealing with military organizations, but a particular aspect of Thurston's personality also likely factored into Hoover's decision to ship him off to the British capital. During his four years in the Bureau, Thurston had gained a reputation as something of a diplomat: He got along well with everyone and could tell hard truths to senior leaders without incurring their displeasure or causing them to dig in their heels. That ability to get the job done without causing undue friction would be a key part of Thurston's assignment in London, since he was being sent there specifically because Hoover had lost all confidence and trust in Prime Minister Winston Churchill's handpicked intelligence representative in the United States.

By the early spring of 1940, Great Britain's military fortunes were at a low ebb. German U-boats were taking a mounting toll of British and Canadian shipping in the North Atlantic, causing increasing shortages of food, oil, and raw materials across the United Kingdom. Nor was the outlook any better on the Continent, for the relative stasis that had prevailed on the Western Front since the outbreak of war the previous September—a period London newspapers sarcastically referred to as the "Phony War" and "Sitzkrieg"—had ended abruptly with Germany's April 9 invasion of Denmark and Norway. A Franco-British attempt to reinforce the Norwegians beginning on April 14 quickly ran into stubborn German resistance, prompting London and Paris to begin withdrawing their forces by the end of the month. Then, on May 10, the precarious position of the Allied armies facing Germany grew infinitely more dangerous, when Hitler's troops, tanks, and aircraft swarmed into Belgium, the Netherlands, Luxembourg, and France.

As dark as that day was, however, it also witnessed an event that was to have a profound effect on both Britain's conduct of the war and America's ultimate participation in the conflict. On May 8, Britain's House of Commons launched a two-day debate on the debacle in Norway, with the often heated rhetoric in the chamber primarily targeting Prime Minister Neville Chamberlain. Widely considered in Britain to be the man who had appeased Hitler at Munich in 1938, the ailing Chamberlain was seen as incapable of effectively meeting the Nazi threat. When, at the end of the second day, the opposition Labour Party indicated it would not serve in a coalition government headed up by Chamberlain, the seventy-one-year-old Conservative Party stalwart had no choice but to resign on May 10. Into his shoes stepped the sixty-six-year-old First Lord of the Admiralty, Winston Leonard Spencer Churchill.

Few men of his generation were as well qualified to serve as Britain's wartime prime minister. A graduate of the famed Royal Military College at Sandhurst, Churchill had seen combat in several colonial conflicts and as an infantry battalion commander in the trenches of World War I. In addition to two stints as First Lord, he had held, as a member of Parliament, such key political appointments as secretary of state for war, minister of munitions, home secretary, and chancellor of the exchequer. Churchill had long been suspicious of Hitler and Nazism and, firmly convinced that Britain would ultimately have to fight for its survival, had throughout the mid and late 1930s gathered around himself a coterie of men both in and outside of politics who shared his beliefs. By the time he became prime minister in May 1940, he was more than prepared to put his long-considered plans into action. Key to the success of those plans was something Churchill confided to his adult son Randolph on the morning of May 18. As the younger man later recalled:

> I went up to my father's bedroom. He was standing in front of his basin and was shaving with his old fashioned Valet razor. He had a tough beard, and as usual he was hacking away.
>
> "Sit down, dear boy, and read the newspapers while I finish shaving." I did as told. After two or three minutes of hacking away, he half turned and said: "I think I see my way through." He resumed his shaving. I was astounded, and said: "Do you mean that we can avoid defeat? (which seemed credible) or beat the bastards? (which seemed incredible)."
>
> He flung his valet razor into the basin, swung around, and said:—"Of course I mean we can beat them."
>
> Me: "Well, I'm all for it, but I don't see how you can do it."
>
> By this time he had dried and sponged his face and turning round to me, said with great intensity:—"I shall drag the United States in."[3]

The elder Churchill's intent to bring the United States into the war on Britain's side was not as far-fetched a notion as it might have appeared in light of the isolationist and antiwar sentiments then prevalent in much of the United States. While still First Lord of the Admiralty, Churchill had in September 1939 begun a back-channel relationship with President Roosevelt (himself a former secretary of the navy), an exchange, carried out by letter and secure telegram, that quickly blossomed into a friendship based on shared beliefs. Key among those mutual convictions was the clear certainty that Nazi Germany posed as much of an existential threat to America's democracy as it did to Britain's. Roosevelt was already dealing with a surge in pro-German propaganda and the increasing popularity of neo-Nazi organizations such as the German-American Bund—the same groups the president had already tasked Hoover and the FBI with investigating. Despite his public pledges to keep the United States out of "foreign wars," Roosevelt was decidedly in favor of Britain's survival and was determined to do what he could to provide the beleaguered island nation with the tools and materiel it needed to stave off the German assault that both he and Churchill believed was inevitable.

Chamberlain's resignation allowed the formerly private correspondence between Roosevelt and newly elevated Prime Minister Churchill to become official, and over the next five years, some two thousand messages would pass between the men.[4] While these communications would cover a broad range of topics—some of which inevitably caused friction between the two leaders—in the first weeks following Churchill's move to 10 Downing Street, one of the primary subjects was Britain's increasing need for American-produced military equipment and supplies. The isolationist U.S. Congress had passed several neutrality acts in the mid-1930s that prohibited the export of war material to belligerent nations of any stripe, but the German and Soviet invasions of Poland in September 1939 prompted increasingly concerned lawmakers to pass revised legislation. Though the Neutrality Act of November 1939 still prohibited the use of U.S.-flagged merchant vessels to transport war materiel to foreign nations, it did allow the sale of American-produced weapons, munitions, armored vehicles, trucks, and combat aircraft on a "cash and carry" basis. Britain had been buying nonlethal materials from American producers for more than a year at that point, and therefore already had a well-organized system in place to purchase needed items and arrange their shipment to various American ports for loading aboard British vessels.

The flow of war materiel from America to Britain—and to a lesser extent, France—inevitably attracted the attention of German agents active on the East Coast. While acts of sabotage aimed at disrupting the supply chain were relatively rare, anti-British agitation among truckers and warehouse and dock workers in ports like Boston, New York, and Baltimore slowed the loading and dispatch of cargo vessels bound for the United Kingdom. More seriously, German agents and their American collaborators recorded the names, sizes, and departure dates of the ships carrying war materiel to Britain and transmitted the information to Germany, from where it was relayed to U-boats prowling the North Atlantic. Churchill and the members of his war cabinet understood that an uninterrupted flow of American war materiel was absolutely vital for Britain's survival, and they determined that the best way to secure the East Coast–based procurement and shipping activities would be to establish a British intelligence presence in the United States. The prime minister and his advisers also understood that to achieve its goals, any such intelligence operation would need both the permission and assistance of the U.S. government. The permission would have to come from the White House, but the assistance would be provided by the U.S. agency already tasked with counterespionage activities within the United States—Hoover's FBI. Fortunately, even before Churchill became prime minister, contact had already been made with the Bureau.

In early April 1940, the head of MI6, Colonel Stewart Menzies (widely referred to for security purposes as "C") dispatched a special envoy to Washington specifically to gauge Hoover's willingness to consider the establishment of close cooperation between the FBI and Britain's intelligence services.[5] The man Menzies chose for the sensitive mission was a wealthy forty-three-year-old London-based Canadian industrialist and entrepreneur named William Samuel Stephenson.[6] During World War I, he'd made a reputation for himself by downing between twelve and eighteen German aircraft while serving as a fighter pilot in Britain's Royal Flying Corps. Awarded both the Military Cross and Distinguished Flying Cross, Stephenson had gone back to Canada at the end of the conflict and attempted several business ventures related to radio and broadcasting. When those endeavors didn't succeed, in 1922, Stephenson returned to England, were he found greater commercial success. By the mid-1930s, he was a millionaire whose business interests included steel, concrete, electrical devices, real estate, motion pictures, and commercial aircraft, and his frequent business trips throughout Europe gave him a first-person view of the rise of Nazism.

Convinced that Hitler would eventually pose a direct threat to the United Kingdom and its dominions, Stephenson created an informal commercial intelligence network made up of business associates and friends scattered across the Continent. He used the information provided by his various "sources" both to benefit his own interests and, beginning in 1938, to supply MI6 with information he'd gleaned about German industrial production, especially in terms of aviation. Stephenson quickly established a close working relationship with Menzies while at the same time becoming a valued member of Churchill's unofficial cadre of part-time advisers. The Canadian had spent much time in the United States for both business and pleasure, was married to an American woman, and had a wide circle of friends in business, politics, and the U.S. military.[7] As a friend and coworker described him at the time, Stephenson

> was a small, slim, erect figure. . . . What you noticed when you first met [him] was a ruddy complexion, crisp grayish hair, a pair of most penetrating eyes, a soft speaking voice with hardly a trace of accent, and, as one observer accurately noted, a mouth that slipped easily into a wry grin. Although he could argue with conviction and even eloquence, as a rule he preferred the other chap to do the talking at an interview, a characteristic which prompted the American dramatist Robert Sherwood to describe him as "a quiet Canadian."

> Not that he was in the least unsociable. His capacity for absorbing dry martinis was astonishing, the more so as they never seemed to have the slightest effect upon him.[8]

Affable, outgoing, well connected on both sides of the Atlantic and, importantly, not officially part of His Majesty's government, Stephenson struck Menzies as the perfect man to reach out quietly to Hoover.

Given his instructions from Menzies to keep a low profile, Stephenson found a decidedly roundabout way to approach the FBI director. Before leaving England, the Canadian wrote to an old friend, the celebrated American heavyweight boxer Gene Tunney, whom he knew to be on good terms with Hoover.[9] Tunney later recalled that he received a confidential letter from Stephenson, asking him to try to set up a covert meeting for Stephenson with the FBI chief. The director responded to Tunney's subsequent query by saying he would make Stephenson his "first appointment." The Canadian and his wife, Mary, arrived in New York on April 15, 1940, aboard the United States Line's SS *Manhattan* and, true to his word, Hoover met with Stephenson at the Justice Department the following afternoon.[10] The meeting apparently went quite well, with the director telling his Canadian guest that the Bureau would welcome a close working relationship with MI6. There were significant caveats to that cooperation, however. Hoover pointed out that if the intelligence liaison were to be made public, it could be seen as a violation of American neutrality, and that the FBI would therefore only cooperate with MI6 if directed to do so by President Roosevelt. Moreover, the director said, any cooperation between the two agencies would be conducted strictly on a "close hold" basis between himself and Stephenson, with only a few key FBI leaders to be advised of the operation. Finally, Hoover said, the existence of the MI6–FBI liaison was to be kept secret from all other arms of the U.S. government, especially the State Department.[11]

More than pleased with Hoover's response to his overtures, Stephenson set out to win the American president's approval for the proposed intelligence cooperation. The Canadian's approach to Roosevelt was, of necessity, as circumspect as it had been with the FBI director. Stephenson reached out to another influential friend with Oval Office connections, this time a New York lawyer named Ernest L. Cuneo. A graduate of Columbia Law School—where he had studied under then Professor Adolf Berle—and former legal aid to New York Mayor Fiorello La Guardia, in 1936, Cuneo had been named associate legal counsel to the Democratic National Committee. This gave him frequent access to Roosevelt, and a few days after Stephenson's request, Cuneo used that entrée to ask the president whether he would approve the covert liaison with British intelligence. Roosevelt was wholeheartedly in favor of the bilateral relationship, Cuneo reported the same day to both Stephenson and Hoover, and in addition, FDR wanted "the closest possible marriage between the FBI and British intelligence."[12]

After hearing the president's positive response and getting Hoover's agreement to cooperate, Stephenson returned to London and reported to Menzies. The MI6 chief is said to have asked the Canadian to lead the liaison effort in New York as Britain's Passport Control Officer—a cover title often used when working abroad by officers of the Secret Intelligence Service (SIS; official name of MI6, not to be confused with the FBI's Special Intelligence Service). Stephenson was unsure about taking the position, however, until he was convinced by no less a person than Churchill himself.

On May 12, the Canadian-born Max Aitken, 1st Baron Beaverbrook and about to become minister of aircraft production, hosted a small dinner party at Stornoway House, his elegant eighteenth-century home overlooking London's Green Park. During an after-dinner discussion with Churchill, Stephenson repeated one of the conclusions he had shared with Menzies after returning from New York. Though any secret British intelligence organization based in the United States would, of necessity, be founded on the relationship with Hoover and the FBI, Stephenson said, the British effort should be far broader. It must encompass everything that could possibly be done to assure sufficient aid for Britain, to counter the enemy's subversive plans throughout the Western Hemisphere and eventually to bring the United States into the war—and "everything," Stephenson said, included counterespionage, political warfare, and special operations.[13] When the Canadian repeated his doubts about taking the New York position, Churchill reportedly led him over to a quiet corner and said,

> You know what you must do at once. We have discussed it most fully, and there is a complete fusion of minds between us. You are to be my personal representative in the United States. I will ensure that you have the full support of all the resources at my command. I know that you will have success, and the good Lord will guide your efforts as He will ours. This may be our last farewell. Au revoir and good luck![14]

Churchill's entreaty obviously convinced the wavering Stephenson, who agreed to return to America to undertake what he considered to be the next step in the creation of the U.S.–British intelligence liaison—a face-to-face meeting with President Roosevelt.

Stephenson flew to the United States within the week, and while waiting for his appointment at the White House to be arranged, he met with another American who was to prove vitally important to the U.S.–British intelligence liaison effort. That man was Roosevelt confidant "Wild Bill" Donovan, whom Stephenson had apparently known for some time.[15] Immediately upon landing in New York, the Canadian is said to have called Donovan, and the two apparently met within the hour.[16] The primary topic of conversation was Britain's urgent need for war materiel, specifically warships with which to better protect the vital Atlantic convoys, and Donovan—a firm supporter of Britain—quickly arranged for Stephenson to meet with Secretary of State Cordell Hull, Secretary of the Navy Frank Knox, and Secretary of War Henry Stimson. The ultimate result of those meetings was the arrangement by which the United States would transfer to Britain some fifty World War I–era destroyers in a way that would not violate American neutrality laws or inflame the nation's still strong isolationist movement. In return, the U.S. Navy and Army Air Corps (which in June 1941 would be renamed the Army Air Forces) would be granted access to British bases in Bermuda, Canada, the Caribbean, and the northeast coast of South America. Donovan's vocal support was crucial to the success of the deal, an indication of how much influence the lawyer had both in Congress and at the White House.

Stephenson's meeting with Roosevelt took place in the Oval Office within a week or so of his return to the United States. Also present was Philip Kerr, Lord Lothian, the British ambassador to the United States. Though already suffering from the kidney infection that would kill him in December 1940, Lothian strongly urged the president to support the transfer of destroyers to Britain, and lobbied equally hard for the formalization of the U.S.–U.K. intelligence liaison. The meeting was "warm and friendly," according to Stephenson, who cabled London that Roosevelt supported a close relationship between MI6 and the FBI—though he added that the president wanted that relationship to remain a secret, at least initially. After a few days of discussions with other American officials, Stephenson flew back to Britain so that he and Mary could prepare for their move to the United States.

The couple arrived in New York on June 21, 1940, aboard the Cunard-White Star liner *Britannic*. Stephenson immediately began organizing his new agency, which initially occupied offices on the twenty-fourth floor at 43 Exchange Place in lower Manhattan. The 5,800-square-foot premises consisted of fifteen private offices and an open central area for typists and file cabinets. This space was adequate for the twelve officers, twenty-one secretaries, and six filing clerks who comprised Stephenson's staff in the first weeks of operations, but the organization's rapid expansion quickly prompted a move to roomier—and far loftier—digs.[17] While subordinate sections were scattered across Manhattan, Stephenson's headquarters element was soon housed on the thirty-fifth, thirty-sixth, and ultimately, parts of the thirty-eighth floor of what was then known as the RCA Building at 30 Rockefeller Plaza. The Canadian's office was in room 3603, with his deputy, the Australian-born career MI6 officer Charles Howard "Dick" Ellis, in 3604. From far above the hustle and bustle of New York City's streets, Stephenson and his minions continued their work, their activities initially coordinated with Special Agent "Sam" Foxworth. As head of the FBI's SIS operations in New York, Foxworth used the alias "Sam Eldridge" in his dealings with the British. Hoover, for his part, gave himself the alias "Henry E. Jones" (based on the reversal of his initials) when passing information to MI6 chief Menzies.[18]

The speed with which Stephenson's organization grew came as something of a surprise to Hoover and the few others in the U.S. government who were aware of the existence of the "liaison group." Indeed, within days after Stephenson's January 14, 1941, return to New York from meetings in London, the FBI director told the Canadian his "covert" group had grown so large and its activities so widespread that to comply with American law, it had to be registered with the State Department as an official foreign agency. Hoover himself is said to have come up with the suitably generic name British Security Coordination (BSC), by which Stephenson's group was thereafter known.[19] In its State Department registration papers, BSC described its overt purpose this way:

> Consequent upon the large scale and vital interests of the British Government in connection with the purchase and shipment of munitions and war material from the United States, coupled with the presence in this country of a number of British official missions, a variety of security problems has been created, and these, affecting closely as they do the interests of the British Government, call for a very close and friendly collaboration between the authorities of the two countries. . . . With a view to coordinating the liaison between

> the various British missions and the United States authorities in all security matters arising from the present abnormal circumstances, an organization bearing the title British Security Co-ordination has been formed under the control of a Director of Security Co-ordination, assisted by a headquarters staff.[20]

This deliberately vague and decidedly disingenuous explanation of BSC's purpose gave no hint of just how extensive the organization's interests and activities were in the United States. As Stephenson himself stated in an October 1941 memo:

> Security Coordination is the counterpart in the United States and the Western Hemisphere of Imperial Security Services, London. As such, Security Coordination is wholly responsible for the protection in the United States of all British interests, including personnel and production.[21]

BSC's protection of "all British interests" in America certainly included such mundane but essential activities as advising on the physical security of the U.S. factories turning out weapons and materiel bound for Britain; overseeing the inland transportation of those items from the point of production to the East Coast ports; assisting local and federal law-enforcement agencies in protecting the ports themselves; and vetting the American citizens involved in each stage of the process. BSC's remit also included passing information to the FBI on a wide range of topics bearing on national security and counterespionage, and in 1941 alone, Stephenson's staff provided the Bureau with some one hundred thousand memoranda, reports, and other documents.[22]

Despite the apparent avalanche of information passed from BSC to the FBI, there was much that Stephenson *wasn't* telling his American colleagues. As part of Churchill's effort to "drag America" into the war, BSC was also conducting what today would be called a massive "information warfare" campaign intended to shift U.S. public opinion away from isolationism and toward a much more positive view of Britain and its fight against Nazism. That effort saw BSC using friendly American journalists to plant pro-British stories in newspapers, magazines, and on syndicated radio programs, while pro-German publications and organizations were targeted for "black" propaganda meant to discredit them and their views. Moreover, BSC's operations were not always passive: Stephenson's agents recruited Americans to provide classified information, carried out covert surveillance of suspected Axis operatives and their sympathizers, forged documents, burgled the homes and offices of perceived enemies, and intercepted mail and bugged telephones.[23]

These violations of both the intent and the agreed upon rules of conduct of the U.S.–U.K intelligence liaison agreement—and in some cases, the actual breaking of U.S. laws—did not go unnoticed at the highest levels of the U.S. government. On the last day of March 1941, Adolf Berle wrote to Undersecretary of State Sumner Welles that while BSC was supposed to simply be "in charge of providing protection for British ships," Stephenson's organization was instead "rapidly evolving" into a "full size secret police and intelligence service." Berle added that BSC was not simply an extension of MI6, but collectively represented nine distinct secret organizations, including MI5, the Special Operations Executive, the Government Code and Cipher School, and the Ministry of Economic Warfare.[24] At a February 1942 meeting, attended by Hoover, Berle, and representatives of ONI and G-2, specifically to discuss concerns about BSC's activities, Attorney General Francis Biddle said that while some ninety people were registered with the State Department as employees of Stephenson's organization, the actual number of operatives was believed to exceed three hundred. Indeed, BSC's New York office was well on its way to becoming what former CIA Staff Historian Thomas F. Troy would later call the "largest clandestine foreign intelligence station" ever established in the United States.[25]

As if BSC's "off book" activities weren't concerning enough, Hoover was also increasingly convinced that Stephenson and his organization were not sharing anywhere near as much useful information with the FBI as the U.S.–U.K. liaison agreement required. On March 5, 1942, the FBI director raised his concerns during another BSC-related meeting called by Attorney General Biddle. Also present were Adolf Berle and Edward Wood, 1st Viscount Halifax, who had been named British ambassador to Washington following Lord Lothian's death in December 1940. As Berle later recorded in his diary, under direct questioning about BSC's activities, Halifax told the group that Stephenson never acted without FBI permission, and that BSC provided "all the information it gathered" to the Bureau. Hoover completely disagreed, saying that Stephenson sometimes reported his activities after the fact, and often not at all. Though the FBI chief said that he liked Stephenson personally, he added that he didn't think the Bureau and BSC could continue to have close relations, because Hoover was never sure Stephenson was telling him everything, and in some cases, he was sure the head of BSC was deliberately withholding vital information, especially material generated by MI5.[26]

Hoover's distrust of Stephenson was almost certainly exacerbated by the fact that the BSC chief was known to be in close and frequent touch with one of the FBI director's least favorite people—"Wild Bill" Donovan. Stephenson had held numerous meetings with Donovan since arriving in New York, and in several messages to Menzies at MI6, the Canadian had accurately portrayed the American lawyer as a true friend of Britain, a man who had the ear of Franklin Roosevelt, and one possessed of a calm and steady manner (as opposed to Hoover, whom Stephenson found to be "a mercurial partner").[27] When, in July 1940, the president tapped Donovan to undertake a secret trip to Britain to ascertain that nation's ability to survive the expected German cross-Channel invasion, Stephenson had urged Churchill to extend FDR's emissary the broadest possible cooperation. Whether as a result of the BSC chief's insistence or, more probably, because the prime minister knew very well how influential a man Donovan was in Washington, Churchill met with the presidential envoy himself and ensured that he spoke with virtually everyone of political or military importance in the British Isles, including King George VI and Queen Elizabeth. Donovan toured factories and military installations throughout England, consulted with the heads of the military services and key government ministers, and held extensive discussions with MI5 head David Petrie and Rear Admiral John Godfrey, the director of British naval intelligence.[28]

Hoover's irritation with Donovan's growing political stature and influence with Roosevelt had only increased when the lawyer made a second, more wide-ranging fact-finding trip for the president. In early December 1940, Donovan had departed for London, the first stop on a months-long tour of the Mediterranean theater of war that included visits to Portugal, Spain, Gibraltar, Malta, Egypt, Greece, Bulgaria, Yugoslavia, and Albania. The fact that Stephenson had done much to facilitate the journey and had personally accompanied Donovan as far as London, only solidified Hoover's distrust of the BSC chief. The FBI director likewise saw Roosevelt's July 1941 appointment of Donovan as head of the Office of the Coordinator of Information as a personal affront, since Stephenson was widely assumed to have been the architect of that agency's creation.[29] The June 13, 1942, metamorphosis of COI into the Office of Strategic Services—the blueprint for which was largely the work of Stephenson's BSC deputy, "Dick" Ellis—and Donovan's elevation to the directorship of the agency with the Army rank of brigadier general infuriated Hoover. The FBI director not only saw OSS as an interloper on FBI territory, he was convinced that Stephenson was deliberately withholding information from the Bureau and was instead passing it to Donovan. Hoover also believed that Stephenson was continuing to run covert agents within the United States, in violation of the intelligence liaison agreement and despite the BSC chief's repeated protestations that no such agents were at work.[30]

Hoover's suspicions about Stephenson were confirmed, ironically enough, by a senior British intelligence officer. Guy Liddell, the chief of MI5's B Branch (its counterespionage division), was in the United States for talks with FBI officials and Donovan the week before the formation of OSS was announced. After lunching with the soon-to-be OSS chief in Washington on June 5, Liddell described Donovan as "a very likable personality" who "is full of good ideas but bad at organization."[31] Back in New York the following day, Liddell had lunch with a BSC operative named Ingram Fraser, who said that he and a colleague named Pepper had been running covert agents in the U.S. before Pearl Harbor. After America's 1941 entry into the war, the agents had been "turned over" to Donovan, who, according to Ingram, had asked the BSC operatives to continue running the agents and simply hand over to COI any interesting information they might uncover. Liddell noted in his diary that the continued running of covert agents by the two BSC members was "certain to be found out before very long and the damage will be considerable, since Hoover hates Donovan's guts."[32] Ten days after his disquieting lunch with Fraser in New York, Liddell met with Hoover in the latter's Justice Department office. The British intelligence officer noted that while the FBI director was "obviously the prima donna type," he was nonetheless "very cordial" and had apparently not yet discovered that Donovan was essentially allowing BSC to run covert agents in the United States on OSS's behalf.[33]

Following his return to Britain, Liddell compiled a lengthy report covering his meetings with Hoover and his subordinates. When discussing the increasing friction between BSC and the FBI, Liddell wrote that while all the Bureau officials he'd spoken with "seemed to desire whole-hearted collaboration" with Britain's intelligence services, it had been made quite clear to him that the director and his senior lieutenants did not believe the British were living up to the liaison agreement and were, in fact, "holding back information which might readily be given" to the FBI. Liddell added that Wyndham Bruce, the Royal Canadian Mounted Police assistant commissioner serving as the RCMP's liaison officer at FBI headquarters, had offered the opinion that the Americans believed BSC was "cagey," and that Stephenson and his top subordinates did not trust the Bureau.

That lack of trust was mutual, and by early November 1942, Hoover had decided that he needed to completely circumvent Stephenson—and, for that matter, MI6 in general—and instead establish a direct relationship with MI5. It was a logical move, given that David Petrie's agency was in many ways the FBI's closest analog within the British government. Whether the FBI director was aware that there was increasing support within MI5 for just such a close relationship—support in large part generated by Guy Liddell—is unclear. However, in a November 15 diary entry, Liddell mentioned Hoover envoy Art Thurston by name and noted that he had been tapped to travel to London "for a visit," and four days later, the MI5 officer noted that the young FBI agent was "on his way" and upon arrival would establish himself as a "legal attaché" at the U.S. embassy.[34] How Liddell knew of Thurston's itinerary and mission is unclear, though it is logical to assume that he was told by someone in the FBI, quite possibly Bruce, the well-informed RCMP liaison officer.

Liddell's source—whoever it was—was remarkably accurate. The MI5 counterintelligence chief was apparently aware of Thurston's progress across the Atlantic from the moment the FBI agent boarded *Yankee Clipper* at LaGuardia Field's Marine Air Terminal in New York.[35] It's also entirely likely that Liddell, whose job included keeping track of all foreign operatives arriving in Britain, whether friend or foe, was informed when the embassy car bearing Coe and Thurston left St Pancras station and headed toward Mayfair, less than two miles to the southwest.

Art Thurston's first minutes in London were disquieting, to say the least. On the drive from St Pancras Station to Claridge's, the young FBI agent got a quick but eye-opening introduction to the realities of wartime life in the British capital. The already inky early winter darkness was made all the more stygian by the nearly complete blackout that enveloped the city, with only the slitted headlights of the few vehicles on the roads providing dim pinpoints of illumination. In a letter to his parents Thurston later wrote that while New York City's dimout had been "dismal," it was nothing compared to the blackout in the British capital, which he described as "complete and just a little depressing at first."[36] Despite the darkness, the widespread damage caused by the Blitz—the German Luftwaffe's nearly nightly intense bombing of London and its environs that had ended more than a year earlier—was clearly visible. Bombed-out buildings dotted the roadsides, and the embassy car had to detour more than once to avoid unfilled craters in the streets. Barrage balloons, briefly illuminated by occasional shafts of moonlight, floated above the city to deter the German bombers that still made sporadic nuisance raids, and sandbagged antiaircraft guns and searchlight emplacements could be seen tucked into small parks and empty lots.

The following day dawned cold and clear, and shortly before 9 a.m., Thurston set out to walk the 250 yards from Claridge's to the U.S. Embassy at No. 1 Grosvenor Square. While the six-acre green space in Mayfair had long been associated with American diplomacy—in 1785, John Adams established the first U.S. mission to the British court in a residence on the northeast corner—the Embassy itself had been built in 1936–37 on a plot formerly occupied by a row of private homes on the north side of the square. The seven-story building's neo-Georgian façade allowed it to blend in with neighboring structures, and during construction, the interior walls connecting the new building to the two former homes directly adjacent had been removed to significantly increase the diplomatic mission's interior workspace.[37] Nor was the embassy the sole American presence on the square—a variety of U.S. military organizations had offices in buildings fronting the green space, with still others tucked away on nearby side streets. Arguably, the most important of the nondiplomatic American workplaces belonged to then Lieutenant General Dwight D. Eisenhower. "Ike" had been named single overall American commander in the European Theater of Operations, United States Army (ETOUSA) the previous June and established his headquarters at 18–20 Grosvenor Square, essentially next door to the Embassy. Operation Torch, the Allied invasion of North Africa, had begun less than two weeks before Thurston's arrival in London, and it must have seemed to the young agent that the entire square was alive with U.S. military personnel scurrying from building to building on vital errands.[38]

After presenting his FBI credentials to the Marine guards in the Embassy's entry hall, Thurston was met by Robert Coe and led up a wide staircase and down several long hallways. Somewhat to the agent's surprise, Coe passed the entrance to the ambassador's main office and continued into the wing of the building that contained living quarters for senior staff. Coe stopped at Apartment 30, rapped on the door, and then led Thurston into what looked much like a comfortable suite of rooms in an upper-class hotel. That genteel image was somewhat marred, however, by the battered wooden desks spotted around the main room and the several clerks banging away on typewriters or speaking urgently into a battery of telephones lined up along one wall.

As Thurston took in the scene, he was approached by a tall, slender, and very distinguished-looking man whom the agent immediately recognized as John G. Winant, the fifty-three-year-old U.S. ambassador to the United Kingdom. Seeing the somewhat surprised look on Thurston's face, Winant introduced himself and explained that after taking up his post in March 1941 during the last months of the Blitz, he'd decided it was safer and more efficient to live in the Embassy rather than commute from the U.S. ambassador's official residence at No. 14 Princes Gate, a mile to the southwest on the southern edge of Hyde Park. Winant used the apartment as both a living space and an informal office, and had equipped it with secure telephones with direct links to the embassy's basement code room, other key offices, and the various U.S. military agencies located nearby. He said he got more work done in the apartment than he did in the grander but far busier formal offices, though he added that he could be at his desk downstairs in less than three minutes.[39]

Small talk over, Winant told Thurston that his assignment to London had come as a surprise. As a matter of fact, the ambassador said, he hadn't learned of Thurston's impending arrival until just hours before the train from Glasgow pulled into St Pancras. The FBI agent apologized profusely, adding that the mission had surprised him as well. So rapid was his departure from Washington, Thurston said, that he'd had time to pack only one small suitcase and had arrived in Britain with basically just the clothes on his back.[40] The FBI agent then went on to explain at length the reasons for Hoover's loss of confidence and trust in BSC chief Stephenson, and the decision to establish direct contact between the Bureau and MI5 and, if Menzies was willing, with MI6 as well. Thurston's audience with Winant lasted some forty-five minutes, and when it ended, the ambassador assigned the FBI agent a desk in Coe's office and said that the second secretary would act as Thurston's supervisor, at least temporarily. In a sign of support for the young agent's mission, Winant told him that he was free to contact anyone he felt might be useful, with the only caveat being that Thurston should keep Coe—and, by extension, the ambassador—informed. After a brief walk down several hallways to Coe's workspace, Thurston chose an empty desk and smilingly announced the official opening of the FBI's first legal attaché office in the United Kingdom.[41]

The following days were something of a blur for the Bureau's new legat in London. With the help of the embassy's housing office Thurston was able to find a comfortable three-room flat on the second floor of a narrow four-story building at 17 Grosvenor Street, just a ten-minute walk from the office.[42] Not that the agent was destined to spend much time in his new digs; Coe had set up introductory meetings for Thurston with a variety of American military and diplomatic officials, as well as senior officers of London's Metropolitan Police.

Arguably, the FBI agent's most important conversation since arriving in London occurred on November 30, when he met with Guy Liddell at 58 St James's Street in Soho. Despite the huge To Let sign posted outside as camouflage, the building was very much occupied—by MI5's senior staff. After being cleared through security, Thurston was escorted to Liddell's third-floor office, where he met for the first time the man who had been indirectly responsible for his assignment to the British capital. Over the course of the next ninety minutes, the two men discussed a variety of topics, starting with the primary reason for Thurston's presence in London. As Liddell later noted, while the FBI agent's stated purpose was to "liaise with [MI5] . . . he said however that he would be pleased to visit [MI6] if they wanted to see him. If they did not, that would be just too bad." Liddell added that Thurston was "quite frank" in his views about BSC, saying that Hoover believed liaison with London through Stephenson's organization was unsatisfactory for several reasons. The first of these was that there was no proper flow of information; Thurston said that the FBI director thought data transmitted from London and intended for the Bureau was not being passed on by BSC. Second, Thurston said, Hoover was incensed by the fact that BSC was still running covert agents within the United States. Liddell made it clear that Director General Sir David Petrie intended to provide Thurston with all the information at MI5's disposal, and the young agent replied that Hoover was committed to responding in kind.[43]

The initial meeting between Thurston and Liddell was followed on December 3 by the FBI agent's introduction to the director general himself, again at St James's Street. Thurston bore a letter of introduction from Ambassador Winant, in which the diplomat stated that the agent's presence in London would "assist in maintaining the liaison that is being established between the Federal Bureau of Investigation and the Security Service." Winant added that both he and Hoover were "most anxious for Mr. Thurston to be in the closest possible contact with the Security Service for the exchange of information pertaining to counterespionage, counter-sabotage, and security intelligence work."[44] Liddell was present for the meeting and noted that Petrie "was impressed by Thurston and considers the letter a clear invitation for [MI5] to have direct representation in Washington. He proposes therefore to notify Stephenson accordingly."[45]

Petrie was obviously as anxious as Hoover that the new direct relationship between the FBI and MI5 be as close and successful as possible, for he offered Thurston access to MI5's extensive files and a small office of his own in which to examine them. To further emphasize his agency's desire for "complete openness" with the FBI, the day after meeting Thurston the MI5 director general invited the FBI agent to accompany him to the secret trial of a Belgian seaman accused of espionage being conducted at London's Central Criminal Court. As Liddell noted:

> Thurston was immensely impressed with the proceedings and much honoured by being allowed into a trial in camera. He was ever more delighted when the D.G. told him that he could not submit any report on the proceedings to Mr. Hoover until the sentence was made public. This has of course emphasized his feeling that we have taken him completely into our confidence.[46]

While Thurston's comment to Liddell that he would be "pleased to visit" MI6 may have been something of an exaggeration, the FBI agent did in fact journey to the agency's headquarters, late on the afternoon of December 7, in response to a telephone invitation from Stewart Menzies himself. The meeting took place at 54 Broadway, a shabby-looking building just south of St James's Park that, according to a sign near the main entrance, housed the Minimax Fire Extinguisher Company. After a few minutes of polite introductory chat, Menzies asked Thurston what Stephenson and BSC had done to earn the FBI director's enmity and distrust. The young agent calmly recited the litany of sins the Canadian was deemed by Hoover to have committed—the most serious being BSC's withholding of important information and its continued running of covert agents within the United States. When "C" asked whether better behavior on Stephenson's part might repair the rift between the FBI and BSC, Thurston responded that the Canadian had "damaged himself irreparably and would never enjoy the Bureau's confidence again." Having dropped that bomb, the agent then salvoed another: The FBI was aware that the cryptanalysts of Britain's Government Code and Cypher School at Bletchley Park in Buckinghamshire had broken the German Enigma codes and were reading message traffic—collectively referred to by the British as Ultra—generated both by the Abwehr (military intelligence) and the Wehrmacht (the combined German armed forces). Thurston made it abundantly clear to "C" that FBI–MI6 cooperation moving forward depended on the latter agency providing the Bureau with any decrypted Ultra traffic that pertained to Axis intelligence and subversion activities in the Western Hemisphere.[47]

The meeting with Thurston was an eye-opener for Menzies. Yet despite the agent's tough line on Stephenson, the MI6 chief still hoped to preserve some sort of liaison between BSC and the Bureau. To that end, on December 9, Menzies sent a telegram to Stephenson that read, in part:

> I require your categorical assurance that no member of Security Cooperation is at present engaged in any subterranean activities in USA either independently or under the cloak of OSS contrary to the terms of any promise given by you to any USA authority, or will be so engaged in future except with a specific approval of Hoover.[48]

In his long and rather disingenuous December 14, 1942, response to Menzies, Stephenson stated that "there is no fundamental friction between ourselves and FBI and I have received renewed assurance from the latter that they desire closest collaboration." Stephenson went on to reassure "C" that any misunderstandings that had arisen between BSC and the Bureau were due to "incidents involving personalities, departmental jealousies or intricacies of Washington politics in a transition period." The BSC director reported that it was the rivalry between the FBI and OSS that was the root cause for any problems that had arisen between himself and Hoover, and said that those problems essentially disappeared when Hoover accepted the fact that BSC and OSS had legitimate reasons to communicate with each other, despite Hoover's insistence that they should not. Stephenson added that BSC's activities were "defined under terms of [the] registration agreement . . . [with] the Department of Justice acting as agent for SIS of State Department, so that it is not for FBI to say with whom we shall deal." Nevertheless, the BSC chief rather petulantly acknowledged that his organization might "continue to be whipping boy from time to time when FBI come upon some unexplained incident in which we are not in the least involved."[49]

Stephenson's assurances that all was basically well between his organization and Hoover's were undercut during the course of a December 22 meeting attended by Thurston, Petrie, and Liddell. As the latter recorded, when the MI5 director general again pressed the agent on whether there was any way to salvage the relationship between BSC and the Bureau, Thurston "made it very clear that the FBI will not resume relations with Stephenson and in fact that liaison with anybody in New York is likely to be entirely meaningless."[50] The BSC chief's estimation of the situation vis-à-vis the FBI also came into question during a December 23 meeting of Britain's security executive, the committee charged with coordinating the country's counterespionage and countersubversion efforts.[51] Held at Kinnaird House in Central London and led by chairman Alfred Duff Cooper, Petrie, and other key intelligence and security officials the meeting discussed the BSC–FBI issue. As the minutes of the gathering record, if Stephenson's December 14 telegram was in fact an accurate and current representation of his organization's relationship with Hoover and the Bureau, then the situation was "as good as could be expected in present circumstances." But as several of those present noted, the BSC chief's point of view was "in direct conflict with reports which had been made to the Security Service by Mr. Thurston, the FBI representative in London."[52]

By the beginning of 1943, Art Thurston was firmly emplaced in London and receiving the full and enthusiastic cooperation of Petrie and MI5. Moreover, during the first week in January, Menzies of MI6 granted the FBI agent's earlier request for access to decrypted Ultra intercepts pertaining to German covert operations in the Western Hemisphere. Known to the FBI collectively as Ostrich, the intercepts provided a wealth of what is today referred to as "actionable intelligence"—information that allowed the Bureau to locate, surveil, and ultimately neutralize enemy agents both within the United States and, through the Special Intelligence Service, in Latin America. Mining the Ostrich material for useful information soon began to take up so much of Thurston's time that he cabled Hoover asking that an additional agent be sent to London to deal specifically with the increasing volume of decrypted German message traffic. In response to that request, thirty-five-year-old Special Agent John A. Cimperman arrived in London in March 1943.[53]

The first half of 1943 also saw further estrangement between the FBI and Stephenson's BSC. By the beginning of April, the rift had become so wide that many within the upper echelons of British intelligence believed the "liaison" between the two organizations was about to be officially terminated and by no less a figure than Stewart Menzies himself. Following an April 2 meeting with security executive chairman Duff Cooper, Liddell noted that "we are now awaiting C's decision as to Stephenson's ultimate fate." MI5's counterintelligence chief then added that

> in the present situation I did not see how [Stephenson] could continue as our representative, moreover anybody who represented [MI6 in the United States] in the present atmosphere would be regarded with some suspicion, firstly because he would be a member of an organization known to carry out offensive operations on foreign territory, and secondly because the suspicion would always remain that what he got from the F.B.I. he might well pass on to OSS, G2 or ONI.[54]

By midsummer, the BSC–FBI situation had deteriorated to the point that Liddell noted in his diary that Cyril Mills, an MI5 representative with access to Bureau headquarters in Washington, had told him

> that the FBI are undoubtedly out for Stephenson's blood. It is pretty clear that they have got all his telephones [bugged] if indeed BSC is not miked. They are also running a file. They told Mills that they are convinced that Stephenson was carrying out commercial espionage on behalf of the British government. Mills said that he thought this highly improbable. He did however think that Stephenson might be feathering his own nest in commercial circles with an eye to the post-war period.[55]

Whether Stephenson was actually attempting to ensure his own postwar economic prosperity had no real bearing on his relationship with Hoover and the Bureau, simply because in the director's eyes, the BSC–FBI liaison was already effectively over. Thurston had established firm links with MI5, and with MI6's grudging assistance, Jack Cimperman was forwarding extremely useful Ostrich information he'd gleaned through access to the Ultra intercepts. Though Stephenson would spend the remainder of the war attempting to rebuild his alliance with the Bureau—and would repeatedly misrepresent the nature and effectiveness of that connection both during the conflict and after—by the latter half of 1943, BSC's own manifold miscalculations and intentional dissimulations had put paid to what had begun as a promising and mutually beneficial liaison. Ernest Cuneo, who himself had helped bring about the initial contact between Stephenson and Hoover, provided perhaps the most succinct summation of the transgressions that ultimately brought about BSC's fall when he noted:

> Given the time, the situation, and the mood, it is not surprising . . . that BSC also went beyond the legal, the ethical, and the proper. Throughout the neutral Americas, and especially in the U.S., it ran espionage agents, tampered with the mails, tapped telephones, smuggled propaganda into the country, disrupted public gatherings, covertly subsidized newspapers, radios [sic], and organizations, perpetrated forgeries . . . violated the aliens registration act, shanghaied sailors numerous times, and possibly murdered one or more persons in this country.[56]

The effective termination of cooperation between BSC and the FBI had several positive effects, not the least of which was a further strengthening of Thurston's relationship with Petrie and MI5. That association would continue to prove extremely valuable to the Bureau in a variety of ways, particularly so in the furtherance of Hoover's plan to dispatch agents to newly liberated Europe to search out American citizens suspected of treason. MI5's cooperation would be key to the success of the Army Liaison Unit, and Thurston's presence in London would prove vital to gaining and maintaining Petrie's support. The young FBI agent was literally the right man in the right place at the right time.

That the FBI would rely heavily on MI5 in organizing the Army Liaison Unit was completely understandable. Britain's domestic security agency already had several years of experience in identifying, locating, and investigating those individuals who may have betrayed king and country through willing collaboration with the Axis.

Before the September 1939 outbreak of World War II, many Britons had fervently believed in and ardently worked to advance the political goals of Fascist Italy and Nazi Germany. Even after hostilities commenced, many of those who had either given or sold their souls to Rome or Berlin continued to serve the Axis—some as spies within the United Kingdom and the wider empire, some by actually joining the enemy's armed forces, and many more through their work as propagandists in print and on enemy-controlled radio stations. During the early years of the war, MI5 had of necessity focused its attention on neutralizing enemy agents operating on British territory either by apprehension or, preferably, by "turning" them through the XX [Double Cross] System and using them against their former masters.[57]

By early 1943, however, the Allied invasion of Europe was no longer a matter of if but when, and the ways in which MI5 was preparing to conduct treason investigations in newly liberated areas in conjunction with British military forces was of immense interest to the FBI. The Bureau had vast experience in pursuing spies and traitors at home, and some in conducting intelligence-gathering and counterespionage activities in Latin America, but virtually none in carrying out investigations in still-contested conflict zones or recently liberated areas. Indeed, the only such investigation the agency had thus far undertaken—the dispatch of assistant FBI director and former SIS head Sam Foxworth and Special Agent Harold Haberfeld to Algiers in January 1943 to interrogate suspected collaborator Charles Bedaux—had resulted in the death of both agents before they even reached North Africa. The two Bureau men who replaced them reportedly received little assistance from the OSS X-2 detachment and did not conclude their investigation until mid-August.[58]

Hoover was able to discuss his planned Army Liaison Unit face-to-face with Art Thurston when the latter arrived in Washington during the third week of April 1943. Having left Cimperman in charge in London, the young agent had flown back to the United States for a series of extensive meetings with senior Bureau leaders regarding the situation in Britain, the value of the Ostrich intercepts, and the possible establishment of an American equivalent of MI5's XX System. During his nearly three months in Washington, Thurston was also fully briefed on the plan to dispatch agents to Europe, an effort that as a former SIS member himself, he wholeheartedly supported. When Thurston returned to London in mid-July, he met with Liddell, who ensured that the FBI agent would have full access to the MI5 sections planning the hunt for British traitors in newly liberated Europe.

Even while learning the details of how MI5 planned to operate in the liberated zones, Thurston also had to gain the cooperation of the only organization that could support FBI agents in the European war zone—the United States Army. Though G-2 head Brigadier General Sherman Miles's reluctant agreement to the extension of SIS operations to Europe had allowed Hoover's plan to move forward at the executive level, for their actual day-to-day operations in the field, the deployed agents would have to rely on the Army for not only the most basic needs—food, shelter, transportation, and protection—but also for intelligence support.

Fortunately for Thurston, the military people with whom he needed to interact were literally just yards from the FBI agent's office in the U.S.

Embassy. The ETOUSA headquarters at 18–20 Grosvenor Square housed the senior staffs of all the Army Ground Forces organizations then active in the United Kingdom, and Thurston met regularly with many of them over the following months.[59] Among the most important meetings the FBI agent attended were those that involved ETOUSA's counterintelligence (CI) chief, Colonel H. Gordon Sheen. He and his two principal assistants, Major Kirby Gillette and Lieutenant Edward Saxe, would be the primary points of contact for deployed FBI agents during the hunt for suspected American traitors on the Continent. All three officers were well qualified for their vital job: Sheen was the former head of the Army's Counter Intelligence Corps; Gillette was a onetime FBI agent; and Saxe was a Harvard MBA graduate who, since joining the Army, had made an in-depth study of German radio propaganda operations. The men had recently returned to London from North Africa, where they had undertaken counterintelligence operations in support of Operation Torch in North Africa. Sheen assured Thurston that the ETOUSA CI team would do everything possible to assist the deployed FBI agents once they arrived in theater.

As it happened, despite all the work Art Thurston had done to help facilitate the creation of the Army Liaison Unit, he was destined not to meet any of its participants nor to be on hand in London when it began operations. During a January 26, 1944, visit with Guy Liddell, Thurston revealed that he was resigning from the FBI to get into the "shooting war" before it ended. His successor as legat, Thurston said, would be Joseph Lynch, who had previously been the FBI liaison officer in Ottawa with the RCMP, where Liddell had met him during a 1942 visit to the Canadian capital. While hugely disappointed that Thurston was leaving, the MI5 counterintelligence chief noted in his diary that during the earlier meeting Lynch had "made a very favorable impression," adding that "if we have to lose Art we probably could not do better."[60]

On January 29, Liddell hosted a farewell party for Thurston at the Savoy Hotel, and the following morning, the FBI agent set off for Foynes to catch the Pan Am clipper back to the United States. Thurston had been a Navy Reserve officer since his time with SIS in New York, and soon after returning to America, he volunteered for active duty. In what Hoover may have considered a slight, Lieutenant (Junior Grade) Art Thurston volunteered for duty with the OSS and served in China for the remainder of the war.

What the FBI's former man in London didn't know at the time of his departure from the British capital was that the Army Liaison Unit had begun operations some three months earlier. In late October 1943, a single FBI agent had been dispatched to North Africa to begin the hunt for a celebrated American accused of making treasonous radio broadcasts lauding Mussolini and Italian fascism. The agent's quarry was perhaps one of the most influential poets of the Modernist movement: the controversial Ezra Pound.

CHAPTER 3

A Pound of Flesh

LOCATED EAST OF THE TIBER RIVER, just outside the city boundaries of ancient Rome, the two-hundred-foot-tall Pincian Hill has for centuries been renowned for the sweeping views it offers of the Eternal City. Yet in the early morning hours of June 5, 1944, those panoramic vistas went unnoticed by U.S. Army Colonel George S. Smith and the members of his S Force, an organization comprising some twelve hundred troops representing more than twenty American, British, and Italian military intelligence and counterintelligence units. S Force had followed the lead Allied combat units into the open and undefended city late the previous evening, and by 3:20 a.m., Smith had established his field headquarters in tents pitched across one of the ornamental lawns that dotted the hill.

Created the previous January when it became apparent that Rome would be the first Axis capital to fall to Allied troops, S (Security) Force was part of Allied Forces Headquarters (AHFQ), G-2's Intelligence Objectives Subsection (IOSS). The S Force was tasked with two vital missions—to locate and secure potentially valuable German and Italian Fascist documents, records, and archives throughout the city, and to locate and apprehend enemy stay-behind agents and sympathizers. The key to success in both endeavors was speed, and within two hours of arriving atop the Pincian Hill, Smith had dispatched four columns of jeep- and truck-borne troops to predetermined targets across the sprawling capital.

Sitting on a bench seat in the back of one of the trucks was a uniformed, thirty-four-year-old man wearing the insignia of a U.S. Army captain, a .45-caliber Colt pistol in a holster on one hip, and a .30-caliber M1 carbine across his knees. Despite his appearance and the fact that he'd spent nearly a year embedded with various Army organizations in North Africa and southern Italy, he was not a soldier. He was the FBI agent tasked with tracking down Ezra Pound, and he was eager to get his man.

The chain of events that led to the agent's presence in Rome in the summer of 1944 had begun nearly five years earlier.

By the spring of 1939, the widely acknowledged dean of Anglo-American Modernist poetry, fifty-three-year-old Ezra Pound, had lived in Europe for three decades. After leaving the United States in 1908 at the age of twenty-three, the poet had initially settled in London, then moved on to Paris, and in 1924, to the Italian seaside town of Rapallo, fifteen miles southeast of Genoa. A virulent anti-Semite, Pound became an ardent and vocal supporter of Benito Mussolini and Italian fascism. The poet actually met *Il Duce* in person on January 30, 1933, and following Franklin Roosevelt's inauguration as America's thirty-seventh president just over a month later, Pound quickly evolved into a rabid and outspoken foe of the New Deal and all it represented.

Convinced that rising tensions in Europe between the democratic nations on one side and the fascist states on the other would likely lead to war, in April 1939, Pound sailed for America to "educate" Americans about the "folly" of allowing themselves to be drawn into a conflict with his beloved Italy. Deeply disappointed by the apathy with which his pleas were met, he returned to Italy and in mid-November 1940 approached Mussolini's Ministry of Popular Culture with his ideas on ways to counter what he termed "anti-Italian and anti-Fascist propaganda" in Europe, Asia, and the United States.[1] Pound's offer was met with both enthusiasm and caution, the former, because he was still a world-renowned literary celebrity, and the latter, because officials in Mussolini's intelligence service feared he might be an American plant. Suspicion of Pound's motives eased when the Italian embassy in Washington reported that during his visit to the United States, the poet had "displayed his friendly feelings for Fascism and granted courageous interviews."[2]

His fascist *bona fides* having been validated, Pound was given the green light to begin his radio broadcasts. The first took place on January 23, 1941, when the poet spoke in English on Radio Roma's "American Hour." In some two hundred programs over the following eleven months, Pound lauded Mussolini's accomplishments—such as reducing crime and improving Italy's road and railway networks—while also advocating that fascism was the only cure for social injustice, financial inequity, and the "dire threat" posed by "international Jewry." In return for his radio services and his written contributions to Italy's print propaganda outlets, including weekly articles in the newspaper

Meridiano di Roma, Pound received a monthly salary, as well as such perks as reduced train and bus fares.[3]

The poet's pro-fascist beliefs had caught the attention of the U.S. government even before he'd begun his radio programs, and in October 1941, the Federal Communications Commission's Foreign Broadcast Monitoring Service began occasional monitoring and recording of Pound's shortwave broadcasts.[4] That same month, J. Wesley Jones, a State Department official who had just returned to Washington from Rome, raised an additional red flag regarding Pound. In a memo to Ray Atherton, then acting chief of State's Division of European Affairs, Jones said that the poet was "still . . . broadcasting his views," and suggested that Pound's name should be added to "the list of pseudo-Americans" still living in Italy.[5]

The frequency of the FBMS's monitoring of Pound's broadcasts increased dramatically following Japan's attack on Pearl Harbor. On the afternoon of December 7, even as Americans were desperately trying to understand the magnitude and import of Japan's assault on the U.S. Pacific Fleet and Army and Navy airfields on Oahu, Pound was on the airwaves once again extolling the virtues of fascism. Because the program had been prerecorded, it included no mention of the disaster in Hawaii, making the poet's comments seem all the more insensitive to his American listeners. Yet Pound himself was horrified by news of the attack, so much so that he vowed to "stand with my country right or wrong" and insisted he would "never speak over the airwaves again." His resolve lasted a mere seven weeks following America's December 11, 1941, declaration of war against Italy, for he resumed his "American Hour" show on January 29, 1942. With the United States now a belligerent, Pound's broadcasts stopped being seen by senior American officials as merely the ill-advised ramblings of a famously eccentric expatriate and entered a far more serious realm—that of treason.

In a very real sense, it was the president of the United States himself who kicked the American government's investigation of Pound into high gear. On October 1, 1942, Franklin Roosevelt dashed off the following memo to Attorney General Francis Biddle:

> There are a number of Americans in Europe who are aiding Hitler et al on the radio. Why should we not proceed to indict them for treason even though we might not be able to try them until after the war? I understand Ezra Pound, [Robert H.] Best, [Jane] Anderson and a few others are broadcasting for Axis microphones. —F.D.R.[6]

Roosevelt's query prompted Assistant Attorney General Wendell Berge, head of the Justice Department's Criminal Division, to reach out to the FBI regarding the expatriate poet. On October 13, Berge sent a memo to Hoover asking that the Bureau "obtain, if possible, transcripts of [Pound's] broadcasts and transmit the same to this Division, together with any information you may have regarding this subject."[7]

Given that the FBI had been compiling a file on Pound since at least January 1941, Berge got a response to his memo just a day after Hoover received it. On October 14, the Bureau sent the assistant attorney general an eight-paragraph précis of the poet's life, work, and political leanings. The document stated that "in February, 1940, Pound began airing his alien views and contempt for the United States over the Rome radio," and added that a June 4, 1941, dispatch from the American consul general in Genoa "stated that Pound is known to have been very pro-Fascist for a number of years and to have spoken over the Italian radio system against the policies of the United States . . . it was stated that upon entering and leaving the Consular offices at Genoa, he was prone to give the Fascist salute."[8]

On November 20, the FBI provided Berge with three pages of excerpts of Pound's post–Pearl Harbor broadcasts, with the first entry dated July 2, 1942, and the last on July 26. That initial tranche of transcripts was followed on December 12 by another eighteen pages spanning January 29 through June 28, 1942. Just over a month after receiving the additional transcripts, Berge was ready to recommend a course of action. On January 15, 1943, he sent Attorney General Biddle a memo titled "Proposed Indictments for Treason of the Following American Citizens Broadcasting Enemy Propaganda from Axis Countries to the United States," citing Pound and six other individuals.[9] The memo noted that the seven "have for some time been broadcasting enemy propaganda to the United States from Berlin, Germany, and Rome, Italy," and added that if transcripts of their broadcasts and other information thus far gathered about the individuals led to the conclusion that "their activities are considered of sufficient importance to warrant action by this Department, they may be properly be deemed treason within the meaning of Title 18, U.S.C, Section 1." The seven-page document then went into detail on the exact legal meaning of the word *treason*, as well as giving several examples of how earlier treason cases had been handled in U.S. courts.[10]

The building wave of official U.S. government interest in determining whether Pound's broadcasts and writings reached the level of treason prompted Hoover to launch a nationwide, in-depth effort to investigate the poet. The director tasked FBI field offices in sixteen states and the District of Columbia to interview Pound's relatives, friends. and business associates regarding the poet's background, literary activities, and political beliefs.[11] Hoover realized, of course, that the most conclusive evidence of Pound's suspected treason could only be found in Italy, which by mid-August 1943 appeared to be the first Axis country likely to be liberated. Allied forces had completed the capture of Sicily on the 17th and were poised to use the island as a jumping-off point for the invasion of the Italian mainland. Having just gained President Roosevelt's authorization for agents of the FBI's SIS to operate in Europe, Hoover decided to make Pound the first treason suspect to be investigated in the combat theater.[12] The task would require the assigned agent to be embedded with U.S. Army units as they moved across the Strait of Messina and up the Italian peninsula, and the investigation would be a test case for Hoover's test case for the Army Liaison Unit. Given the stakes, the director would have to dispatch the best agent he could find. That man was an Italian American and former lawyer from Wyandotte, Michigan, named Frank Lawrence Amprim.[13]

THE FBI's INITIAL EXPERIENCES with SIS operations in Latin America had clearly shown that agents deployed abroad had to be able to read, write, and speak the language of the country in which they were working. Since teaching agents a foreign tongue from scratch proved to be a time-consuming and less-than-optimal approach to the issue, Hoover had decided early on that whenever possible, agents chosen for overseas assignments in non-English-speaking countries should be either native speakers of the local language or have gained fluency through family, education, or travel *before* joining the Bureau. Frank Amprim was chosen to be the man to investigate Ezra Pound at least in part because the agent was not just fluent in Italian, but also in the Piedmontese dialect common in the region where the poet was expected to be found.

Born in January 1910 in Donora, Pennsylvania, Amprim was one of eight children of Giacomo Marco and Anna Luigia Amprimo. Both were natives of Bussoleno, a town twenty-eight miles west of Turin in Italy's Piedmont region, where they had married in 1899. Seeking to build a better life than seemed possible in Italy at the turn of the twentieth century, the couple decided to emigrate to the United States. Giacomo sailed from Le Havre, France, aboard the SS *La Cascogne* and arrived in New York on September 14, 1903. Anna followed him several months later, arriving on the SS *La Lorraine* on July 2, 1904, accompanied by the couple's first two children, Adeline and Emilio.[14] Fairly soon after reuniting, the couple dropped the final letter of their last name, and Giacomo began going by the "more American" Jack.

Within a few years of their arrival in America, the Amprims moved from Pennsylvania to Michigan, where Jack found work in one of Detroit's many auto plants. The family eventually settled in Wyandotte, eleven miles to the south, where Jack became a leader in the local branch of an Italian American fraternal association. Frank and his siblings grew up completely bilingual, speaking Italian at home and English everywhere else. Intelligent and outgoing, Frank was a straight-A student at Wyandotte's Roosevelt High School and, at eighteen, entered Wayne State University in Detroit. Upon graduation, he enrolled at the University of Michigan Law School in Ann Arbor, earning his Bachelor of Laws degree in 1933. The following year, Frank became a law partner of family friend and fellow Italian American Frank P. Darin.

In the eight years he spent as a lawyer in Wyandotte before World War II, Frank Amprim earned a reputation as a both a dogged and thorough researcher and a fine courtroom advocate for his clients. Among the latter were members of Wyandotte's Italian community, whom Amprim also served as a leading member of his father's Italian American fraternal association. Many of the group's members had fled Italy following Mussolini's rise to power in the 1920s, and the 1939 outbreak of war in Europe prompted widespread concern that Italy and America might end up on opposite sides of the conflict. Amprim himself watched events with increasing anxiety, though unsure of what role he might play should hostilities break out. A native-born and patriotic American, he was nonetheless conflicted about possibly having to go to war against his parents' homeland and, perhaps, against blood relatives.

Like virtually all American men between the ages of twenty-one and forty-five, the young lawyer had registered for the draft in October 1940. His registration card, filed on the 16th, noted that he was then thirty years old and described him as standing 5 feet 9 inches tall, weighing 155 pounds, with brown hair and brown eyes. Somewhat to his relief, Amprim was not called up in the first national lottery in late October, nor in the second lottery held in July 1941. Any unease he may have felt about serving the United States vanished, however, after Pearl Harbor. Within four weeks, he decided on the way in which he could best serve the nation, and in mid-January 1942, he applied to join the FBI. The background investigation done on all prospective special agents noted his Italian heritage and membership in the Italian American fraternal association, but found "nothing subversive" and suggested that his language skills might be "especially useful" to the Bureau.

On April 13, some ninety days after submitting his application, Amprim was offered a position as a special agent at the starting annual salary of $3,200.[15] The proffer was contingent, however, on the young lawyer's completion of the then standard twelve-week new agent training class, which was conducted both at FBI headquarters in Washington and at the recently opened FBI Academy on the grounds of the vast U.S. Marine Corps base at Quantico, Virginia. The seven and a half weeks of instruction at the former largely centered on such academic topics as criminal law and rules of evidence, trials and courtroom procedures, FBI regulations and policies, investigative and interrogation techniques, codes and cyphers, concealed cameras and listening devices, and proper recordkeeping. The four and a half week curriculum at Quantico was decidedly more physical, entailing daily calisthenics, classes in jiujitsu and other styles of unarmed combat, firearms training with revolvers, shotguns, rifles, submachine guns, and the Browning automatic rifle, and extensive field exercises focused on covert surveillance methods and crime-scene investigation. The new agent training was challenging both mentally and physically, but Amprim graduated with flying colors in August 1942.

At this point, the agent's activities become opaque because the pages of his FBI personnel file covering his first field assignments have been heavily redacted. There are anecdotal indications that he spent time in the field offices in Cincinnati and Pittsburgh, and that he was at some point transferred to Miami. While the nature of Amprim's work in Florida is unclear, given his language skills, it is likely he was involved in investigations of Mafia activities in the state. It is also probable that at that point in his early career, he either became an SIS agent or worked in some capacity to support SIS operations in Latin America, most likely those targeting expatriate Italian populations in Argentina.[16]

What we do know for certain is that in early August 1943—less than a month after Mussolini's fall from power—Frank Amprim was selected to be the first FBI agent to deploy under military cover to an active combat zone. The broad outlines of what was termed his "liaison attachment" to Army units in the North African Theater of Operations (referred to as NATOUSA and which included Italy) were established during negotiations between Hoover and Major General George Strong, the head of G-2, with the details to be hammered out when Amprim arrived at NATOUSA headquarters in Algiers.

After a thorough physical at Walter Reed Army Hospital in Washington,

D.C., the FBI agent spent several weeks at Fort Belvoir, Virginia, where he was issued with uniforms and field equipment, and underwent an abbreviated period of basic military training. In addition to physical conditioning and familiarization with such Army-specific firearms as the Colt Model 1911 .45-caliber semiautomatic pistol and M1 Garand rifle, Amprim was educated on Army rank structures, military courtesy, and the current status of Allied operations in North Africa and Sicily. Much of his time was devoted to learning how agents of the Army's Counter Intelligence Corps operated in a tactical environment, since he was expected to be embedded with CIC detachments once he reached North Africa. After being granted an official (though entirely chimerical) leave of absence from the FBI, he was given papers identifying him as a brevetted captain in the Army of the United States.[17] His travel orders, signed by G-2 chief Strong, directed all Army organizations with which the agent came into contact to provide him "all requested support and assistance."

While Amprim's primary overseas mission was to investigate Ezra Pound, when he boarded a U.S. Army Air Forces C-87 in Miami in late September, the agent's orders from Hoover listed a number of other important tasks. These included gathering information on Carmine Senise, head of the Polizia di Stato (Italy's national police), who was thought to have supported Mussolini's overthrow the previous July; details on possibly pro-Fascist activities by U.S.-based chapters of Italy's Dante Alighieri Society; specifics on the organization and operations of the Organizzazione Vigilanza Repressione dell'Antifascismo (OVRA), Fascist Italy's equivalent of the Gestapo; the activities of the Nazi party in Italy; the names and locations of the offices and reporters of the Agenzia Stefani, an international Italian news agency coopted by Mussolini and thought to be a front for espionage; the South American activities of Italy's ItalMar shipping group; and data on Italian companies doing business with German firms operating in Argentina.

Amprim had plenty of time to consider the magnitude of his mission as the lumbering C-87—a transport version of the B-24 bomber—bearing him and a dozen other passengers, fought its way through thunderstorms en route for Natal, Brazil, the jump-off point for the first leg of the Atlantic crossing. Whether the agent also had time to ponder the deaths of Percy Foxworth and Hal Haberfeld along the same route eight months earlier is unknown, but his aircraft encountered no difficulties and reached Casablanca, Morocco, via Ascension Island. After several days spent arranging further transportation, on October 1, Amprim boarded a USAAF Air Transport Command C-47 for the 650-mile flight to Algiers.[18]

Upon arriving in the Algerian capital, the agent made his way to the Mustapha Supérieur district, set atop a low hill overlooking the city's harbor. With its lush gardens and fine villas, the area had long been a favorite of well-to-do tourists and the Franco-Algerian elite. Following the ouster of German and Vichy French forces from the city in November 1942, the historic Hôtel Saint-George—located atop the highest point in the district—had become the temporary home of Allied Forces Headquarters (AFHQ).[19] A joint American, British, and Free French organization commanded by then Lieutenant General Dwight Eisenhower, AFHQ was the administrative nerve center for all current and planned Allied operations in the Mediterranean and southern France. Amprim was given a small room in the Saint-George and spent the next several weeks learning all he could about the ways in which the Allied forces conducted intelligence and counterintelligence operations both individually and jointly at the theater level.

As valuable as those God's-eye view insights were, Frank Amprim would be carrying out his mission at ground level. As he moved across North Africa and, ultimately, into Italy proper, he would be attached to company- and battalion-size U.S. Army formations. At the time of the agent's arrival in Algiers, those units were under NATOUSA's operational control, and Amprim therefore spent several additional weeks working with that headquarters' G-2 section. Housed in a small hotel barely a hundred yards downhill from the Saint-George, NATOUSA's "intel shop" comprised twenty-four men, most of them officers. They were more than happy to educate Amprim on the ways Army units conducted tactical intelligence operations, which were intended primarily to locate and identify enemy maneuver formations, determine their strength and capabilities, and predict their movements.

While this was certainly useful information for the FBI agent, his investigation obviously fell into the counterintelligence realm, and he therefore spent much of his time with NATOUSA's CIC detachment. Second Lieutenant Paul Lyon and nine enlisted soldiers from the 2678th CIC Company not only broadened Amprim's theoretical understanding of tactical counterintelligence operations but introduced him to the practical realities of the job by allowing him to participate in their daily operations. These included evaluating documents captured from the Italian Armistice Commission that had been based in Algiers following France's capitulation in 1940; tracking down, apprehending, and interrogating suspected Axis stay-behind agents—work closely akin to what the FBI agent had been doing in the States; as well as the more mundane task of investigating Army personnel thought to be inadvertently divulging classified information while drinking in Algiers's many and varied watering holes.[20] Amprim also investigated, and reported to Hoover about Communist Party activities in North Africa.[21]

Near the end of his stay in the Algerian capital, Amprim also reached out to the one organization he knew Hoover would definitely not approve of—the Office of Strategic Services. The director's intense personal dislike of "Wild Bill" Donovan and disdain for his group of "amateurs and dilettantes" was well known throughout the Bureau, but very soon after arriving in Algiers, it had become clear to Amprim that the OSS could be a valuable ally. The organization was generally not subject to strict supervision by regular Army units, had operatives already at work in Sicily and behind enemy lines in mainland Italy, and was likely to eventually enter Rome before the bulk of the U.S. Fifth Army. Amprim almost certainly likely believed that Hoover would absolve him of the sin of working with OSS if that cooperation hastened the apprehension of Pound and aided in the collection of pertinent OVRA documents.

The OSS had established its Algiers station during the winter of 1942–43, taking over a sprawling collection of buildings in the Mustapha Supérieur district known collectively as the Villa Magnol. Located less than a half mile from AFHQ headquarters at the Saint-George, the complex housed several hundred people representing all of OSS's branches—Special Operations (SO), Operational Groups (OGs), Secret Intelligence (SI), Morale Operations (MO), Counterintelligence (X-2), and Research and Analysis (R&A). Originally given the intentionally vague designation Experimental Detachment G-3, by the time of Amprim's arrival in Algiers, the organization was known by the only slightly less misleading moniker 2677th Headquarters Company Experimental (Provisional). In overall command was U.S. Marine Corps Colonel William Eddy, but it was the civilian chief of the SI section's Italian division, Vincent J. Scamporino, whom Amprim sought out.[22]

A labor lawyer in Connecticut before Pearl Harbor, Scamporino had been born in Massachusetts of Sicilian immigrant parents and grew up speaking both Italian and French in addition to English. He'd been brought into the world of wartime intelligence by his friend and fellow Sicilian American Biagio Massimo "Max" Corvo, the man who almost singlehandedly created the OSS's Italian-speaking operational groups.[23] By the time he met Amprim, Scamporino was directing all secret intelligence operations in Sicily and mainland Italy. As he noted in a memo to OSS Algiers commander Eddy, Amprim visited the SI office on December 2, identified himself as an FBI agent, and laid out the details of the "special mission" he was undertaking at Hoover's request. Scamporino told him that OSS would be happy to help, on the condition that Eddy approved such assistance.[24]

The SI chief went on to endorse cooperation with Amprim, writing, "It is my opinion that we are in a very favorable position to obtain [the requested] information by virtue of the contacts we have established in Italy. Your approval is recommended." Scamporino then added that he and Amprim had informally discussed the possibility that OSS could support FBI operations in South America by putting the Bureau in contact with "numerous individuals who have excellent contacts with big business," and that any productive information that resulted "could be considered a joint OSS/FBI operation."[25] This last might have been an attempt on Amprim's part to both encourage OSS support of his mission and to preemptively mitigate Hoover's displeasure should he hear about the agent's contact with Scamporino.

After gaining Eddy's authorization to assist Amprim, the SI chief gave the FBI agent a broad overview of OSS activities on the Italian peninsula since the Allied landings at Salerno on September 9 and the liberation of Naples twenty-two days later. Scamporino then pledged his support for Amprim's mission, and gave the FBI agent a letter directing all OSS SI units with which he came in contact to help him whenever the tactical situation allowed. Armed with similar documents provided by both NATOUSA's intelligence chief and its CIC detachment, Amprim was ready for the next phase of his mission—to get boots on the ground in his parents' homeland.

WHILE THE FALL OF NAPLES WAS AN IMPORTANT PART of the Allies' progress up the Italian boot, it did not result in the hoped-for rout of Axis forces on the peninsula. The ouster of Mussolini in July 1943 and Italy's surrender the following September had prompted Adolf Hitler to order the disarmament of all Italian forces and immediate occupation of those parts of the country not already captured by the Allies. German divisions had poured into the country from Austria, France, and the Balkans, overcome resistance by Italian forces, and occupied Rome and other key cities. The Germans also began establishing successive defensive lines immediately ahead of the leading Allied units and stretching across the entire peninsula from the Tyrrhenian Sea to the Adriatic. By making skillful use of the mountainous terrain, the several large rivers in the region, and the harsh weather that characterized the winter of 1943–44, German forces were able to slow the Allied advance to a crawl. On January 22, 1944, U.S. and British troops landed at Anzio, on Italy's west coast, in an attempt to bypass the German defenses and advance on Rome. Though initially unopposed, the landings soon prompted a sustained German response, with the beachhead being encircled and subjected to nearly constant artillery fire. Once again, the Allied advance northward was brought to a halt.

Frank Amprim had arrived on the mainland in late December 1943 and spent several days inspecting documents captured by the British forces that had taken the Adriatic port city of Brindisi. By early January, he had crossed the peninsula and attached himself to the Fifth Army CIC Detachment Naples. The following month, that unit moved some fifteen miles north to the relocated NATOUSA headquarters in the opulent eighteenth-century palace of the Bourbon kings in Caserta, and Amprim took up residence in nearby San Leucio. OSS Algiers's Vincent Scamporino had established an advance base of the redesignated 2677th Headquarters Company Experimental (Provisional) there in February, requisitioning a hillside complex the Americans referred to as "the little palace." Built in the 1770s as an ornate hunting lodge where King Ferdinand IV of Naples could get away from the bustle of the Caserta palace, the building was steadily enlarged and eventually became the cornerstone of a 200-acre model village built around silk making. The mills were still in operation when Amprim arrived, and the more than two hundred OSS members on-site worked, ate, and slept in the palatial former lodge. In a ceremony on March 1, the building's gilded grand hall served as the backdrop for the brevetted FBI agent's promotion to major, with Scamporino pinning on Amprim's gold oak leaves.

By poring through literally thousands of pages of captured Italian and German records held in Caserta and San Leucio, the FBI agent was able to glean and pass on to Bureau headquarters in Washington much useful information pertaining to OVRA and the organization and operations of both the Abwehr and the Sicherheitsdienst (the SS intelligence arm). He was not, however, able to move forward with his primary mission—locating and interrogating Ezra Pound—until the tactical impasse between German and Allied forces was broken in mid-May by the capture of Monte Cassino and the Allied breakout from the Anzio beachhead. On May 21, the resumption of the advance on Rome prompted Colonel George "Budge" Smith to prepare his S Force for movement toward the Italian capital. After assembling at the port of Naples, the unit's men and vehicles were transported by ship to Anzio, arriving at the former beachhead on May 30. Four days later, S Force—with Frank Amprim once again attached to the Fifth Army CIC Detachment—set off for the Eternal

City with the lead elements of the joint American–Canadian 1st Special Service Force (FSSF).

While the breakout from Anzio put Allied forces back on the road to Rome, the thirty-mile advance on the Italian capital was not uncontested. Even though the bulk of German forces had evacuated the city, ambushes by well-placed German infantry and armor along the approach routes repeatedly slowed the lead elements of the U.S. II and VI Corps. It therefore wasn't until 6 a.m. on June 4 that the first Allied troops—a reconnaissance element of the FSSF—slipped into Rome through the Porta San Giovanni.[26] Other units followed, spreading out across the capital, and by 3:20 a.m. on June 5, "Budge" Smith and the members of his S Force were firmly ensconced atop the Pincian Hill.

When two hours later Smith's four columns fanned out across the city to search predetermined locations, Frank Amprim hitched a ride with a group headed toward the city's Della Vittoria neighborhood. Less than a mile and a half northwest of the Pincian Hill on the other side of the Tiber, the historic and elegant part of the city was home to fountains, museums, and a famed basilica. Of most interest to the FBI agent, however, was the massive building at Via Asiago 10, the headquarters of the Ente Italiano per le Audizioni Radiofoniche, Fascist Italy's sole national and international radio broadcaster.[27] It was there where Ezra Pound had recorded his broadcasts and from where they had been transmitted to the English-speaking world, and Amprim was intent on recovering any evidence of the poet's alleged treason. During repeated visits over the following two months, the agent discovered some of Pound's radio scripts, two discs bearing recorded broadcasts, and numerous newspaper clippings in Italian lauding the poet's support for Mussolini and fascism.

Since arriving in Italy in December 1943, Frank Amprim had reported to Bureau headquarters several times that the many aspects of his mission had become nearly overwhelming, and in August 1944, his requests for assistance were finally answered when two special agents arrived in Rome from Washington. Arthur H. Avignone and Raymond J. Bacigalupi were both fluent in Italian, had undergone abbreviated Army basic training, and arrived in uniforms adorned with captain's bars.[28] Experienced field agents and early members of the SIS, the men initially joined Amprim in the hunt for Pound-related materials and aided the lead agent in his October 8 search of the Ministry of Popular Culture, where the trio discovered the poet's personnel file. Eight days later, Amprim tasked Avignone and Bacigalupi with establishing and manning the FBI liaison office in the newly reopened U.S. Embassy, where they focused on the ancillary investigations the senior agent had been undertaking. The move freed Amprim to largely concentrate on the Pound case, which, with Allied forces continuing to move north, would likely require increased travel outside Rome.

As it happened, however, less than two months after the arrival of Avignone and Bacigalupi in Rome, Amprim's dogged investigation of Ezra Pound's possible treason came to an abrupt halt. The agent had been dealing with increasingly debilitating intestinal problems for several months, and when he finally entered the Army's 73rd Station Hospital in the Italian capital on December 1, he was diagnosed with a serious parasitic infection. The following day, he was flown to Naples, and on December 3, he was put aboard an Air Transport Command flight to Washington, D.C. Upon his arrival at National Airport two days later, Amprim was taken to Bethesda Naval Hospital in suburban Maryland, where he was found to be carrying the parasite *Entamoeba histolytica*.[29] The infection is usually connected with unsanitary conditions and contaminated drinking water—both of which are common in combat zones—and the physicians at Bethesda determined that Amprim had likely been carrying the parasite in his gut for a least a year.

Over the following twelve weeks, Amprim underwent several courses of antibiotic therapy at Bethesda, initially as an in-patient and later during weekly visits to the hospital while on physician-ordered home rest. It was not a particularly restful period, however, for the agent was actually working several days a week at FBI headquarters. He spent much of that time briefing Hoover and other senior Bureau leaders on the search for Ezra Pound and information he'd been able to dig up regarding German and Italian intelligence activities in the United States. Amprim also spent time at the War Department, where he was updated regularly on the general military situation in Italy. During the time he'd been in the United States, the Allied advance up the peninsula had continued, though slowly. The Gothic Line—stretching from just north of Pisa in the west to Ravenna in the east—had been breached in August 1944, and the Germans had been slowly pushed back through that fall and early winter. Poor weather, the need to consolidate the gains made thus far, and the transfer of key U.S. Fifth Army units from Italy to France had brought forward movement to a standstill, and by the time Amprim returned to Rome in early March, all of northern Italy from just south of Bologna was still firmly in Axis hands.

That situation began to change dramatically in early April as Allied forces launched several offensives across northern Italy. Moving up the peninsula's west coast, the majority Black U.S. 92nd Infantry Division captured Massa, just sixteen miles southeast of the vital port complex at La Spezia, on April 10. Bologna was liberated eleven days later, and by April 27, the 92nd Division's lead elements had entered Genoa. And it was there, in the city long known as the jewel in the crown of the Italian Riviera, that Frank Amprim finally came face-to-face with the man he'd been doggedly investigating for nearly two years.

On the afternoon of May 3, 1945, Ezra Pound was alone in the cottage he shared with both his wife, Dorothy, and his longtime mistress, Olga Rudge.[30] Located in the hillside hamlet of Sant'Ambrogio di Zoagli, a little over a mile from the seaside resort town of Rapallo, the two-story cottage at Casa 60 had been Rudge's primary home since she rented it in 1929 to be closer to Pound. The poet and his wife had moved from Paris to Rapallo that year, living in a rented attic apartment in the Palazzo Baratti, an imposing building on the seafront. In May 1944, occupying German troops ordered all the buildings near the harbor to be evacuated in anticipation of a possible Allied amphibious landing. Pound's wife had known for years about his relationship with Rudge—indeed, for more than a decade the poet had essentially been dividing his time between the Rapallo apartment and the cottage in Sant'Ambrogio—but she must have been stunned when her husband casually suggested that the two of them move in with Rudge. It can't have been a comfortable arrangement for the two women, given that they loathed each other, but at that point, the three of them literally had no place else to go.

The tense atmosphere that must certainly have pervaded the Sant'Ambrogio cottage was compounded by the steady approach of Allied forces in the spring of 1945. Pound knew of his indictment for treason and naively believed that he could escape charges by simply turning himself in to the first American troops he encountered and explaining his motivations for broadcasting on behalf of the Italian Fascists. On April 25, the lead elements of the 92nd Infantry Division occupied Rapallo, and three days later, Pound set off down the hill in search of an American official to whom he might explain himself. He didn't find anyone, however, because the soldiers had moved on toward Genoa. Pound returned to the cottage.

On May 2, follow-on units of the 92nd Division entered Rapallo, and Pound again trudged down the path from the cottage in search of someone in authority. The several Black soldiers he ultimately encountered had better things to do than listen to the disjointed ramblings of a wild-haired eccentric who wanted to be taken to Washington because he had "important information for the State Department."[31] When he could find no one willing to take him seriously, the poet walked back to the cottage and returned to work on an English translation of a text by the Confucian philosopher Mencius. The next morning, with Dorothy and Olga both out of the house on errands, Pound was again hard at work on the translation. Just before noon, two heavily armed Italian partisans forced their way through the front door and demanded that the poet accompany them to their unit's outpost in Zoagli. As he was being hustled out, Pound picked up a small Chinese dictionary and the Confucian text and shoved them in his pockets.[32]

When Olga returned to Sant'Ambrogio and heard from the cottage's downstairs tenant that Pound had been taken, she rushed to Zoagli. She and the poet were then taken to the partisan unit's headquarters in Chiavari, some four miles down the coast. Understandably nervous that he might be shot out of hand, Pound told the partisan commander he would like to be sent to the nearest U.S. unit. Somewhat to the poet's surprise, the commander agreed, and within minutes, the two Americans were seated in the back of a jeep bound for Lavagna, just on the other side of a small river from Chiavari. Upon arrival at the headquarters of the U.S. infantry regiment occupying the city, Pound and Rudge were given some sandwiches, after which the unit's commander had the pair driven to the 92nd Division's CIC Detachment at Via Fieschi 6 in Genoa.

The detachment had entered Genoa on April 30, as part of an S Force comprising some four hundred infantrymen, to provide security and a variety of American and Allied intelligence and counterintelligence operatives. Their mission was to locate and apprehend German-controlled saboteurs and stay-behind agents, and secure all enemy documents that might prove to be of intelligence value. The CIC detachment had also been told to keep an eye out for Ezra Pound, who was known to be living in or near Rapallo. The detachment commander, Special Agent in Charge (1st Lieutenant) Ramón Arrizabalaga, had orders to hold the poet until he could be questioned by an FBI agent who would come up from Rome.[33] When the S Force had passed through Rapallo a few days earlier, the CIC detachment didn't have time to look for Pound, but on May 2—once the unit had established its headquarters in Genoa—Arrizabalaga sent Special Agent George Merriman back to search for the poet. Having been told by one source that Pound might be in

Portofino, the CIC man lost a day searching that city and didn't get to Rapallo until May 3. By that time, the poet and Olga Rudge were in partisan custody and already on the way to Lavagna. A few hours later, Arrizabalaga got a call from Colonel Donald MacWillie, the 92nd Division's G-2 chief, telling him that Pound and his mistress were en route to Via Fieschi 6.

For Arrizabalaga, a thirty-one-year-old Nevadan of Basque heritage,[34] the impending arrival of Ezra Pound was an unwanted distraction. His detachment was already extremely busy tracking down Italian and German stay-behind agents, and the idea of having to babysit the poet and his mistress until an FBI agent arrived from Rome was more than a little irritating. Thus, when Pound and Rudge were delivered to Via Fieschi 6 on the evening of May 3, Arrizabalaga had them locked into a sixth-floor anteroom where they spent the night sitting on hard-backed chairs. Their conditions improved the following morning, however, when they were moved to a vacant office that had cushioned armchairs on which they could comfortably recline. Arrizabalaga provided the pair with boxes of C-rations—which Rudge later said she and Pound found to be "excellent"—and with hot coffee by the Italian *carabinieri* who acted as guards for the CIC detachment and the small OSS unit that shared the sixth floor.[35]

Frank Amprim arrived at Via Fieschi 6 from Rome at about 2 p.m. on May 4 and immediately sat down with Arrizabalaga to explain his mission. The FBI agent had come bearing several hundred pages of Pound-related documents he'd found in the Italian capital, and after thoroughly briefing the CIC detachment chief, he asked whether Arrizabalaga would like to assist in interviewing the poet. Perhaps because Amprim laid out such a convincing case of Pound's importance as a possible traitor, or maybe because the soldier and the G-man immediately recognized each other as like-minded professional investigators, Arrizabalaga agreed to assist Amprim as much as he could, given the CIC detachment's heavy workload.

When the FBI agent began interrogating Pound on the morning of May 5, the poet apparently believed the uniformed Amprim was, like Arrizabalaga, a CIC officer. The revelation that he was actually dealing with a Bureau agent prompted Pound to make two requests. First, he wanted to send a telegram to President Harry Truman offering his help, as a longtime student of Confucianism, in brokering a "just peace" between the United States and Japan. Second, he wanted to make a final radio broadcast in which he would plead for America to be a benevolent victor over the defeated Axis nations. That Pound was shocked when Amprim declined both requests gives a clear idea of the poet's stunning naïveté and overwhelming sense of self-importance. After five hours of questioning, the poet was returned to the room where he and Rudge had spent the previous night, and both were again provided with food and hot coffee. As the pair settled in, Amprim dispatched a cable to Hoover stating, "EZRA POUND IN CUSTODY CIC, NINETY SECOND DIVISION, GENOA. ADMITS VOLUNTARY BROADCASTS FOR PAY."[36]

Amprim and Arrizabalaga continued their questioning of Pound on May 6 and 7, and at the end of the final session, the poet voluntarily signed two important documents. The first was the final version of a six-page typewritten sworn statement in which Pound outlined his early life and his initial move to Europe in 1908, his relocation to Italy in 1924, his fascination with and approval of Mussolini and fascism, and his writings and broadcasts both before and after Pearl Harbor. Pound admitted making the transmissions under his own name and at least two aliases, and acknowledged being paid by the Ministry of Popular Culture for his radio and print work. He also said that after the fall of the Mussolini regime, he had approached the Salo Republic about doing more radio broadcasts.[37] He said he was given 3,000 lire in "living expenses" by Carl Giorgio Goedel, a German who had worked for the Ministry of Popular Culture in Rome and then for the same entity in Salo—on organization Pound would certainly have known to be completely controlled by the Nazis. The poet also admitted that after Fascist Italy declared war on the United States on December 11, 1941, he said in one of his broadcasts that America was getting into a "whale of a debt" and should get out of the war immediately. In the statement, which was witnessed and signed by both Amprim and Arrizabalaga, Pound also acknowledged that he understood the document could be used against him in court and that he was "willing to return to the United States to stand trial on the charge of treason."[38]

Though consisting of just a few handwritten lines, the second document Pound signed on May 7 was in many ways equally important. Scrawled in the poet's distinctive cursive hand, it read simply: *I hereby authorize Frank Amprim to examine and search my premises at Santa* [sic] *Ambrogio 60 and to remove therefrom any and all documents of interest to him.*[39] That same evening, the FBI agent and Arrizabalaga drove Olga Rudge back to Casa 60, where they presented Dorothy Pound with her husband's signed search authorization. Amprim had brought along some ground coffee, milk, sugar, canned corn, chocolate bars, and other items that the women ate before providing the two men with several hundred items. These included drafts of Pound's radio scripts, letters to and from various Ministry of Popular Culture officials in both Rome and Salo, and a few books. In his written report to Hoover, Amprim noted that Dorothy was "very cooperative in finding incriminating evidence against her husband and did not seem to be the least disturbed" by the search.[40] A few days after that visit, Dorothy left Casa 60 to stay with Ezra's aged mother in Rapallo. Amprim returned to the Sant'Ambrogio cottage several times over the following weeks and, with Olga's permission, removed additional documents and Ezra Pound's Everest Model 90 portable typewriter. While many of the documents and books initially taken from Casa 60 were returned after they'd been copied, the typewriter was ultimately shipped to Washington to be used as physical evidence.[41]

In addition to his sworn statement and the written authorization to search Casa 60, on May 8, Pound provided Amprim with two additional written "supplements." The first, titled "Outline of Economic Bases of Historic Processes," was an exceptionally dense and rambling treatise quoting, among others, John Adams and Vladimir Lenin. The second item, "Further Points," while also rather disjointed, includes a few concrete statements Pound wanted Amprim—and presumably the U.S. court that might eventually try him—to know. At one point, the poet wrote, "I do not yet know at what date the mere use of a radio in a foreign territory became a crime. I certainly had no news of its being illegal before the date, whenever it was, that I heard I was accused of treason." He then added, "I do not believe I have betrayed anyone whomsoever." In a later additional typed statement that day, Pound wrote, "I am not anti-Semitic, and I distinguish between the Jewish usurer and the Jew who does an honest day's work for a living." This latter statement would have rung false to Amprim, who was aware that the poet had publicly sought to justify Mussolini's Nazi-inspired "race laws" and the Germans' treatment of Italian Jews following the 1943 capitulation. Moreover, Pound added two lines to the statement that were to haunt him for the rest of his life: "Hitler and Mussolini were simple men from the country. I think that Hitler was a saint, and wanted nothing for himself."[42]

Amprim maintained a calm and friendly manner throughout his extended contacts with Ezra Pound despite such statements, and the poet later wrote that Amprim "expressed himself as convinced that I was telling the absolute truth . . . and has since with great care collected far more proof to that effect than I or any private lawyer would have got at."[43] Pound had obviously misconstrued the FBI agent's "good cop" interview style, for Amprim was often irritated by the poet's glib, offhand pronouncements in favor of Mussolini, Hitler, fascism, and anti-Semitism. The agent was especially incensed that on several occasions, when Pound was being interviewed between May 5 and May 17, the poet routinely gave the Fascist salute when entering the room. Nor were Amprim and Arrizabalaga the only ones to whom the poet made the loathsome gesture—on May 8, he rendered the salute to Colonel Donald MacWillie when the 92nd Division intelligence chief visited Via Fieschi 6. Pound then attempted to shake the officer's hand, and was obviously bewildered when MacWillie refused.

After returning to Rome following his initial interviews of Pound, Amprim cabled Hoover requesting an urgent decision about the poet's ultimate disposition. Arrizabalaga was also asking his higher headquarters about what should be done with the poet, who had become so comfortable in the CIC detachment's offices that when not being interviewed, he had gone back to work on his Confucian translation. On May 22, both Amprim and his CIC colleague were finally notified that orders regarding Pound had been signed by Lieutenant General Matthew B. Ridgway, the commander of the U.S. Army's Mediterranean Theater of Operations (MTOUSA):

> American civilian Doctor Ezra Loomis Pound . . . under federal grand jury indictment for treason. Transfer without delay under guard to MTOUSA Disciplinary Training Center for confinement pending disposition instructions. Exercise utmost security measures to prevent escape or suicide. No press interviews authorized. Accord no preferential treatment.[44]

Ramón Arrizabalaga later recalled how several jeeps full of military police soldiers arrived in Genoa on May 24 to remove the celebrated prisoner:

> It was actually rather a sorry sight to see the big six foot MP's commanded by a captain relieve [Pound] of his shoestrings, belt, necktie and clamp a huge pair of handcuffs to one of his wrists, the other end to an MP's wrist and take him away. We had treated him courteously and he couldn't understand it. He said to me, "I don't understand it." I said, "Mr. Pound, you are no longer under my jurisdiction, and I can't help it." He then said, "Do they know who I am?" I answered, "Yes they do."[45]

Pound's six-month stay at the Disciplinary Training Center (DTC), outside Pisa, was initially a tremendously unpleasant one. The facility housed

American military personnel convicted of, or awaiting trial on, charges ranging from black marketeering and rape to desertion and homicide. Those inmates whose crimes were less odious and who were thought to be "redeemable" were put through rigorous training intended to get them back into the field as combat troops. The worst offenders—murderers and those believed to have thrown in their lot with the enemy—were held until they could be executed or transferred Stateside. Nearly sixty, Pound was by far the oldest prisoner in the facility, but his age did not prevent him from at first being held under truly harsh conditions. Set within a larger stockade surrounded by tall double fences topped with razor wire, the poet's twelve-foot-square "cell" consisted of a concrete floor, four walls of strong steel mesh, and a wooden roof. Pound and the men in the identical adjoining enclosures—referred to by guards and prisoners alike as "Murder's Row"—wore Army dungarees, slept on blankets rather mattresses, were denied all reading material but a Bible, used buckets for latrines, and were fed once a day. Open to the weather, the cells were cold at night, stifling hot in the daytime, dripping wet when it rained, and illuminated from dusk to dawn by bright floodlights.[46]

It's no surprise that after three weeks in such conditions, Pound's mental state began to obviously decline. Captain (Dr.) Walter H. Baer, the second of two DTC psychiatrists to examine the poet, wrote, "Due to his age and loss of personality resilience, prolonged exposure in the present environment may precipitate a mental breakdown, of which premonitory symptoms are discernable. Early transfer to the United States or to an institution in this theater with more adequate facilities for care is recommended."[47] During several visits to the DTC, Frank Amprim had also noticed Pound's mental deterioration and cabled Hoover of his belief that the poet should be returned to America without delay.[48] When no transfer was immediately forthcoming, Pound was moved into a tent by himself in the medical compound, where he was eventually given access to a typewriter and books.

Pound's seemingly endless sojourn at the DTC ended abruptly on the night of November 16, when he was informed that he would be leaving for the United States in two hours. After gathering together his few belongings, he was handcuffed and put in a jeep with guards and driven to the USAAF Air Transport Command terminal at Rome's Ciampino Airport, where the party arrived just before 5 a.m. Soon afterward, the three Judge Advocate General's Corps officers tasked to escort Pound—Lieutenants Colonel Holder and Donaghy and Captain Manus—took official custody of the poet and all four boarded a waiting C-54E transport. The aircraft departed Rome at 8:30 a.m. and made brief stops at Prague, Brussels, and RAF Bovington in England before proceeding to the Azores. There Pound and his escorts transferred to a C-54 bound for Bermuda, from where the aircraft set a course for Bolling Field in Washington, D.C.[49] Holder kept extensive notes of his conversations with Pound during the journey and later summed up his impressions of the poet by saying, "He is an intellectual 'crack pot' . . . who resented the fact that ordinary mortals were not sufficiently intelligent to understand his aims and motives."

The aircraft, carrying Pound, his escorts, and—just by coincidence—the French ambassador to the United States and his secretariat chief, arrived at Bolling at 9:40 p.m. on November 18. The poet was immediately taken into custody by two U.S. marshals and driven to the District of Columbia jail. Over the following week, Pound's attorney, Julien Cornell, determined that the elderly poet was too mentally fragile to stand trial, and at a formal arraignment on November 27, Cornell argued that Pound was incapable of entering a rational plea. Judge Bolitha J. Laws ordered Pound to be transferred to the Gallinger Municipal Hospital Psychopathic Ward in D.C. for "observation and evaluation."

Though Frank Amprim had interviewed Pound a few times after the latter's transfer to the Disciplinary Training Center, the FBI agent largely shifted to different investigations. Assisted by two new agents sent to replace Art Avignone and Ray Bacigalupi, Amprim investigated other cases of possible treason, including that of American-born propaganda broadcaster Rita Zucca.[50] However, Amprim had continued to have health issues following his return to Italy from Bethesda Naval Hospital, and Hoover ultimately ordered him home. Amprim sailed from Naples aboard the SS *Sea Tiger* on November 15, 1945, arriving in New York eleven days later. He reentered Bethesda, where he was found to be suffering from full-blown amoebic dysentery. The agent's illness did not take him off the Ezra Pound case, however, for on December 18, 1946, senior Bureau leaders notified Amprim that the psychiatrists who had examined Pound were going to report to the court on December 20 that the poet was insane and not able to stand trial. Though still recovering, Amprim launched into an exhaustive review of all the documents and other evidence gathered in the case, and turned in a comprehensive case review late on December 19.

In the end, Ezra Pound was never tried for treason. He was found mentally unfit to stand trial and transferred to Washington, D.C.'s St. Elizabeths Hospital for the criminally insane. Pound spent thirteen years in the institution, and upon his release in May 1958, he returned to Italy to live in Venice with Olga Rudge. Pound died in 1972, followed by Rudge in 1996.

CHAPTER 4

Agents to Officers

At about the same time Frank Amprim was undergoing Army basic training in Virginia, Frederick Ayer Jr. was summoned to the office of the special agent in charge (SAC) of the FBI's Boston Field Office. The twenty-eight-year-old Ayer had been in the Bureau for just over two years, and for months after Pearl Harbor, his repeated attempts to enlist in the armed forces had been rebuffed because of his extreme nearsightedness and the resultant need to wear glasses. He had then begun desperately lobbying his superiors for an overseas Bureau assignment that had something to do with the war effort. Now, on a humid summer day in 1943, it finally seemed as though his repeated requests were about to bear fruit, for after closing the office door and directing the young agent to be seated, the SAC lowered his voice conspiratorially.

"Fred, I understand that you have been clamoring to go overseas," the older agent said. "Well, the Bureau wants you for a highly sensitive assignment out of the country where you will get to use your knowledge of a foreign language. Are you willing to accept such an assignment?"[1]

Envisioning himself playing a key role in the growing Allied war effort in Europe, the French-speaking Ayer eagerly responded that he was "already packed" and ready to depart at a moment's notice. Two days later, after handing his active cases off to fellow agents and saying goodbye to his wife and their infant son, Fred boarded a train for Washington with images of victory parades down the Champs-Élysées in Paris dancing in his head.

Unfortunately, those ephemeral scenes of martial triumph quickly dissipated under the harsh light of reality. Upon arriving in the nation's capital, the young agent was told that the mission for which he'd been selected would not take him to embattled Europe, but to the steamy tropical backwater of Haiti. The French-speaking Caribbean nation, which shared the western third of the island of Hispaniola with the Spanish-speaking Dominican Republic, was thought to harbor German and Vichy French sympathizers who might secretly be refueling Axis submarines. Despite his extreme disappointment, Fred accepted the mission, only to be intensely relieved when it was canceled hours before his scheduled departure.

Having said fulsome farewells to family and friends before leaving Massachusetts, the young agent rather sheepishly returned to the Boston field office less than a week after his departure for Washington. Once again facing a desktop covered in case files and the certainty of fourteen-hour workdays largely spent pounding the pavements of the city's less-desirable neighborhoods, Fred sadly assumed that the chance to "get into the war" had passed him by.

He would soon find out just how wrong he was.

That the scion of one of the wealthiest and most prominent families in Massachusetts would end up wearing a badge, carrying a gun, and chasing criminals was a surprise to many people, including to Fred Ayer himself.

Born December 28, 1915, in Topsfield—nineteen miles northeast of Boston—he was one of four children of Frederick and Hilda Ayer.[2] Young Fred grew up in a decidedly privileged household, largely because his grandfather—Frederick Charles Ayer—was a multimillionaire who had made his fortune in the patent medicine business, as a prominent financier, and as the cofounder of the American Woolen Company.[3] On the day in 1914 when Fred's parents were married, grandfather Ayer gifted the young couple with Copper Beech Hill estate, a 10,200-square-foot mansion on 24 acres of land in Wenham, a few miles southeast of Topsfield.[4] Young Fred grew up there, attended by butlers, maids, housekeepers, and the family's private nurse, and spent much of his youth riding horses from the estate's extensive stables, playing polo and tennis at the private Myopia Hunt Club, and acquiring the cultural "polish" expected of a young gentleman. Part of that process was being tutored in French from the age of ten onward, and undertaking a three-month-long European trip with his parents and siblings in 1928.

In the fall of 1930 fifteen-year-old Fred entered the prestigious Hill School in Pottstown, Pennsylvania, which his father had also attended. Then one of the finest and most exclusive male-only college preparatory academies in the United States, the institution prided itself on turning out young men intellectually qualified for admission to the nation's finest universities. That academic preparation was matched by an emphasis on physical fitness, and during his three years at the Hill School, Fred played football and baseball, ran track, and was a leading member of the trap shooting team. In his spare time, he was also a captain of the debate team and edited both the class newsletter and the school newspaper.

While the majority of Hill School graduates tended to go on to Princeton, Fred again chose to follow in his father's footsteps by enrolling at Harvard. He entered in 1933, and over his four years, he not only excelled academically but also played football and polo, ran track, was on the rifle team, wrote for the *Lampoon*, and to top it all off, was a member of the Hasty Pudding Club. After graduating in 1937 with a *cum laude* A.B. degree, Fred took a solo month-long trip to France. Upon his return, he enrolled in Harvard Law School, and it was there that on October 16, 1940, he registered for the draft. His registration card described him as 6 feet tall, 180 pounds, with blue eyes, brown hair, and a "ruddy" complexion.

While still a law student, Fred had interned with the eminent Boston firm Adams, O'Brien and Weinberg, and it was widely believed (particularly by Ayer's parents) that after graduation from Harvard Law and passing the Massachusetts bar, the newly minted attorney would quickly be offered a full-time position with the firm. Fred himself had a different plan, however. Following the outbreak of World War II in September 1939, he had begun exploring the possibility of joining America's armed forces, but was repeatedly told that his poor eyesight would preclude any military service. During a criminal justice class early in 1941, Professor Sheldon Glueck mentioned in passing that he strongly felt the FBI "was the best possible experience and finest training ground for a young lawyer."[5] The comment stuck with Fred, who waited only a few weeks before applying to the Bureau.

The FBI did not seem to see Fred's nearsightedness as a serious disadvantage, for after the usual thorough background investigation, the young attorney was accepted for training as a special agent. Just days after his law school graduation and passing the Massachusetts bar, he reported to Bureau headquarters in Washington for initial orientation. On Monday, June 16, 1941, Fred and forty-seven other eager young men began ten weeks of training. Conducted largely at what Fred called the "tropic miasma" of Quantico, the course ran seventy hours per week, with each day split roughly between academics and field work. Fred did well at both, and not surprisingly, given that he was a good shot before entering the FBI, he qualified "expert" with the .38-caliber revolver, shotgun, .30-06 Springfield rifle, and Thompson submachine gun.

Fred and his fellow fledgling lawmen—forty-three law school graduates, three certified public accountants, and one PhD in languages—were "turned out into a crime-ridden and war-threatened world" on August 25, 1941.[6] Days after the graduation, twenty-six-year-old Fred married twenty-year-old California native and longtime family friend Anne P. Moody in a lavish ceremony at the Copper Beech Hill estate. There was no time for an extended honeymoon, however, for Fred was due to report to his first duty station in early September.

Much to his wife's chagrin, the city where Fred's career as a special agent was to begin was the one place the young bride had said she really would prefer not to live—the nation's capital, where Fred was assigned to the Washington field office on Lafayette Square. To add insult to injury, less than a month after the couple moved into a small apartment, Fred was called into the office of the SAC. The man asked if the young agent read, wrote, and spoke French. When Fred said he did, he was told he was being assigned to a special surveillance operation that would likely keep him away from home for days or weeks at a time. Though Anne was understandably disturbed by the news, she assured Fred that she could, and would, cope on her own during his absences.

Over the following six months, Fred and a team of agents undertook microphone and personal surveillance of various foreign organizations and individuals, both in the D.C. area and farther afield. Fred had been brought into the project specifically to transcribe recordings of various targets believed to be agents of Vichy France, but was also occasionally called upon to transcribe English conversations. The young agent found the work boring, given that the majority of what he listened to, whether live or recorded, had little to do with espionage. His interest was definitely piqued, however, when, in early January 1942, he recognized one of the voices on a recording to which he was listening.

The conversation Fred had to transcribe had taken place the previous evening between twenty-nine-year-old Danish-born reporter Inga Arvad and a young U.S. Navy officer with whom she was having an affair. Arvad was a "person of interest" to the FBI, because during the 1936 Summer Olympics, she had interviewed Adolf Hitler, Hermann Göring, and Heinrich Himmler, among other key Nazis. She had then gone to work for the *Washington Times-Herald*, a D.C. newspaper with a decidedly isolationist editorial viewpoint. The Bureau's interest had intensified considerably when in the fall of 1941, the married-yet-separated Arvad had begun a relationship with the Navy ensign, who worked in the Office of Naval Intelligence. Convinced the reporter was likely a German spy, J. Edgar Hoover ordered round-the-clock surveillance of her, including phone taps and the bugging of her apartment, and of the hotel rooms in which she stayed while traveling.

It was one of the latter recordings that Fred Ayer had been tasked to transcribe. The first sounds the young agent heard were of enthusiastic lovemaking, which eventually gave way to languid conversation. Fred had just turned up the volume when he realized with a shock that the young Navy officer in bed with Arvad was his former Harvard classmate, John F. Kennedy. After noting that the lovers' postcoital conversation consisted solely of innocent intimacies, Fred signed off on the finished transcript and with a wry smile dropped the document into his outbox. In an attached note to his supervisor, Fred reported his past association with the "male subject" and was not surprised when days later he was taken off the special surveillance operation and sent back to normal duties.[7]

The workload to which Fred returned was crushing, with agents routinely working eighty-hour weeks. As he later recounted:

> The problems [were] strange and complex. The Bureau had only recently been named coordinating agency for all matters of espionage, sabotage, sedition and subversion. The Selective Service System was in full sway with its myriad accompanying investigations of draft dodgers, deserters, and self-styled conscientious objectors. The personnel of nearly every foreign embassy or legation was, for some reason or another, suspect. Hundreds of new bureaus and agencies were being staffed, and, as a result, tens of thousands of personnel fitness and loyalty investigations were under way. And, as usual, crime was paying.[8]

Nor did the situation improve following Fred's June 1942 transfer to the Cincinnati Field Office. An agent, as he later said, "unless he were reviewing complex files or dictating reports was to be out of the office each morning by 9 a.m. and was to remain on his investigative rounds until at least 4 p.m."[9] Even after normal working hours, agents, like doctors, were on call and had to leave a telephone number where they could be reached. They were expected to report to the office or a crime scene within an hour of getting a call, no matter what time it was.

After just over nine months in Cincinnati, Fred was again transferred, this time to the Boston field office. While the workload was still onerous, the move back to Massachusetts allowed more frequent visits to family and friends, and it also meant that on May 15, 1943, Fred and Anne's first child was born just miles from where Fred himself had come into the world. Following family tradition, the baby boy was named Frederick Ayer III.[10]

Though happy to be back on his home ground, Fred Ayer was increasingly dissatisfied with his work. His desire to join the armed forces and participate directly in the war against the Axis had only increased over time, and since the summer of 1942, he had, as he later recalled,

> been rather frantically striving to escape what I then considered a phony war against internal enemies. I wanted desperately to go overseas. I begged, I wrote, I telephoned, and I pounded on desks, as it seemed, uselessly. What did it matter that I couldn't see without glasses? I would carry six pair with me. I was young. I considered myself physically tough, spoke fluent French, could operate a typewriter, could shoot well with any type of firearm and had a fair knowledge of Europe and things European. In short, it was perfectly clear in my mind that I was just the man the U.S. intelligence service had been frenziedly seeking to fill a very important role abroad.[11]

When Fred's nearly constant official requests for some kind of war-related overseas work failed to produce the desired response, the young agent reached out to a relative who he believed was in a unique position to aid him in his quest. That person was his uncle, Major General George S. Patton Jr., who was married to Fred's father's sister, Bernice. Just days before the man who would soon become famous as "Old Blood and Guts" departed the United States to lead the Western Task Force in the November 1942 Allied invasion of North Africa, Fred begged his uncle to take him along in any capacity, "no matter how humble or menial." To the young agent's dismay, Patton refused, saying,

> Freddie, there are a lot of people trying to weaken this country from within. When this war is over there will be a lot more. We are being lied to in many cases about what is really going on. . . . Stalin is selling us a bill of goods, and we should not help him. We should use our arms to lick the German ourselves in the West. The Russian has been and will continue to be a menace. . . . The best thing for you to do is to stay home and do the job for which you have been trained.[12]

Fred was still brooding over his uncle's refusal when the summons came from the SAC at the Boston field office regarding the job in Haiti. The ultimate cancellation of that mission, Fred's sheepish return from Washington after saying his goodbyes, and the crushing workload that loomed before him all contributed to his increasing sense of gloom. His dejection quickly evaporated, however, when, during the first week of January 1944, he received another summons from the nation's capital. To Fred's delight, he was finally going to have the chance to get into the war.

HAVING SUCCEEDED IN SENDING FRANK AMPRIM TO ITALY under Army cover, despite myriad administrative and political hurdles, by December 1943, J. Edgar Hoover was ready to expand the Army Liaison Unit in Europe. On his orders, staffers began combing through Bureau personnel files looking for men with the right set of skills—fluency in French, German, or Italian; former residency or extensive travel in Europe; and proven investigative talent. Though existing membership in the Special Intelligence Service and prior military experience were desirable, they were not absolutely required, and to widen the pool of possible candidates, Hoover agreed to consider married men. Fred Ayer more than met the director's requirements, and the fact that the young agent was directly related to a senior Army commander in the European Theater was a definite plus.

Fred traveled to FBI headquarters in Washington in mid-January to undergo a battery of interviews. While most were conducted by senior Bureau officials—including on at least one occasion by Hoover himself—and had to do with Fred's experiences as a field agent, two of the sessions were conducted entirely in French by a native speaker from Georgetown University's foreign languages faculty. Fred's command of written and spoken French was rated as "superior," and the interviewer noted that the young agent's accent was "elegant" and decidedly Parisian. Fred was also grilled on his knowledge of the current war situation in Europe, and was repeatedly asked whether he was sure he could leave his wife and child for "an extended period." Having passed the interview process with flying colors, Fred was surprised when at the end of his week in D.C. he was directed to return to Boston "briefly" to await further instructions.

The agent's time back at the Boston Field Office was hardly brief, in that he was not summoned back to Washington until the end of April. After two days spent filling out paperwork at headquarters, Fred was put on a bus with

12 other agents and driven to Camp Ritchie, Maryland. Located some 60 miles northwest of Washington in the hill country just south of the Pennsylvania border, the installation was home to the Army's Military Intelligence Training Center (MITC).[13] Army Counter Intelligence Corps agents were also trained there, and Hoover had gained the Army's permission for his chosen agents to receive both basic military instruction and mission-specific training at the CIC "schoolhouse."

Fred and the other agents who accompanied him on the bus to Camp Ritchie were meant to form the nucleus of what Hoover intended to be a much larger organization.[14] Like Fred, each man had undergone interviews and language tests at headquarters, with several of the agents demonstrating fluency in more than one European tongue. The men ranged in age from 27 to 39, and had been drawn from both the SIS and field offices across the country. In addition to Ayer, the original group included the following men.

William Harrington Clark Jr., 27*

Bill Clark was born in Washington, D.C., and grew up in nearby Alexandria, Virginia. He graduated from Pennsylvania's Haverford College in 1938 with a BS degree in German and completed a master's in German literature at Columbia University in 1940. He joined the FBI almost immediately after graduation, and his first assignment following initial agent training was San Francisco, where, in November 1941, he married Margaret Garmey. In addition to fluent German, Clark spoke decent French and passable Italian. His extensive language skills made him a logical choice for the ALU, and he was among the first special agents called to Bureau headquarters for personal and language evaluation.

John Irish Condon, 29

A native of Bryn Mawr, Pennsylvania, Jack Condon attended Cornell University and spent his entire senior year in Heidelberg, where he became fluent in German. Condon joined the FBI after graduating from the University of Pennsylvania Law School, and his first assignment was the Dallas field office. In mid-1941, he was transferred to Honolulu, where he and his wife, Margaret, lived in a small, rented house near John Rodgers Airport.[15] During the December 7, 1941, Japanese attack on Pearl Harbor, the young agent fired his .45-caliber pistol at enemy aircraft strafing the field. Over the following months, Condon was a member of the FBI team that investigated

* Each agent's age is given as of the time of his selection for the Army Liaison Unit.

various aspects of the assault on Hawaii, and his reports became part of the official record of the 79th Congress's joint committee hearings on Pearl Harbor. By early 1944, Condon was assigned to the San Francisco field office, and it was from there that he was summoned to Washington for the interviews that led to his selection for Europe.

John Eldon Dunn, 32

Born in College Ward, Utah, Joe Dunn was one of at least two Mormon agents recruited for the ALU because of the time each had spent as a missionary in prewar Germany.[16] The presence there of young American men of the Church of Jesus Christ of Latter-day Saints was part of a very active missionary program begun in Europe following World War I. The missionaries in Germany spent two years both proselytizing and working with established congregations, in the process becoming fluent in German and learning much about the nation's history, culture, and politics. Dunn was in Germany from 1931 to 1933, and upon his return, he enrolled at the University of Utah, graduating in 1936. He married Edith Green the following year and joined the FBI in January 1941. He was brought into the ALU from the Milwaukee field office. His fellow agents jokingly referred to him as the "Blond Beast," a reference to his 6-foot height, 210-pound weight, blond hair, and blue eyes.

Joseph George Fellner, 33

Joe Fellner was born in Arnoldstein, Austria, came to the United States with his parents at the age of two, and grew up in Milwaukee. He spent extended periods of time with relatives in Austria in both 1927 and 1930, and spoke fluent German with an Austrian accent. He also spoke passable Italian, given that Arnoldstein is barely three miles from the Italian border and his parents and most of his Austrian relatives used both languages. Fellner attended the University of Wisconsin at Madison, then its law school, where he met his future wife, Christine Torkelson. Both graduated in 1936 with LLB degrees and practiced law in Milwaukee. Joe joined the FBI in 1937, and was assigned to the field offices in Pittsburgh, Detroit, Seattle, Chicago, Milwaukee, and New York. It was while working at the latter that he was approached about serving in Europe. During his interviews at Bureau headquarters, he was rated as fluent in both German and Italian.

Erling Harald Kloster, 28

A colleague of Fellner's at the New York field office, Hal Kloster was born in Iowa to Norwegian immigrant parents. He graduated from St. Olaf College in Minnesota and from Harvard Law School in 1941. His younger brother, Lief Kloster, an Army Air Forces pilot captured by the Japanese in the Philippines, died in captivity.[17] Hal's first assignment after joining the FBI in late 1941 was to the San Francisco field office, where he worked with Bill Clark. Following America's entry into the war, Hal's fluency in both Norwegian and German (which he'd taken in college) led to his being assigned to internal security investigations of enemy aliens. Hal and his wife, Mary, moved to Los Angeles following his early 1943 transfer to that city's field office. Near the end of 1943 the couple moved again, this time to New York, where Hal worked closely with Fellner. It is likely that Fellner recommended Kloster for the ALU.

Roland Octave L'Allier, 34

Roland L'Allier was born in Somerset, Wisconsin, to a French-speaking and deeply Roman Catholic family with roots in Québec. He grew up completely bilingual and spent most summers with relatives in Canada. After graduation from St. Lawrence College,[18] a Catholic boy's high school in Mount Cavalry, Wisconsin, he attended the Université de Montréal. L'Allier graduated from the school's faculty of law in 1938, married distant cousin Gabrielle Charlotte Legare, and took a job in St. Paul, Minnesota. He joined the FBI in early 1941 and was assigned first to Philadelphia and then to the St. Paul field office. Though L'Allier worked a variety of cases, he specialized in those dealing with communist and socialist organizations, and it was that particular skill set—coupled with his fluency in French—that led to his inclusion in the ALU.

Arthur Matthew O'Connor, 30

Art O'Connor was born in New Haven, Connecticut, the last of four children of Joseph and Elenor O'Connor. His mother died soon after his birth, and Art, his three siblings, and their father all moved in with Joseph's three older sisters. In high school, Art displayed a talent for foreign languages, especially German and French, and wanted to further his studies in college. That proved beyond his family's economic abilities, however, and in 1934, Art got a job as a stenographer but remained in the extended household. By the time in registered for the draft in 1940, he was still working as a stenographer, but by then for the FBI's New Haven field office. As a current Bureau employee with valuable language skills, he was able to apply for training as a special agent, which he completed in early 1942. He then returned to the New Haven office, from where he was recruited for the ALU.

Bernard Walter Rucks, 27

Minnesota-born Walt Rucks's parents were first-generation Americans born to German immigrant parents, and Walt grew up speaking both English and German. After high school, he enrolled at the University of Minnesota, graduating in 1939 with a BA degree in business administration. He went to work for the IBM Corporation in Saint Paul and joined the FBI in early 1942. His first assignment was to the Kansas City, Missouri field office, but in 1943, he was transferred to New York. There he worked with both Hal Kloster and Joe Fellner, and it was the latter who recommended Walt for the ALU.

Boyd Verne Sheets, 28

The second former Mormon missionary to join the ALU, Boyd Sheets was born and raised in Salt Lake City. One of thity-six young Mormons sent to Germany in 1936, he worked in Wuppertal until 1938 and learned to speak fluent German. He earned a BA degree in speech pathology at the University of Utah, and was working on a master's in the same subject at the University of Minnesota when he joined the FBI in early 1942. After completing agent training, he married Barbara Snow at the LDS temple in Salt Lake and then took up his first posting, at the New York field office. He was ultimately transferred to the Salt Lake field office, and it was from there that he was brought into the ALU.

Richard Charles Thompson, 34

A native of Deer Park, Wisconsin, Dick Thompson first traveled to Germany, in October 1935, to bicycle through Bavaria with several friends. He graduated from the University of Wisconsin at Madison in 1937 with a BA in education and soon afterward married June Hosier. In 1938, the young couple departed for Germany, where Dick spent a year in a graduate German-language program at the University of Freiburg. He took a month off from his studies to take another bicycle tour of southern Germany, this time with his wife. Upon the couples' return to the United States, Dick enrolled in UW–Madison's law school. He joined the FBI in February 1941, and he was assigned to the Los Angeles field office. Among other duties, he was assigned to interview such well-known German émigrés as Thomas Mann and Berthold Brecht. At 6 feet, 4 inches tall, he must have been an imposing figure, doubly so in that he was able to conduct the interviews in flawless German. It was that language ability, his travels in Germany, and his experience investigating German nationals that led to his selection for the operation in Europe.

Hans Frederick William Wenthur, 39

The son of German immigrants, Hans Wenthur was born and raised in Milwaukee. He did not follow the usual career route into the Bureau, in that he had no background as a lawyer or accountant and wasn't a college graduate. After high school, Hans had, like Art O'Connor, taken a stenography course, and soon after completing it, he got a job as the chief clerk of the Wisconsin state legislature's Committees on State Affairs and on Excise and Fees. He then worked in the Milwaukee Police Department's Bureau of Identification, where his fluency in German soon led to his being called upon to take part in investigations dealing with members of Milwaukee's large German and Austrian immigrant communities. He quickly became adept at interrogating German-speaking suspects, often by adopting the persona of a rigid and uncompromising Prussian aristocrat, and was ultimately taken on as an MPD detective. Following the September 1939 outbreak of war in Europe, Hans was often "loaned" to the FBI's Milwaukee field office to take part in investigations of suspected German sabotage and espionage activities, and soon after Pearl Harbor, the FBI offered him a position as a special agent. He was brought into the SIS and worked for several months tracking German agents in Argentina before becoming the oldest man to be selected for the ALU.

Howard Peter Winter, 30

Like Art O'Connor, Pete Winter was a Connecticut native. Born in Hartford, he attended that city's elementary and high schools and then enrolled in nearby Trinity College. Pete graduated in 1936 with a BA in modern languages (with emphasis on French, German, and Spanish), and at the time he registered for the draft in October 1940, he was working at the Pratt & Whitney aircraft engine assembly plant in East Hartford. He joined the FBI soon afterward and was immediately selected for SIS duty in Latin America. From December 1941 to July 1942, he was undercover in Torreón, Mexico. He then served as legal attaché in Guatemala City, from August 1942 to July 1943, and in Port au Prince, Haiti, from August 1943 to January 1944. At the time he was chosen for the ALU, he was assigned to the New Orleans field office.

While Fred Ayer and the other men chosen for the Army Liaison Unit would be undertaking fairly straightforward investigations of American renegades, as Hoover called the suspected traitors, the agents' working conditions would differ in two very significant ways from those they routinely encountered in the States.

First, though domestic field work could obviously be dangerous—there was a reason FBI agents trained with and employed various sorts of firearms—Europe in 1944 remained a war zone in which the ALU members might well be exposed to far more lethal weaponry. Artillery and mortar barrages, land mines, small-arms fire, and even air attack were distinctly possible threats. Lacking any prior military experience, the ALU men would need to be trained how to operate in a tactical environment, as well as learning the basics of Army organization, rank structures, military courtesy, and the rules of warfare.

Second, and in some ways more important, the ALU agents would need to learn all they could about four German adversaries far more dangerous and vastly more powerful and resourceful than any individual or criminal organization they had ever faced. The first of these enemies was the Wehrmacht, Germany's combined land, sea, and air forces. The second was the Abwehr, the military intelligence service of the armed forces. The third, the Sicherheitsdienst, was the intelligence service of the SS and Nazi Party. The fourth and in some ways the most fearsome of the organizations the ALU agents might have to confront was the Gestapo, Nazi Germany's secret police.[19]

In early 1943, a couple of rudimentary weeks at Fort Belvoir had been considered enough military groundwork for Frank Amprim before his departure for North Africa. A year later, the significantly altered military situation in Europe convinced both J. Edgar Hoover and the Army that Fred Ayer and his colleagues needed far better preparation before being dispatched overseas. Camp Ritchie was deemed the ideal location, and it was that determination that led to the ALU agents' bus ride through the early spring chill of northern Maryland.

Fred and the others spent their first few days at the Army post in "admin mode," filling out forms, being issued uniforms and field equipment, and receiving the first of many inoculations meant to protect them against an impressive array of diseases. While the agents were billeted in officers' quarters on base, Fred elected to stay in a nearby residence hotel. There he roomed with his uncle, a former Army Air Forces officer who had come back into service to teach the basics of aerial reconnaissance photo interpretation to students at the military intelligence school, and another man, a World War I veteran undergoing training at the Counter Intelligence Corps School before taking up an assignment with the OSS.[20] The apartment the three shared was distinguished "by the size and number of its cockroaches," according to Fred, which won the building the almost universal appellation of 'Vermin Towers.'"[21]

Once the ALU agents began their training, each twelve-hour day was divided into three four-hour periods of instruction. The first block began with physical conditioning, followed by Army-specific classwork covering ranks, basic unit organization, military courtesy (which the agents wryly referred to as "salute school"), familiarization with standard Army firearms and explosives, and an in-depth examination of military law and the ways in which it differed from civilian federal law.

The second instruction period—military intelligence methods and operations—was taught by representatives of the MITC and dealt with the organization and activities of the German intelligence services both in Europe and within the Western Hemisphere. The classes also covered military- and intelligence-specific terms in German and French, basic codes and cyphers, secret inks, the use of microdots to covertly pass information by mail, aerial photograph interpretation, how to compile order-of-battle intelligence,[22] the ways in which civilians and law-enforcement agencies in occupied Europe either collaborated with or resisted the Germans, and the operations of U.S. Army intelligence units, both in the field and at higher command echelons.

Each day's final class period was spent on counterintelligence (CI) methods and operations and was conducted by CIC personnel. Whereas intelligence agents seek to find out things about the enemy, the purpose of CI is to prevent the enemy from discovering information about friendly forces and to either neutralize or "turn" hostile operatives. The basic methods used to conduct CI operations were already very familiar to the ALU agents, since successful investigations by both CIC and FBI agents were built on similar foundations. These included identifying possible targets through exhaustive "shoe leather" field work, keeping extensive and detailed files on individuals and groups, working with informants and undercover agents, undertaking surveillance of persons and locations of interest, and interrogating suspects. Since the conditions under which CIC agents worked were obviously different, in that they often conducted investigations in combat zones and recently liberated areas in which enemy stay-behind agents might still be present, the CIC instructors' insights were especially valuable to Ayer and his colleagues.

Near the end of the training at Camp Ritchie, momentous news arrived that stunned the ALU men. As Fred recalled:

> I vividly recall sitting by a radio in Vermin Towers, waiting through the small hours of the morning exalted and prayerful, confident as well as afraid, along with tens of millions of others, as the early news of Normandy reached our ears. I remember feeling, perhaps stupidly, that I had been cheated by being left behind at home.[23]

The news of the June 6, 1944, D-Day landings affected the other members of the ALU in much the same way. All were eager to get into the war before it ended, and feared that if the invasion forces were unable to break out from the beachheads or, God forbid, were pushed back into the sea, the ALU mission would be canceled outright. That possibility seemed increasingly likely when, a few days after completing the Camp Ritchie training, Fred and his colleagues received orders from Bureau headquarters in Washington to return to their home field offices and "await further developments."

As it happened, it wasn't the military situation in France that was imperiling the ALU's deployment to Europe. It was a much closer and far more familiar adversary—the Office of Strategic Services.

Several weeks after arriving in Algiers in October 1943, Frank Amprim had made contact with Vincent Scamporino, the civilian head of all OSS special intelligence operations in Sicily and Italy. It was a risky meeting for both men, in that their respective bosses—J. Edgar Hoover and William Donovan—loathed each other both personally and professionally. Yet Amprim and Scamporino were able to forge a mutually beneficial working relationship, one that helped the FBI agent in his ultimately successful quest to locate Ezra Pound. Ironically, it was the news that Amprim was closing in on the poet that stirred Donovan's ire.

Long convinced that the FBI had no business operating in war zones, the OSS chief was incensed by the increasing likelihood that it would be a Bureau agent who would apprehend one of the highest-profile America renegades. Even before Amprim rolled into Rome with the S Force, Donovan was using his close relationship with President Roosevelt to sow doubt about the need for Hoover's Army Liaison Unit. The OSS was more than capable of tracking down U.S. citizens who had stayed in Axis-occupied territory after Pearl Harbor and subsequently collaborated with the Axis, Wild Bill argued. He insisted that a mere handful of FBI agents would be incapable of doing the job that rightfully belonged to the scores of OSS X-2 operatives that would soon be following Allied ground forces across Europe. While Donovan's arguments ultimately did not erode Roosevelt's support for the ALU, they caused enough of a kerfuffle among Washington's political movers and shakers that Hoover was ultimately forced to slow-walk the ALU's deployment. Fred Ayer and his colleagues were therefore directed to return to their field offices while Hoover and Donovan continued their bureaucratic turf war.

While Fred was undoubtedly happy to be back in Boston with his wife and son, he was increasingly anxious about the possibility that continued delays in the deployment of the ALU would ultimately result in the entire mission being canceled. He was therefore understandably relieved when a month or so after returning from Camp Ritchie, he got the call he'd been nervously awaiting. A senior Bureau member directed him to be at the USAAF Air Transport Command passenger terminal at National Airport the following morning, in uniform, his bags packed, and his travel orders in hand. After hurried goodbyes, he boarded a train at Boston's South Station for the overnight run to Union Station in Washington, D.C., then took a taxi across the Potomac to National Airport in northern Virginia.

Fred made it to the ATC terminal with time to spare, only to be told that his departure would be delayed because the Bureau had not secured him a high enough passenger priority number to get him a seat on a flight to Europe. Outbound aircraft were packed with senior military officers, politicians, State Department officials, and others rushing to the Continent in the wake of the Normandy landings, and a lowly FBI agent without a priority boarding number had no chance of securing a seat. Fred spent the following nine days roaming the halls of Bureau headquarters attempting to get someone with authority to request the priority number for him, but it seemed that all of the FBI's senior leaders were too busy with other, more pressing matters. He finally, and dejectedly, took the train back to Boston to yet again "await further developments."

Just over a week later, another call summoned Fred back to Washington, this time for a face-to-face meeting with the director himself. When the young agent entered Hoover's office, he was pleased to find Special Agent Donald L. Daughters, a friend from the Boston field office, also in attendance. The two agents, Hoover said, would be the first ALU members sent overseas, and Don was to be Fred's second-in-command.

It was welcome news for Fred, because he and Don had known each other for several years. Their paths had first crossed when both were Harvard undergraduates, though the older Fred was two years ahead of Don. The two men struck up a friendship despite their different backgrounds: Fred had known a life of privilege on the family estate in Wenham, while Don grew up in Watertown, a Boston suburb.[24] One of the things that first drew them together was their shared love of French. Fred had been schooled in the language from early on, and he had actually spoken it before he'd learned English. When he was a child, his parents had enrolled him in a nursery school run by a French woman. From there he went to Ste. Jeanne d'Arc, a Roman Catholic French-immersion school in Lowell, Massachusetts, until the age of eleven. Don, for his part, had taken French in high school, where, in addition to being a star athlete, he was president of the French Club. At Harvard, Don was named an All-American football tight end and majored in Romance languages, and following his graduation in 1939, he taught French and Spanish at a Catholic high school in Boston.

Don had intended to use his foreign-language skills as a foundation for a career in international business, but something else he'd done at Harvard put that plan on hold. The university had one of the best Army Reserve Officers' Training Corps programs in the country, and Don took ROTC all four years. The Harvard unit was field artillery–specific, and upon graduation, Don was commissioned a second lieutenant in that branch. He then attended an intensive two-week follow-on course, after which he was promoted to first lieutenant. In March 1941, while Don was teaching in Boston, he was called to active duty and deployed to Puerto Rico as part of America's shift to a war footing. To his surprise, the assignment was to a military intelligence company rather than a field artillery unit, a change made because of his language skills. While Don found the work interesting, he was soon faced with a choice: He had applied to the FBI soon after graduation from Harvard, and after just two months in Puerto Rico, he was notified that he'd been accepted. With his commanding officer's support, Don was able to gain a release from active duty, and in June 1941, he reported to Quantico for initial agent training—where one of his classmates was none other than Fred Ayer.

Upon completion of their training, the two men went their separate ways, with Fred headed to the Washington, D.C., field office and Don to Seattle. Don worked there until early January 1942, when he was transferred to Los Angeles. His time in the City of Angeles didn't last long, however, for after just two months, he was summoned to Bureau headquarters for assignment to the SIS. Once again, his language abilities were the reason for the move, and after completing SIS training, he was sent to Santiago, Chile. He spent the next eighteen months in Latin America, working primarily out of the legal attaché's office at the U.S. Embassy. While in the Chilean capital, Don met and fell in love with Yvonne Fath, a local-hire embassy employee of Swiss-French descent. When Don was transferred back Stateside, Yvonne followed, and the couple was married in Washington, D.C. Soon afterward, Don was transferred to the Boston field office, where he and Fred renewed their friendship.

Despite the fact that Don had not attended the Camp Ritchie training period, Fred knew he was the perfect choice for the ALU. Don would be the only member of the team who had actual military experience, and he had even worked—albeit briefly—in military intelligence. He was obviously more than qualified in the foreign-language department, and the fact that he and Fred knew, liked, and respected one another was a definite plus. Before allowing the two men to leave his office, Hoover looked at them solemnly and, after reminding them of the importance of tracking down American renegades, added that there would be another, equally important aspect of their mission. As Fred later remembered, the director said:

> You two have been picked to go first. The other men will follow. You have both been well grounded in the workings of the communist conspiracy. You have now been trained to go to Europe and take a logical part in the military counterintelligence set-up. You have a plausible reason to be there. Germany is defeated, although it might take her two years to realize it. I am, therefore, not so much interested in what the Nazis have done as in what the Russians are doing and plan to do. Find out all you can on this score, but remember that they are our allies and that the Powers That Be won't like it if they find you operating outside your charter.[25]

With that sobering thought in their heads, Fred and Don left the building and headed to Union Station to catch a train back to Boston. They would have just forty-eight hours to say goodbye to their families before reporting to the ATC terminal at National Airport, this time bearing the necessary priority tickets. Barring any last-minute glitches, the two men would be in London just twelve hours after boarding a Europe-bound flight.

Unfortunately, fate had something else in store for them.

CHAPTER 5

City of Light

FRED AYER AND DON DAUGHTERS SPENT THE DAY before their scheduled departure for Europe attending to a myriad of bureaucratic details involving both the FBI and the Army.

The men first turned in their Bureau credentials and badges, and signed forms in which they acknowledged they were willing to be temporarily relieved of normal Bureau responsibilities in order to undertake "special activities" in the European Theater of Operations (ETO). The time they spent on those duties would count toward their FBI retirement, the forms stated, and should they be killed in the line of duty, their identified beneficiaries would receive the standard federal life insurance payout. Moreover, upon completion of the European assignment, both agents would be offered the field assignment of their choice.

Having shed their Bureau personas—at least on paper—Fred and Don spent the rest of the day at the newly completed Pentagon building acquiring their military "cover." They received orders signed by Major General Clayton Bissell, the Army's director of military intelligence,[1] identifying them as temporary majors, with SECRET-level clearances, engaged in classified work authorized at the highest levels. The documents specified that the men were to be accorded all the rights and privileges of their rank, and allowed them to use military transportation and facilities, to carry personal weapons, and to travel anywhere in the ETO that their official duties might require. Perhaps most significantly, the orders directed that the men be given "any and all necessary assistance" by any Army individual or organization to which their orders were presented.

Fred and Don spent their last night in Washington at the Carroll Arms Hotel on Capitol Hill and the next morning were driven across the Potomac to the Air Transport Command passenger terminal at National Airport. Both men were well-enough acquainted with the realities of wartime air travel to assume that their Atlantic crossing would be neither quick nor trouble free, and were therefore pleasantly surprised when after a short ATC briefing and the signing of a few additional forms they boarded their C-54 and departed on time. The flight was full, with the other passengers including senior military officers, State Department personnel, civilian journalists, and a party of replacement Army nurses bound for frontline field hospitals.

The first leg of the flight took the C-54 northeastward across New England, over Nova Scotia, and into the major ATC hub at the Royal Canadian Air Force base in Stephenville, Newfoundland, where the gremlins of wartime air travel caught up with Fred and Don. As it turned out, their priority tickets didn't prevent the two agents from being "bumped" so that two senior British officers could have their seats. Then, a combination of bad weather over the Canadian Maritimes and North Atlantic and a series of mechanical issues with the C-54 on which Fred and Don had been assigned new seats kept the men on the ground for five days. Once finally on their way again, the agents transited through Prestwick, Scotland, and on to Croydon Airport, nine miles south of London.

While checking in at the airport's security office, Fred and Don were forcefully reminded that they were now in a war zone. As Fred later recalled:

> We heard certainly the loudest explosion of our young lives. Pictures crashed from the wall, an inkwell jumped from the desk, and I jumped from my skin. With what I felt was becoming calm, however, I observed, "I don't suppose that was a V-1 was it?" "No, old chap," said an RAF officer. "That was The Rocket, but we don't admit it yet."[2]

By "The Rocket," the man meant the explosive-laden ballistic missile the Germans referred to as the *Vergeltungswaffe Zwei* (retaliation, or vengeance, weapon two, the V-2), rather than the smaller V-1 the British referred to as the "buzz bomb" because of the characteristic noise made by its pulsejet engine. The V-1 had started hitting targets in Britain just after D-Day, while the first V-2 had fallen on September 8, just days before Fred and Don's arrival.[3]

Having cleared British customs and passport control, the agents left the Croydon terminal in the early evening to be met by a driver from the U.S. embassy. The man dropped them at Claridge's, the same hotel Art Thurston had stayed at upon his arrival in the British capital, where a note from Joe Lynch awaited them. The legal attaché said a car would pick them up in the morning and take them to Supreme Headquarters Allied Expeditionary Force (SHAEF) headquarters, located in Bushy Park, ten miles southwest of Central London. In the meantime, Lynch suggested the agents enjoy their stay at Claridge's with the embassy's compliments. After dinner in the hotel restaurant, Fred and Don decided to take a walk around the neighborhood, only to find themselves in streets that, as Fred later recalled, were "as nearly black as dark can be." As the two men groped their way forward, Fred "crashed into a two-star general . . . knocking him into a dank and dirty gutter." The incident ended with a few choice words from the senior officer and an abject apology from Fred, with Don struggling to stifle his laughter.[4]

The agents' visit to SHAEF headquarters the following morning initially seemed to also be headed in a negative direction. After cooling their heels in the outer office of the assistant chief of staff for intelligence, they were ushered before a rather stern-looking Army major named Anthony Nicol, who demanded to see their FBI credentials. When Fred explained they had left their badges and identity cards back in Washington on Hoover's orders, Nicol brusquely asked how he could be sure the men were who they purported to be. Fred offered to produce their travel orders, only to have Nicol respond that such documents meant nothing to him, since they had been signed "by some sergeant in the Pentagon." Fred and Don were beginning to think their mission to Europe would end right there, when Nicol dissolved in laughter and explained that he knew who they were and was only getting even for the times that people in the New York field office made him feel "like a saboteur" when he'd gone there on business. He then slapped both men on the back and, still chuckling, led them into the first of the day's briefings.[5]

Just before noon on their third day in the British capital, Fred and Don sat down with Joe Lynch in his office overlooking Grosvenor Square. The legal attaché since not long after Art Thurston's departure, Lynch was one of the busiest people in the embassy.[6] In addition to being the Bureau's main liaison with MI5, MI6, and those British military intelligence departments that had not yet crossed the Channel to France, he supervised Jack Cimperman's continued oversight of the decrypted Ultra intercepts (which the FBI referred to as Ostrich). In the months since the D-Day landings, Lynch had also been instrumental in coordinating with Colonel H. Gordon Sheen, SHAEF commander Dwight Eisenhower's counterintelligence chief, for the arrival and support of the Army Liaison Unit agents. Sheen and his staff had moved with the advance element of SHAEF headquarters from London to Versailles following the August 25 liberation of Paris and were awaiting Fred and Don's arrival.

Before the two agents could cross the Channel, however, there were dozens of additional people—American, British, and Free French—with whom they needed to meet. The first of these was Ambassador John Winant, who hosted them for two hours in his apartment-cum-office in the embassy. Though obviously tired from long hours of work with little sleep, Winant succinctly explained the then current political situation in France, beginning with General Charles de Gaulle's establishment of a provisional Free French government. De Gaulle's post-liberation proclamations that all France was once again united were wildly inaccurate, Winant told Fred and Don. First, and most obviously, because much of the eastern part of the country was still held by the Germans, and second, because France's powerful Communist Party—which had fielded effective Résistance units against the Germans during the occupation—was determined to take over the reins of government. Though Paris was still reveling in the joy of liberation after four years of brutal occupation, Winant said, the struggle to save France from communism was just beginning.

That sober assessment was echoed by others with whom Fred and Don met during their time in London, including David Petrie of MI5. The communists already controlled a variety of political and labor organizations, the director general noted, and party members were seeking to insert themselves into every level of the still-organizing de Gaulle government. The penetration of the police and intelligence services was especially troubling, Petrie said, and he warned Fred and Don to be wary of any French law-enforcement or security official with whom they came into contact. Nor were communists the only adversary in newly liberated France, the MI5 chief added, for German stay-behind agents were still active, especially in Paris and its environs.

Suitably forewarned, the two agents began wrapping up their meetings in London and preparing for the cross-Channel journey to France. During their final days in the British capital, the men were again reminded that the war was far from over, and that the low-tech V-1 flying bombs remained a real threat even with the advent of the more advanced V-2. Walking along blacked-out streets, they would, as Fred later wrote, hear

> a noise as if some giant motorcycle were racing across the heavens. An angry streamer of red would appear heading north. After a while the

noise of the motor would cut out, the streamer fade and disappear. At this point one could but wait. . . .[7]

The silence would soon be shattered by the sound of a massive explosion, a brief but intense flash of brilliant light, and if the men were close to the impact point, a shock wave that would blow out the windows of nearby buildings. And it wasn't just distant parts of the city that suffered—the area around Grosvenor Square had been hit several times, and the wreckage of damaged and destroyed buildings still blocked several nearby streets on the morning Fred and Don climbed into an embassy car for the drive to Hendon airdrome and the flight to Le Bourget.

As the two agents entered the French airport's battered arrivals terminal several hours later, they were greeted by an Army enlisted soldier holding up a hand-drawn sign bearing their names. The man led Fred and Don to a waiting olive-drab Dodge staff car, and once the agents were settled in the rear seat and their duffel bags stowed in the vehicle's trunk, the soldier pulled the car away from the curb and set off for Versailles, eighteen miles to the southwest, on the other side of Paris. The driver skirted the center of the French capital to the north, generally following the left bank of the Seine through the western suburbs. Once in Versailles, the car pulled up in front of the opulent Trianon Palace hotel, at 1, boulevard de la Reine. Until a few months before the headquarters of the Luftwaffe in occupied France, the building was now home to the advance elements of SHAEF.[8]

Among the building's occupants was Colonel H. Gordon Sheen. A native of New York City, Sheen had spent much of his youth in Germany, where his Army officer father had taken part in the post–World War I Allied occupation. Sheen's ability to read, write, and speak German inevitably drew him into intelligence after he was called onto active duty from the Army Reserve in 1940, and following the 1942 establishment of the Counter Intelligence Corps, Sheen was named its first director.[9] Described by one of his early agents as "an outgoing, dynamic, physical specimen of man who was one of the first Americans to win black belts in judo and karate,"[10] Sheen was also keenly intelligent, analytical, and willing to tell the unvarnished truth to his superiors. In late 1943, Eisenhower had personally tapped the highly respected officer to become SHAEF's CI chief.

Sheen greeted Fred and Don warmly when they were ushered into his office in the Trianon Palace's Room 140, and over the following few hours, he gave the agents a thorough overview of the CI situation in Paris and the other areas of liberated France. The Army was still apprehending German stay-behind agents and French collaborators, Sheen said, and he would be happy to turn over to the FBI men the names of U.S. citizens the French believed had thrown in their lot with the Nazis. While he realized that tracking down American renegades was the Bureau's primary goal in newly liberated Europe, Sheen was aware that Fred and Don were also tasked with investigating the extent of communist infiltration into de Gaulle's government. The CI chief offered his full cooperation in that task as well and only asked that Fred and Don keep him informed if they found anything he ought to know. Sheen, Fred later wrote, "was not only a delightful and gallant gentleman, he was also very much a realist. He accepted the presence of uniformed civilians and recognized the nature of our mission."[11] To increase the chances of that mission's success, Sheen saw to it that the agents were issued with SHAEF "blue passes." The documents ordered U.S. military personnel "not to interfere with the bearer in the performance of his official duties" and authorized the bearer to "take such steps as he may deem advisable to obtain information of any nature of any subversive activity by the enemy" and to "carry cameras and firearms."[12]

Following their initial meeting with Sheen, Fred and Don were driven in to downtown Paris to the hotel that would be their temporary billet until they could find other accommodations. Though the liberation had occurred weeks earlier, the city's residents were still joyously celebrating the end of the German occupation, and Allied troops of several nationalities were more than pleased to find themselves the recipients of very intimate expressions of appreciation from the women of the city. The hotel chosen for the FBI agents was apparently a frequent venue for these usually temporary and often commercial interactions, for when Fred and Don checked in, they noticed a large sign hanging behind the front desk that read, in both French and English, "No women permitted upstairs under any circumstances. Violators will be arrested by the Military Police." Just as the two agents were collecting their room keys they noticed, as Fred later remembered, "a blonde and a redhead, both obviously and delectably a woman, walk calmly up the stairs. I raised my left New England eyebrow and pointed to the sign. The concierge shrugged, sighed, and complained, 'But mon commandant, what a tragedy it is that I suffer from eyes of the most myopic.'"[13]

As entertaining as the staff and clientele of the hotel might have been,

Fred and Don immediately began searching for a residence more suitable for J. Edgar Hoover's personal representatives in the City of Light. Somewhat to their surprise, it took only a few days to find a place. An officer on Sheen's staff suggested they look at an apartment at 15, avenue Mozart in the 16th *arrondissement*, an upscale residential district on the Right Bank of the Seine less than a mile west of the Eiffel Tower. Located near two Métro stations in an eight-floor building erected in 1931, the apartment had been confiscated from a wealthy French family in 1940 and had been home to a senior German diplomat until his hasty departure the day before Free French troops entered the capital.[14] One of the larger of the building's twenty-two units, the fully furnished apartment took up the entire fifth floor and was laid out in a U shape around an open courtyard. With three bedrooms, two bathrooms, two studies, a kitchen, a formal dining room, and a large living room, the apartment was more than adequate for Fred, Don, and the occasional official guest.[15] The agents quickly obtained the keys from the Army Billeting Office and moved in less than a week after their arrival in France. Days later, an Army truck delivered to the apartment two desks, a large safe, a supply closet, a battered wooden file cabinet, and two portable typewriters, allowing the living room to be turned into the FBI's first official office in the liberated French capital.

Though generally pleased with their new digs, Fred and Don soon realized the apartment had a couple of drawbacks. The elevator would frequently stop working, meaning they had to climb five flights of stairs, often while carrying file boxes, groceries, and other items. And as Fred noted, looters

> had denuded what had once been a fine wine cellar. What was worse, they had completely emptied the coal bin. This second problem we were able partially to solve after an aesthetic decision that Nazi taste called for far too much heavy oaken furniture. When reduced to manageable proportions, it burned beautifully in an old fashioned potbelly stove.[16]

The apartment's shortcomings were unfortunately highlighted not long after the agents moved in. MI5 director general David Petrie had come to Paris for an Allied intelligence conference and—out of respect for J. Edgar Hoover—wished to pay a call on what was, for better or worse, the FBI's official headquarters in France. Petrie used a cane, and Fred offered him the use of the building's elevator despite misgivings about its dependability. All seemed to be going well initially, for the open-lattice car rose slowly and steadily. That is, until it reached a spot halfway between the fourth and fifth floors, when it stopped dead. As Fred recalled:

> I was just barely able to see the general's cap, his monocle, his mustache, and the rank insignia on his shoulders. . . . The general's aide seemed to be quite upset about the whole matter, and demanded that something be done. The British security chief, however, was wholly relaxed and benign. "Type of thing happens all the time, don't you see. Bloody war and all that, you know." Shortly thereafter . . . our janitor . . . managed to insert a new fuse in the right socket. We were then able to put our international amenities on a more formal footing. We did have a fire blazing in our grate. Sir David studied it for a while. "Some of those pieces look a lot like chair legs, you know." "They are," I said. After all, security officers are trained to be observant.[17]

Following Petrie's departure, Don stood thoughtfully for a moment before turning to Fred. "You know," Don said, "I just can't imagine J. Edgar Hoover stuck in an elevator. I bet the damned thing wouldn't dare break down if he were in it."[18]

FRED AND DON HAD BEGUN SENDING REPORTS to Bureau headquarters while still in London for their briefings by Joe Lynch and representatives of MI5 and MI6. Those initial documents had essentially been "backgrounders" on such topics as the ways in which Britain intended to deal with its own renegades, the organization and activities of the OSS's London station, and the names of several individuals the British believed had transited through Commonwealth territory on the way to undertake espionage missions in the United States. The move across the English Channel only added to the flow of information back to the Bureau—the agents' first report had gone out via SHAEF's secure mail pouch on Sunday, October 1, just twenty-four hours after they had landed at Le Bourget.[19]

That document had dealt with communist infiltration of the French Forces of the Interior—the umbrella anti-German resistance organization—and was largely based on information provided by Gordon Sheen during his first meeting with the FBI agents.[20] That was also likely the case with the second report, "Administrative Set-Up of Allied Counter-Intelligence," which went out on October 2. The third report, "Food Prices and Food Rationing in

Paris," was compiled by Don and was mailed two days later.[21] All three documents were written while the two agents were still billeted in the Paris hotel with the colorful clientele.

Once settled in the avenue Mozart apartment, the agents began researching and writing a series of "survey reports" for Hoover and other senior Bureau leaders dealing with the current intelligence situation in the liberated parts of France. Based largely on interviews with Sheen and other American, British, and Free French officers, the reports covered such topics as the working relationships among the various Allied military intelligence organizations and short biographies of their senior leaders, the operations of the Services de Renseignements (intelligence services) and civilian police agencies of de Gaulle's provisional French government, the wartime activities of the major French Resistance groups and how they were being integrated into the Free French army, the continuing hunt for German stay-behind agents, and the ways in which French citizens who had collaborated with the Nazis were being dealt with by the French legal system.

Even while compiling these reports, Fred and Don were starting to put together their list of "targets," which fell roughly into four categories. The first comprised those American renegades whose collaboration with the Nazis was already well documented because the individuals had made radio broadcasts or written print propaganda pieces on behalf of Joseph Goebbels's propaganda ministry, much as Ezra Pound had done for Mussolini's Ministry of Popular Culture. Most of the people in this first category were not likely to be found in liberated France, having fled to Germany, though information on their past activities and current whereabouts could well be. The second category included Americans still in the greater Paris region who were suspected of collaborating in other ways, including providing material or financial aid to the Germans. Collaborators and German agents who knew of or supported Axis intelligence operations in the United States made up the third category, and the fourth comprised communist agents or fellow travelers—American or otherwise—who were working to infiltrate French institutions or support covert Soviet activities in the U.S. or South America.

Fred and Don well understood that locating and interrogating any of their intended targets would require good working relationships with a variety of military and civilian agencies. In addition to their already close ties with Gordon Sheen, the agents therefore held extensive meetings with senior officers in the U.S. Army's Military Police, Provost Marshal, and Judge Advocate General branches, as well as with the leaders of the analogous British army organizations. Given that it was the French police and intelligence services that were likely to have files on American citizens who had remained in occupied France and were suspected of having collaborated with the Germans, Fred and Don made a special effort to reach out to key figures in both services. Their primary contacts were Commissaire Charles Badin, director of the civilian Police Judiciaire in Paris, and Commandant Paul Paillole, head of the Direction de la Sécurité Militaire (DSM), the French military counterintelligence organization.

A lifelong Parisian *flic* (cop), Badin had risen through the ranks and investigated some of the French capital's most notorious crimes and criminals. Following France's 1940 capitulation to Germany, he, like many of his fellow police officers across the occupied zone, had been forced to work for and with the Germans. While the Police Judiciaire continued to handle the normal range of crimes—theft, fraud, murder, and the like—the organization also aided the Kriminalpolizei and Gestapo when ordered to. Following the liberation, Badin's superior was fired for having been too cozy with the Germans, and the younger officer stepped in to the office. By the time Badin began interacting with Fred and Don, he had been cleared of any suspicion of collaborating with the Germans and was eager to cooperate with the Bureau. In return for providing Fred and Don with leads on the whereabouts of suspected American renegades and open access to the Police Judiciaire's files, Badin asked that the FBI provide him with updates on the latest trends in criminal investigation. He was particularly interested in modern laboratory and technical innovations, and in fingerprint recording and filing systems. In Fred's report to Hoover, he strongly recommended that the Bureau take Badin up on his request, and it subsequently did.[22]

Paillole of the DSM was an especially important figure in the larger realm of French counterintelligence and would prove a stalwart supporter of the Army Liaison Unit's activities in France. Born in 1905 and raised by his mother in Marseilles following his father's death in World War I, Paillole was a graduate of France's Saint-Cyr military academy. Assigned to the army's intelligence service, he quickly showed an aptitude for the work and gained a reputation for both efficiency and political savvy. Following France's surrender and the resultant creation of Vichy (unoccupied) France, Paillole headed a clandestine organization known by the innocuous name Travaux Ruraux (Rural Works), or TR.

Ostensibly an agricultural agency, TR was in reality a counterintelligence organization headquartered in Marseilles's Villa Éole and tasked with ferreting out Nazi agents working covertly in Vichy and its overseas territories in violation of the Franco-German armistice agreement.[23] The Vichy government reorganized its intelligence services in August 1942 and Paillole was put in charge of the Service de Sécurité Militaire (Military Security Service). When the Allied invasion of French North Africa the following November prompted the Germans to occupy Vichy, Paillole fled to Spain and then to London, where he offered his services to the Free French. By early 1943, he was head of the DSM in Algiers, where he worked closely with U.S. military intelligence and the OSS. Paillole much preferred Americans to the British, whom he had long suspected of having designs on France's colonial empire, and likely met with Frank Amprim before the FBI agent moved on to Italy in search of Ezra Pound. Paillole was embedded with the Free French units that liberated Paris, and within days of his arrival in the capital, he had the DSM up and running. By the time Fred and Don reached the city, the French counterintelligence chief was uniquely positioned to help them with their mission.

To ensure that cooperation, the two FBI agents held three days of meetings with Paillole and his deputies, Captain Claude Jouannais and Lieutenant André Debes—the latter DSM's liaison officer to SHAEF, who had met personally in London with both Joe Lynch and Jack Cimperman. According to Gordon Sheen, the two subordinate French officers were as pro-American as their boss, and though both spoke fair English, they were delighted the FBI agents were fluent in French. Fred and Don first explained that they were in France at the express invitation of the combined Allied chiefs of staff, and that the purpose of their mission was to investigate American renegades, collect information on espionage cases that bore directly on the internal security of the United States, and establish a close liaison with the French police services. As Fred noted in his report to Hoover on the meeting:

> The DSM officers were exceedingly cordial and expressed a keen interest in the work of the Bureau and the methods it has used in combatting crime in the United States and in smashing the enemy espionage rings in the United States and South America. They expressed also a real desire to enter into liaison with the Bureau through its representatives in an exchange of information on enemy activity and the methods of combating them.[24]

The cable to the Bureau's director also included the details of a memorandum in which the FBI agents and the French officers set out what each group hoped to obtain from the other. The Bureau, as represented by Fred and Don, asked for all information dealing with the security of the Western Hemisphere, American renegades, and all French documentation on the methods employed by the German intelligence services. In return, Paillole requested outlines of the major espionage cases handled by the Bureau (including the methods by which the enemy agents had been recruited and trained, and the ways in which they communicated with each other and with their handlers in Germany), information on the methods used by the FBI to combat enemy sabotage and espionage activities (including laboratory techniques), and physical descriptions and photographs of French citizens who may have worked for the German intelligence services in the United States.

There was also an addendum to the memo that Fred knew Hoover would be keenly interested in. Paillole said the DSM saw no conflict between the counterespionage operations undertaken in liberated France by the FBI and the OSS. He understood that the former operated in Europe only insofar as it protected the Western Hemisphere, while the latter's X-2 branch was a tactical and strategic service dealing with CI activities within the theaters of military operations. That administrative distinction aside, both Jouannais and Debes said they were aware that OSS was not consistently furnishing Bureau headquarters in Washington with all of the information OSS obtained that was of primary jurisdictional interest to the FBI. The officers also indicated that in its relationship with them, OSS had adopted a policy of "taking everything and giving nothing." The French intelligence officers, Fred wrote, made it perfectly clear that they were "irritated by this attitude and would prefer to deal with the FBI, whose reputation was exceedingly well known to them."[25]

Fred added that he and Don understood and sympathized with the French officers' opinions of the OSS. The FBI agents had found the civilian heads of the Paris office of Donovan's organization to be "apparently completely under the thumb of MI6 . . . [and] regarded as rank amateurs by experienced Army G-2 men, and because of all these factors are cooperative only against their will." While the military members of OSS were somewhat more willing to share information, Fred said, most were "of the school-teacher or socialite type and accordingly appear not mature enough in intelligence work to compete not only with the German intelligence system, but that of the French and the British as well." Summing up, Fred noted that the friction between the OSS and the French presented an excellent opportunity for the Bureau to solidly establish itself in the European Theater:

> It seems likely the best method of accomplishing this is for the Bureau . . . representatives to avoid the errors made by the OSS. . . . Rather than being demanding on the basis of military position it would appear well for the agents to be cooperative and helpful, insofar as it is consistent with Bureau policy, with the members of the French intelligence services.[26]

Friendly cooperation with the DSM quickly proved as useful as Fred had predicted. In addition to opening the DSM's voluminous files to the two FBI agents, Paillole was able to offer them something they sorely lacked—space in which to securely confine and question suspects. Gordon Sheen's hotel headquarters in Versailles was too far from central Paris and obviously had no detention facilities, nor did the apartment at 15, avenue Mozart. At Paillole's suggestion, Fred got in touch with Lieutenant Henri Desormeaux, commander of the DSM interrogation center at 18, boulevard Suchet in Paris.[27] Located on a wide, tree-lined street in the 16th *arrondissement*, the five-story building was less than a ten-minute walk from avenue Mozart. Despite its outward elegance, the building had something of sinister history. In September and October 1940, German Vice Admiral Karl Dönitz, head of the Kriegsmarine's submarine force, lived and worked there with his senior staff while planning the expansion of the "wolf pack" tactic that was already wreaking havoc on Allied shipping in the North Atlantic. During Dönitz's stay, the building's 4,500-square-foot basement was converted into a bomb shelter, with reinforced ceiling and walls. After the liberation of Paris, the DSM took over the structure, using its upper floors as offices and living spaces, while the basement was divided into windowless holding cells and interrogation rooms. Desormeaux offered Fred and Don use of the facilities whenever they might need them.

Exactly when the FBI agents would have someone to interrogate in the boulevard Suchet facility was at that point something of an open question. Fred and Don were waiting on Bureau headquarters in Washington to provide the names of American renegades charged with broadcasting on behalf of the Nazis, though most of those suspects would likely not be available for interrogation until the Allied armies rolled into Germany. And the targets the two agents would themselves pursue in liberated France had first to be identified either by Army intelligence or the French police and intelligence services. Fred and Don had secured the support of SHAEF through Gordon Sheen and laid the groundwork for effective cooperation with Charles Badin and

Paul Paillole, but it would take time to develop credible leads. In the meantime, the agents still had much prep work to do.

THE DAY AFTER MEETING WITH DESORMEAUX, Fred left Don in charge in Paris and set off on a six-day road trip. The purpose of the journey was to meet the intelligence officers at the higher levels of the forward-deployed U.S. Army units advancing eastward against the slowly retreating Germans.[28] After a short meeting with Sheen in Versailles, Fred and Colonel Edward H. Osgood Jr., SHAEF's deputy G-3 (plans, operations, and training) officer, set off in a jeep.

Several hours later, the pair met with Brigadier General Edwin L. Sibert, G-2 officer of Lieutenant General Omar Bradley's Twelfth U.S. Army Group (Twelfth USAG), and Sibert's counterintelligence chief, Colonel Thomas J. Sands.[29] Fred explained that the Bureau's representatives in Europe were looking for information pertaining to the internal security of the United States and the rest of the Western Hemisphere. He also outlined the search for American renegades and Hoover's concerns about communist infiltration of the French military and civil society. Sibert then granted permission for Fred to meet with Major Henry H. Marsden and Captain John Shewbridge of Twelfth USAG's captured documents section, who said they would send to Paris any items responsive to the FBI agent's request. To his surprise, while walking through the headquarters building, Fred ran into Major Edward Saxe, an old friend from Harvard Law School. After a short reunion with Saxe and before returning to the French capital, Fred and Osgood headed for Nancy, in Lorraine, to meet with Colonel Oscar Koch, G-2 of Third Army. Sitting in on that meeting was another of Fred's Harvard classmates, Captain James B. Hallet, one of Koch's deputies. Upon the conclusion of the meeting, Osgood went to visit friends on the Third Army staff, while Fred headed for dinner with his favorite uncle—and the Third Army commander—Lieutenant General George S. Patton Jr.

Fred had thus far had no chance to clean up after the jeep journey and arrived at Patton's headquarters appearing rather disheveled. That his appearance made him look more than a little out of place was driven home to him by the fact that every person in sight, both enlisted and officer, was clean-shaven, wearing tie and helmet, and had freshly polished shoes.[30] When Fred was ushered into his uncle's office, Patton barked out, "What in hell are you doing over here? I thought I told you to stay home and catch commies." Then, after looking Fred up and down with apparent distaste, the famously by-the-book general added, "And that's the God-damnedest poorest excuse for a uniform I've ever seen. If you're going to have dinner with me tonight, you'll have to do better than that."[31] Patton then sent his orderly in search of suitable attire, and minutes later, Fred was resplendent in pressed trousers, shirt and tie, waist-length Eisenhower jacket, and polished shoes. Now smiling broadly, Patton led his somewhat sheepish nephew into dinner and introduced him to several senior Third Army officers.

With the meal over, Fred and his uncle had time for some personal conversation. After catching Patton up on the latest family news, the younger man commented on the way the general was often portrayed in the press—rough, foulmouthed, and swaggering—attributes that Fred and his family knew to be exactly opposite to Patton's actual nature. In response, the Third Army commander said:

> Freddie, please remember two things: first, an officer, whether he be a kid lieutenant or general of an army, must each day send to certain death a percentage of his men. Some of these men he knows intimately, but to everyone he owes all of the protection he can afford. If he is any kind of man, this officer will want to sit down and ball [sic] like a baby. It is far better that he swagger a little and swear; second, the press has created for me a character in which my army has come to believe. So, if I don't wear my pearl-handled guns, if I don't swank around, if I don't rant and rave a little, the word will get out, "the old man is sick, he's on his way downhill."[32]

The conversation then turned to Eisenhower's decision some weeks earlier to halt Third Army's eastward advance in order to transfer much of its fuel and ammunition stocks to British Field Marshal Bernard Montgomery's combined airborne and ground assault into Holland to capture key bridges over the lower Rhine River. Market Garden, as the operation was named, was intended to create a corridor for an Allied advance into Germany but had only been partially successful. The Germans retained control of the final and most important bridge, in the Dutch city of Arnhem, and killed, wounded, or captured the majority of the British airborne troops tasked with that bridge's capture. When Fred asked his uncle if he felt discouraged or disgusted about having to halt his own advance in order to make Market Garden possible, Patton replied, "Of course I am, but the day is going to come when I have enough gasoline, guns, munitions and planes. Then, by God, I'll break out of here. Come and I'll show you what I'm going to do."[33] After pointing out, on a huge wall map, where and how he planned to advance, the general explained one of the key reasons for his confidence in his ability to defeat the enemy forces arrayed against Third Army:

> I've studied the German all my life. I've read the memoirs of his generals and political leaders. I even read his philosophers and listened to his music. I have studied in detail the accounts of every damn one of his battles. I know exactly how he will react under any given set of circumstances. He hasn't the slightest idea what I'm going to do. Therefore, when the day comes, I'm going to whip hell out of him.[34]

The evening following his meeting with Patton, Fred (presumably still wearing his "suitable" borrowed uniform) and a few other officers attended a dinner party in honor of Marlene Dietrich. The German-born American actress and singer was in Europe doing performances for Allied troops, often in positions very close to the front lines. When Fred introduced himself as an FBI agent, Dietrich expressed her admiration for the Bureau and said that when she finished her current round of shows, she planned to stay in Paris for a few months. She told Fred she might have information that would be of use to the FBI regarding her many contacts in Europe, and Fred responded that she could reach him and Don via Gordon Sheen, whom the actress already knew, or the U.S. embassy.[35]

Upon his return to Paris, Fred wrote a series of reports to Hoover regarding the journey to the front lines and the insights gained from speaking with the various senior G-2 officers. One of the most important topics, from Fred's point of view, was raised by Colonel Tom Sands, the Twelfth USAG's counterintelligence chief. Sands said that he had been tapped to head counterintelligence operations in the American-controlled sectors of defeated Germany, including Berlin, and that he very much wanted German-speaking FBI agents to be assigned to those sectors. One would work directly with Sands in the former German capital, while the other agents would be individually assigned to the four Army corps resident in the larger American sector.[36] Sands also told Fred that the agents should be brought into the European theater under Army cover and assigned to SHAEF well in advance of Germany's capitulation. That would allow the men to study the "vast amount of material being assembled regarding Germany and to be thoroughly briefed on the problems of occupation and the manner in which the American intelligence and counterintelligence units were planning to deal with them."[37] Sands added, however, that the matter should be discussed with SHAEF G-2 before any final decisions were made.

Don Daughters subsequently outlined Sands's comments for Gordon Sheen, who agreed completely on the idea of sending German-speaking Bureau agents to Europe. He also agreed that sooner would be far better than later, and told Don that he would take the matter up with British Major General Kenneth Strong, SHAEF's senior intelligence officer, at his first opportunity. Sheen said that Strong could then contact Major General Clayton Bissell, who in February 1944 had replaced Major General George Strong as the Army's top intelligence officer.[38]

The fact that it would be a British general, albeit one on the SHAEF staff, contacting Bissell about the deployment to Europe of German-speaking Bureau agents was likely a cause of concern for Fred and Don. While the two men had been warmly received by David Petrie in London and had hosted him at avenue Mozart, their relationships with the British members of the joint intelligence services on the ground in Europe had been more than a little frustrating for them and, indeed, for Army intelligence officers as well. Fred believed that the situation resulted, at least in part, from the fact that as newcomers to the intelligence war against Nazi Germany, the U.S. intelligence services were seen by the British to be fairly naive and very ignorant. As he later wrote:

> We had been separated by 3,000 miles of water from the continent instead of a mere 25. We were not part of the business, social and political life of Europe as Englishmen had, perforce, to be. As a result we were at the beginning of our war, and for a long time thereafter, dependent on our allies for information concerning the personnel and organization of the enemy services which it was our job to neutralize and overcome.
>
> In one of the earliest reports which Don and I submitted to Washington we emphasized these facts and pointed out that the British members of the joint intelligence services, and most particularly the counterintelligence people, largely ran the show and dictated

> the policy. This was not pleasing to the Bureau. How was it, we were asked, that representatives of the FBI were not by now taking the lead and running things as they had been taught to do in police work at home? I again in writing tried to explain, but suggested that the best answer would be for the Bureau to send over an inspector who could accompany us on our rounds, attend some staff conferences and, in short, see for himself.[39]

While waiting for a response from the Bureau regarding the dispatch to Paris of a senior inspector, Fred forwarded a request Gordon Sheen had made during his talk with Don about sending German-speaking agents to Europe. SHAEF's CI chief had reiterated his belief that communist agents were attempting to infiltrate the French military, intelligence, and police services, as well as media outlets and other segments of society. He had also expressed concern that the U.S. forces currently in the European theater would themselves be targeted for penetration and admitted that current American policy as implemented by the various Army Groups in the theater precluded the direct investigation of communist activity by military counterintelligence personnel. Fred had heard essentially the same thing from the senior officers he'd spoken with during his trip to the front—that Army CI units would accept and file any communist-related information uncovered during their scrutiny of German subversive activities but were barred by SHAEF policy from actively investigating communist activity.[40]

The Army's "no investigations of communists" policy had been established at the highest levels of the U.S. government for very practical—if somewhat shortsighted—reasons. The Soviet Union was an important ally in the war against the Nazis, and Washington did not want to derail cooperation with Moscow by looking too closely at the activities of Soviet agents and surrogates in Western Europe until Germany had been soundly defeated. While Sheen understood and adhered to the SHAEF policy, he told Don he was nonetheless keen to stay well informed about communist activities, because he was firmly convinced that when the war in Europe had been won and SHAEF had been disbanded, "the Reds" would become the primary long-range focus of American counterintelligence operations. Sheen said he believed the FBI was the best-informed agency in America regarding communist methods and goals, and that he would consider it a privilege to have assigned to SHAEF headquarters a special agent from the Bureau's Communist Section. Fred forwarded Don's report of the meeting with Sheen to Hoover, adding that the

Bureau would soon receive an official request from SHAEF for the deployment to Europe of an agent specializing in communism.[41]

IN EARLY NOVEMBER, FRED AYER was on the road again—or, more accurately, in the air. Leaving Don Daughters in charge in Paris, Fred flew to London for several days of talks with Joe Lynch on a number of topics. These included Gordon Sheen's desire to have additional Bureau agents assigned to SHAEF, briefings on Fred's recent visits to the Twelfth Army Group headquarters and with Patton at Third Army, and the as yet unscheduled visit of a Bureau inspector to the avenue Mozart office.

The latter open question was answered just days after Fred's return to Paris. A cable from Washington stated that Inspector Myron E. Gurnea would soon be dispatched to the French capital to ascertain both the suitability of the avenue Mozart apartment as a "field office" and to evaluate Fred's statement that British counterintelligence officers were exerting undue influence over SHAEF's CI operations. While it was not mentioned in the cable, Gurnea and Special Agent Thomas E. Naughten would also have several other tasks while in Europe. They would be meeting with incoming U.S. Ambassador to France Jefferson Caffery in regard to the possible opening of a legal attaché office in the Paris embassy, making a quick side trip to Rome to check in on Frank Amprim and the other FBI agents in the Italian capital, and sounding out senior U.S. and British officials about the proposed dispatch of German-speaking Bureau agents to the Continent.[42]

That Myron Gurnea was on his way to Paris undoubtedly sent a few shivers of anxiety through Fred and Don. Though just forty-two, Mike Gurnea was already a legend in the FBI. Born in Oregon but raised in California, he had joined the San Francisco Police Department at twenty-one and transferred to the Los Angeles Police Department in 1934. His championship skills as a pistol shot brought him to the FBI's attention, and in 1936, he joined the Bureau as both a special agent and a firearms instructor. The following year, his pistol skills were put to a real-world test when he was one of the agents attempting to apprehend the three members of the infamous Brady Gang. In just two years, the trio had committed some 150 robberies, a number of vicious assaults, and the suspected murder of a police officer. When confronted by Gurnea and other FBI agents outside a gun shop in Bangor, Maine, on October 12, 1937, gang leader Al Brady feigned surrender but pulled a hidden pistol and started shooting. Gurnea and another agent returned fire, killing Brady instantly. In the following years, Gurnea was part of several major cases, earning a reputation as a tough but fair G-man.

Gurnea and Naughten arrived in Paris on December 19, with Gurnea visiting avenue Mozart on his own that afternoon. Fred's first impression of the famed inspector was of a man

> tall and gangly and slow moving, except in time of emergency, when he could strike like lightning. He resembled more than anything else a beardless Abraham Lincoln cast in the role of the grand inquisitor. I believe that it would have been wholly impossible to lie to him. I know that I did not try.[43]

Over the following weeks, Gurnea and Naughten examined every detail of Fred and Don's activities in Paris—including the effectiveness of the agents themselves. In his later report to Hoover, Gurnea gave both men "Excellent" performance ratings. Of Fred, the inspector noted:

> Special Agent Ayer has an excellent background for European work in that he has traveled extensively in Europe and speaks French fluently. Because of his family connections, he is capable of establishing contacts that otherwise would be very difficult to make. . . . His ability to obtain information in a foreign country is above average. I feel that irrespective of what our espionage program may be in France, he should remain in charge of our operations there.[44]

Of Don, Gurnea said:

> Special Agent Daughters speaks French, Spanish and some German. He is intelligent, alert, and has a good personality. Daughters has been successful in developing some excellent contacts among the French political and intelligence circles. He has the ability to develop informants and obtain information in foreign countries.[45]

After several weeks in the French capital, Gurnea was able to join Fred and Don at one of their intelligence staff conferences at SHAEF headquarters in Versailles. The conference began with a review of recent intelligence-related events in the greater Paris region and then moved on to a discussion of who would set the top priorities on the target lists for

German intelligence installations, key personnel, and captured documents. As Fred later remembered:

> Then came up these questions: who would set the top priorities on the target lists for enemy intelligence installations, personnel and records? Who would have custody of the important personages when, and if, captured? Who would have the first chance to interrogate them? The senior officer present was an American. This had no bearing whatsoever upon the outcome of the discussion. A very bored appearing English lieutenant colonel let the conversation go on for a while. Then he leaned back, took his pipe at last from his mouth, and announced, "It's really all quite simple, don't you know. We happen to have most of the information and we control nearly all of the good sources. Now, don't you see, the fellow who does that, he's the fellow that dictates the policy.

Fred turned to Gurnea and said, "You see?"

With a bemused expression, the inspector arched an eyebrow and responded simply, "I see."[46] In his report to Hoover, Gurnea agreed completely with Fred's earlier assertion that the air of smug paternalism displayed by the lieutenant colonel was pervasive among the British members of the joint intelligence services, particularly the counterintelligence staffers, and resulted in their largely running the show and dictating much of SHAEF's intelligence and CI policy in terms of dealing with the Germans.

On the positive side, however, Gurnea noted that since their arrival in Paris, Fred and Don and been able to pursue—largely without British interference—the primary reason for the deployment to Europe: the hunt for American renegades. And as luck would have it, one of their first targets was a man with White House connections.

CHAPTER 6

The Curious Case of W. Dawson

LATE ON THE AFTERNOON OF AUGUST 17, 1944, Dr. Peter Widlöcher hurried down the front steps of the German embassy in Paris with several bundles of bulging dossiers clasped tightly in his arms. The front courtyard of the Palais Beauharnais—the ornate eighteenth-century townhouse at 78, rue de Lille, in the 7th *arrondissement*—was crowded with vehicles. Pandemonium reigned as scores of soldiers and diplomats sought to load personal items and even entire filing cabinets into sedans, trucks, and confiscated French delivery vans. Clerks from the basement code room threw armfuls of paper onto blazing fires while others used sledgehammers to wreck what just minutes before had been highly sophisticated Enigma cypher machines. Widlöcher had to dodge and weave his way to a waiting Daimler-Benz staff car, its closed trunk already packed with files. He threw his latest load of documents into the rear seat, jumped behind the wheel, and roared out the embassy's narrow front gate, paying no heed to the startled sentries who jumped out of his path.

Widlöcher's haste was understandable. The Allies were less than fifty miles from Paris and advancing steadily, Résistance groups within the city were beginning to openly attack German installations and personnel, and the fall of the French capital that four years earlier had seemed impossible was now inevitable. On August 12, the Militärbefehlshaber in Frankreich—Germany's military high command in France—had issued a widely anticipated but nonetheless shocking order for all nonessential personnel to evacuate the city and head eastward toward Germany.

Like many of his embassy colleagues, Widlöcher had quite a few loose ends to tie up before he could flee. His official title was director of the Sprachendienst des Auswärtigen Amtes (Foreign Office Language Service) office, which handled translation services for the embassy's various directorates. A thirty-year-old graduate of Frankfurt's Goethe University, with a doctorate in political science and international economics, Widlöcher was completely fluent in both French and English as well as German. The same language skills, intelligence, and engaging personality that made him an excellent translator also made him useful to the German intelligence services. Soon after being assigned to the Paris embassy in 1941, he began working as an informal "talent scout" for the Propaganda-Abteilung Frankreich, the Germans' main disinformation and "fake news" office in France. Widlöcher's specific task was to cultivate French citizens and those of other countries who could be used to produce pro-Nazi propaganda for distribution in print and by radio. He had been very good at that particular task, and the documents that he was so desperate to protect on August 17 were the personnel files of all of his recruits.

While Widlöcher ultimately made it back to the Fatherland, his files did not.[1] On October 13, a reconnaissance patrol of General Philippe Leclerc de Hauteclocque's 2nd French Armored Division discovered the German's Daimler-Benz staff car abandoned on a narrow farm track in Alsace. The vehicle's fuel tank was empty and three of its tires were flat, but the files in its trunk and back seat were undamaged. Members of the Direction de la Sécurité Militaire attached to the recon unit did a quick survey of the files before sending them back to Paris. They flagged one of the dossiers for the personal attention of DSM chief Commandant Paul Paillole, because the subject of the file was an American widely known to have friends in the highest ranks of French society.

The American's name was Francis Warrington Dawson.

A longtime fixture in Paris's large community of expatriate Americans, Dawson had what was widely referred to by friends and enemies alike as a "colorful background."

He was born September 27, 1878, in Charleston, South Carolina, the scion of a well-to-do and outwardly traditional post–Civil War Southern family. Yet his lineage had some distinctly nontraditional roots. Dawson's father, Austin John Reeks, was born in the Shoreditch area of London in May 1840, a member of one of the oldest Roman Catholic families in England. When the American Civil War broke out in April 1861, the young man—a romantic who believed the American South was a bastion of chivalry under attack by the rapacious North—decided to fight for the Confederacy. Reeks assumed the name of a dead uncle, Francis Warrington Dawson (likely in case of capture by Union forces), and in early 1862, signed on as an able seaman aboard CSS *Nashville*, a Confederate Navy commerce raider blockaded in Britain's Southampton harbor by Union warships. When the vessel eventually escaped and reached Beaufort, North Carolina, Frank Dawson—as he now called himself—joined the Confederate Army as an officer and fought in several major actions, including Gettysburg. After the war, Dawson married Mary Fourgeaud and became a newspaper reporter in Richmond, Virginia, and eventually moved to Charleston. In 1867, he and a partner bought the local *Charleston Daily News*. Some six years later, the *Daily News* merged with the *Charleston Courier*, which Dawson had also co-purchased. The renamed Charleston *News and Courier* became one of the leading newspapers in the postwar South, and Dawson himself one of the region's leading editors.

Frank Dawson's wife, Mary, died of tuberculosis in 1873, and the following year, the young editor married Sarah Ida Morgan. The daughter of a Louisiana plantation-owning family that had not fared well in the years during and just after the war, Sarah had been writing editorials for the *News and Courier*, under the pen name "Mr. Fowler," on the plight of women in the postwar South. The Dawsons' first child, daughter Ethel, was born in 1874. Their first son, Francis Warrington Dawson Jr.—whom the family called Warrington—arrived in 1878, and in 1881, a second son, Philip, died at just five months. In 1889, Frank Dawson was shot to death by a married man who had been making sexual advances toward the family's young Swiss governess, Hélène Burdayron.[2] Warrington was barely ten years old when his father was killed, and his grieving mother showered all her attention and love on him. Frank Dawson's death robbed his son of a strong male role model, and various authors have suggested that his grieving mother's smothering love undermined his masculinity for the rest of his life.[3]

One thing Warrington inherited from both his parents was a love of writing. The young man had begun contributing reviews of children's books and magazines to the *News and Courier* the year before his father's death. At sixteen, after returning from school in Paris and Geneva, Warrington began penning occasional feature stories on Colonial and Revolutionary War topics for the paper. He also wrote short stories in French, a language he'd grown up speaking thanks to his well-bred and bilingual Louisiana-born mother, and his schooling abroad made him fluent in the language. After his return to South Carolina, he wrote occasional articles for French newspapers while attending the College of Charleston. Though a good student, he never graduated, owing to what some scholars believe was a series of psychosomatic illnesses.

In November 1899, the twenty-one-year-old Warrington Dawson sailed for France, soon establishing himself as a freelance reporter in Paris. His family money allowed him to rent an apartment on the fashionable rue de Varenne—just east of the historic Hôtel des Invalides in the wealthy 7th *arrondissement*—where his mother joined him in early 1900. The pair soon moved to a larger apartment just to the north of Invalides on the rue de l'Université, where mother and son both continued to write. Sarah Dawson used her considerable social and literary connections to further her son's career, and it was largely through her efforts that he was named Paris bureau manager of the jointly operated Publishers Press and Scripps-McRae Press. In 1907, the two groups were merged with Scripps News and became the United Press Associations.[4] In addition to his journalism work, Dawson wrote two novels—*The Scar* in 1906 and *The Scourge* two years later.[5] From 1905 to 1908, he was also the secretary-general of the Paris-based Association de la Presse Étrangère, the Foreign Press Association. As the liaison between the French government and all members of the foreign press based in Paris, Dawson became so influential that he was the first American reporter to be granted a permanent seat in the observer galleries of both houses of the French parliament.[6] The relationships he was able to develop with influential politicians were to serve him very well in the coming years.

Shortly after U.S. President Theodore Roosevelt left office at the end of his second term in March 1909, he announced that he would be embarking on an African expedition to gather wildlife specimens for the Smithsonian Institution's new natural history museum, then under construction on the National Mall in Washington, D.C. Underwritten by millionaire philanthropist Andrew Carnegie, the expedition was scheduled to last more than a year and include hunts in British East Africa, the Belgian Congo, and the Anglo-Egyptian Sudan.[7] Despite Roosevelt's loudly and widely professed desire that the expedition be private, news organizations in the United States and Europe immediately began trying to get their respective reporters attached to the former president's retinue. The United Press Associations' headquarters in New York cabled Warrington Dawson to secure a place on the expedition "at any cost." Roosevelt and his party were about to set sail across the North Atlantic, bound for an intermediate stop in Naples, and Dawson had to think fast. As was often the case, he relied on his mother's connections to make things happen. She got her son an appointment with U.S. ambassador to France Henry White, a mutual friend of both hers and Roosevelt's. Unfortunately, it was the last time Sarah would be able to help her son, for she died unexpectedly at their Paris apartment on May 5. She was the last woman with whom Dawson would have any sort of emotional connection.

After holding a small funeral in the French capital and arranging for his mother's body to be returned to South Carolina for burial, Dawson called on White at the embassy. Pointing out that the purpose of the Roosevelt expedition—the killing of thousands of animals, albeit for scientific reasons—would ultimately compel the former president to defend his actions whether he wanted to or not, Dawson said that he would like to be there to help Roosevelt deal with the press. The reporter asked White to provide him with a letter of introduction, and said that he would go to Naples to meet Roosevelt and ask his permission to join the expedition. "If he says no, I shall come back to Paris," Dawson said. "If he says yes, I'm ready to promise not to worry him."[8] With the ambassador's letter of introduction in hand, Dawson met Roosevelt's ship in Italy. The former president's only words to him then were "you may come with me as far as the African coast if you promise not to follow me afterwards and not to ask for any interviews."[9]

Dawson did indeed sail with Roosevelt to the African coast, and during the voyage apparently impressed the former president enough to earn himself a place on the safari itself. On July 23, 1909, Roosevelt officially hired Dawson as a private secretary, his primary tasks to be taking dictation and managing correspondence. It was welcome news for the young reporter, who had taken a huge chance in essentially throwing himself at a man who, though out of office, remained a major force in American politics. Dawson quickly proved himself to be more than a secretary, for he was also adept at "spinning" potentially unfavorable news about the former president. On one occasion, for example, Roosevelt set out to bag a male hippo but repeatedly fired indiscriminately into a semisubmerged group of the animals. While he bagged a large bull, he also killed three cows. Shamed by his own performance and afraid that he would be humiliated in the press, Roosevelt turned to Dawson for help. "Warrington," the former president said, "the most awful thing has happened." When the story eventually broke, it was not a tale of wanton slaughter by someone who had long labeled himself a conservationist, but rather a simple case of self-defense—in Dawson's version the event was "an attack by, rather than on, the herd of hippos."[10]

This and other incidents in which Roosevelt's reputation was saved or even enhanced as a result of Warrington Dawson's ability to "massage" the facts led the former president to further broaden the scope of the young man's position. At one point, Roosevelt even suggested that Dawson should negotiate the French language rights for the series of newspaper articles the former president was writing about the expedition, suggesting a $20,000 contract for both serial and, ultimately, book rights.[11]

Roosevelt was not the only one whose literary fortunes would benefit from the African expedition. While in Nairobi with the former president, Dawson was introduced to Edward Lancelot "Ted" Sanderson and his wife, Helen. The British couple had arrived in Kenya in 1904 from South Africa, where Second Boer War veteran Sanderson had been the headmaster of an elite boy's school in Johannesburg. At the time of Roosevelt's expedition, Sanderson was Nairobi's town clerk, but it was a different distinction that caught Dawson's attention. Some sixteen years earlier, Sanderson and his close friend John Galsworthy (later the author of *The Forsyte Saga*) had been returning from Australia to Britain aboard the three-masted passenger clipper *Torrens* when they struck up a friendship with the vessel's first mate. It was that sailor's last voyage, for upon reaching Britain, he intended to give up seafaring in order to become a writer. He was more than successful, gaining fame as novelist Joseph Conrad, and he and Sanderson remained stalwart friends.[12] Dawson had long been an avid fan of Conrad's work, and he cajoled Sanderson into giving him a letter of introduction to the novelist, hoping at the very least to interview him at some point and sell the piece to newspapers in France and the United States.

In the meantime, Dawson set about capitalizing on his relationship with Roosevelt—despite the fact that their association had lasted less than three months. After resigning from the United Press Associations in the fall of 1909, Dawson sailed for America to embark on a lecture tour largely based on "Hunting With Roosevelt in East Africa," an article he'd written for the November 1909 issue of *Hampton's Magazine*. He also started work on the memoir that would become *Opportunity and Theodore Roosevelt*, which he later had privately printed. In addition, Dawson began lecturing on Conrad, who at that time was not as well known or as widely read in the United States as he was in Britain.[13]

Dawson's chance to meet Conrad in person came in the spring of 1910. King Edward VII of Great Britain died on May 6, and his state funeral was scheduled for exactly two weeks later in London. Dawson decided to travel to Britain in order to write freelance articles about the solemn occasion—likely for the North American readers of his erstwhile employer, United Press Associations. Before leaving home, Dawson wrote to Conrad at the address given to him the year before by Ted Sanderson, asking the novelist if they could meet. Apparently impressed by Dawson's acquaintance with Roosevelt and Sanderson's letter of introduction, Conrad invited the younger man to his home in Kent. Dawson's focus on that meeting apparently overcame his usually sharp journalistic instincts, for he filed only a few perfunctory stories about the funeral, an event that attracted most of the still reigning crowned heads of Europe and literally millions of people, who lined the streets of the British capital to catch a glimpse of the procession.

The thirty-two-year-old Dawson and fifty-three-year-old Conrad met at the latter's small country cottage on May 28. Conrad's wife, Jessie, was also present, and the gathering marked the beginning of a friendship the trio would enjoy for several years. Despite the difference in their ages, the two writers had much in common—including their mutual fluency in and love of French. Dawson appreciated Conrad's genius as a novelist, and the older man was more than happy to provide advice on the craft of fiction and insights on Dawson's style. The two met some ten times between 1910 and 1914, always at Conrad's home and for periods ranging from a few days to several weeks. They also kept up a voluminous correspondence, trading opinions on a vast range of topics. Dawson became one of Conrad's most ardent supporters, lecturing on his work in Europe and America. In 1914, the younger man was apparently instrumental in arranging a meeting between Conrad and Frank N. Doubleday that resulted in the latter becoming the British novelist's sole U.S. publisher.[14]

Though Dawson hoped to one day become as great a novelist as his idol Conrad, the only book-length works he turned out before the two men drifted apart following the 1914 outbreak of World War I were nonfiction. The first, published in French in 1912, was *Le Nègre aux États-Unis* (*The Negro in the United States*). Perhaps not surprisingly given his Southern heritage, the book was overtly white supremacist and vehemently racist—so much so that it was actually panned in the pages of *Dépêche Coloniale*, a French magazine famous for its xenophobic and bigoted content. The second volume, published in 1913, was an edited collection of his mother's Civil War diary entries titled, fittingly, *A Confederate Girl's Diary*. During this same period, Dawson also began expressing virulently anti-Semitic views, a likely consequence of his affiliation with and acceptance by the French upper classes.

After France was engulfed by World War I, Dawson's activities become somewhat harder to discern. We know that in 1915, likely because he was a citizen of still neutral America, the French government appointed him a member of special commission formed to investigate the German army's first use of chemical weapons, near Ypres, Belgium. He also continued to freelance articles to British, French, and American publications, including the July 1916 story "Refugee: The Experience of a War Correspondent" for *The Atlantic*. But Dawson had always had a propensity for unwarranted self-aggrandizement, and he long claimed to have spent at least some of the war years as a secret agent performing unspecified missions for both the French and American governments. It was one such covert operation, he claimed, that led to his becoming a lifelong invalid. As he told the story—often with significant variations—he was served poisoned coffee by a pro-German Swiss waiter. Whether the story was true or not, Dawson began suffering increasing paralysis to his lower limbs and bouts of unspecified spinal cord–related problems.

Whatever their origins or severity, Dawson's infirmities did not keep him from obtaining gainful employment. From March 1915 to September 1917, he was a confidential adviser to U.S. ambassador to France William G. Sharp, a position Dawson later said he'd secured upon the personal recommendation of President Woodrow Wilson.[15] Dawson's novel *The True Dimension* came out in 1916, followed in 1923 by the nonfiction *Opportunity and Theodore Roosevelt* and the novel *The Sin*. In 1926, a World War I story, his book *Le don de Paul Clermont* (*The Gift of Paul Clermont*) won Dawson a prestigious medal from the French Academy and ultimately became his most commercially successful novel. In addition to his literary efforts, Dawson continued to work for the Paris embassy, serving from 1917 to 1928 as the chief of the Press Bureau. During that same period and into the 1930s, he was also a special assistant to Ambassadors Hugh Wallace, Myron Herrick, Walter Edge, Isidor Straus, and William Bullitt.

It was during his time as a special assistant in the Paris embassy that Dawson began communicating with another prominent member of the Roosevelt clan—the thirty-second president of the United States. Franklin D. Roosevelt, the fifth cousin of Theodore Roosevelt, began his first stint in the White House on March 4, 1933. Days later, Dawson wrote to FDR on Paris embassy letterhead congratulating him on winning the 1932 election and mentioning the time he, Dawson, had spent time with Teddy Roosevelt in Africa. On March 13, Dawson wrote again, this time mentioning the remarks made by May Birkhead, a Paris-based reporter for the New York *Herald* who had attended one of the soirees Dawson frequently hosted at his Versailles apartment. Birkhead was an enthusiastic FDR supporter, Dawson wrote, as were many of her newsroom colleagues. "She tells me that on all sides, among

Americans in Paris, she hears the most complete confidence expressed in you with unreserved approval of the measures you are taking," Dawson added.[16] The letter also included a copy of one of the "confidential dispatches" Dawson had written as part of his embassy work. In a reply dated March 28, the president thanked Dawson for his letter regarding Birkhead's comments, and said that he would henceforth have copies of all of Dawson's dispatches sent directly to the White House.[17]

Roosevelt's positive response to Dawson's postal overture ensured that the White House would be treated to further missives on a range of topics. As time went on, the tenor of Dawson's letters evolved from professional and formal to gossipy and almost simperingly deferential. Where in his early letters Dawson had closed by declaring himself "respectfully yours," by mid-1934, he was "devotedly yours." He also asked for, and received, an autographed photo of FDR, which he hung in a prominent location in his apartment. Yet Dawson's opinion of, and devotion to, FDR would eventually undergo a radical change.

Soon after William C. Bullitt Jr. was named the U.S. ambassador to France in October 1936, he came to believe that Dawson's poor health significantly reduced his ability to effectively perform the tasks assigned to him. Bullitt's suggestion that a retirement for medical reasons might be the best course of action sparked both panic and anger in Dawson, who treasured the contacts available to him as an embassy employee almost as much as he liked the regular paychecks at a time when his writing income had dropped off precipitously. Always one to work every available angle, Dawson sought to secure his position by gaining the support of none other than Franklin and Eleanor Roosevelt. His approach was circuitous—rather than present his case directly to FDR, Dawson first reached out to his brother-in-law, Herbert Barry. He, in turn, contacted an acquaintance who had direct access to the First Couple, Susan Ludlow Parish, a first cousin of Eleanor Roosevelt's mother and Eleanor's godmother.

In mid-May 1937, "Cousin Susie," as Parish was known within the family, passed on several letters to Eleanor in which Barry pleaded for intervention in Dawson's case. In one of the letters, Barry pointed out that if the embassy severed its connection to the ailing writer, he would have to begin paying French income taxes, something that would definitely put a crimp in Dawson's extravagant lifestyle. Eleanor sent a note to her husband outlining Barry's concerns, and on June 1, the president asked Under Secretary of State Sumner Welles to "speak with me about this the next time I see you."[18] When the two men talked about the matter, Welles pointed out to FDR that Barry had written to Secretary of State Cordell Hull with the same request to intercede on Dawson's behalf. Hull had responded to Barry on May 22, saying that nothing could be done to prevent Dawson's forced medical retirement. On June 11, the president sent his wife a memo saying simply, "Sumner has written to Cousin Susie. Forget it!"[19]

That brief memo from husband to wife effectively killed any chance Dawson had of retaining his embassy job. Susan Parish passed the bad news to Herbert Barry, who conveyed it to his brother-in-law. Dawson was ultimately called before Ambassador Bullitt, who made it abundantly clear that he was extremely displeased with the attempt to go over his head. Dawson was given the choice of voluntarily resigning for health reasons or being fired for ignoring State Department protocol. Given that the first option would allow Dawson to keep his Civil Service pension while the second would not, he made the logical decision. He later told friends that he had chosen to resign because it was in the best interests of the country, and apparently never told anyone of his attempts to get FDR and Eleanor to somehow prevent his ouster. From that point on, Dawson was a vocal and vitriolic critic of Franklin Roosevelt.

After ending his association with the embassy, Dawson focused on his writing and his social life. Increasingly confined for whatever reason to a wheelchair, he turned his Versailles apartment into one of the most popular salons in greater Paris. Politicians, military leaders, artists, and musicians were frequent guests, and Dawson himself often gave opera recitals while dressed in extravagant robes and headdresses. His social circles widened even more following France's 1940 capitulation, with German military officers and diplomats making the drive from central Paris to mingle with his other guests. It seems likely that it was at one of Dawson's soirees that he first met Dr. Peter Widlöcher.

It was that association between the rabidly anti-Roosevelt American writer and the German translator-cum-propagandist that would ultimately land Dawson face-to-face with Fred Ayer.

Almost two months before the discovery of Peter Widlöcher's abandoned staff car and the dossiers it contained, Warrington Dawson was finding ways to ingratiate himself with the U.S. Army. During the liberation of Paris, the Versailles area had come under the control of Twelfth USAG, and almost as soon as American troops appeared in the street outside his apartment,

Dawson sent his maid to hand a letter to the first senior officer she encountered. The missive eventually made its way up the chain of command to Brigadier General Robert W. Hasbrouck, Twelfth USAG's chief of staff. He was intrigued that a person styling himself a "former State Department official" was offering to assist the U.S. forces, and a few days later met Dawson at his apartment.[20] Over the following weeks, the latter wrote some thirty briefing documents for Hasbrouck and other senior commanders on the political situation in the region, with particular emphasis on the growing strength and influence of the French communist party. In a September 15 note, Hasbrouck thanked Dawson for his assistance, adding:

> Your intimate knowledge of the French people and of the somewhat involved political situation now existing in Versailles and the Seine-et-Oise department have assisted us materially in our contacts with French officials. . . . Your reports . . . have been forwarded to the proper authorities and will no doubt be of considerable value to them.[21]

Encouraged by Hasbrouck's kind words, and at his suggestion, on September 17, Dawson wrote a letter offering his services to SHAEF's senior intelligence officer, British Major General Kenneth Strong. Dawson offered to put himself at Strong's disposal because, as he put it:

> I believe I can be of use to you, my connections and resulting information extending beyond the Versailles region and often dealing with matters of general interest to the entire Paris region and even for our Army in France.[22]

Among the character witnesses Dawson listed were Hasbrouck, retired Brigadier General Dennis Nolan (World War I intelligence chief for General John Pershing), and several high-level American diplomats, including newly designated U.S. ambassador to France Jefferson Caffery. Dawson's rather vaguely addressed letter made the rounds of various Allied bureaus in Paris, and finally made it to Strong's office at the Trianon Palace hotel—barely four hundred yards from Dawson's apartment—on September 26. Having finally received the letter, Strong passed it to his counterintelligence chief, none other than Gordon Sheen. Dawson's offer to put himself at SHAEF's disposal apparently didn't excite the CI officer, however, because he took no action on the proposal. Initially, that may simply have been because Sheen was an extremely busy man, but by late October, it was almost certainly the result of the discovery of Dawson's file in Widlöcher's abandoned car.

The dossier and many of the other items found in the Daimler-Benz in Alsace had been sent back to Paris as part of a larger cache of captured German documents, and by Tuesday, October 17, the Dawson file was sitting on Paul Paillole's desk. The DSM chief knew who the American writer was, though they had never met, and was well aware that Dawson had friends throughout the upper echelons of French society. Paillole took some time to carefully consider all the possible political ramifications that might arise from investigating the American, and by the morning of Friday, October 20, he'd made up his mind. Paillole dispatched Captain Claude Jouannais and three other officers to Versailles to confront Dawson and search his apartment.

A few minutes before noon, Dawson's housekeeper burst into his bedroom without knocking, exclaiming that uniformed men had forced their way through the front door.[23] The DSM agents crowded around Dawson's bed, flashing their identity cards. Jouannais said they had information the writer had collaborated with the Germans and announced that he and his men intended to search the apartment. Dawson protested their presence on the grounds that he was an American citizen, and demanded he be allowed to contact the U.S. embassy and SHAEF headquarters at the Trianon Palace. Jouannais flatly refused, and when Dawson said no search could be conducted without an American representative being present, the DSM captain said that just such an official was on his way. Jouannais left the apartment in search of a telephone, and on his return announced that the search would be postponed until the American arrived—sometime after lunch.

The Army lieutenant who finally showed up appeared extremely young, an impression bolstered by his slight stature.[24] Dawson's estimation of him improved significantly, however, when he addressed the DSM agents in fluent Parisian-accented French. Introducing himself simply as Robins, the officer explained the discovery of the German dossier containing documents that implicated the American writer. When Dawson admitted that he knew Widlöcher, Robins and Jouannais begin firing questions at him—did he know a Werner Plack or a Dr. Grimm? Had he written pro-German propaganda for broadcast to the United States? Had he ever used the pen name Ivan Starold? Why would the Germans have a file on him if he wasn't working for them? The interrogation went on for four hours, with Jouannais's subordinates searching the apartment the whole time. Robins and the

DSM agents eventually left with several boxes of Dawson's papers, despite the writer's protestations that they had no right to do so. Robins simply smiled and responded that they did.[25]

The following day, Dawson was finally able to get in touch with the embassy in Paris. He related the story of his interrogation and the removal of many documents from his apartment, and the embassy, in turn, passed the information to the Counter Intelligence Corps Field Security Office attached to SHAEF headquarters. On Saturday, October 23, two CIC officers—Captain Tait and Lieutenant Harrison—visited Dawson and took down his statement about the events of the 20th. The writer vehemently denied having collaborated in any way with the Germans, and suggested that the documents found in Widlöcher's car were forgeries created by French communists. That, Dawson said, was in retaliation for the reports he had been providing to Brigadier General Hasbrouck and other senior leaders regarding the "communist threat" in post-liberation France. Dawson also told the CIC agents that he feared for his life, saying that the communists would target him. Tait and Harrison were apparently concerned that the threat might be real, for they assigned CIC Special Agent Donald Cannon to spend that night at Dawson's apartment.[26]

Cannon was replaced by a CIC special agent named West on the afternoon of October 24.[27] In his report on the visit, the agent stated that he and Dawson had had a wide-ranging discussion that touched on music, literature, politics, and life in Versailles during the German occupation. On the latter topic, Dawson said that he was one of some ten Americans who had remained in the city following the United States' entry into the war. Because of his serious physical limitations, he had been excused from the usual daily check-in with the German field police but was instead visited once a week by officials from the German embassy. Dawson said several of the other Americans had also been excused from daily reporting despite the fact that they were in good health, and he said that he was "suspicious of them." West noted that Dawson showed unusual interest in the Field Security Office, asking probing questions about its organization, staffing, and the scope of its operations. The writer's intense curiosity struck the CIC agent as odd, but then West was already decidedly unimpressed with Dawson, writing that:

> He is a poseur, a man who wishes, by a theatrical manner of speech and dress, by surrounding himself with a wealth of books and objets d'art, by discoursing elegantly on artistic subjects and

FBI Director J. Edgar Hoover was convinced the Bureau was the agency best suited for tracking down and interrogating American citizens who had remained in Axis-occupied Europe and were suspected of providing "aid and comfort" to America's enemies. *Library of Congress.*

gadier General William J. ild Bill" Donovan was ally certain that his Office of tegic Services (OSS) should esponsible for tracking down erican "renegades." *ional Archives and ords Administration.*

Though personal friends with Donovan, President Franklin D. Roosevelt was ultimately convince by Hoover that the FBI's Special Intelligence Service (SIS) was the organization best equipped to undertake the hunt for American traitors in Europe.
National Archives and Records Administration.

Hoover tapped FBI Assistant Director Percy E. "Sam" Foxworth as the first head of the SIS. On January 15, 1943, while on his way to Algeria to question an American treason suspect, Foxworth was among 33 people killed in the crash of a USAAF C-54 transport in what was then French Guiana.
FBI.

In November 1942, 28-year-old Special Agent Arthur M. Thurston became the FBI's first legal attaché in Great Britain. Before taking up the post, Thurston had worked closely with America's military intelligence and counterintelligence organizations.
FBI.

ıurston's office was in the U.S. Embassy London's Grosvenor Square. At the time the FBI agent's arrival, more than 2,000 nericans worked in the embassy and nearby ilitary offices, leading the British to call the ea "Eisenhower Platz," a waggish reference European theater commander General wight D. Eisenhower's German ancestry.
3I.

The first FBI agent dispatched to Europe under Army cover, 34-year-old Frank Amprim. His quarry was perhaps the most influential and controversial poet of the Modernist movement, accused traitor Ezra Pound.
Omar S. Pound Archives, Hamilton College.

On May 3, 1945, Pound w
taken into custody in Genoa, Ita
by members of the Count
Intelligence Corps detachme
of the U.S. 92nd Infantry Divisio
The poet's first interrogator w
the detachment's command
1st Lieutenant Ramón Arrizabalag
Omar S. Pound Archive
Hamilton Colleg

In between interrogations by Amprim and Arrizabalaga, Pound typed out a multipage sworn statement outlining his wartime pro-Fascist propaganda activities. *Omar S. Pound Archives, Hamilton College.*

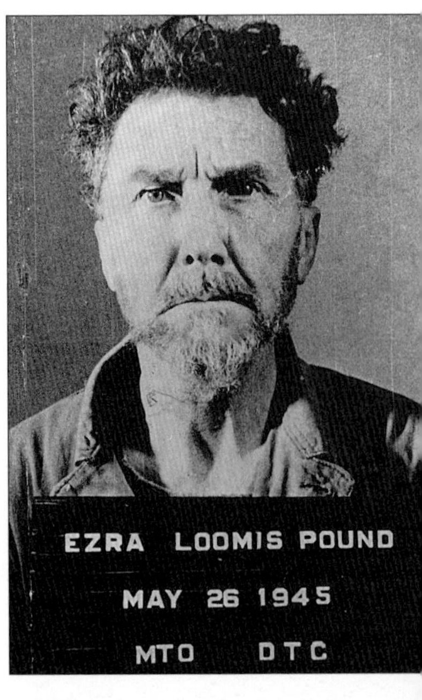

On May 24, Pound was transferred to the custody of the U.S. Army's Disciplinary Training Center (DTC), outside Pisa, to await transfer to the United States to stand trial for treason. *Omar S. Pound Archives, Hamilton College.*

At the DTC, Pound was initially held in "Murder's Row"—a series of covered outdoor cages set within a larger stockade surrounded by tall double fences topped with razor wire.
Omar S. Pound Archives, Hamilton College.

Among the FBI agents who joined Frank Amprim in Italy was Alfred Pease, a 34-year-old Italian-speaking SIS member from Pennsylvania.
Courtesy Anthony L. Pease.

While a devasting blow for France, the German occupation prompted several American citizens resident in Paris to throw in their lot with the Nazis.
National Archives and Records Administration.

The liberation of Paris by Free French and U.S. forces in August 1945 helped speed up the FBI Army Liaison Unit's (ALU's) search for American renegades and collaborators.
National Archives and Records Administration.

Fred Ayer (left) and Don Daughters arrived at Le Bourget airport outside Paris on September 30, 1944, the first ALU agents to set foot in liberated France.
Courtesy David R. Daughters.

Colonel H. Gordon Sheen, SHAEF commander Eisenhower's counterintelligence chief, warmly welcomed Ayer and Daughters and provided wholehearted support to the fledgling ALU.
Courtesy David R. Daughters.

Ayer and Daughters often accompan
Sheen on forays outside the c
Note that in this photo Ayer we
the holster for the Model 1911 C
semiautomatic pistol, apparen
having replaced his Bureau-iss
.38-caliber revolver with the stand
Army handg
Courtesy David R. Daughte

Author Warrington Dawson (seen here in 19
was suspected of collaborating with the Nazi
during the German occupation of France.
Though Ayer was convinced of Dawson's gu
the writer was never charged with treason—
largely owing to his social and political
connections. Ironically, the photo was signed
by Madame Cosette Harcourt, founder of
Paris's renowned Studio Harcourt. She was
Jewish, and during World War II Dawson
would prove himself a virulent anti-Semite.
*Studio Harcourt/David M. Rubenstein Rare
Book & Manuscript Library, Duke Universit*

In February 1945, the Paris-based ALU was asked to assist in the recovery of a missing U.S. Army M-134-C cipher machine. Referred to by the code name Sigaba, the top secret device was used for the highest-level tactical and strategic communications. *NSA/National Cryptologic Museum.*

A strong supporter of the ALU's activities, Supreme Allied commander General Eisenhower helped get more desperately needed FBI agents assigned to newly liberated Europe. He was less than pleased, however, when it appeared the ALU was investigating the daughter of one of his favorite generals. *National Archives and Records Administration.*

A prewar friend of Florence Gould, Otto Abetz returned to occupied France as Nazi Foreign Minister Joachim von Ribbentrop's representative to the German military command as well as Berlin's ambassador to Vichy. It was likely because of Abetz's patronage that Gould fared far better than most Americans who chose to stay in Paris. *U.S. Holocaust Memorial Museum, courtesy of National Archives and Records Administration, College Park, Maryland.*

Joachim von Ribbentrop, himself a close friend of Florence Gould and André and Ruth Dubonnet, used Werner Plack to recruit American expatriates in Paris for radio propaganda work on behalf of the Foreign Ministry. *Wikimedia Commons/Bundesarchiv Bild 183-H04810.*

Howard "Pete" Winter was one of six FBI special agents and two Bureau stenographers who joined Fred Ayer and Don Daughters in Paris in late May 1945. An experienced SIS operative, Winter had worked undercover in Mexico in 1941 and 1942.
H. P. Winter Family.

Winter and the other members of the ALU all initially carried Army-issued AGO (Adjutant General's Office) cards identifying them as "administrative assistants."
H. P. Winter Family.

NOT A PASS – FOR IDENTIFICATION ONLY

WAR DEPARTMENT
THE ADJUTANT GENERAL'S OFFICE
WASHINGTON, D.C.

NONCOMBATANT'S
CERTIFICATE OF IDENTITY

ONLY IF CAPTURED BY THE ENEMY

Howard P. Winter
NAME
AdministrativeAssistant
DESIGNATION
Howard P. Winter
SIGNATURE

DATE ISSUED 18 May 1945

COUNTERSIGNED Major W.D., A.G.O. 65-8

LOSS OF THIS CARD MUST BE REPORTED AT ONCE

Tapped to be the legal attaché in newly liberated Paris, Horton Telford chose Clement "Bud" Rousseau to be his deputy. The two men had earlier worked together in Cuba, where this picture of Rousseau was taken.
John Rousseau.

Captured in Austria by U.S. forces on May 1945, Luftwaffe commander Hermann Göri (seen here while on trial at Nurembu was questioned by ALU member Joe Dur The agent's German language ability a interrogation skills so impressed the form *Reichsmarschall* that he presented Du with his gold-braid rank epaulett
National Archives and Records Administratic

Among the first American renegade cases to be concluded by the ALU agents working in Berlin was that of Max Otto Koischwitz. The college professor turned Nazi propagandist and lover of fellow renegade Mildred Gillars wa found to have died in 1944 of tuberculosis.
Archives and Special Collections, Hunter College Libraries, Hunter College of the City University of New York, New York City.

Dr. Walter Schellenberg, the last head of Nazi Germany's foreign intelligence service, turned himself over to the Allies in June 1945. When questioning the spy chief, Fred Ayer was particularly interested in why he had possessed a U.S. passport with the same number as that of Maurice Gagnon, the suspected American traitor who in February 1945 had hanged himself while in custody. *National Archives and Records Administration.*

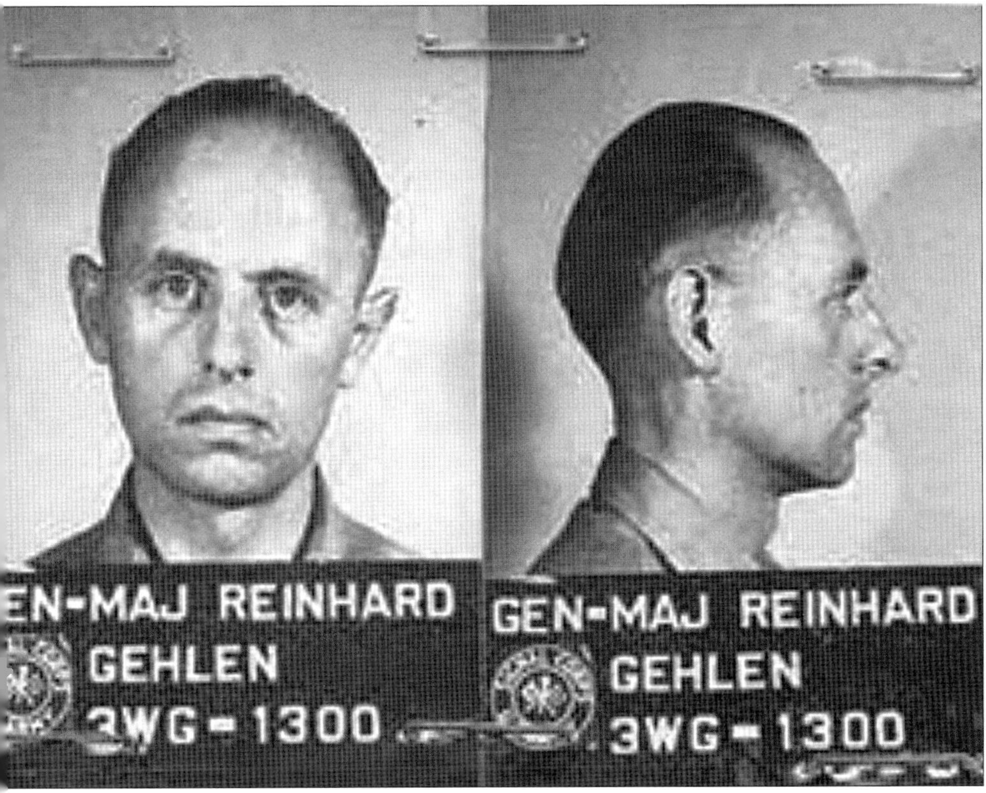

Generalleutnant Reinhard Gehlen's wartime position as commander of Fremde Heere Ost—the German general staff's intelligence branch dealing with Soviet military capabilities and intentions—made him extremely valuable to the Allies. So valuable, in fact, that after the war he was installed as the director of the West German intelligence service. *National Archives and Records Administration.*

The first of two ALU agents assigned to Austria, Hans Wenthur (seen here, far right, during a visit to Hitler's mountaintop Eagle's Nest in Bavaria) handled several important cases while based in Salzburg. He was later joined by fellow ALU member Joe Fellner, who worked primarily in Vienna. *Wenthy Marcy.*

One of the key cases Wenthur handled in Austria in 1945 had its roots in prev America. Before Pearl Harbor, pro-Nazi organizations flourished in the United Sta with the best-known group—the German-American Bund—parading throu major cities and hosting a Madison Square Garden rally in 1939 that dr 22,000 people. One of the smaller pro-Hitler organizations, Friends of New Germa gave rise to a New York–based German spy ring. *F*

The leader of the ring, German-born Dr. Ignaz T. Griebl, was a committed Nazi and virulent anti-Semite who had a knack for recruiting valuable agents. He ran an effective espionage organization despite his membership in Friends of New Germany and a reputation as a serial womanizer. *FBI.*

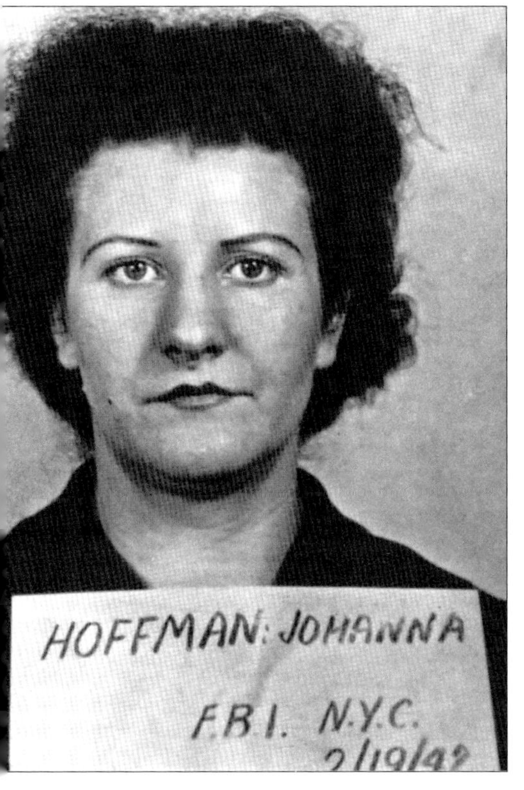

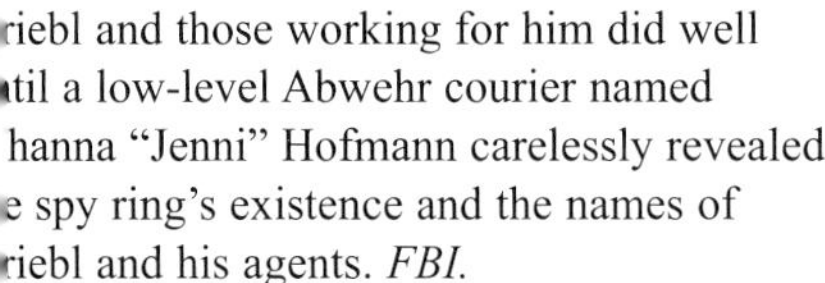

riebl and those working for him did well
ıtil a low-level Abwehr courier named
hanna "Jenni" Hofmann carelessly revealed
e spy ring's existence and the names of
riebl and his agents. *FBI.*

Widely considered the FBI's best investigator and interrogator, Special Agent Leon Turrou led the case against the Griebl ring. Though initially successful, Turrou earned Hoover's ire by publicizing the case for his own benefit and by allowing Ignaz Griebl to escape to Europe in May 1938. Seven years later, Hans Wenthur interrogated the fugitive physician in ıustria, only to have Griebl disappear yet again. *FBI.*

Despite the excellent work the men of the ALU had done in newly liberated Europe, in early October 1945 Brigadier General Edwin L. Sibert—intelligence chief for U.S. Forces European Theater—abruptly decided to reduce the ALU to just two agents. *National Archives and Records Administration.*

Convinced that Sibert's decision to reduce the ALU to just two agents would make it impossible for the FBI to operate in postwar Europe, Hoover ordered Ayer and his men to return to the United States. Most of the agents journeyed home by sea. In this photo, (left to right) Joe Fellner, Hans Wenthur, Dick Thompson, and Pete Winter enjoy a moment in the sun while waiting for their ships in the port of Le Havre. *Wenthy Marcy.*

claiming acquaintance with celebrities, to give the impression of being a man of culture and importance.[28]

Despite Commandant Paul Paillole's suspicions about Dawson, Gordon Sheen, and others within the SHAEF intelligence hierarchy had initially been inclined to accept the writer's assertions that the dossier found in Widlöcher's car was a communist forgery. But many of the documents removed from Dawson's apartment on October 20 seemed to implicate him further, to the extent that Paillole told Sheen the French government intended to charge the American writer with "Activities Against the Best Interests of the State" and try him in a French court. This was in keeping with an agreement between the U.S. and Free French governments that the latter had primary jurisdiction over any violation committed in France and against the safety of the French nation, no matter the citizenship of the perpetrator. Moreover, the reports by the various CIC agents who had spoken at length with Dawson revealed so many troubling inconsistencies, especially regarding the writer's activities during the occupation, that Sheen and others within SHAEF decided that the Widlöcher documents must be genuine. It was at that point, on the afternoon of October 26, that Sheen brought in the FBI.

The first thing Fred Ayer and Don Daughters did when Gordon Sheen told them about Dawson and his suspected collaboration with the Germans was to request access to the material found in Widlöcher's car and the reports written by the various U.S. military personnel who had interacted with the writer. They also asked Paillole for an inventory of all the items removed from Dawson's apartment, and the DSM chief said he would provide it when his agency had completed processing the materials. In the meantime, the two FBI agents did their own translations of the German files, which, as Sheen had told them, put Dawson in a very bad light.

The most potentially damning documents were a series of letters between Widlöcher and various senior German functionaries. The first, dated June 26, 1942, was addressed to a Captain Bergmann of the German Censorship Office at 93, boulevard du Montparnasse. In it, Widlöcher stated that he was enclosing three letters written in English, one each to the U.S. ambassadors in Argentina, Brazil, and Sweden.[29] He told Bergmann that the unnamed writer of the letters "seems to know code," which "is to be remembered when these letters are censored."[30] The reason Widlöcher wanted the documents examined wasn't given. On July 1, Bergmann replied that the letters had been "appropriately censored and have been chemically examined without disclosing any evidence of secret writing."[31]

The letters were, in fact, written by Warrington Dawson and relayed his impressions of the then current situation in Europe. The recipients were all diplomats whom Dawson had previously known or worked with in France. The ambassador to Argentina, Norman Armour, had been the *chargé d'affairs* in Paris from 1929 to 1932. Jefferson Caffery in Brazil had been part of President Woodrow Wilson's staff at the 1919 Paris Peace Conference, which Dawson attended. Herschel Johnson in Sweden had served in France in World War I, then stayed for several months after the war in Burgundy and Paris, where he met Dawson socially. The two men renewed their acquaintance following Johnson's first diplomatic posting, to the U.S. legation in Berne, Switzerland in 1921.

Exactly what happened to the three letters after they were cleared by Bergmann is unclear, though there are indications they eventually reached their intended recipients. In a December 3 memo to a Herr Schlottman at the Paris office of the German radio service, Widlöcher enclosed another report he said had been written by his "American informant." The document—likely a précis of current events in France similar to the one previously sent to the three ambassadors—could be used on the radio, Widlöcher wrote, a strong implication that the document was pro-German. Further reports could be prepared for radio use, the translator added, though his "partially paralyzed" informant would need the assistance of an English-speaking German stenographer.[32]

On January 20, 1943, Widlöcher wrote to Dr. Paul Karl Schmidt, the chief of the Foreign Office press department in Berlin, regarding the U.S. government white paper "Peace and War: United States Foreign Policy, 1931–41." That 144-page document had been released in book form in North America on January 2, and then published in full four days later in *The New York Times*. A scathing indictment of Nazism and Italian fascism, the white paper prompted an immediate counterpropaganda effort by the Germans. In the letter, Widlöcher named Warrington Dawson as his "American informant" and said that as a former employee of the U.S. embassy in Paris who "not only dislikes Franklin Roosevelt but hates him," he could "be of great service to us" in refuting the white paper. Widlöcher then added:

> I have often had occasion to chat with Warrington about American problems and, little by little, a mutual friendly understanding developed which led Warrington, toward the end of 1942, to offer me for our use commentaries and talks, edited by him, for radio transmission. . . . Warrington still keeps copies of all of his reports addressed to the State Department from 1920 to 1938. Therefore, it would be entirely possible to contradict with them certain passages of the white paper, making use of his material and demonstrating with especially striking examples the arbitrary tone of diplomatic communiques of the U.S. State Department.[33]

In the body of the letter, Widlöcher also mentioned that he had spoken about Dawson to Werner Plack, the man responsible for recruiting foreigners to write and broadcast programs aimed at Britain and the United States.

Berlin-born Plack had traveled to California in 1928 at the age of twenty-one, apparently because he wanted to be a film star. He had, in fact, gotten bit parts in several Hollywood movies, but supplemented his meager acting income by working as an assistant to the German consul general in Los Angeles. Following Adolph Hitler's rise to power, Plack also became a stringer for the Deutsches Nachtrichtenbüro (DNB), the official Nazi press agency. Suave, debonair, and fluent in English and French in addition to his native German, Plack and his South African–born wife became fixtures on the Hollywood social scene. While not too subtly promoting the views of the German government, Plack also attempted to tone down anti-Nazi sentiments in Hollywood movies by telling actors, producers, and distributors that "unfavorable" films would be banned in Germany and any other countries that might come under Reich control.[34]

Whatever value Plack's work in America might have had, his spendthrift ways with consulate funds and penchant for heavy drinking soon became issues his superiors could not ignore. The last straw was in June 1940 when a severely inebriated Plack got into a very public fistfight at a popular nightclub with a Hollywood screenwriter who had taken umbrage at the German's frequent shouts of "Heil Hitler!"[35] Plack and his wife were sent packing back to Germany, where both found employment with the Press Department of the German Foreign Office. By 1942, Plack was splitting his time between Berlin and the German embassy in Paris, with the sole duty of recruiting British and American citizens resident in occupied Europe (and

Allied prisoners of war being held in German camps) to broadcast pro-Nazi propaganda over Radio Berlin.

Accompanied by Dr. Friedrich Grimm, the head of German propaganda research in France, Plack met Dawson on a visit to Paris in February. During their conversation, the American complained that his lack of a radio was preventing him from staying informed about U.S. politics and policies he might end up writing about. In a March 11 memo to Schlottman, Widlöcher wrote that a radio had been purchased for Dawson, who "will furnish talks to the America Broadcasting Section of the Radio Division." The cost of the radio was 7,480 francs, and Widlöcher asked that Schlottman "remit this sum, due for two months, at your early convenience."[36]

The several references to Dawson in Widlöcher's recovered letters and memos certainly implied that the American writer had collaborated with the Germans. Any lingering doubts Fred Ayer and Don Daughters may have had regarding Dawson's willingness to literally sell out his country were erased by one of the last documents in the captured dossier. In an April 9, 1943, memo to Rudolf Schleier of the German embassy, Widlöcher wrote:

> I have been collaborating with the American diplomat W.D. (alias Ivan Starold) who lives in Versailles. Since Berlin regards his work as of great importance, I even entered into a contract with the man under which royalties will be paid to him for turning out periodic talks.[37]

The revelation that Dawson had signed a contract guaranteeing him a financial reward for turning out pro-German propaganda put him squarely in Fred and Don's sights. But the Free French government's claim of primary jurisdiction in the case meant that the FBI agents had to tread carefully, at least initially. Anxious to confront Dawson face-to-face, Fred turned to Commandant Paul Paillole for help.

Fortunately, the DSM chief was able to devise the perfect way to keep his earlier promise to assist the FBI in any way he could, while at the same time avoiding any affront to Free French sovereignty.

The morning of Saturday, October 28, 1944, was dreary and frigid in Versailles. Leaden skies, a biting wind, and periodic snow squalls presaged a winter that would be the coldest in European history to that time. The windows of the black Citroën Traction Avant sedan that pulled up in front of Warrington Dawson's apartment building were veined with ice, and the engine's exhaust formed a hazy, slow-moving cloud in the subzero temperature.

The vehicle belonged to the Direction de la Sécurité Militaire and two of its occupants—Capitaine Simonin and Sous-Lieutenant Chauvel—had been dispatched by Paul Paillole, ostensibly to interrogate Warrington Dawson. The third person in the Citroën was Fred Ayer, whom the DSM chief had designated as an "interested observer." The reality was that Fred was there to do the interrogating, while the presence of the two DSM agents ensured that the Franco-American agreement on primary jurisdiction was observed—at least in appearances.

Dawson was sitting in a wheelchair next to the living room fireplace when his elderly housekeeper led the visitors in. Though the writer was obviously startled by the trio's unannounced arrival, he appeared surprisingly hale, not at all the sickly invalid Fred had expected to confront. Dawson's composure slipped somewhat when the man he'd taken for an American Army officer revealed that he was an FBI agent, and still more when Fred began questioning him.

Asked how he knew both Widlöcher and Grimm, the writer replied that he'd been introduced to them by René Martel, a pro-Nazi French historian and journalist. As to Werner Plack, Dawson said he believed the radio propaganda chief had come to Versailles simply to "keep an eye on him." When Fred queried him about his large and obviously expensive radio, Dawson nervously responded that he'd bought it himself but couldn't produce a receipt. He also strongly denied that he'd ever furnished written reports to the Germans for propaganda purposes, but allowed that some of his writings might have been used without his knowledge or permission. When Fred asked about the English-speaking stenographer Dawson had hired, the writer insisted the young woman had "appeared spontaneously" and offered her services. He claimed he thought she was Irish because she said her last name was Cairn, but that he started to suspect she was German when he noticed she spelled it Kern. Asked about how he managed to afford a sumptuous apartment, a housekeeper, a stenographer, and the radio, Dawson was "exceedingly evasive."[38]

Fred was more than a little dissatisfied with the writer's responses. As he wrote in his report of the meeting:

> All in all his replies were totally unsatisfactory and failed to explain the correspondence which had been recovered from the German embassy papers. Every time the man was asked a direct question he either answered that he did not know, that he had forgotten, or else he launched into a flood of oratory concerning his acquaintanceship with important American statesmen and other figures. On the basis of the existing evidence it would be impossible to prove definitely that the man was guilty of working for the Germans, but it would seem almost impossible to believe that such a chain of circumstances could all have been coincidental, or that the subject was a man of such international importance that the Germans would have gone to such elaborate lengths to make it appear that he was working for them.[39]

Fred added that the French were continuing to work on Dawson's case and that, among other things, they were planning to question the writer's housekeeper about the number of times senior German officials had visited the apartment. Moreover, Fred wrote, Selden Chapin—the *chargé d'affaires* at the U.S. embassy—had been made aware of all aspects of the Dawson investigation and was satisfied with the way the case was being handled.

However, not everyone at the embassy was apparently as pleased with the Dawson inquiry. Within days of Fred's initial interrogation of the writer, a very high-ranking American official asked the FBI agent to use his influence with the French to have Dawson released from house arrest and spared further indignities. "I remembered my Dale Carnegie," Fred later wrote, "and assured the official that I would do no such damned thing . . . and that, furthermore, I was firmly convinced that the old gentleman was guiltier than original sin." The response by the unnamed official was simply, "Ayer, you must be wrong, this man cannot have worked for the Germans. After all, I knew him socially."[40] It was the first indication that influential or high-ranking friends of the "renegade Americans" would likely attempt to obstruct Fred and Don's investigations to protect themselves, the alleged collaborators, or a particular organization.

Over time, pressure on Fred and Don regarding the Dawson case only increased, despite the fact that the French still had official jurisdiction and had announced that the writer would be tried by a military tribunal. An October 31 cable from Fred to Hoover noted that Jefferson Caffery, the newly arrived but not yet officially installed U.S. ambassador to France, had asked to see copies of every report the FBI agents sent to the Bureau regarding Dawson. Fred noted that Caffery was

> exceedingly perturbed about the whole affair and is very much worried about the scandal which may result because of the fact that Dawson was at one time an employee of the State Department, was the friend or acquaintance of so many prominent persons, including Caffery himself, and because he was so well known in France.[41]

Fred had been called to the ambassador's office twice in the forty-eight hours following the FBI agent's interrogation of Dawson, with Caffery ultimately announcing that the embassy would "take a stand" intended to force the French to call off their prosecution. The diplomat also said he had dispatched his friend Major George Sharp to see Dawson. Sharp, the chief of the SHAEF mission to the Free French government and son of a former ambassador to France, reported to Caffery that Dawson could not possibly be guilty. In his report, Fred noted that Sharp was, in fact, a former very close friend of Dawson's who likely could not reconcile himself to the possibility that the writer might be guilty of treason. In addition, Fred said that during his conversations with the ambassador, he'd gotten the "definite impression" that Caffery wanted him to use his contacts with the French to ensure that there would "not be too much publicity given to the case."[42]

Unknown to Fred and Don at the time, the ambassador had that same day cabled Secretary of State Cordell Hull about the case, saying in part that Dawson, "whose special relationship to the Embassy in Paris in the past is well known to the Department, may have become involved during the German occupation in some questionable activities." That seems a very bland description of acts that were being considered by the Justice Department to have constituted high treason. Moreover, in the same report, Caffery seemed to imply that Dawson should be considered not responsible for his actions. "Even before his infirmity Mr. Warrington Dawson had shown signs of eccentricity as regards dress, habits and fixation of ideas," he wrote. "This is mentioned not in any way to excuse the conduct of which he may have been guilty but rather in explanation thereof."[43]

In the six weeks following Fred's interrogation of Dawson, a flurry of cables regarding the case passed back and forth between Paris and Washington. On November 19, Fred informed Hoover that the DSM had turned Dawson's prosecution over to the Justice Militaire—the French equivalent of the U.S. Army Judge Advocate General's Corps—which intended to try the writer before a military tribunal to be held in Versailles. Fred noted that George Sharphad retained prominent Paris attorney Pierre Paulle to defend Dawson. The FBI agent also included various memoranda prepared by SHAEF's counterintelligence branch concerning Dawson, which indicated that the writer was "a braggart and a man appearing to suffer from delusions of grandeur. It seems obvious, however," Fred continued, "that [Dawson] is exceedingly clever and . . . a very evasive and slippery character."[44]

Ambassador Caffery, for his part, cabled Secretary Hull on December 4 about Sharp's hiring of Paulle, "a well-known member of the Paris bar." Caffery also noted that Sharp, "who has studied the whole matter carefully, is convinced of Dawson's innocence."[45] What the ambassador did not mention was that in late November, Paulle had contacted four of the writer's current and former physicians for statements he hoped would prove Dawson not guilty of collaboration by reason of physical and mental deterioration. Each of the doctors stated that Dawson's paralysis, spinal issues, and claims of excruciating pain from the slightest movement were real. Moreover, the physicians agreed that the writer's poor physical health greatly contributed to a declining mental state. Dr. Julien Rouart, the former head of a neuropsychiatric clinic, examined Dawson on November 26 and found him to be suffering from recurring amnesia, exaggerated emotive reactions, and disturbances of logical capacities and judgment. Dr. E. Humbert, who had treated Dawson since 1928, examined him on November 27 and noted "a deterioration of his general state, along with a great diminishment of memory and often the near-impossibility of expressing himself."[46] These findings were completely at odds, of course, with the impression Dawson gave to Fred Ayer and the other American and French investigators who dealt with him at length—despite often seeming evasive and manipulative, the writer struck them as erudite, effusive, and intellectually agile.

While the physicians' statements might well have bolstered Dawson's defense when his trial was eventually held before a French military tribunal, by the first week of 1945, there were forces at play that would ultimately ensure Dawson would never be prosecuted for the treason he almost certainly committed.

From the moment the Free French government announced that Warrington Dawson would be tried in a French court under French law, the

U.S. departments of War, Justice, and State were collectively faced with a series of thorny issues. The primary concern was one of jurisdiction.

If an American citizen suspected of treason was detained by the police or military forces of an ally during wartime and charged with crimes against that friendly government, which nation had the right to prosecute the individual first? If the person was apprehended by American military forces operating within the allied nation, should the individual first face the U.S. treason charge or the charge leveled by the ally? How should the U.S. government respond if the allied nation chose to hold the American citizen in indefinite custody on the grounds that the person's freedom would be prejudicial to national security? If the person being held by the allied government was of unsound physical or mental health, should the U.S. government demand the individual's release from custody or transfer to a secure medical facility?

The War Department was essentially of the opinion that France should be allowed to try Dawson in keeping with the mutually agreed upon "Activities Against the Best Interests of the French State" concept. His collaboration with the Germans had first been discovered by the French, after all, and he had been placed under house arrest and first interrogated by the DSM. To alter the agreement could well disrupt Franco-American military cooperation in the continuing battle against the Axis, the Pentagon argued. That Dawson was a civilian rather than a U.S. servicemember may well have influenced the War Department's position, of course.

The State Department's opposition to a Dawson trial was apparently based on an overwhelming desire to avoid adverse publicity—both for the agency as a whole and for certain individuals. Ambassador Caffery and others pointed out that should the charges against Dawson become public, they were certain to be trumpeted both in France's resurgent communist press and in the American media. The revelation that a longtime Foreign Service officer and confident of a former U.S. president had willingly aided the Nazis would humiliate the State Department, and the news that the accused was a longtime friend or acquaintance of still serving senior American diplomats could well focus suspicion on the patriotism—and perhaps even the lifestyles—of those individuals.

The issues were somewhat more clear-cut for the Justice Department. There was considerable evidence that Warrington Dawson had, in fact, committed treason against the United States as defined by Article 3, Section 3, Clause 1 of the Constitution: "Treason against the United States shall consist only in levying war against them, or in adhering to their enemies, giving them aid and comfort." The recovered Widlöcher papers and other incriminating documents discovered by French investigators and Fred Ayer and Don Daughters clearly showed that Dawson had intentionally produced written materials for propaganda use by the Germans, and that he had been compensated in return.[47] Unfortunately, the Constitution also states that "No person shall be convicted of treason unless on the testimony of two witnesses to the same overt act, or on confession in open court."[48] Neither the French authorities, Army counterintelligence officers, nor Fred and Don had been able to locate the requisite number of witnesses for any of Dawson's alleged treasonous acts. All of the Germans who could have witnessed his writing of, presentation of, or payment for propaganda were obviously unavailable. Moreover, the American and British radio-monitoring agencies could find no evidence of Warrington Dawson or "Ivan Starold" having voiced German propaganda.[49]

In the end, it was the Justice Department that ultimately decided that Warrington Dawson would not be tried for treason. In a December 26 letter to Hoover, Assistant Attorney General Tom C. Clark wrote, "The facts presently developed do not indicate a violation of the Treason Statute for which prosecution would be warranted." The bad news was passed to Fred and Don three days later by cable. While certainly disappointed the two agents were not all that surprised. As Fred later wrote, "All of us who have been in the intelligence reporting business have, far too often, seen the prejudices or warped judgment of some . . . Washington bureaucrat eventually override the precise reporting and seasoned powers of observation of a man of twice the caliber in the field."[50] The possibility that France would prosecute Dawson for his dealings with the Germans also faded over time, both because the French government had far more important homegrown traitors to prosecute and because Paris didn't want to embarrass the nation that would likely provide the majority of the funding necessary to rebuild postwar Europe.

By the summer of 1945, Warrington Dawson was back to hosting lavish parties at his Versailles apartment. Despite his famously poor health, he lived another seventeen years, and none of the obituaries published following his death in 1962 at the age of eighty-five mentioned his wartime collaboration with the Nazis.

CHAPTER 7

Renegades and Monuments Men

As important and time-consuming as the Warrington Dawson case was for Fred Ayer and Don Daughters, it was just one of many treason investigations they undertook simultaneously during the final months of 1944.

The agents had arrived in France with seven names already on their target list—Fred Kaltenbach, Constance Drexel, Robert Best, Edward Delaney, Jane Anderson, Max Koischwitz, and Douglas Chandler. These were the Americans who, along with Ezra Pound, had been indicted for treason in July 1943 for broadcasting enemy propaganda. However, Pound was already in custody and the others were believed to be in Germany. So, with the help of Gordon Sheen and the French police and intelligence services, the Paris-based agents had begun compiling a list of more readily accessible suspects that ultimately included the names of twenty-two people.[1]

Still only a two-man team, the FBI agents necessarily had to prioritize their investigations. One of the criteria they used was the prominence of the suspect. Individuals whose names were better known in the United States or Europe because of celebrity or political connections—or both, as in the case of Warrington Dawson—were likely to have been more effective as spokespersons for the Third Reich. In combing their list of targets, one of the first names that caught the agents' attention more than fulfilled the "celebrity" requirement. He was a man small in stature but gigantic in the hearts of European horse racing fans—and his name was Frank Joseph O'Neill. Though retired by the time he came to Fred and Don's attention, the American expatriate had for more than two decades been the most successful professional jockey in Europe.

Born in Newton, Kansas, in 1885, Frank O'Neill grew up in St. Louis. At the age of ten, he divided his time between delivering newspapers and exercising horses at a nearby racetrack. At thirteen, he rode in his first amateur race, and at fifteen, made his professional debut as a jockey. He won his first race in 1901, and two years later, began riding in New York state. Though just 5 feet, 3 inches tall and weighing less than 100 pounds, O'Neill was an extraordinarily gifted rider and a fierce competitor. By 1905, he'd won some two hundred local races and nine major ones, including the Brooklyn Derby (twice), the Saratoga Special, and the Manhattan Handicap. Arguably one of the most successful and best-known jockeys in the United States, in July 1905, O'Neil made two important decisions—he married the former Mary McCafferty, and he temporarily retired from riding to open his own stables with partner Fred Burlew.[2]

The business initially prospered, but in 1908, tough antigambling laws passed by the New York state legislature prompted O'Neill and Burlew to sell their stable and take ship for Europe.[3] Horse racing was hugely popular on the Continent, especially in France, and O'Neill was soon riding again. In 1909 alone, he won 72 races as a freelancer, and after winning the French Derby the following year, O'Neill joined American millionaire William K. Vanderbilt's Haras du Quesnay stable as principal rider. The jockey and his family—wife Mary, son Frank, and daughters Ella Frances and Mary Margaret—moved into a grand house in the affluent Paris suburb of Maisons-Laffitte, adjacent to both the racetrack of the same name and to Vanderbilt's sprawling stable complex. Over the next fifteen years, O'Neill won every major race on the French and British circuits and was named France's champion rider ten times between 1910 and 1922. Following Vanderbilt's death in 1920, O'Neill rode for American millionaire A. Kingsley Macomber and France's Baron Édouard de Rothschild, and in 1925, he was paid $25,000 to ride for one year in Germany for the Halma Stable.[4] Even when not in the saddle, O'Neill spent much of his time at the various racetracks in and around Paris, often in the company of fellow jockeys and friends, such as a promising young writer named Ernest Hemingway.[5]

By the late 1920s, the aging and increasingly portly O'Neill had successfully transitioned from jockey to highly regarded trainer, a career change that allowed him to continue living in the manner to which he and his family had become accustomed. That lifestyle changed abruptly, however, following France's 1940 capitulation. Most of the country's top stables were shut down and their horses were confiscated and transferred to new owners in Germany.

Though the occupiers allowed horse racing to continue in France, the sport was tightly controlled, with most of the proceeds being used to fund the German war effort. These factors resulted in a sharp decline in O'Neill's income, which in mid-1941 forced the former jockey and his family out of their opulent home in Maisons-Laffitte and into a still elegant but decidedly smaller apartment at 306, rue St. Honoré in Paris's 1st *arrondissement*.

Why the O'Neills chose to stay in German-occupied France is unclear, though it may have been because, in 1938, Frank—unable to make a living as a horse trainer—had bought a profitable bar on the rue Volney, in the 2nd *arrondissement*. Located barely five hundred yards from the rue St. Honoré apartment, the short street was home to several small but highly regarded restaurants and to Chez Elle, one of the most renowned cabarets in Paris. O'Neill's bar was a popular watering hole and, following the outbreak of war in 1939, became something of a home away from home for expatriate Americans. Following the French surrender in 1940, Chez Elle became a favorite with German soldiers, many of whom enjoyed a pre- or after-show libation at O'Neill's. The bar became known among the occupiers as "German-friendly" and, like Chez Elle, was among the Paris venues approved by the arm of the Reich's official tourist office tasked with ensuring that German service members enjoyed their time in the City of Light.[6]

Frank O'Neill's willingness to entertain Germans apparently stood him in good stead following the 1941 Japanese attack on Pearl Harbor. America's December 8 declaration of war against Japan prompted Germany, as Tokyo's ally, to declare war against the United States on December 11. That declaration was followed by an order from the Militärbefehlshaber in Frankreich—Germany's military high command in France—that all U.S. citizens remaining in the occupied part of the country register with the German authorities by December 17 or face arrest and imprisonment. The vast majority of Americans affected by the decree lived in Paris, and most of them registered before the deadline expired. Those who did not, some 340 men under the age of sixty, were arrested and imprisoned. Initially housed at the former French army Caserne Vauban in Besançon, two hundred miles southeast of Paris, near the Swiss border, the men were soon moved to the Royallieu-Compiègne internment camp, forty miles northeast of the French capital.

Among the Americans who failed to register in time were Frank O'Neill and his now thirty-five-year-old son, Frank.[7] Unlike most of the other men who were swept up by the Germans within days of the deadline's passing, the two O'Neills remained free for weeks. When they were finally arrested, they were transported to the Royallieu camp, but were held for less than twenty-four hours before being released and allowed to return home. This struck the other American internees as exceedingly suspicious, and word soon filtered back to the U.S. expatriate community in Paris that the O'Neills must have received favorable treatment because of their "German-friendly" attitude.

Once released from Royallieu, the two Americans went back to business as usual at the bar on rue Volney. The elder O'Neill handled the books and played the convivial and gregarious host while his son tended bar and supervised the several young German-speaking French women who served as waitresses.[8] Business was good, with the clientele almost exclusively German save for some pro-Nazi French functionaries and a few die-hard American patrons. Among the latter was Joseph Luhan, the man who introduced German-friendly barkeep Frank O'Neill to the Third Reich's top recruiter of American renegades.

JOSEPH EMIL LINCOLN LUHAN WAS BORN in New York City in 1898. His parents had immigrated from Bohemia—then a part of the Austro-Hungarian Empire—in the 1870s, and their children grew up speaking German in the home. Luhan Sr. was a very wealthy Manhattan physician who tended to spoil his son and three daughters, and that indulgence essentially guaranteed that Joseph grew up never having to take responsibility for his often careless actions. A string of relatively minor scrapes with the law culminated in 1915 with young Luhan crashing his father's car while driving drunk, an accident that left a young female passenger critically injured. Dr. Luhan paid off the girl's parents—and apparently the police as well—and no charges were ever filed. Two years later, the now nineteen-year-old Joseph was named in a paternity suit, and rather than deal with the situation honorably, the young man took a different way out.[9]

On April 23, 1917, just seventeen days after the United States entered World War I, Joseph Luhan enlisted in the U.S. Army at Governors Island in New York. After basic training, he was assigned to the Quartermaster Corps and, likely much to his dismay, was trained for graves registration work. He deployed to France in July 1917, where he spent the following eighteen months helping to locate, collect, identify, and prepare for burial the bodies of American soldiers killed in action. He learned to speak French and must also have had some aptitude for his military work, for he was a sergeant by the time of his honorable discharge in June 1919.

Life back in old New York apparently didn't suit Luhan, for after just weeks with his parents, he convinced an uncle to dispatch him to Europe as a clerk for the American-Bohemian Mining and Exploration Company. The young veteran spent five months traveling in France, Switzerland, and Czechoslovakia, though what sort of business he undertook is unclear. He returned to the United States in November 1919 but stayed less than a year before taking ship back to Europe. From late 1920 to 1922, he worked as a civilian staff member for the U.S. Army Graves Registration service in France—a fairly logical use of his wartime skills. He then moved to Prague but, in 1926, returned to the French capital, and the following year, went to work as a clerk in the *Chicago Tribune*'s Paris bureau. In 1928, he married Lucienne Janin, a native of Grenoble working as a teacher in an exclusive girls' school, and the couple ultimately had two sons.[10] Following his marriage, Luhan worked at several jobs, including as a liaison between American expatriates and French insurance companies. It was likely that position that introduced him to bar owner Frank O'Neill.

Like the former jockey, Luhan stayed in France after war broke out in September 1939. He had been doing freelance reporting for a few U.S. magazines and newspapers, which allowed him to join the American Press Association of Paris. That, in turn, meant that when most American reporters left France following the 1940 surrender, Luhan was able to land a reporting job with the United Press bureau in the French capital. Following the United States' entry into the war in December 1941, Luhan—again like O'Neill—was only briefly held at Royallieu, apparently because he offered to work for the Germans as a translator. In March 1942, he was ordered to visit the German embassy, where he was told that he was being sent to Berlin to meet with an "important official." That turned out to be Werner Plack.

Once in Berlin, Luhan was interviewed by Plack and other senior members of the Foreign Office and of Joseph Goebbels's Ministry for Public Enlightenment and Propaganda. The American was also given a voice test, after which he was told to return to the French capital and "await further instructions." Those were delivered by Plack in person when he met with Luhan in early April 1942 at the Hôtel Le Bristol in Paris.[11] It was then that Plack instructed Luhan to begin finding "social subjects" that could form the basis for English-language propaganda broadcasts. The topics—fashion shows, nightclub life, films, and sports events—were intended to prove to audiences in America and Britain that life was still happy and going on as normal in France under German rule. Plack also told Luhan to attempt to recruit other Americans in Paris for radio propaganda work, and one of the first people he approached was Frank O'Neill.

The former jockey was an ideal choice to help do radio commentary for horse races, and he did so at least three times during the summer of 1942, at tracks including Vincennes and Longchamp. It was these broadcasts, made over German-controlled Radio Paris and Vichy's Radio Nationale, that ultimately led O'Neill to be designated a suspected American traitor.

Frank O'Neill's name had first come up a few days after Fred Ayer and Don Daughters arrived in Paris in September 1944. During one of their initial meetings with Gordon Sheen, the SHAEF counterintelligence chief had provided the FBI agents with a list of the last known addresses of Allied nationals who had been released from internment in Royallieu under suspicious circumstances. Frank O'Neill and his son were on the list, as was Joseph Luhan. Fred had passed the roster on to Bureau headquarters in Washington and to Gerald Drew, the first secretary of the American Mission to France (soon to become the U.S. Embassy). In an October 4 message to Hoover titled "Frank O'Neal, aka O'Neill Sr., Sedition, Treason,"[12] Fred indicated that he would be reaching out to his French police and intelligence contacts to develop more information on the O'Neills and Luhan.

Progress on the O'Neill and Luhan cases, among several others, was somewhat slowed by the crush of work Fred and Don had to deal with during their first weeks in Paris, as well as by Fred's six-day road trip to visit Twelfth Army Group and his brief visits to London in late October and early November to meet with Joe Lynch. It was therefore not until mid-November that the FBI agents got their first real break. The O'Neills and Luhan had earlier been put on a SHAEF CIC target list, and on November 18, Fred and Don were notified that Luhan had been located and was apparently about to flee the French capital. Accompanied by several CIC soldiers and one of Commandant Paul Paillole's operatives, the two FBI agents apprehended Luhan and deposited him in the DSM interrogation center at 18, boulevard Suchet.[13]

Don was the first to interrogate the suspected traitor, who was initially cocky and self-assured. But then, as Don later recalled:

> We had a recording of [Luhan's] that we had picked up somewhere, so right in the middle of this interrogation, in one of the pauses while Joe was talking, we turned on this recording and played it from

> behind a screen so that Joe's voice was coming through the screen to us in the room. It was obviously Joe's voice. Here he was, spouting all this German propaganda to be sent over to America. Joe turned all colors of green and yellow, I mean, the poor guy practically fainted.[14]

Confronted with proof that he had made radio broadcasts for the Germans, Luhan became apologetic and said that he had only worked for the occupiers so he could eat. He vehemently denied that he had been an informant for the Gestapo—something Fred and Don had heard from several French sources—and said that he had only gone to Berlin because he didn't want to anger Werner Plack by refusing.

Fred then joined the interrogation, playing "bad cop" to Don's "good cop." As Fred later wrote:

> Under constant [verbal] hammering . . . he confessed to more and more . . . actually admitting a great deal that we had not known about him in the beginning. Among the most damaging of his admissions was his acknowledgement of personal acquaintance with various members of the Nazi security and intelligence services. He would most certainly have never had access to these individuals unless he had been highly trusted by the occupation authorities.[15]

When Luhan realized how much the FBI agents already knew about his activities and the ways in which he had implicated himself, "he began practically to grovel, acting more like a whipped dog than a man," Fred recalled. "He wept for his family—how they would be disgraced. At one point, he actually went down on his knees."[16]

Likely in hopes of currying favor with Fred and Don, the now thoroughly broken Luhan asked for paper and pencil so he could give "a complete account" of his activities. He acknowledged being recruited by Plack and related all he knew about the German's background and activities, and provided a wealth of information on the other Nazis with whom he had dealt in both Paris and Berlin. Luhan admitted making "many" radio broadcasts for the Germans, including commentary on horse and dog races, boxing matches, and cultural events. He also confessed to making one broadcast "ridiculing the Jews and their money-grabbing and draft-dodging tactics in time of war."[17] Finally, and of particular interest to Fred and Don, Luhan listed the names and addresses of several other Paris-based American expatriates he claimed had also done propaganda work for the Germans. Among the individuals he implicated was Frank O'Neill, whom Luhan said he had recruited in the spring of 1942.

Fred and Don continued to interrogate Luhan intermittently over the following days while also pursuing the many leads his written statement had provided. The agents were especially interested in locating Frank O'Neill, and on November 25, they had another bit of good fortune. That day, Army Criminal Investigation Division officers acting on a tip arrested the former jockey at the home of a friend. O'Neill's son—who was also on the CIC target list at the FBI agents' request—was not found at the same location.[18]

O'Neill was taken to the boulevard Suchet interrogation center, where Fred and Don spent several hours walking him through the details of his involvement with the Germans. Unlike Luhan, O'Neill was immediately forthcoming. When asked about why he and his son had been so quickly released from the Royallieu internment camp, he explained that it was a simple act of friendship rather than the result of collaboration. One of the camp officers was a regular at the rue Volney bar, and after ensuring that the O'Neills were not wanted by German authorities for acts committed against the occupation, father and son were cautioned to "behave themselves" and were then released. O'Neill acknowledged that he had done radio commentary for three horse races at Luhan's request, but said that he hadn't realized that doing so could be considered a treasonous act. He had not been compensated in any way for the broadcasts, he said, and had never met Werner Plack. O'Neill also said that he had continued to serve Germans at the rue Volney bar not to provide "aid and comfort" to the enemy, but simply to stay out of trouble with the occupiers and to earn a living.[19]

Fred and Don generally accepted O'Neill's account of his actions and did not believe that he or his son had committed treason. Since there was no indication that the younger O'Neill had worked for the Germans (other than serving them alcohol at the rue Volney bar), his name was taken off the CIC target list. His father was held in custody for several weeks while the details of his statement were validated, and when, in late December, the Department of Justice declined to prosecute him, Frank O'Neill was released. How he spent the remainder of his life is unclear, though we know that the man once known as the world's greatest jockey died in relative obscurity in New York City in 1960 at the age of seventy-five.

Joseph Lincoln Luhan's fate is much clearer. Following a U.S. Justice Department decision not to prosecute him (for reasons that remain opaque, given his admitted guilt), he was handed over to the French for possible trial.

He was held in custody while his case was investigated, and in April 1947, the DSM discovered something the Army Liaison Unit had not. While going through the records of Germany's wartime embassy in Paris, French intelligence agents found a ledger containing the names of individuals paid out of the embassy accounts. Luhan's name was among those listed, with a date of July 22, 1944, the terse notation "transmitter Siegfriedlinie," and a payment of 80,000 francs. The sum was apparently compensation for Luhan's pro-German broadcasts, though he denied any knowledge of the money.

The American renegade remained in French custody until 1948, at which time he was released without charge—again, for reasons unknown. Perhaps he was freed in exchange for testimony against other collaborators, or perhaps he knew too much about the wartime activities of persons who by that point were important members of the postwar government. Whatever the reason, Luhan spent the rest of his life in Paris with his wife. The couple lived well, and neighbors often said that the American seemed to have more money than his wife's job as headmistress of yet another exclusive girls' school would explain. Luhan died in the mid-1970s, taking many unanswered questions with him to the grave.[20]

When Fred Ayer and Don Daughters landed at Le Bourget Airport on the last day of September 1944, certain peculiarities in the agents' appearance or equipment may have led some sharp-eyed onlookers to assume that the two men were members of the "Monuments Men." That inter-Allied organization—officially known as the Monuments, Fine Arts, and Archives Section Unit (MFAA)—was established in 1943 to help safeguard cultural heritage in combat zones.[21] Academic experts in architecture, archeology, painting, sculpture, manuscripts, textiles, and other disciplines were brought into military service and sent out to locate, identify, and protect culturally and historically important items. The first Monuments men (and women) were active in the Mediterranean Theater of Operations before the Allied invasion of Sicily and then moved up the Italian mainland with the combat forces. In northern Europe, MFAA members arrived in France shortly after the Normandy landings and one, 1st Lieutenant James J. Rorimer, rode into newly liberated Paris atop a Sherman tank.[22]

Though Fred and Don had been briefed about the MFAA and its activities before leaving Washington, both agents probably assumed they would have no interactions with the organization. After all, the various missions J.

Edgar Hoover had tasked them to undertake in Europe did not include protecting cultural items or investigating the theft of such treasures by the Germans. Moreover, before D-Day, the MFAA and William Donovan's OSS had agreed to work together, which eventually led to the latter's creation of the Art Looting Investigation Unit (ALIU). Hoover's deep-seated antipathy to Donovan and his organization was well-known throughout the Bureau, and Fred and Don would not have been eager to incur the director's wrath by cooperating with Donovan's organization. That hesitation would have been reinforced by the agents' own low opinion of the "amateurish" OSS members with whom they'd come into contact, an evaluation shared by SHAEF CI chief Gordon Sheen. For all these reasons, it must have come as a huge surprise to the FBI agents when they found themselves working with the Monuments Men to unravel a convoluted case involving an American traitor, a crooked Swiss art dealer, the Abwehr, brutal French gangsters, and Nazi Germany's ruthless looting of France's cultural heritage.

What Fred and Don ultimately referred to as the "art affair" began simply enough. During his initial meetings with the FBI agents at SHAEF headquarters in Versailles, Gordon Sheen had produced a list of suspected American renegades who were currently either in Allied custody or on CIC target lists. One of the individuals still being sought was a Tony Heilenstein, said to have been born in New York around 1900. A cabled request to Bureau headquarters for a background check revealed that the man's name was actually Anthony Gerard Helfenstein, born, in Brooklyn in 1898, to German immigrant parents. Helfenstein had joined the U.S. Army at Fort Slocum, New York, in April 1915 and was trained as a medical orderly. In the spring of 1917, he joined Base Hospital No. 36, a thousand-bed unit staffed by faculty and students of the Detroit College of Medicine and Surgery. On October 24, Helfenstein married Mary E. McGrath in Detroit, and three days later, he deployed with his unit to Europe. The hospital was established in Vittel, France, where it occupied a former resort hotel.[23]

While details are scarce regarding Helfenstein's time with Base Hospital No. 36, he must have been fairly good at his job. He was a sergeant first class by July 1918, at which point he was transferred to Medical Supply Depot No. 3, some hundred miles southeast of Paris. Three months later, Helfenstein was promoted to second lieutenant, and spent the remainder of the war as the officer in charge of the depot section that provided bed linens, surgical and patient gowns, and other textiles to U.S. Army medical facilities throughout France. Despite generally good efficiency evaluations, on August 25, 1919,

Helfenstein went absent without leave from the depot. Thirty days later he was declared a deserter and his name was added to those of more than five thousand other American servicemen who abandoned their posts and disappeared during the conflict.

Fred Ayer and Don Daughters continued to investigate Helfenstein along with their several other suspects, and during the first week of November 1944, were pleasantly surprised when the SHAEF provost marshal's office notified them that the man had been arrested. Helfenstein was transferred to the boulevard Suchet interrogation center, and during questioning, filled in many of the blanks in his personal history. He had deserted from the Army in 1919, he said, because he had been told that rather than being sent home for discharge, he was to be part of the Allied occupation force in Germany. He was fed up with the military, he added, and the young woman he'd married just days before going overseas had subsequently divorced him on grounds of abandonment. Fluent in German from childhood, Helfenstein had learned French during the war. After going on the run as a deserter, he had adopted the name Anton Krammer and spent the following years dividing his time between France and Germany.[24]

When the war broke out in 1939, Helfenstein was living in Paris and working as an accountant. Following the French capitulation, his language and financial skills won him a position with a German organization known as Dienststelle Otto (Bureau Otto). Established and run by a Munich-born engineer and Abwehr agent named Hermann "Otto" Brandl, the group was one of many so-called *bureaux d'achats* (purchasing offices) established by German military and civil authorities specifically to strip France of anything that might possibly prove useful to the Nazi war effort. Initially focused on industrial machinery, metal, oil, rubber, textiles, chemicals, medicines, and similarly vital products for the Reich's military forces, the *bureaux d'achats* quickly broadened their shopping lists to include virtually any item they could lay hands on that could be offered to a German civilian population hungry for consumer goods. The increasingly hard-pressed French sold off family heirlooms, jewelry, artworks, furs, leather products, clothing, automobiles, and a host of other items. In many cases, the goods that ended up in the warehouses of the more than two hundred *bureaux d'achats* that dotted the French capital had been confiscated from the homes of leading Jewish families. No matter what the provenance, everything had to be evaluated and inventoried before it could be sold onward. Anthony Helfenstein was in charge of the Bureau Otto section that dealt with textiles, located at 23, square du Bois de Boulogne, in the 16th *arrondissement*.[25] Brandl had subsidiary offices in Portugal and Spain, through which he shipped some looted items—and apparently funds meant to support Abwehr activities in the Western Hemisphere—to South America, and at one point, Helfenstein spent several weeks in Madrid organizing a shipment of tapestries. While in the Spanish capital, the American also met and married Josefina Castro, a woman nineteen years his junior.

That Brandl and the operators of the other *bureaux d'achats* were able to establish ancillary operations outside France was possible because of the huge profits the Paris-based organizations generated. And the secret to their financial success was that the money the *bureaux* spent to buy items wasn't actually theirs, but belonged to the French themselves. Following the capitulation, the Germans imposed crushing monetary reparations on France, which had to pay all the costs of the occupation. The *bureaux d'achats* thus essentially used French reparation money to buy French goods, which were then sold to German consumers or foreign buyers at a massive profit. Many of those who ran the various *bureaux* quickly amassed vast personal fortunes and, as head of the most successful operation, Brandl's was among the largest.

But it wasn't just about the money; the head of Bureau Otto was first and foremost a dedicated Abwehr agent. While his operations in Paris certainly generated a significant revenue stream both for himself and for the intelligence agency—funds that were for the most part unknown to the Gestapo, the SS, and even Hitler himself—Brandl's primary task in Paris was to gather intelligence on behalf of his longtime friend, Abwehr chief Admiral Wilhelm Canaris. This he did by having operatives scattered throughout the French capital at all levels, from pimps and enforcers in the city's many brothels to the heights of Parisian society.

One of Brandl's key agents was a Swiss citizen named Max Stöcklin.[26] The two men had known each other since 1934, and in 1936, Stöcklin had become a paid Abwehr agent with Brandl as his primary handler. A sometime art dealer in his home country, in 1938, Stöcklin and an associate compiled a list of all the important paintings, sculptures, and other works belonging to France's leading Jewish families—items that could be "requisitioned" should Germany occupy France at some point. By 1939, the Swiss operative was living in a rented house in the Paris suburb of St. Cloud, and in the weeks before the outbreak of war, he began sending clandestine radio reports to Germany on French military preparations. Stöcklin's transmissions did not go unnoticed, and in mid-May 1940, he was arrested by French counterintelligence agents.

Tried for espionage and sentenced to death, Stöcklin was able to escape during the German invasion and reconnected with Brandl in newly occupied Paris.

In October 1940, the head of Bureau Otto paid for Stöcklin to set up a subsidiary office at 1, rue Lord Byron, barely five hundred yards east of the Arc de Triomphe, in the 8th *arrondissement*. While the new location would deal in many of the same items as other *bureaux*, Brandl wanted Stöcklin to specialize in artworks—specifically high-end paintings and such historic and valuable decorative textiles as tapestries and Persian carpets. The Swiss operative used his 1938 catalog of Jewish-owned art works as a shopping list and ultimately was directly involved in the illegitimate seizure and transfer out of France of such masterpieces as Henri Matisse's *The Open Window, Étretat*, and *Female Nude in a Yellow Chair*, among others.[27] Stöcklin often worked in cooperation with the Einsatzstab Reichsleiter Rosenberg (ERR), a special task force under the command of senior Nazi Alfred Rosenberg that Hitler had ordered to seize the cultural holdings of Jews and other "enemies of the Reich." The ERR quickly became Germany's premier art looting entity, plundering works from all the occupied territories, with France a particularly lucrative hunting ground.

But paintings were not Stöcklin's only quarry. Historic textiles were also on his target list, and just before America entered World War II in December 1941, the Swiss operative reached out to Otto Brandl's textiles expert for help. Helfenstein had access to French documents listing important tapestries and other items held by individuals and museums, and he shared that information with Stöcklin. Helfenstein also evaluated and inventoried looted items, and arranged for their packing and shipment to Germany. He was well paid by both Brandl and Stöcklin, and it was apparently because of their intervention that Helfenstein—like Frank O'Neill and Joseph Luhan, whom he apparently knew—only spent only two days in internment following Germany's declaration of war on the United States.

It was the American deserter's admitted involvement in the looting of French art, and his close relationships with Brandl and Stöcklin, that prompted Fred Ayer and Don Daughters to reach out to the Monuments Men. Specifically, the two FBI agents contacted 1st Lieutenant James J. Rorimer, the man who had ridden into newly liberated Paris atop a tank. A thirty-nine-year-old Harvard graduate and former curator of medieval art at New York's Metropolitan Museum of Art, Rorimer had landed in France soon after D-Day. By November 1944, he was the chief of the Monuments and Fine Arts Section within the SHAEF mission to France. His initial meeting with Fred and Don was at the MFAA office in Room 308 at 41, rue Cambon, but subsequent talks took place in the more relaxed atmosphere at 15, avenue Mozart.

During their discussions, the FBI agents were able to fill Rorimer in on what Helfenstein had told them about the ways in which Brandl and Stöcklin acquired artworks, and the names of individual pieces Helfenstein had seen in the men's possession. Rorimer, for his part, revealed that the French had apprehended Stöcklin and his mistress, Odette Poirier, in late October and were holding them at Fresnes Prison, south of Paris. The Monuments man offered to arrange for Fred and Don to speak to Stöcklin, which they were eager to do in order to determine whether Helfenstein had become an Abwehr agent in addition to helping loot French artworks. On December 6, Fred notified Hoover of Stöcklin's arrest—though he neglected to inform the director of who had relayed the news to him—and added that it was his intention to "interview Stocklin [sic] at the earliest possible moment relative to Helfenstein's activity with the German Abwehr and obtain from [Stöcklin] a signed statement thereto."[28]

Suspicions about Helfenstein's ties to the Abwehr had been raised during Fred's early December interrogation of a Dutch member of Bureau Otto named Gédéon van Houten. An Abwehr agent since the late 1930s who went by the alias Baron d'Humieres, van Houten said he had heard that Helfenstein—whom he'd originally known as Anton Krammer—had taken part in intelligence operations on the behalf of Brandl and Stöcklin, but could provide no concrete details. At the time Fred spoke with him, van Houten was in prison and about to be tried for espionage against France, a crime that carried the death penalty. Fred believed that the possibility of execution made van Houten especially interested in helping the Allies in exchange for a commuted sentence, and he thought the Dutchman seemed anxious to convince him of "his good faith in the matter of Helfenstein's connection with Abwehr operations."[29]

Fred's interview with Stöcklin took place at Fresnes Prison in mid-December. The two met in a windowless interrogation room, with the Swiss suspect still managing to look dapper despite handcuffs and rumpled clothes. Two guards stood against a wall, talking quietly between themselves and smoking what seemed to Fred like an endless succession of cheap, foul-smelling cigarettes. Stöcklin, for his part, seemed relaxed and more than willing to cooperate. He, too, said that he had originally known Helfenstein as Anton Krammer, but that the American had revealed his real name once the men had worked together for a while. Stöcklin said he'd first met Helfenstein in May or June of 1942 at Brandl's bureau at 23, square du Bois de Boulogne, where the American was working as head of the textiles section.[30]

When Fred mentioned van Houten's statement that Helfenstein had worked for the Abwehr, Stöcklin responded that he firmly believed the American had never done so. In fact, the Swiss said, Brandl had told him in no uncertain terms that Helfenstein was "strictly an office employee and had nothing whatever to do with Abwehr activities." That likely struck Fred as hair-splitting of a high degree, given that Bureau Otto's profits were used at least in part to fund Abwehr operations in France. Stöcklin added that insofar as he was personally involved in Brandl's operations, he was confident that Helfenstein's activities were confined to the office from 9 a.m. to 6 p.m. daily. Nor had the Swiss ever discussed with the American his reasons for working with Brandl, or what he'd done before the war.

When pressed for further details about the nature of Helfenstein's relationship with Brandl, Stöcklin responded that the two men got along very well. That is, the Swiss said, until the middle of 1942, when Jeanne Karpeles, a young Italian secretary of whom Brandl was quite fond, announced that she was pregnant.[31] Helfenstein was the father of the child, and in a fit of anger, the chief of Bureau Otto banished the American to Prien am Chiemsee, in Bavaria. The small resort town was home to one of several personal repositories where Brandl hid cash, jewels, manuscripts, artworks, and other treasures he intended to keep for himself. Helfenstein spent two months laboriously cataloging, cleaning, labeling, and packaging every item in the storehouse.[32] By the time Brandl allowed him to return to Paris, Jeanne Karpeles and her child were living in an apartment that, ironically, was just two blocks from the boulevard Suchet building that would ultimately become the DSM interrogation center used by the Army Liaison Unit agents.[33] A few months later, Helfenstein was dispatched to Brandl's office in Madrid, where the American ultimately married Josefina Castro.

While Stöcklin's statements seemed to exonerate Helfenstein of any direct involvement in Abwehr operations, they did reveal that the American had not been entirely forthcoming during his interrogations by Fred and Don. He had not mentioned his involvement with Jeanne Karpeles or the fact that they had a child, nor had he disclosed that he had traveled to Prien am Chiemsee. These omissions obviously brought into question the veracity of Helfenstein's other statements, and the FBI agents grilled him several more times until they were relatively sure he'd finally been completely honest with them. By the last week of December, Fred and Don felt they had enough information to send a complete report to the Bureau, in which they asked for guidance on the final disposition of Helfenstein's case. The response they received from the Department of Justice (DOJ) through the office of the Army's adjutant general on December 31 was straightforward:

> Department evidences interest in case but cannot formulate prosecutive opinion based on basis presently available information. Through witnesses to treasonable acts et cetera [request] efforts be made to substantiate and corroborate subject's admissions.[34]

Here again was the requirement that any indictment for treason had to be based on the act being witnessed by at least two people. As with Warrington Dawson and Frank O'Neill, in Helfenstein's case the chances of locating and deposing the necessary two witnesses were slim. Brandl and most of his Bureau Otto staffers were nowhere to be found, and Stöcklin's statement on its own was insufficient.

Fed and Don continued to look into Helfenstein and his activities, but a January 9, 1945, decision by Assistant Attorney General Tom C. Clark not to prosecute the American renegade ultimately brought the agents' investigation to a halt. Why the DOJ also chose not to prosecute Helfenstein for his 1919 desertion from the Army is unclear, though it was likely a pragmatic decision not to expend time and resources on a relatively minor case at a time when much larger postwar prosecutions were looming.[35] Upon his release from U.S. custody, Helfenstein was immediately arrested by the French, tried on charges of aiding the Germans against the best interests of France, and sentenced to prison. Available records indicate that he was released after seven years and returned to Paris. He died there on June 7, 1954, at the age of fifty-six and was buried in a local cemetery. A cryptic notation on the consular report of his death—"See Department's instruction (restricted) of August 6, 1945, to Paris, France, regarding decedent's identity," likely refers to his longtime use of the alias Anton Krammer.[36]

Hermann Brandl and Max Stöcklin were also held to account for their wartime activities. The former was arrested on August 6, 1945, in Munich and incarcerated in Stadelheim Prison, where he was found hanging in his cell on March 24, 1947. The latter was sentenced to death by a French court, and many sources—including the records of the OSS Art Looting Investigation Unit—say that he was executed in 1946. He was, in fact, sentenced to life in prison and was held at the Centre Pénitentiaire de Saint Sulpice-la-Pointe until released from custody in June 1952—after which he immediately disappeared.[37]

December 1944 was an incredibly busy month for Fred Ayer and Don Daughters. Not only had they been working on several important cases simultaneously, they had been turning out in-depth background reports for Hoover on a variety of topics. The two agents had also hosted Inspector Mike Gurnea as he evaluated their operation in Paris, while at the same time interacting with the French police and intelligence services, and Jim Rorimer of the Monuments Men. The crushing workload prompted Fred to increase the frequency of requests for additional agents he'd been making almost since he and Don had arrived in France, and the day after Christmas, his entreaties finally got a positive response. Three agents were to join the Army Liaison Unit, he was informed by cable, and would arrive in the French capital during the first week of January.

Fred's requests for additional manpower had actually covered two areas. First and foremost, he had been asking for French-speaking agents who could join him and Don in Paris. But following his return from his six-day road trip to visit the forward-deployed Twelfth Army Group, he had also been urging the Bureau to begin planning for the deployment of men fluent in German. In a November cable to Hoover, Fred pointed out that Gordon Sheen believed the dispatch of German-speaking agents was an "immediate necessity." The CI chief had written a memo to Brigadier General T. J. Betts, SHAEF's assistant chief of staff for intelligence, in which he said, "It is considered essential to the proper functioning of American intelligence in Europe that at least five FBI agents having a knowledge of the German language be without delay assigned to SHAEF for eventual work in Germany."[38] Betts had carried the memo with him on a subsequent trip to Washington, where he broached the subject with Clayton Bissell, the head of Army intelligence.

The three FBI agents tapped to travel to Paris via London in the second week of January 1945 were German-speakers Bill Clark, Joe Dunn, and Dick Thompson. Though there was no official explanation from the Bureau as to why additional French-speakers had not also been sent, the newly arrived men believed it was because of Bissell. Seeking to protect the Army's primacy in overseas intelligence operations, and already leery of the growing capabilities of William Donovan's OSS, Bissell was extremely reluctant to also give the FBI what he saw as an early foothold in postwar Germany. Hoover, who was equally determined that the Bureau should play a much larger role in foreign intelligence operations, apparently believed that the dispatch of Clark, Dunn, and Thompson could solve two problems at once. As fluent German speakers, the men could move into the Reich as needed, and their initial assignment to France would likely escape Bissell's attention. Moreover, the newly arrived agents could help off-load work from Fred and Don, with Clark's ability to speak passable French an added benefit.

After settling into the avenue Mozart apartment/office, the newcomers spent several days at SHAEF headquarters in Versailles. Much of that time was spent in the G-2 "war room," a second-floor suite in the Trianon Palace hotel that had been converted into an intelligence and counterintelligence nerve center. American, British, and French staffers working twelve-hour shifts tracked the latest information coming in by telephone, field radio, and courier. The location of known and suspected enemy agents was constantly updated on the maps that covered the walls, and enlisted men at a dozen desks compiled and revised target lists based on data provided by the French security services, prisoner-interrogation reports, tips from informers, and a host of other sources. The processed data was then passed both up the SHAEF chain of command and out to Allied field units in the form of daily intelligence/counterintelligence summaries. Because a certain volume of the processed data concerned possible American renegades, at the end of the new agents' orientation, Fred assigned Dick Thompson as the Army Liaison Unit's representative on the war room staff. The agent was soon spending so much time in Versailles that he moved out of the avenue Mozart apartment and into a shared room in the Trianon Palace itself.

While Clark and Dunn were able to take over many aspects of the day-to-day operations of the ALU's Paris office—writing reports, handling correspondence with Washington, tracking expenses, and so on—they were also tasked with a particular type of investigation that made the most of their language skills. Since arriving in France, Fred and Don had been receiving reports from Allied military units regarding their capture of uniformed German military personnel who claimed to be Americans forced against their will to work or fight for the Nazis. Most of the subjects were being held in prisoner of war camps between Normandy and Paris, and Fred decided to give Clark and Dunn responsibility for investigating the men.

These Americans caught wearing the wrong uniforms—which in and of itself was a treasonous act—were known as the *Volksdeutschers*.

CHAPTER 8

Volksdeutschers, Renegades Redux, and the Lost Sigaba

Most scholars agree that the term *Volksdeutshe* was likely coined by Adolf Hitler himself. Literally translated as "German folk," the word referred to people whose language and culture had German origins but who did not hold Reich citizenship and were living in other countries. In Eastern European nations such as Poland, Czechoslovakia, Romania, and even the Soviet Union, the presence of large groups of *Volksdeutshe* gave Berlin an excuse to lay claim to the areas in which the people lived.

In the Western Hemisphere, however, the Nazis took a different approach. After Hitler became Germany's chancellor in January 1933, his government began calling for German- and Austrian-born *Volksdeutshe* in North and South America to "return to the Fatherland"—and to bring their families with them. In the case of the United States, this often meant that the American-born spouses and children of immigrants who chose to return to Germany ended up living in a country they did not consider their own. Whatever their feelings toward their new fatherland, the *Volksdeutschers* (males) of military age became subject to service in the German armed forces.[1] Those who never officially renounced their U.S. citizenship were therefore liable to be charged with treason if they fell into American hands.

Fred Ayer had actually worked the first *Volksdeutscher* case himself, though it turned out to have an unexpected result.

Walter Frederick Elmer Windisch

In October 1944, elements of Twelfth U.S. Army Group's 94th Infantry Division operating in Brittany captured a group of young men who had been building fortifications around the German-held French port of Saint-Nazaire, at the mouth of the River Loire just north of Nantes. The 94th's Counter Intelligence Corps detachment quickly determined that the prisoners were mostly Frenchmen forced to work as slave laborers for the Nazis under the Service du travail obligatoire (compulsory work service) program, though one of the captives identified himself as a twenty-two-year-old American citizen named Walter Windisch. While the young man said he, too, was an involuntary worker, others in the group told the American troops that Windisch was actually a paid member of the German organization overseeing military construction in occupied France. The workers claimed that Windisch had been on very friendly terms with the Germans, had expressed exceedingly anti-American sentiments, and had even been seen wearing an SS uniform. These allegations were enough to ensure that when the French workers were released, Windisch remained in the custody of the 94th's CIC detachment.

News of the young American's capture was quickly passed up the chain of command to Lieutenant Colonel Harold MacDonald, the division's adjutant general. He, in turn, notified Colonel Earl C. Berquist, the 94th's chief of staff. In keeping with a SHAEF directive regarding the capture in the field of American citizens serving with or in support of German military forces, the two men kicked the Windisch problem upstairs. In an October 19 message to Dwight Eisenhower's headquarters, Berquist said the issues and policies involved in dealing with a U.S. citizen voluntarily working for the Germans "are of such importance and so serious in nature as to preclude the assumption of [legal] jurisdiction by this combat command." He then added that the Windisch matter "could be more appropriately and expeditiously disposed of by some other headquarters."[2] Berquist's message ultimately resulted in Windisch's case being passed on to Gordon Sheen's CI office in Versailles, and the young American prisoner was transferred to a detention facility in the Paris suburbs.

It was at that point that Fred Ayer entered the Windisch case. In a November 19 message to Hoover, the agent laid out the basic facts as determined by an initial report provided by the 94th's CIC chief and a follow-on interrogation of Windisch conducted at the boulevard Suchet facility. The young suspect had been born in Williamson, Illinois, in 1925, son of an American father and a French mother. Windisch said that in 1933, the entire family had moved to his mother's birthplace, Nantes, intending to reside permanently in France, though he kept his American citizenship. After primary and secondary schools, Windisch said he enrolled in one year of technical training, after which he took a job with a French manufacturing firm. When France capitulated in 1940, that company had been taken over by the Germans and converted to the production of military aircraft parts. The plant was destroyed by Allied bombing in June 1944, and at that point, Windisch went to work for the group building German fortifications.[3]

During the course of his various interrogations, Windisch confessed that his work for the Germans had been voluntary and that he had been well paid. He denied that he knew about the Allied landings at Normandy and said he'd never worn an SS uniform, but he admitted that he had spoken against the American bombing campaign and had told fellow workers that any attempted British landing in France would be thrown back into the sea. In his report to Hoover, Fred pointed out that it was "fairly well-established" that Windisch had German sympathies, but that "it seems exceedingly doubtful that he ever belonged to the SS."[4] Though the young American obviously did not fall into the *Volksdeutscher* category, his voluntary civilian service on behalf of Nazi Germany while still a U.S. citizen made him liable to the same treason charge that would face Americans who had actually served in the German military.

Fred also told Hoover that Colonel C. R. Langdon, the adjutant general of Twelfth USAG, had stated that he believed the U.S. Department of Justice had primary jurisdiction over the Windisch case because of Article III, Section 3, of the Constitution (the "aid and comfort" clause). But, the officer had added, both the American and French military tribunals could also make a justifiable claim of jurisdiction. Though Windisch was currently being held in Paris, Fred said, he still technically "belonged" to Twelfth USAG. Langdon thus wanted DOJ to render an opinion—should the case be handled by the Army through the military tribunal system or be handed over to the French or be dealt with by U.S. federal courts?

Before making a decision, Fred said, DOJ should consider a few relevant facts. First, for unknown reasons, the 94th Division CIC officers who first interrogated Windisch had not obtained written, signed statements from the captured workers stating that they'd seen the American voluntarily work for the Germans. The Frenchmen had already been released and couldn't be found, and the lack of signed statements by two eyewitnesses was a problem, given the requirements of the treason statute. Second, while the young American had admitted that the Germans had paid him, no pay vouchers had been found. And third, should DOJ decide to prosecute Windisch in a U.S. federal court, it would be necessary to transport many people—including the American troops who had first encountered the group of French workers—to the U.S. for the trial. Fred added that if no decision had been made by DOJ within a month, "it is [SHAEF's] intention to instruct that [Windisch] be handled according to military law and the articles of war . . . most probably in a trial before a United States military commission."[5]

It took DOJ one day longer than the month mandated by SHAEF to make a decision on the case of Walter Windisch. On December 20, Fred received a cable routed through Army G-2 chief Bissell's office that stated simply, "Department declines prosecution on basis presently available information." While no explanation was given, it's likely the DOJ's decision was based on the same combination of factors that pertained in other cases the Paris-based Army Liaison Unit had investigated: Without the two eyewitnesses required, there was little hope of a conviction; there were no corroborating German pay vouchers or other incriminating documents; the suspect was essentially a "little fish" whose actions apparently did not directly harm U.S. military personnel; and for those reasons, the costs of mounting a prosecution simply weren't justified.

Windisch was subsequently turned over to the Army for trial by a military tribunal, but for the same reasons cited by DOJ, that prosecution never happened. He was ultimately released, and in November 1945 was living and working in Paris. Windisch registered for the draft that same year as an American citizen living abroad, and returned to the United States in 1947. On the outbreak of the Korean War in 1950, he was drafted into the U.S. Army, but served for less than a year before being discharged. He died in Sarasota, Florida, in 1984, at the age of sixty.

Though Fred's investigation ultimately did not involve a *Volksdeutscher*, there would be several following cases that most certainly did. And the first of those, undertaken by Bill Clark and Joe Dunn, turned out to be eerily similar to the Windisch case—with a few added twists.

Fritz Franz Mohr

By December 13, 1944—almost exactly a month before the three additional FBI agents arrived in Paris—the more than forty infantry and armored divisions comprising Lieutenant General Omar Bradley's Twelfth U.S. Army Group were arrayed in an eastward-facing arc running through Belgium and Luxembourg in the north to the French–German border in Alsace to the south. The planned final push into the Reich had been stalled by two primary factors—the wettest winter in Western Europe in more than a century, and Dwight Eisenhower's still hotly debated decision to divert the Allies' limited fuel resources from George Patton's Third Army to Field Marshal Montgomery's Operation Market Garden in Holland.

While the fuel shortage may have halted Patton's headlong rush toward Germany, Twelfth USAG's American (and Free French) divisions were by no means inactive. Third Army had launched its campaign to clear the Lorraine region of eastern France in early September, and by the beginning of December had taken Nancy and Metz. However, the German garrisons occupying several of the nineteenth-century fortifications surrounding the latter city held out for weeks following the capitulation of the bulk of the German forces. The last of the fortresses, Fort Jeanne d'Arc, finally surrendered on December 12. Among the prisoners taken by American forces were members of the Reichsarbeitsdienst (RAD), the German civilian labor service. Comprised largely of young men and women between eighteen and twenty-five, RAD units aided frontline combat forces by carrying out logistical supply operations and undertaking military construction projects. As had happened in the Windisch case, one of the civilians taken captive identified himself as an American citizen, though he spoke English with a noticeable German accent. When searched, the young man was found to be carrying a torn and somewhat faded U.S. birth certificate in the name of Fritz Franz Mohr.

The young captive's claim of U.S. citizenship and his age—just over sixteen—ensured that he was quickly separated from the other prisoners and transferred under guard to Twelfth USAG's CIC detachment. On December 13, that organization notified SHAEF G-2 of Mohr's capture, saying, as in the Windisch case, that disposition of the prisoner would be more appropriately undertaken by some other headquarters. SHAEF G-2 responded the same day that "Mohr should be held pending instructions from Department [of] Justice. Send information from birth certificate soonest. . . . If notification received that Department Justice has no interest in subject Mohr may be tried by Military Commission in view his voluntary service with enemy."[6]

SHAEF's request for information "soonest" fell on temporarily deaf ears, for on December 16, German forces launched the surprise attack through the Ardennes that became known as the Battle of the Bulge. Twelfth Army Group's attention was immediately focused on helping to respond to the assault—primarily by shifting Patton's Third Army from Lorraine north to attack the flank of the German advance. It was therefore not until December 30 that Twelfth USAG was able to send a response to SHAEF's request for further information on Mohr. That message, sent to Eisenhower, over Bradley's signature block, said that according to the birth certificate, Fritz Franz Peter Heinrich Mohr had been born in Jersey City, New Jersey, on August 9, 1928. His father was listed as Franz F. P. Mohr, and his mother's maiden name was given as Martha H. Toyak. Bradley's message added that Mohr was being detained by First Army "awaiting further instructions."[7]

On January 2, 1945, Fred Ayer sent a message to the Bureau regarding Mohr, who by that point had been transferred to the custody of the Twelfth USAG provost marshal. As had happened in the Windisch case, Bradley's headquarters had mandated that if DOJ did not make a decision regarding Mohr's legal status within ten days, the suspect would be subject to trial by military commission. While waiting to hear from Washington, Fred dispatched Joe Dunn to personally interrogate Mohr.

Over the course of two days, Dunn learned quite a bit about the young man's background. His parents, Franz and Martha, were natives of the German port city of Bremerhaven. Franz had been a steward on passenger ships of the North German Lloyd Line sailing to American ports, and he and Martha married in 1927. The following year, they were visiting Martha's relatives in New Jersey, when Fritz was born. Over the next eleven years, the family split its time between Germany and the United States, and when war broke out on September 1, 1939, Martha, Fritz, and two younger sons were living in Wesermünde, a section of Bremerhaven. Franz was actually on his way back from New York, having arrived there aboard the SS *Bremen* on August 28.[8] He finally rejoined the family in mid-September, and soon after was apparently drafted into service working in one of Bremerhaven's many shipyards.

By early 1944, Allied bombing had put Franz and thousands of his colleagues out of work, at which point Fritz volunteered for the RAD to help support the family. Given the state of Germany's war effort by that point, the young man was accepted for service despite his age, and he worked in the greater Bremerhaven region until his group was sent to Metz in September. He and his fellow workers had remained in Fort Jeanne d'Arc throughout the siege by Allied forces, he said, and they were all more than happy to finally surrender. Fritz had never been in the Hitler Youth and was not a Nazi, he told Dunn, and all he wanted was to return to his family.

The FBI agent obviously believed the young man's story of simply being caught up in the maelstrom of war, for Dunn's interrogation report recommended that Fritz not be prosecuted for treason. Fred Ayer concurred when he forwarded the report to Washington, and in a January 15 message to Twelfth USAG, Gordon Sheen wrote that the "Department of Justice has no interest in Fritz Franz Mohr and decision re: disposal of him is left to you."[9] Inundated by tens of thousands of German prisoners by that point, Twelfth USAG decided to free Fritz Mohr. He did indeed return to his family, and by 1949, he was living with them in Hoboken, New Jersey. Like Walter Windisch, Mohr registered for the draft and in 1950 was called up for duty in Korea. He served in the Army for two years and left as a corporal. Like Windisch, Mohr eventually settled in Sarasota, Florida, where he died in May 2013 at the age of 84.

Wilhelm Ludwig Augustin

Though Walter Windisch and Fritz Mohr were both taken into custody while working for unarmed support units, the third American citizen investigated by the Paris-based Army Liaison Unit was most definitely a combatant.

In late January 1945, troops of the U.S. Seventh Army operating northwest of Strasbourg captured eighteen-year-old Wilhelm Augustin. Though wearing a German uniform and carrying a rifle, the young man immediately told captors that he was an American citizen who had been pressed into Wehrmacht service against his will. As proof, he presented his *Soldatbuch* (individual service record), which listed his birthplace as "Passaic, USA, Amerika." Interrogated by the Seventh Army CIC detachment, Augustin said he had indeed been born in New Jersey in January 1927, the son of Austrian immigrants, Stefan and Appollonia. In 1937, the then ten-year-old boy traveled with his father to the latter's birthplace, the small town of Punitz, seventy-five miles directly south of Vienna and hard on the border with Hungary. The intention was that the boy would live with his paternal grandmother while attending school and eventually learning a trade. The elder Augustin's intention was to have his son rejoin the family in New Jersey once the schooling and job training were completed.[10]

That plan changed significantly following Nazi Germany's March 1938 annexation of Austria. Wilhelm Augustin continued his education in Punitz, though under increased scrutiny by local officials owing to his American citizenship. The boy was able to maintain mail contact with his parents in New York until the United States' 1941 entry into the war on the Allied side. When, in 1944, Wilhelm was called up for a preinduction physical, he objected on the grounds that he was an American citizen. Unaware that the Swiss legation's representatives in Vienna might have been able to help him avoid military service, the young man was inducted into the Wehrmacht on August 18, 1944. After training in a primarily Austrian *ersatz* (replacement) battalion, Wilhelm was assigned to one of the units committed to Operation Northwind. That final major German offensive on the Western Front launched some 300,000 troops backed by armor and aircraft against Allied forces in

Alsace and Lorraine. Despite initial successes against thinly stretched U.S. and French units, the German attack was finally halted in late January 1945.

By that time, Wilhelm Augustin had already been interrogated by Bill Clark, who had traveled from Paris to a POW cage just west of Strasbourg. The FBI agent noted that the young man—and possibly even his grandmother—would have been shot had he refused military service, and relayed Augustin's testimony that he had done everything possible to avoid engaging American troops. Clark was firmly convinced that Augustin had had no choice but to enter the Wehrmacht, he wrote, adding that the young man "made a good impression." In response to Ayer's report to the Bureau, the Justice Department declined to prosecute Augustin. Nor did the Army choose to try him by military commission, and following Germany's May 7 surrender, Augustin was released from custody.

Available records indicate that the young man returned to Punitz following the war and was residing there when Burgenland was allocated to the Soviet occupation zone. Augustin remained in Punitz until the 1955 signing of the Austrian State Treaty ended the Soviet presence, at which point he and his wife, Anna, immigrated to the United States. The pair ultimately settled in Fort Mill, South Carolina, where Augustin worked as a foreman for the Duff-Norton industrial products company, just over the border in North Carolina. Anna Augustin passed away in 2006 at the age of eighty, and her husband—who had once been a young American trapped in the wrong place when the world went to war—died in 2012, at eighty-five.

Charles H. Reininghaus

Although the Army Liaison Unit launched its fourth and final *Volksdeutscher* investigation in France in mid-February 1945, the case had its origins some four months earlier and more than a thousand miles north of Paris.

On October 25, 1944, a Luftwaffe Ju-52 trimotor transport equipped with floats lifted off from a small bay on an eastern arm of Norway's Trondheim Fjord. The aircraft was ostensibly on a brief flight to another field, but the two crewmen aboard had another plan. Under cover of poor weather, the pilot, Oberfeldwebel Heinz-Jakob Murk, and his observer/crew chief, Obergefreiter Hans Maas, turned west and headed for Iceland.[11] Both men believed the war was already lost and intended to surrender themselves and their aircraft to the Allies. Bad weather over the Norwegian Sea caused the Ju-52 to wander far off course, and low fuel ultimately forced the aircraft down at sea. Murk and Maas were rescued by an armed British fishing trawler and were astounded to learn that they were just thirty miles from Aberdeen, on the east coast of Scotland. The two Germans eventually ended up in a POW camp in northern France, and it was there that Murk made a surprising revelation while being interrogated by U.S. Army intelligence officers during the first week of November 1944.[12]

Some months earlier, Murk said, he'd been temporarily assigned as a flight instructor at the Luftwaffe airfield in Schönwalde, sixteen miles northwest of Berlin. There he'd met and interacted with a young enlisted man named Charles Reininghaus, who'd said he was deeply depressed because he was an American citizen who had been drafted into the Luftwaffe against his will. The young airman had just been released from three days in the base stockade for some minor infraction, Murk said, and was "filled with anger and hatred for the deprivation of his freedom." Reininghaus was "further tortured by the danger, which he recognized, that if his position was not soon changed, his American comrades would capture and even shoot him." Reininghaus had confided to the sympathetic older man that he was planning to steal one of the airfield's Me-108 trainer aircraft and fly it to Allied territory. Out of sympathy for the young airman—and because of his own anti-Nazi beliefs—Murk had offered to help Reininghaus in his airborne escape plan. That attempt had never taken place, Murk said, because two days after their meeting, the American was transferred to the paratroops and disappeared from Schönwalde.[13]

Murk's statement ensured that Reininghaus's name ended up on the SHAEF CIC target list, and on September 22, 1944, the young American gave himself up to a U.S. Army patrol in the Netherlands. He was transferred to Continental Central Prisoner of War Enclosure No. 15 in Attichy, some fifty-eight miles northeast of Paris, where he was first interrogated on December 12.[14] During that initial session, Reininghaus said he'd been born in Miami, Florida, on May 16, 1922, but grew up in Pinewald, New Jersey. His father, Kurt, was a German immigrant, and his mother, Olga, was an American citizen. Reininghaus told his interrogators that in July 1939, when he was seventeen, his father sent him to Germany to collect money that was part of a family inheritance.

His father had lied to him, the young man said. There was no inheritance—Kurt Reininghaus was a member of the German-American Bund in the United States and he wanted his son to join the Wehrmacht. The younger Reininghaus lived with his uncle's family, and following the outbreak of war in September 1939, he was not permitted to leave Germany. He said he worked for the Fieseler aircraft company as an apprentice mechanic until October 1942, when he was drafted into the Luftwaffe. After his involuntary transfer to the paratroops, he was deployed to the Netherlands as part of the German response to Operation Market Garden, but he deserted from his unit and hid with a Dutch family until his surrender to troops of the U.S. 82nd Airborne Division.

The interrogators at the POW camp found Reininghaus's story credible, though owing to the massive number of German troops being taken prisoner in the first weeks of 1945, it wasn't until February 10 that the Army Liaison Unit was finally notified of the case. Joe Dunn reviewed Reininghaus's file, and on the 18th, Fred Ayer was able to send a message to Bureau headquarters outlining the young man's story.[15] Fred noted that Reininghaus was still in custody at that point, awaiting a determination by the Combined Chiefs of Staff on how *Volksdeutscher* cases should be handled within the European Theater. Fred added that the ALU agreed with a suggestion made by SHAEF's assistant adjutant general to his higher headquarters in Washington: In a January 26 letter, Major R. E. Lewis wrote that Kurt Reininghaus's actions as a member of the German-American Bund should be investigated by the Department of Justice as possible treason or as violations of the Espionage Act.[16]

In the end, neither Charles Reininghaus nor his father were charged for their actions during World War II. The younger man returned to the United States after the war, married, and worked as a carpenter in Florida until his death in April 1988. His father outlived him by just six months.[17]

THOUGH THE *VOLKSDEUTSCHER* CASES WERE an interesting introduction to the Army Liaison Unit for Bill Clark and Joe Dunn, investigating people who had been forced against their will to support the Nazi war effort was not the primary task for any of the Paris-based FBI agents. J. Edgar Hoover wanted his G.I. G-men to focus on *real* threats: the ways in which the German intelligence services might be supporting espionage and sabotage operations in the Western Hemisphere and the growing influence of Soviet-backed communist parties in Western Europe.

But above all, Hoover wanted the men of the ALU to find and interrogate Americans who had willingly sold out their country, whether for money, power, or even love. By early 1945, it looked increasingly as if Adolf Hitler and his barbaric Reich were on the verge of imminent collapse, which only made the hunt for American renegades more important. Those who had rooted against their native land, who had chosen fascism over democracy, had to be found and brought to justice before they could disappear into the shadows . . . or find new authoritarian masters to serve.

And the clock was ticking.

In the first month of 1945, the five agents of the Army Liaison Unit then in Paris were steadily working through their list of Americans suspected of voluntarily collaborating with the Nazis during the occupation of France. Among the people on whom they focused their collective efforts was a man first implicated by Joseph Lincoln Luhan. The suspect, Maurice Sylvester Gagnon, was, like Warrington Dawson, a prominent and longtime member of the American expatriate community in the French capital. But Gagnon's case would have a conclusion vastly different from that of the Versailles-based invalid.

Born in Concord, New Hampshire, in April 1888, Gagnon's parents were both French speakers—his father a native of Québec and his mother a member of a Francophone family in Vermont.[18] The young man grew up completely bilingual, and often spent time with his relatives in Canada. After finishing high school, Gagnon first tried his hand at selling real estate but ultimately became an insurance agent. By 1913, he was working for the Fidelity and Casualty Company of New York in Hartford, Connecticut, and that same year, he married Canadian-born Jennie Bertrand in Salem, Massachusetts. Gagnon avoided the World War I draft by claiming to be the sole support of his wife, though in 1925, he divorced her and moved to Paris to be his company's primary European representative. Not long after arriving in the French capital, Gagnon became the manager of the local office of the London-based Indemnity Marine Insurance Company. He subsequently married a woman named Claude Pinel, and over the following two decades, the couple became wealthy and prominent in Parisian society.

Given his line of work, it was inevitable that Gagnon would make the acquaintance of another American providing insurance services in Paris—Joe Luhan. The two men came to know each other very well, and it was that relationship that ultimately brought Gagnon to the attention of Fred Ayer and his fellow ALU agents. When Luhan was interrogated at 18, boulevard Suchet in mid-November 1944, he implicated Gagnon as having done broadcasts for the Germans and, in addition, accused his fellow insurance agent of having denounced French citizens to the Gestapo.[19] As had happened with Frank O'Neill, Gagnon's name was added to a target list circulated throughout SHAEF and to the French police and intelligence services. It turned out that he was much easier to locate than the jockey had been, since Gagnon's home at 73, boulevard Montmorency was less than a mile to the southwest of the DSM interrogation center.

Arrested by SHAEF CIC agents on November 28, Gagnon sat in a cell at 18, boulevard Suchet for some six weeks while Fred and Don dealt with a host of other issues. The arrival of Clark, Dunn, and Thompson in January allowed Gagnon's case to move up the priority list, and Fred was able to begin interrogating the man not long after the three new agents moved into the avenue Mozart apartment. It's clear from Fred's report to Hoover that the suspect made a decidedly poor first impression: "Gagnon is a most unattractive type of individual, definitely a spineless, crawling type of man," the FBI agent wrote. "He whines continually and tearfully protests that he never worked for the Germans and never denounced anyone to the German authorities."[20]

Despite his initial protestations of innocence, after further questioning, Gagnon made several self-incriminating admissions. He had met Werner Plack socially after France's capitulation, he said, and at the German's urging had eventually made three all-expenses-paid trips to Berlin. During his first visit, in October 1940, Gagnon met with Plack and other propaganda ministry officials, and dined with them at the prestigious Hotel Adlon. Gagnon admitted that after that first meeting, he had agreed to do pro-German broadcasts from both Berlin and Paris, in return for which he received an initial payment of 50,000 francs and a monthly living allowance in deutsche marks.[21] He only ever made one recording, Gagnon said, and that was in December 1942, when, as part of a wrap-up of the year's events, he and others had performed an anti-Semitic skit. He confessed that the Germans allowed him to keep and drive his personal automobile in Paris, and that the occupation forces had frequently even provided him with gasoline. He admitted that the German officials who paid him and granted him privileges worked out of the Gestapo's Paris headquarters at 72, avenue Foch, though he claimed he had no idea what went on in the building.[22]

During the course of his interrogation, Gagnon repeatedly said that he had done everything possible to avoid doing any real work for the Germans and only did what was necessary to keep him at liberty and "out of the clutches" of the Gestapo. He claimed that he had deliberately broken the disk bearing one recording made at the Radio Paris studio and added that his increasingly anti-German comments eventually got him arrested. The prisoner did not elaborate, but Fred already knew the details courtesy of MI5. Gagnon had been having an affair with a woman named Suzanne Louise Booth, a British subject by marriage, and voice actress who did propaganda broadcasts for the Germans. During a July 1944 tryst at the woman's apartment at 82, rue de la Faisanderie, Gagnon had said some things that Booth reported to the Gestapo, and the American was subsequently briefly detained. By the time Gagnon was released Booth had left Paris and was rumored to be in Berlin.

The American's brief stint in German custody for anti-Nazi comments he may or may not have murmured to his mistress did nothing to improve Fred's opinion of him. The FBI agent wrote that

> the impression that has been formed by [Gagnon's] activities and speech is that he is so yellow that he will talk in favor of whoever he feels to be the winning side, but that he would not have the courage to participate actively in favor of anyone except himself. It seems probable that he did not do much of any radio or any of their work, but just participated to the extent which he felt would keep him at liberty. . . . There is no question but that he did receive some pay from the Germans and that he did speak at length and loudly in favor of them when they were around.[23]

Whatever the extent or fervor of Gagnon's pro-German feelings, the fact that he voluntarily aided the enemy in time of war in exchange for money certainly earned him a treason charge. In the end, however, the man Fred deemed "so yellow" escaped trail and imprisonment. On February 9, 1945, while still awaiting a Department of Justice decision on whether he would be indicted, Maurice Gagnon hanged himself in his cell at the 18. boulevard Suchet facility. He was temporarily interred on the grounds of a small country house he and his wife owned in Clachalôze, on the River Seine, northwest of Paris, before his 1946 burial in the French capital's Bagneux cemetery.[24]

The assumption that the renegade broadcasters indicted for treason by the Department of Justice in July 1943 were still in Germany and temporarily beyond the FBI's reach had initially persuaded Fred Ayer to focus the Army Liaison Unit's investigations on closer targets. But in late November 1944, a report from Commandant Paul Paillole of the Direction de la Sécurité Militaire indicated that another American who had spoken on Radio Berlin might actually be in France.

The information provided in the initial French report was meager. The

American was identified as one Marvin Harold Fritz, who had apparently been born in California sometime between 1914 and 1917. He was known to have spoken on German shortwave propaganda broadcasts originating from Königs Wusterhausen, a village southeast of Berlin to which most Nazi radio operations had been moved when Allied bombing raids damaged production facilities in the German capital.[25] Fritz was said to have a mistress, and possibly a child, living in Alsace. While his current whereabouts were unclear, the chance that the renegade broadcaster could be captured in France—and thereby become a source of valuable information on the Americans still beyond reach in the Reich—prompted Fred to add Fritz to the list of suspects being investigated by the ALU. Fred also requested Bureau headquarters in Washington to undertake a thorough background check on the suspect.[26]

That inquiry revealed the suspect was born in Los Angeles on June 17, 1916, the son of German immigrants. Raised by his mother following his father's death in 1919, Fritz attended local schools and became a leading player in the L.A. Tennis Club's junior division. In early 1936, the young man was in New York City, where he signed on as a crewman aboard the Hamburg America Line steamship SS *Hansa*. The job was temporary, in that it enabled Fritz to get to Germany to attend the Berlin summer Olympics (as a spectator). He returned to California following the games, but went back to Germany in 1937. Fritz worked at a hotel in Heidelberg until February 1941, then took a clerk position in the visa section of the U.S. consulate in Stuttgart. When that facility closed after America's entry into World War II, Fritz chose to remain in Germany and subsequently dropped from sight.

While the background data on Fritz provided by the Bureau was helpful, Fred really couldn't launch a full investigation on the suspected renegade until after the January 1945 arrival in Paris of the three additional agents. Once Clark and Dunn had completed their *Volksdeutscher* inquiries, they were tasked with looking into reports of Fritz's presence in France. They were able to determine that after the closure of the Stuttgart consulate, the young American had indeed spent some time in occupied Paris, where he was likely recruited for propaganda work by the industrious Werner Plack.[27] Several sources interviewed by the two FBI agents believed Fritz did indeed have a mistress (or wife) in France, but Clark and Dunn were unable to immediately locate the woman or her rumored child. Moreover, all indications pointed to Fritz being in Germany and, like the other accused renegade broadcasters, therefore temporarily out of the ALU's reach. Fred nonetheless added the man's name to the SHAEF CIC target list, determined to track him down following the Reich's now inevitable collapse.

ALTHOUGH THE FINAL DEFEAT OF NAZI GERMANY was certainly within sight by February 1945, the war in Europe was by no means over. Allied forces had advanced into the Reich at several points during the last months of 1944 but had not yet crossed the Rhine River. There was the very real possibility that another surprise German ground assault might derail the long-planned Allied spring offensive, and Operation Bodenplatte—launched on New Year's Day—was a potent reminder that the Luftwaffe wasn't quite as toothless as many senior Allied leaders had assumed.[28] Nor was all the action on the front lines—though virtually all of France had been liberated, German forces still held the Atlantic coast ports of La Rochelle, Saint Nazaire, and Royan, and would do so until the end of the war.

There was considerable concern among the Allied counterintelligence services that small German commando units operating from the French coastal enclaves might disrupt the massive logistics operations that were supporting the buildup to the spring offensive against Germany. Moreover, enemy stay-behind agents were known to be active in southern France, especially in the areas bordering Italy north of Cannes and Nice. And finally, several American renegades were thought to have fled Paris for the Mediterranean coast between Toulon and Marseilles, ports from which they might be able to escape to Spain, Portugal, or North Africa.

Given these concerns, the telephone call that Don Daughters took at the avenue Mozart apartment early on February 21 was not unexpected. On the other end of the line was Lieutenant Colonel James Edler, chief of the Criminal Investigation Division (CID) section of the Communications Zone (Com Z) Theater Provost Marshal's Office at Paris's Hôtel Majestic.[29] The call was actually an invitation, Edler said. Lieutenant Colonel N. C. Atwood, the chief of the military police section in the Provost Marshal's office, was going to visit the Delta Base Section in Marseilles. That organization was responsible for managing the vast logistics operations supporting the U.S. Army troops and equipment flowing into southern France in preparation for the spring offensive into Germany. Atwood wanted a member of the ALU to travel with him to Marseilles to discuss with the local CID detachment the ways in which Bureau agents might be able to assist in the investigation of crimes that could disrupt the vital buildup—"ordinary" offenses like theft, fraud, smuggling, and even murder. Moreover, Edler said, the trip would also allow an ALU representative to meet face-to-face with the Delta Base Section's counterintelligence detachment. Atwood and his assistant, 1st Lieutenant William C. Yerg, were leaving for Marseilles by air that very afternoon, Edler said. After consulting with Fred Ayer, Don told Edler he would meet Atwood and Yerg at Le Bourget for the C-47 flight to Marseilles.[30]

Following their arrival at airfield Y-14, just northwest of the French port city, in the town of Marignane, Don and the two officers were driven to the nearby Delta Base Section headquarters.[31] In meetings the following day, Major Karl Nash, chief of the organization's CID detachment, told Don that as a congressional investigator for the prewar House Committee on Un-American Activities, he had worked closely with the FBI and would greatly appreciate the ALU's investigative help.

There was one caveat, however. Nash pointed out that the majority of his CID investigators were enlisted soldiers whose pay was significantly less than that of an FBI agent. He was concerned that the salary discrepancy might lead to "dissatisfaction" among his men should they end up working full time with the Bureau representatives. Don then suggested that rather than having FBI agents permanently assigned to the Delta Base Section, Paris-based ALU representatives could deploy temporarily to southern France to conduct special investigations on specific cases, thus freeing CID personnel for other tasks. Don added that while he could make no commitments regarding the number of Bureau agents that might be available at any given time, he assured Nash the ALU would provide as much assistance as possible. The CID chief liked the "temporary special assignment" concept, and he and Don worked out a mutually acceptable agreement.

As constructive as the first part of his junket to southern France was, what came next was of greater importance to Don. After his meetings with Nash, the FBI agent sat down with Major C. E. Reid, commander of the Counter Intelligence Corps detachment within the Delta Base Section's larger G-2 branch. A former Chicago police officer, Reid had worked with the FBI in the past and was enthusiastic about cooperating with the ALU on its core tasks—investigating American renegades and the European aspects of Western Hemisphere espionage cases. The CIC chief said that he and his detachment hadn't yet developed any leads in the latter category, but they were looking into a few cases of American citizens who had remained in the greater Marseilles area throughout the Italian and German occupations and may have given material assistance to the enemy. Their strongest suspect, Reid said, was one John E. Loskot. The name was familiar, Don replied, because it had been on a list of suspected renegades given to the ALU by Gordon Sheen a few weeks earlier. The SHAEF CI chief had also provided a file on Loskot, and on February 3, Don had sent a preliminary report on the suspect to Washington. He promised Reid he would delve deeper into the case when he returned to the French capital.

Using a jeep and driver provided by Reid, Don next traveled to Cannes. Some eighty-five miles east of Marseilles, the famous resort city on the Côte d'Azur was also the headquarters for the CIC detachment responsible for the Mediterranean coast of France stretching from the Bay of Cannes all the way to the Italian border. The man in charge, Lester Blumner, had worked briefly with Frank Amprim in Italy and welcomed the opportunity of further cooperation with the FBI. He told Don there were a few cases in the region that merited the Bureau's attention and identified several people who might be reliable sources of information on possible American renegades. Blumner also arranged for Don to visit Nice and speak with Captain Jeff Jones, the chief CID officer for the area. Jones, in turn, introduced the FBI agent to 1st Lieutenant Herbert Armstrong, the head of the OSS X-2 (counterintelligence) detachment in Nice. Don already knew Armstrong, with whom he had interacted in Paris and now found "very cooperative and anxious to help in any way possible with the investigation of American renegades in the Cannes–Nice area."[32]

Before leaving for Marseilles and the return flight to Paris, Don also met with two French counterintelligence officers—captains Nicholas Burg and André Froment. The three worked out an agreement whereby the Frenchmen would provide the ALU with a list of resident American citizens who were suspected of collaborating with Axis elements during the occupation. One man they assured Don would be at the top of that list was an expat named Hector O'Connor—whom Blumner, Jones, and Armstrong had all also mentioned. The suspect was at that moment being held in a Nice jail cell on suspicion of having worked with the Gestapo. Don explained that he needed to return to Paris to take charge of the ALU office, because Fred Ayer had been unexpectedly called away. Burg and Froment provided the FBI agent with copies of their files on O'Connor, and Don assured the French officers he would look into the case.

Upon his return to Paris and the avenue Mozart apartment, Don pulled the file on the man in whom Delta Base Section CIC chief Reid had expressed such interest. Background information gathered by Army sources and provided by Gordon Sheen indicated that John Emerel Loskot had been born, in Nebraska in

1879, to immigrants from the Bohemia area of the Austro-Hungarian Empire. Loskot grew up in Iowa and, in 1898, was deployed to the Philippines as an enlisted member of the 51st Iowa Infantry Regiment. Following the end of the Spanish-American War, Loskot chose to remain in Manila, where he worked as a civilian quartermaster clerk for the Army. There he met Edith Mason, a nurse from Michigan. The two married in Santa Cruz, California, in 1904, returned to the Philippines, and ultimately had one child. Edith died in Manila in 1908, after which Loskot and his son went back to the United States and settled in Iowa. Loskot worked as a civilian for the War Department but rejoined what by then had become the Iowa National Guard. In 1911, he married the former Kettie Ackert, with whom he eventually had four children.

In 1917, Loskot—by then a commissioned quartermaster officer in the Iowa Guard's 133rd Infantry Regiment—deployed to France with his unit. He returned to the United States following the 1918 Armistice, and in June 1919, left the Army as a major and went back to his civil service job. In 1929, Loskot was granted disabled-veteran status based on injuries sustained during his military service, though the type of injury was not stated. The following year, he and his family were known to be living in Michigan. The dossier provided by Gordon Sheen noted that Loskot had sailed to France alone in 1920, 1934, and 1937, and in 1939, had registered with the U.S. embassy in Paris as an American living in France.

As Don had noted in his February 3 message to the Bureau (sent over Fred's signature block), Sheen had passed along photostatic copies of prewar letters Loskot had sent to senior members of the American and German governments and to the American embassy in Paris. There were also copies of several letters between Loskot and William Joyce, the British renegade broadcaster widely known as "Lord Haw Haw." And finally, Sheen had provided a copy of a letter Loskot sent to the German commander of the Compiègne internment camp in October 1942.[33]

In his message to the Bureau, Don had stated that the content of Loskot's various letters indicated quite clearly the suspect's "anti-Roosevelt, anti-English, antisemitic and generally pro-Hitler" sentiments. Given Loskot's age and his apparent lack of influence, Don had asked that before the ALU began an extensive investigation into the subject—whose present whereabouts were then unknown—the Bureau

> submit [the photostats of the letters] to the [Department of Justice] and sound them out as to possible treason violations. In the event that

> [DOJ] should decide that prosecution for treason is inadvisable in this case, the facts of the case will be presented to the American Embassy which will take appropriate action with regard to re-validation of the subject's passport and his recognition by the American Government as an American citizen with residence abroad.[34]

Don had also asked the Bureau to respond at its earliest convenience, but as of the day he returned from southern France and reviewed the file on Loskot, no response from Washington had yet been received. Don sent a message to Reid at Delta Base Section filling him in on all the facts thus far in the ALU's possession and promising to pass on any further information that might be uncovered. Then he returned Loskot's file to the secure cabinet and set about compiling a dossier on Hector O'Connor.

The documents provided by Burg and Froment indicated that O'Connor was born October 19, 1904, in Paris. He and his three brothers were the children of American parents resident in France, and were thus themselves American citizens. Their father was noted sculptor Andrew O'Connor, who maintained a studio, at 17, rue de Bièvre in Paris, from 1904 to the 1914 outbreak of World War I. The family moved first to London, and in 1916, to Washington, D.C. Completely fluent in both French and English, Hector O'Connor obtained a position on the secretarial staff of the U.S. government delegation to the 1927 Conference for the Limitation of Naval Armaments in Geneva. He briefly returned to the United States following the end of the conference, but in late December 1927, he had notified the U.S. embassy in Paris that he was residing full time in Monaco. He opened and ran a successful art gallery in Monte Carlo, where he was known to be living as of November 1942. That month, Italian troops invaded the neutral principality Monaco, only to be replaced by German troops following Italy's September 1943 capitulation to the Allies.

O'Connor's activities during the Axis occupation were destined to remain largely unknown until months after the liberation, when they would come to light as the result of a related—and much larger—investigation of a very different type of American renegade.

On February 23, while Don Daughters was still in the south of France, Fred Ayer received a telephone call from Gordon Sheen that would ultimately present a challenge none of the Paris-based agents—or anyone in Bureau headquarters—had anticipated. The SHAEF counterintelligence chief asked that Fred meet him in Versailles immediately. He needed to discuss an extremely sensitive and highly classified national security issue, he said, one that might very well swing the war back into Germany's favor.

Fred arrived at the Trianon Palace hotel less than ninety minutes later. Rather than being ushered into Sheen's office, however, the FBI agent was led downstairs to a large basement storage area that had been walled in and converted into a secure conference room. After closely scrutinizing Fred's credentials, the armed military police soldier standing guard checked his name off a list on his clipboard and then motioned the FBI agent through a heavy metal door and into a sparsely furnished room. Sheen, an anxious look on his face, quickly explained the reason for his urgent summons.

Eighteen days earlier, on the night of February 5, an unguarded "deuce-and-a-half" (two-and-a-half-ton) truck with a small attached trailer belonging to the headquarters element of the Army's 28th Infantry Division had been stolen. The theft of Allied military vehicles was not uncommon, Sheen told Fred, with the culprits usually being French civilians or even U.S. or British soldiers seeking to make money by selling the gasoline in the machines' tanks on the black market. But this incident was vastly more serious, because the rear cargo area of the stolen truck was occupied by a portable, secure code room equipped with a massive safe. Inside the safe, Sheen said, was an example of the most advanced and secure cryptographic tool used by the U.S. Army and Navy. Officially designated the ECM (Electric Cipher Machine) M-134-C but commonly referred to as the Sigaba,[35] the device was used for the highest-level tactical and strategic messages and was the cornerstone of the joint U.S.– U.K. combined communications network in both the European and Pacific theaters of war. Should an example of the machine fall into enemy hands, the results would be catastrophic, most immediately for the Allies' planned spring offensive into Germany.

That dire possibility was now a very real probability, Sheen said. The truck bearing the device had disappeared overnight from in front of the 28th Division's just established message center in newly liberated Colmar, in Alsace.[36] The German border was barely ten miles to the east, and significant enemy forces were still operating less than four miles north of the city. When the theft was discovered early on February 6, members of the division's message center staff launched an immediate search of the surrounding area. They soon found the truck's small trailer, its unclassified contents undisturbed. Tire tracks indicated that the truck itself had apparently been driven toward Colmar's eastern suburbs.

When told of the theft, the 28th's intelligence chief, Lieutenant Colonel Harry S. Messec, alerted division commander Major General Norman D. Cota and then directed the unit's military police and CIC soldiers to establish checkpoints on every road leading out of the greater Colmar region. Told they were looking for "highly classified documents," troops from the division's three infantry regiments were ordered to search all outlying buildings capable of concealing the deuce-and-a-half, including barns, large sheds, and slaughterhouses. When SHAEF commander Dwight Eisenhower was notified of the Sigaba's disappearance, he immediately ordered Sixth Army Group's General Jacob L. Devers to find the device at all costs. Devers, in turn, put his counterintelligence chief, Colonel David G. Erskine, in charge of the search. As a first step, Erskine directed that all two-and-a-half-ton trucks within Sixth Army Group's area of operations be inventoried and searched, and have their serial numbers verified. He also put small L-5 liaison aircraft to work doing aerial searches, and even reached out to covert Allied agents operating in Switzerland to determine whether the Sigaba might have passed through that neutral nation on its way to Germany.

As extensive as the theater-wide hunt for the machine had been, Sheen said, no trace of the cryptographic machine had yet been found. That lack of success had prompted Brigadier General Eugene Harrison, Sixth Army Group's intelligence chief, to seek the Army Liaison Unit's help. He wanted two agents to travel immediately to Vittel, the current location of Devers's headquarters, to act in a "consulting capacity" with respect to the ongoing search. Fred told Sheen the ALU would be happy to be of assistance but noted that inasmuch as nearly three weeks had elapsed since the theft, he couldn't promise a successful outcome.[37] The SHAEF CI chief responded that any assistance the FBI could offer would be greatly appreciated.

With Don still in the south of France, on the morning of February 24, Fred and Dick Thompson set out for Vittel equipped "with a jeep, a driver, plentiful firearms . . . a case of rations [and] authority to issue any needed orders to anyone."[38] The two agents made the 173-mile journey to Sixth Army Group headquarters in one long day of driving and immediately went into a long conference with Harrison and Erskine. The officers were completely open about what they saw as the various shortcomings of the Army's search for the Sigaba and gave the FBI agents free reign to conduct their own investigation. It was immediately obvious to Fred that the inquiry would have to start in the place where the theft occurred, so just after dawn the next day, he, Dick Thompson, and their driver set out for the 65-mile drive to Colmar. As Fred later wrote:

> The environs of Colmar were a mess. Two towns in the immediate vicinity had virtually ceased to exist, largely as a result of artillery fire. Smashed up vehicles lined the roads and there were a great number of German corpses still lying around. Sporadic shooting was going on in the city itself, and the methodical Prussian was still dropping very large caliber shells at mathematically predictable intervals into the center of the place.[39]

Upon checking in with the CIC detachment commander in the city, the two FBI agents were taken to the exact spot from which the truck had been stolen—a dead-end dirt road that terminated at the bank of the River Lauch. Fred and Dick examined the area and then asked the accompanying CIC soldiers whether any other Army vehicles had gone missing in the same general area. One of the soldiers sheepishly replied that, as a matter of fact, one of the CIC detachment's own jeeps had disappeared, just the previous night, from the courtyard of the house where the team was billeted. When Fred asked the man if such thefts happened often, he replied that over the previous two months, nearly a thousand vehicles belonging to Seventh Army had been stolen. In many cases, the CIC agent said, the perpetrators were found to be French military personnel who believed their units weren't being issued with suitable or sufficient transportation.

Over the following two days, Fred and Dick met with all the American and French military personnel working on the case, and with representatives of the Sûreté Nationale. The two FBI agents also went house to house in the area, looking for witnesses to the truck's theft, though the locals remained determinedly closemouthed. On their last full day in Colmar, Fred had occasion to talk with another CIC officer about the "appropriation" of American vehicles by French troops. The rate of theft had declined considerably in the previous forty-eight hours, the man said. As Fred later remembered the story, some unnamed American soldiers

> had left another jeep sitting unchaperoned at night, but with a hand grenade in its gas tank under the seat, and the release pin of the grenade attached by piano wire to the gear-shift lever. [The French]

lost a junior officer, and the rate of vehicle thefts dropped to and remained at a new low.[40]

Before leaving Colmar, Fred and Dick prepared an in-depth memorandum outlining the circumstances of the Sigaba's theft, the investigative procedures they had undertaken, and those carried out by the CIC detachment. The document also included suggestions on further steps that could help recover the cryptographic machine and prevent any similar problems in the future. Harrison and Erskine agreed that the FBI agents' suggestions were logical and should be acted upon, and suggested that Fred contact Gordon Sheen immediately so that the SHAEF CI chief could brief Eisenhower. Fred made the call from Verdun during a fuel stop on the return drive to Paris.[41]

As it turned out, fears that the Sigaba had fallen into enemy hands ultimately turned out to be baseless. On March 9, the missing truck was found in a forest near Rambervillers, thiry-nine miles northwest of Colmar. The vehicle's bumpers had been removed and the serial numbers on both sides of its front hood painted over, but other than that, it was intact. The safes and the all-important Sigaba were missing, though later that day, the larger safe containing the cryptographic machine was found, in the small Gressen River, halfway between the towns of Châtenois and Scherwiller, about fifteen miles north of Colmar. The second safe containing instructions and spare parts for the Sigaba was found eleven days later, about a hundred feet downriver from the location of the first find. Tests showed the cryptographic machine had not been tampered with, and the entire Allied intelligence apparatus was able to heave a collective sigh of relief.

Several weeks later Fred, Don, and the three other agents of the ALU joined members of the SHAEF intelligence staff for a ceremonial opening of the second safe, whose combination lock had been clogged and frozen by silt from the river. A soldier with an acetylene torch attempted to cut a whole in the side of the safe, but was unable to do so. That turned out to be a blessing in disguise, for when the safe was finally opened some days later, two large thermite bombs and a huge block of TNT were found inside, wired to detonators. The charges were not intended as booby traps, but were meant to destroy the Sigaba if it were about to be captured by the enemy. Still, a hot torch caressing a block of TNT might well have resulted both in an unintentional remodeling of Versailles's elegant Trianon Palace hotel and in the abrupt dissolution of the Army Liaison Unit.

CHAPTER 9

"Horizontal Collaborators," Angry Generals, and a Momentous Day

WHILE MEN WERE MOST OFTEN THE TARGETS of the Army Liaison Unit's treason investigations, women also came under suspicion. Like their male counterparts, the female suspects could be roughly divided into two categories: There were those thought to have sold out their native land because of ideological conviction and those who did it for love, money, or simply to maintain a privileged lifestyle to which they believed they were entitled by birth, social status, or wealth. Of the several American women the ALU investigated, few were as privileged and felt as entitled as Florence Gould and Ruth Dubonnet.

ON SEPTEMBER 11, 1944, LONDON-BASED LEGAL ATTACHÉ Joe Lynch sent J. Edgar Hoover a message regarding an American woman living in Paris who was thought to have collaborated with the Nazis during the occupation. He had been advised by MI5, Lynch wrote, that a Mrs. J. Gould had entertained officials of the Sicherheitsdienst—the intelligence service of the SS—and was believed to have worked with members of German military intelligence. The information had come from a Wehrmacht prisoner interrogated in the U.K., who said he was told about Gould by an Oberleutnant Stoll of the German army. Lynch asked the Bureau to identify the woman and determine whether she was, in fact, a U.S. citizen. The London legat also said that he would provide the woman's name and any available information on her to Fred Ayer and Don Daughters when they arrived in Britain en route for France.[1]

Lynch's request for background information had elicited no response from Hoover by the time Fred and Don left London for Paris, so the two agents arrived in the French capital knowing nothing about Gould beyond her last name. Indeed, it wasn't until November 4—nearly two months after Lynch's message to Hoover—that the director responded. He told Lynch that "it has not been possible to identify [Gould] with any information presently appearing in the Bureau's files. We are so advising Special Agent Ayer and in the event you are able to secure any other pertinent data . . . you should, of course, relay [it] to the Bureau.[2] Hoover sent almost the identical letter to Fred on the same day. That the FBI could provide no information about Gould seems difficult to understand, given that she was the wife of one of America's richest men.

The woman who would become Florence Gould was born Florence Antoinette Juliette Lacaze in San Francisco in 1895, the eldest of French immigrants Maximin and Berthe Lacaze's two daughters.[3] Florence and her sister, Isabelle, grew up speaking French in the family's Belvedere home and, thanks to their father's position as editor of the newspaper *Le Franco-Californien*, enjoyed a certain social status in the Bay area's close-knit French community.[4] The Lacazes were moderately wealthy, due in large part to San Francisco real estate owned by Florence's maternal grandmother, Florinte Rennesson. That formidable woman lived with the family and was an outsized influence on her daughter and granddaughters, and a frequent and vocal critic of Maximin Lacaze's parenting skills and financial acumen. When the cataclysmic April 1906 earthquake devastated San Francisco—destroying the family's investment properties in seconds—it was *grande-mère* Florinte who decreed that she, Berthe, and the two daughters would henceforth live in Paris. Maximin chose to remain in his beloved ruined city by the Bay, hoping to rebuild a home and life to which his wife and children—if not his mother-in-law—would someday choose to return.

Maximin Lacaze actually succeeded in his quest, up to a point. Within eighteen months of the 1906 earthquake, he'd managed to redevelop and even expand his mother-in-law's real estate portfolio, likely with funding from state and federal governments eager to resurrect what had arguably been the most economically important city on the West Coast of the United States. The revenue generated by Florinte's properties—for she was still their owner of record, despite decamping to Paris—allowed Lacaze to further strengthen his own finances. By December 1907, he was well enough off to travel to Paris to plead with his wife and daughters to return to the Golden State. They categorically refused, Berthe and her daughters arguing that France was safer and offered brighter futures for them all than would California. Lacaze returned to San Francisco and was likely not deeply saddened when, in February 1911, a letter from Berthe informed him of Florinte's death. Lacaze survived his quarrelsome mother-in-law by barely nine months, passing away at just fifty years old.

In the years following the deaths of her grandmother and father, Florence grew into a beautiful, beguiling, vocally talented, and unabashedly ambitious young woman. When her dreams of becoming an opera star failed to pan out, she turned her sights to becoming a *salonnière*. Those prominent upper-class women who showcased artists, writers, and musicians at lavish in-home gatherings known as salons were in many ways the ultimate arbiters of Parisian style, culture, and even fashion. A *salonnière*'s patronage could ensure a new talent's success or the revival of a fading star's career, and in the process enhance the hostess's social standing and reputation. The allure of such behind-the-scenes power attracted Florence like a seductive drug, because in her evolution from child to young adult, she had become supremely self-centered, self-aggrandizing, and epically self-confident in her ability to charm, seduce, and manipulate her way to the top of Parisian society. Unusually attractive, vivacious, and secure in her ability to entice any male between puberty and infirmity, she lacked only one vital ingredient in her recipe for personal success—money, and lots of it.

While Berthe Lacaze was the potential beneficiary of both her mother's and estranged husband's considerable financial assets in America, those funds remained frustratingly unavailable. Lawyers in California argued that the money belonged to Maximin Lacaze's San Francisco–resident brother and other relatives, because Berthe's abrupt departure for Europe following the earthquake and her apparent decision to live permanently in France meant she had effectively renounced her U.S. citizenship. Under the terms of a somewhat obscure piece of American legislation known as the Expatriation Act of 1907, Berthe was therefore disqualified from inheriting the funds.[5] Her Paris-based American lawyer was continuing his efforts to convince the San Francisco probate court that Berthe had never intended to renounce her U.S. citizenship, but the money remained out of reach. At that point, it seems that Berthe and Florence settled on a different strategy.

In July 1914, Henry Chittenden Heynemann, the twenty-three-year-old scion of a well-to-do California family, arrived in Paris with his mother and brother. Henry had recently graduated from the University of Pennsylvania with a degree in architecture, and his announced reason for visiting the French capital was to enroll in the École des Beaux-Arts. But the Heynemanns and Lacazes had been neighbors in Belvedere during Florence's childhood, and she and Henry had known each other as children. Whether the couple had maintained a correspondence over the years and planned the reunion in France or their encounter in the French capital was a simple coincidence isn't clear. What is apparent, however, is that Florence and her mother saw the young man as a possible solution to their increasingly dire financial situation. Until lawyers could determine if Berthe would inherit any of her husband's and mother's American assets, a marriage between the young, obviously besotted Henry Heynemann and the younger but far more calculating Florence Lacaze would allow Berthe and her two daughters to continue to live in the style to which they'd become accustomed.

The young couple's burgeoning romance was only slightly hindered by the August outbreak of a general European war. Florence, Berthe, and Isabelle left Paris for the south of France, where they were eventually joined by Henry, after he'd put his mother on a ship back to the United States.[6] The group returned to Paris in September and—following the signing of a financial agreement between Henry and Berthe that the latter found suitably generous—the twenty-three-year-old groom and his nineteen-year-old bride married in the French capital on October 27.[7] The wedding automatically conferred U.S. citizenship on Florence—though she had apparently never renounced or lost it following the childhood move to France with her mother.[8] Now undeniably an American citizen by marriage, Florence was in an excellent position to help her mother inherit the funds and properties in California initially denied her by the Expatriation Act.

Gaining the release of her father and grandmother's assets was apparently Florence's top priority when she and Henry finally arrived in San Francisco in December 1914. She soon discovered that whatever funds Maximin had left behind had been almost completely consumed by legal fees and payouts to his brother and other relatives in California. But Florinte's considerable estate remained intact, and Florence proved unusually adept at using her mother's power of attorney to gain ownership of the property and bank accounts. The young bride achieved that goal within five months of her marriage, then promptly left her stunned and distraught young husband, declaring her intention to return to Paris. Henry initially pleaded with her to change her mind, but ultimately accepted the fact that she had cynically used him. He did not contest Florence's August 1916 petition for divorce, and less than two weeks after it was granted, the now twenty-two-year-old woman sailed from New York for France.

Florence—now spelling her family name La Caze in order to make it sound aristocratic—returned to a nation embroiled in war, a circumstance that understandably limited her attempts to establish herself in Parisian society.[9] Whether out of patriotism for her adopted home or a calculated desire to polish her somewhat tarnished reputation as a divorcée, she became a volunteer nurse and spent much of the last year of the war ministering to wounded soldiers. When the conflict ended, she briefly turned to singing and dancing at the Folies Bergére, and it was during that time that she met the expatriate American millionaire Frank Jay Gould.

The son and grandson of robber barons who had made their fortunes in railroads, telegraph companies, and real estate, Jay Gould had lived permanently in France since 1913. Owner of champion race horses—whose jockeys included none other than Frank O'Neill[10]—and valuable real estate in the best districts of Paris, Gould was also an inveterate womanizer with a penchant for chorus girls. Already on his second marriage when he first saw Florence onstage, Gould was immediately smitten. Florence, now twenty-three, saw the forty-one-year-old millionaire as her entrée into the life of wealth, fame, and social prestige to which she had always aspired. She turned the full force of her considerable charms on him, and in April 1919, he divorced his second wife in a case that made international headlines.[11] Florence finally became Mrs. Jay Gould in a Paris ceremony on February 10, 1923.

In the years following their marriage, the Goulds spent much of their time in the south of France, reveling in the warmth and beauty of the Mediterranean coastline between Cannes and Nice. They were not alone, for the Cote d'Azur attracted many well-to-do American expats in addition to famous and soon-to-be-famous artists, writers, and musicians from throughout Europe. It was a milieu guaranteed to capture Florence's heart, for her husband's wealth ensured that she received the deference and recognition for which she hungered. There were other appetites at play, too. The Goulds' marriage had from the start been an open one, and though devoted to each other on many levels, they each enjoyed a series of dalliances carried out with the full knowledge and acceptance of the other.[12] Indeed, so enamored were the Goulds of the Riviera and all it had to offer that they invested in a local casino and ultimately opened three upscale resort hotels in the formerly sleepy fishing village of Juan-les-Pins, near Antibes.

From that point on, Jay Gould spent the majority of his time in "Juan," as he called it, while his wife alternated between there and Paris. It was during her increasingly prolonged stays in the French capital in the mid-1930s that Florence first met Joachim von Ribbentrop and Otto Abetz, Francophile Germans ordered by Adolf Hitler himself to strengthen the bonds between Nazi Germany and the far-right elements within France's government and society. That mission included such things as forming Franco-German "friendship societies," placing pro-Nazi articles in French newspapers and journals, and generally seeking to create a narrative in which Great Britain, rather than Germany, was France's true adversary.

Abetz and Ribbentrop not only insinuated themselves into Florence's social circle, they also reportedly found their way into her bed. Whether out of real affection or simply as another method of influence, the Germans' relationships with Florence allowed them to pump her for information on the wealthy Britons she and her husband hosted in Juan-les-Pins and the various right-wing French politicians and journalists with whom she socialized in Paris. By August 1934, at Hitler's request, Ribbentrop was running what amounted to a shadow foreign ministry known as the *Dienstelle* Ribbentrop. The group provided Hitler with information that the still tradition-bound German Foreign Office—not yet purged of career diplomats in favor of party loyalists—could not or would not. Florence was likely a useful source of information for Ribbentrop even after he was named Nazi Germany's ambassador to England in 1936, and certainly once he became the actual foreign minister two years later. Most of her observations were apparently passed to her part-time German lover through her *other* part-time German lover, Abetz.

As Europe drifted ever closer to war, Florence focused her attention on two things—managing the Goulds' properties and business affairs, and continuing to live a glittering social life both in Paris and on the Cote d'Azur. She was in the French capital when war broke out in September 1939, but in March 1940, she rushed to Juan-les-Pins, because her mother's already frail health had taken a turn for the worse. Berthe Lacaze died in April, and the following month, Florence joined many of her wealthy upper-class women friends in volunteering as a nurse's assistant. Whether she did so out of patriotism or simply because she believed it would burnish her reputation is unclear, though she did help care for combat casualties evacuated from the front lines to the capital's Val-de-Grâce hospital.

The rapid advance of German forces toward Paris in May prompted Florence to flee back to Juan-les-Pins, where her husband had already secured tickets for the voyage to America. The couple ultimately chose not to leave, however, fearing that their departure would lead to the seizure of their many properties throughout France by business rivals or, worse, by the *Boche*, should they actually manage to conquer the country.[13] Their decision was also likely influenced by the fact that America's neutrality offered them some protections not afforded to the French, and it was to determine the breadth of those protections that upon her return to Paris following the capitulation in June Florence sought the counsel of William Bullitt.

The American ambassador was already an acquaintance—his official residence was rented from the Goulds—and he was more than happy to help in any way he could. That desire to be of service only increased when the recently divorced diplomat became yet another of Florence's romantic conquests. The lovers initially spent time together at the Gould estate in Maisons-Laffitte and then at a luxurious duplex apartment Florence bought at 2, boulevard Suchet.[14] As with many of Florence's amorous liaisons, her relationship with Bullitt provided many side benefits. One of the most important was the ambassador's agreement to move many of the Goulds' art treasures into the embassy's secure basement storage area to keep them out of the hands of the increasingly rapacious Einsatzstab Reichsleiter Rosenberg.

The German conquest of France was undoubtedly a disaster of epic proportions, especially for Jews, communists, Freemasons, Roma, and many others the Nazis considered enemies of the Reich. Yet the occupation allowed Florence to finally fulfill her long-held desire to become a *salonnière*. Soon after purchasing the boulevard Suchet apartment—and in between trysts there with Bullitt—Florence began holding weekly gatherings that were soon drawing a wide range of writers, actors, musicians, and other luminaries. Many of the guests at her "Thursdays," so called because of the day on which they were most often held, were right-wingers who collaborated with or at least tolerated the Germans. When the boulevard Suchet apartment and Maisons-Laffitte mansion were requisitioned by the Germans, Florence simply moved her weekly salons into a rented suite of sumptuous rooms at the prestigious Hôtel Le Bristol in the 8th *arrondissement*. Her guests—now including members of the Wehrmacht, Luftwaffe, and the German embassy staff—feasted on food and wine secured on the black market, and the events often stretched from midday until late evening.

America's entry into the war, in December 1941, led to the hurried departure of Bullitt and his embassy staff but did nothing to dampen the mood or restrict the gastronomic extravagances of Florence's salons. Otto Abetz returned to Paris as Ribbentrop's representative in the German military command in occupied France as well as Berlin's ambassador to Vichy, and it was likely because of Abetz's patronage that Florence fared far better than most Americans still in the occupied zone. She was not interned, nor was she required to register weekly with the local police. A special permit allowed Florence to continue driving her Bugatti sedan (using fuel drawn from German motor pools) at a time when most Parisians had to resort to bicycles, and she was given a pass granting her unhindered passage into Vichy to visit her husband at Juan-les-Pins. Not surprisingly, Florence's already busy romantic life also benefited from the occupation. Though now in her mid-forties, she looked a decade younger and retained the ability to seemingly mesmerize any man—or woman—who took her fancy or from whom she wanted something. Following her April 1942 move to a large third-floor apartment at 129, avenue Malakoff, Florence reportedly took as lovers, among others, the famed German novelist turned Wehrmacht officer Ernst Jünger, Helmut Knochen, the Gestapo chief in Paris, Carl Oberg, the senior SS and police officer in France, Gerhard Heller, the chief censor within the embassy propaganda bureau, and Ludvig Vogel, a German aeronautical engineer working for the Paris office of the Focke-Wulf aircraft company.[15] Vogel was so smitten with Florence that he took an apartment at 133, avenue Malakoff so that he could be at her beck and call.

In addition to her own dalliances with Germans, Florence joined her friend Marie-Louise Bousquet in organizing the *souris grises* (gray mice) network of well-to-do French women willing to have sex with senior Nazi officers and diplomats in return for money and other favors.[16] Florence used information the "horizontal collaborators" learned from their "clients" to further her own financial interests by concluding several lucrative contracts with the Germans.[17] It was that same willingness to do business with the occupiers that in mid-1944 led Florence and, by extension, her husband to help the Germans establish a bank in putatively neutral Monaco.[18] Known as Banque Charles, the Monte Carlo institution was essentially a front for Berlin's Reichsbank and was intended to help move Nazi money out of Europe in anticipation of what was by then an almost certain German defeat. The 5 million francs the Goulds transferred to the bank was supposed to appear as legitimate seed money, but the entire operation floundered following the Allied landings in southern France (Operation Dragoon) in August 1944.

Florence's activities during the German occupation did not go unnoticed, of course. At least three frequent visitors to her Thursday salons were covert members of the Résistance. All reported on her to their superiors, who in turn channeled the information back to Free French headquarters in London. De

Gaulle's intelligence people passed their file on Florence to Guy Liddell at MI5, who in turn handed it over to both the OSS X-2 branch and to Joe Lynch. It was the latter's September 1944 request to the Bureau for more information on Florence Gould that ultimately led to J. Edgar Hoover's belated response that Lynch—and, by extension, Fred Ayer—should keep the Bureau apprised of any "pertinent information" they might uncover.

Even as the FBI's interest in Florence as a possible traitor was gearing up, she herself was doing what she could to quickly repair her damaged reputation. Soon after Vogel's arrest by the DSM on September 11, she made a large cash contribution to the Forces Françaises de l'Intérieur (French Forces of the Interior), the umbrella organization under which France's various resistance groups were gathered after D-Day. Florence also began encouraging British and American military and diplomatic personnel to attend her salons at avenue Malakoff, which had become sparsely attended since the liberation had prompted many of her right-wing French guests to go underground to avoid arrest on charges of collaboration. Florence also started boasting to anyone who would listen that during the occupation she had been secretly in the employ of both the OSS and Free French intelligence, though no one who knew her accepted the obvious lies.

The same Free French intelligence group with which Florence claimed to have worked was the first Allied organization to take her into custody. And, somewhat ironically, the arrest took place during one of the American millionairess's Thursday salons. On October 19, 1944, Florence was hosting three guests for a pre-discussion lunch at the avenue Malakoff apartment when her butler came in and whispered something in her ear. She calmly excused herself and left, but when she had not returned several hours later, the butler said to the puzzled visitors, "I think, ladies and gentlemen, that it would be better not to wait any longer. Madame has been arrested."[19]

Florence had been taken into custody by agents of de Gaulle's DGER (Direction Générale des Études et Recherches), a division of the Free French intelligence service known as the Bureau Centrale de Renseignements et d'Action. She was held and interrogated for twelve days and among those quizzing her on her dealings with the Nazis was 1st Lieutenant Charles C. Michaelis.[20] A member of the OSS's Paris-based Special Counterintelligence Unit 105, the thiry-four-year-old specialized in financial cases. Much to Florence's surprise, he had no interest at all in how many Germans she had slept with during the occupation or whether she had actually denounced anyone to the Gestapo. He was *very* interested, however, in the part she'd played in helping to establish the by then defunct Banque Charles and was intensely skeptical of her repeated protestations under oath that she hadn't known it was a cover for Nazi attempts to move money out of Europe.

Florence was released from custody on November 1 on the understanding that she'd remain in Paris. She wouldn't have had time to flee the capital even if she'd wanted to, for on November 2, she was taken back into custody, this time by U.S. Army CIC agents acting at Michaelis's behest. Unbeknownst to Florence, he had been interrogating Ludvig Vogel for the previous week. Both the French and Americans suspected the German was a covert Gestapo agent who had been involved in both deporting Jews to the concentration camps and in attempting to move Nazi money out of Europe. In order to save his skin, he offered to spill all he knew about Banque Charles and the Goulds' involvement in the scheme. His information was apparently quite useful, for on October 29, he'd been released from French custody and taken under the protection of the OSS—and eventually went to work in some capacity for X-2. When confronted by Michaelis with Vogel's sworn statements, Florence continued to deny any wrongdoing. Unable to break her, the OSS agent ordered her released after only a few days.

When there had been no further interaction with Allied authorities for four months, Florence started to relax, apparently believing that she was now in the clear. That illusion was shattered during the fourth week of March 1945, when she was once again picked up by CIC agents. Taken to the DSM interrogation center at 18, boulevard Suchet, Florence found herself sitting across a table from Don Daughters. The FBI agent had been investigating her case for several weeks and in the process had spoken at length with the French security services, Michaelis of OSS, and several Army counterintelligence agents. Among the latter was Lester Blumner, the man in charge of all CIC operations on France's Mediterranean coast. He had been looking into the Banque Charles affair himself, and when Don contacted him, Blumner had said that one of his most useful sources of information had been Hector O'Connor. The man who had been incarcerated in Nice during Don's March visit to the Cote d'Azur had turned out to know quite a bit about the Goulds' involvement in the bank scheme, and in a March 8 sworn statement to Blumner had revealed all he knew in return for leniency on any punishment that might result from his suspected collaboration with the Germans.[21]

Much of what O'Connor had sworn to under oath directly contradicted Florence's previous statements to the OSS and CIC. Questioned for several hours by Don Daughters regarding the inconsistencies in her stories, Florence nevertheless refused to admit to any wrongdoing regarding either her personal relationships with Vogel and other Germans or the Banque Charles affair. She must have been rattled by the interrogation, however, for within days she submitted to the counselor for economic affairs at the U.S. embassy several testimonial letters written on her behalf by prominent friends. The writers stated that Florence had given large sums of money to various resistance organizations, had sheltered *résistants*, and had financially supported their families.[22]

Whether Don saw the testimonial letters is unclear, but he didn't mention them in his April 6 report of Florence's interrogation. After reviewing the basic facts of her birth, marriage to Jay Gould, and prewar life in France, the FBI agent used information provided by "Source B" (a Captain E. Schaeffer of the DGER) to list the various German officials with whom she had been romantically and/or economically involved. Don then cited "Source C" (Hector O'Connor), who said the Goulds were "important stockholders in the proposed Banque Charles, which was being founded in Monte Carlo by Baron von [sic] Charles, acting under the supervision of . . . a representative of the German Economic Ministry."[23] The FBI agent added that

> it is the opinion of Source B that although the subject FLORENCE GOULD merely used these German officials to enhance her own possessions and possibly to protect the financial interests of the family, it can be concluded that these officials also used her in order to obtain favors in exchange.[24]

Don concluded his report by saying that he would seek further information from Hector O'Connor and from Captain Gerard Dubos of the DGER, "who is reported to be well advised on the collaborationist activities of [Florence Gould]."[25]

Don was not the only one in the FBI looking into the Goulds' wartime activities. On April 25, the supervisory agent in charge of the Washington, D.C., field office, Guy Hottel, reported to Hoover on information obtained through confidential sources within the Department of State dealing specifically with the Banque Charles affair. The sources had provided copies of several messages sent from the U.S. embassy in Paris to the State Department, and Hottel included the full text of each communication in his report. That document went into detail regarding Florence Gould's financial involvement in the Reichsbank-backed scheme and speculated about the roles played by Vogel and other Germans in her orbit.[26]

As thorough as Hottel's report was, Don Daughters did him one better. On July 31, the Paris-based ALU agent dispatched to the Bureau an exhaustive nine-page report that not only reviewed much of the information already gathered regarding the Goulds, but listed every known piece of property owned by the couple in France and the names of the various corporate entities through which those properties were managed. Further, in a thirteen-page appendix to the report, Don gave the names and short biographies of seventy-four people (French, German, American, Swiss, and Italian) with whom the Goulds had interacted between September 1939 and February 1945, many of whom Don had personally interviewed since submitting his April 6 report. Several of the individuals listed in the appendix were known members of the German intelligence and security services or proven collaborators with the Nazis, and Don pointed out that four of his sources admitted outright that Banque Charles was specifically created "to conceal funds of the German Reich in . . . a neutral country." The agent added that he would continue his investigation and update the Bureau as necessary.

As it turned out, further inquiries by the ALU were not required. On September 17, Hoover passed the Bureau's voluminous Florence Gould file to the Criminal Division at Main Justice, along with a memo indicating his strong desire that she be indicted for treason. He heard nothing in response until November 2, when a terse memo from Assistant Attorney General Theron Caudle informed the director that the Criminal Division "is of the opinion that no further efforts are justified in order to develop a treason case against the subject. You are requested, however, to furnish this Division with any further information which you may receive concerning this case."[27] Caudle provided no reason for DOJ's decision, though Hoover assumed it was because the Goulds had hired former United States Attorney for the Southern District of New York John T. Cahill to defend them against any possible court action arising from allegations of treason or financial wrongdoing. Or possibly, it was because the wealthy couple had called in favors owed them by senior American diplomats or jurists who had enjoyed the many prewar delights of Juan-les-Pins.

Hoover's quest to indict Florence Gould may have been stalled by Caudle, but the director took to heart the assistant attorney general's offhand suggestion to forward any "further information." Over the following fourteen years, Hoover ordered repeated investigations of the Goulds and two of their longtime women employees who the director believed were either "notorious lesbians" or communists, or both. Jay Gould died in his beloved Juan-les-Pins in 1956, but not before Florence had begun showering cash on a variety of charities, foundations, libraries, and educational institutions in both France and the United States. By the time of her death in 1983, Florence had finally achieved the status she had hungered for since the end of World War II—that of a widely respected, influential, and in some quarters, beloved philanthropist and patron of the arts.

The final denouement of the Florence Gould case was still years in the future, when the men of the Army Liaison Unit were tasked to investigate yet another wealthy American woman suspected of treason during the German occupation of France. Indeed, that second individual actually came to the ALU's attention less than a month after Joe Lynch first mentioned the name Gould in his September 11, 1944, message to Hoover. There was little chance that anyone in the FBI would fail to recognize the second suspect's name, for it was also the name of the most famous *apéritif* in France.

THAT THE LONG-REVERED HOUSE OF DUBONNET would ultimately come into disrepute during World War II was largely the result of an event that took place in the wealthy Paris suburb of Neuilly-sur-Seine on April 12, 1937.

On that day, Pierre André Dubonnet—grandson and heir of the *apéritif*'s inventor—wed the former Countess Ruth de Vallombrosa. The wedding made news on both sides of the Atlantic, for in addition to his inherited wealth and social status, the forty-year-old twice-married groom—known to friends and family as André—was also a much decorated World War I flying ace, a bobsledder in the 1928 Winter Olympics, a successful race car driver, an automotive engineer, and an inventor. His thirty-seven-year-old bride was the widow of famed American portrait artist Walter Dean Goldbeck, who, after the painter's death, had wed the Harvard-educated Count Paul Manca de Morès Vallombrosa. That marriage had broken up soon after the countess met the dashing Dubonnet, reportedly because the count's fortune hadn't been large enough to keep his wife in the style she considered appropriate.

Though the onetime countess had lived an aristocratic life in France for nearly two decades before marrying into the Dubonnet clan, her origins were decidedly plebian. Born Ruth Angela Obre on New York's East Side in January 1900, she spent the first decade of her life on the sprawling 2,800-acre estate of American multimillionaire John Jacob Astor IV in Rhinebeck, in the Hudson River Valley. Ruth was not a member of that illustrious family, however. Her parents, William and May, helped run and maintain the vast estate, and Ruth grew up in the Astor mansion's servants' quarters as the pampered favorite of the "backstairs aristocracy"—the senior household staff. Being "wealth adjacent" for most of her early life gave Ruth an appreciation for money and the power and position it could bring. She also came to love fine art, and as a young adult she moved to Greenwich Village to study painting. Her youth and beauty attracted the attention of Goldbeck, eighteen years her senior, who both taught her and used her as a model for many of his compositions. The artist quickly fell in love with Ruth, and the two married in 1921.[28]

Soon after their wedding, the Goldbecks departed for France, where the artist introduced his young bride to celebrities of every stripe. Ruth soon learned to speak fluent French, though with a distinctly American accent, and the couple were welcome guests of many of the French capital's most famous residents. After spending several months in Munich—where Ruth learned to speak good German—the Goldbecks returned to Paris. Ruth so loved life in the City of Light that she remained there when her husband returned to the United States for what was supposed to be a brief business trip. Unfortunately, Walter Goldbeck fell ill soon after his arrival in New York. He died at St. Mark's Hospital on October 13, 1925, at the age of forty-two. Ruth sailed home from Europe as soon as she was notified of Walter's passing, and was by all accounts devastated by her loss. Her circumstances were greatly helped, however, by the considerable fortune left to her in Walter's will, and she spent the next few years circulating among the well-to-do of Palm Beach, Manhattan, the Hamptons, and Boston.

In was in the latter city that Ruth first met Paul de Vallombrosa, and the two were married in New York's St. Patrick's Cathedral in January 1928. They settled in Paris, where Ruth's social life quickly became much the same as it had been when she was married to Goldbeck. Soon after returning to the French capital, the Vallombrosas were introduced to Jay and Florence Gould, and the two couples often spent time together in Juan-les-Pins.

Following her divorce from Vallombrosa and marriage to Dubonnet, Ruth and André saw quite a bit of Joachim von Ribbentrop, who managed Dubonnet's marketing in Germany and Austria before his move into politics. Through the soon-to-be diplomat, the Frenchman and his American wife also met Otto Abetz and other members of the French capital's expatriate German colony. The Dubonnets traveled to Germany, where they met and were entertained by senior members of the Nazi party. At a dinner party in Paris following their return, Ruth was heard to say that the Nazi idea "was the fascinating one of the future."[29]

The Dubonnets' relationships with important Germans—and with French members of Abetz's Franco-German friendship organization—obviously became something of a liability following the September 1939 outbreak of war. Rumors regarding the couples' pro-German sympathies were put to rest—at least for the time being—when André lied about his age in order to rejoin the Armée de l'Air. Initially assigned as a flight instructor, he eventually transferred into a fighter squadron. André flew dozens of sorties, apparently shooting down at least one German aircraft, and participated in the French air force's last combat sortie before the country's June 1940 surrender. Ruth, for her part, volunteered with the French Red Cross and helped transport wounded soldiers from the front lines back to Paris until the capitulation.

The couple's situation did not appreciably change following the German occupation of Paris. André became an adviser on aviation affairs for the Vichy government, and Ruth organized and ran her own private ambulance corps in conjunction with the Red Cross. She always seemed to have plenty of gasoline for her several vehicles, and much like Frank and Florence Gould, the Dubonnets did not seem to suffer from the food shortages that affected most Parisians. Indeed, André and Ruth often held lavish dinner parties at their Paris mansion, to which they invited both senior Germans and leaders of the French extreme right wing. It was one of those parties that caused a rift between Ruth and another American woman living in the French capital.

Drue Tartière was a well-known actress in American films of the 1930s who had gone by the name Drue Leyton until marrying French American actor Jacques Tartière in 1938.[30] After her marriage, Drue did broadcasts for Radio Mondial in Paris, voicing programs in both English and passable French (the latter acquired while attending a girls' school in Switzerland and the Sorbonne) using the last name Leyton rather than Tartière. Her frequent criticisms of Hitler and Nazi Germany earned her the undying enmity of Joseph Goebbels and his promise she would be executed on sight if caught. In April and May 1940, Jacques fought in Norway with the French Foreign Legion, but after the French capitulation in June, he escaped to England to join de Gaulle's forces. Unaware of Drue's unpopularity with senior Nazis, in the fall of 1940, Ruth Dubonnet asked the former actress to attend a dinner party being given for the wives of Joachim von Ribbentrop and Luftwaffe chief Hermann Göring. When Drue flatly refused, Ruth archly responded, "Why shouldn't you be friendly with them? The Americans have never broadcast that Americans in France shouldn't be friendly with the Germans here."[31]

In October 1940, Drue moved to the village of Barbizon, thirty miles southeast of Paris.[32] She rented a small villa and several acres of farmland and began raising poultry and growing a variety of crops. She would barter with local residents for beef and lamb, and would then take the meat and some of her produce to the capital to sell. Drue kept the lowest possible profile to avoid attracting the attention of the Gestapo, though her life was shattered when she received news in September 1941 that her beloved Jacques had been killed the previous June during the Free French campaign to wrest Syria and Lebanon from Vichy forces. When America entered the war the following December, the young widow's absence from Paris prevented her internment, though on September 22, 1942, she was arrested at the house in Barbizon. That her French identity card was issued in the surname Tartière rather than Leyton kept her captors from realizing that she was the American broadcaster whom Goebbels had promised to execute.

That lifesaving anonymity was threatened, however, as Drue and several others were about to board a bus in Paris bound for the women's internment camp at Vittel in the Vosges mountains. From across the street, a loud voice rang out, "My God, Drue, you still in this country?" The voice belonged to none other than Ruth Dubonnet, who was dressed in her Red Cross uniform and was helping wounded German soldiers into a waiting ambulance. "What are you doing here?" Ruth added. "Why haven't you called me all this time or let me know what happened to you?" Then, to Drue's horror, Ruth shouted, "Is it true what I've heard about Jacques being killed?"[33]

In an effort not to arouse German suspicions about her or Jacques, Drue had been telling everyone for months that her husband was traveling on business. If relayed to the Gestapo, Ruth's thoughtless question could well have led to an investigation that would reveal both Jacques's membership in the Free French forces and Drue's identity as the woman from Radio Mondial. Shuddering, Drue shouted, "No, I don't think so, that's the first I've heard of it!" Ruth called back that she would get Drue out of internment and that her fellow American shouldn't worry.

That Ruth was not herself in custody because of her U.S. citizenship and felt that she would have no trouble securing Drue's release from Vittel were both indications of the strength of the Dubonnets' relationships with senior German and Vichy French officials. Not only had Ruth not been interned, she was not even required to make weekly check-in visits with the local police. She still had no trouble obtaining fuel for her ambulances, which were now largely dedicated to transporting German wounded, and she and André were frequent hosts of German dignitaries at gatherings that continued to offer foods and wines about which the average French citizen could only dream. In her spare time, Ruth shopped and dined out with the wives of French collaborators and was a frequent guest of Coco Chanel and her German lover at the fashion icon's lavish suite in the Hôtel Ritz.

It was the Dubonnet's close and rewarding relationships with Nazis and French collaborators both before and during the occupation that brought the couple to the attention of Free French intelligence officers following the August 1944 liberation of Paris. When it became obvious to Ruth and André that they were about to be arrested, the couple sought out Drue Tartière. She had managed to get herself released from Vittel using a faked terminal cancer diagnosis and then spent the remainder of the occupation sheltering downed Canadian, British, and American aviators and helping the Résistance move them out of France and back to Britain. Drue had returned to Paris after the liberation and when visiting friends was told that the Dubonnets had been there looking for her.

"They knew you were coming to lunch," her friend said, "and Ruth thinks you owe her protection because she claims you wouldn't have got out of Vittel if it hadn't been for her influence. She wanted us to ask you to intercede for them because they think they may be arrested at any moment."[34] Days later, Ruth herself suddenly appeared at Drue's door in abject terror, pleading with her fellow American to "let bygones be bygones" and do what she could to help keep the Dubonnets out of prison.[35] Drue—a true heroine of the French Résistance—understandably had no desire to aid people who had consorted with Nazis and apparently told Ruth exactly that before closing the door in the woman's face. Days later, on September 20, 1944, the Dubonnets were arrested by DSM agents.

Very soon after being taken into custody, André and Ruth were sent to the Drancy internment camp in the northeast suburbs of Paris. Until just weeks before, the facility had been run by the SS as a holding area for French Jews who were to be sent to concentration camps in the east. Now it was used to house refugees and, in a separate area enclosed by barbed wire, people believed to have collaborated with the Germans. The Dubonnets were separated on arrival, André being housed in the men's barracks and Ruth in the women's. While André was apparently released from detention fairly quickly—owing, no doubt, to his social and political connections—his wife was still being held in late October when several reporters were allowed to visit the detention center. In the women's barracks, journalist W. A. S. Douglas encountered Ruth, whom he described as "fortyish, wearing a rough tweed jacket," and sitting on an upturned wooden box. She said that she had retained her American citizenship and had been doing "charity work among the poor" throughout the occupation, though she admitted that in order to get certain needed items for her work she "had to approach the authorities."[36] She neglected to mention, of course, that during the occupation she had also been entertaining senior German officials and their wives in her home.

During the first week of October 1944, the DSM notified Fred Ayer of Ruth Dubonnet's detention and provided the FBI agent with a copy of her dossier. After going through the file and undertaking some additional background research, on October 6, Fred sent a message to Hoover outlining the details of the case. Fred wrote that, according to the DSM, Ruth

> was known to be pro-German in her attitude, to have entertained them lavishly in her home after the fall of France and to have associated with them after the entry of the United States into the war. . . . According to the French sources there was not any doubt concerning the pro-German attitude of both of the Dubonnets.[37]

But, Fred added,

> There were no specific allegations that either of them actually materially aided the German cause or furnished information to the enemy. In her defense Madame Dubonnet had argued that her associations with German leaders and . . . influential Vichy personages had been for the purpose of obtaining material comforts for interned Americans and in attempting to have many released from internment camps. According to the dossier on the woman there did not seem too much question but that some of her claim at least was true. The fact that stood out, however, was that the German occupation authorities at no time interfered with the activities of the Dubonnet family.[38]

After telling Hoover that he had provided the U.S. embassy with the basic facts of the Dubonnet case, Fred added that he had also reached out to Gordon Sheen at SHAEF to see if he had any additional information. Sheen responded that the DSM had determined that it was no longer interested in Ruth Dubonnet "from the espionage or treason angle" and had turned her case over to the French civilian police because she was regarded as an undesirable resident. The CI chief added that despite André's widely known pro-German sympathies, he was relatively well regarded in France because he'd fought for the nation in both world wars. Ruth, on the other hand, was considered merely a "rich and vicious parasite." Sheen speculated that perhaps one of the reasons Ruth had not yet been set free from Drancy was "because of the terrific clamor which the communists would raise if a woman of her wealth were set free." While Sheen added that the U.S. Army had no intention of acting through any channels—official or otherwise—to secure Ruth's release, he was certain that she soon would be. When that happened, Sheen was equally certain that as a face-saving measure, the French would announce that she'd been freed because of pressure from the United States.

Fred told Hoover that he had passed Sheen's information and comments on to the embassy, and that the diplomats were apparently content to "let matters ride for a while and see what developed." Accordingly, Fred wrote that the ALU would take no additional action on the Ruth Dubonnet case unless there were a further request from the embassy. He allowed that the French security services might uncover more information, and that should such additional facts come to light, the Bureau would be promptly notified.

Fred's unusually nonchalant attitude toward Ruth's case likely arose from two factors. First, unlike with Florence Gould, there was no evidence that Madame Dubonnet had given aid or comfort—either material or sexual—to the Nazis or their French supporters. And second, the understaffed ALU was simply too busy to put time and effort into investigating a woman who may certainly have been a "rich and vicious parasite" but who had apparently not actually been a "horizontal collaborator" and had not committed overt acts of treason against the United States. Fred believed that any punishment Ruth or her husband might ultimately receive should rightfully be meted out by the French, an attitude with which Hoover and the Department of Justice ultimately concurred. The United States quietly dropped its nascent case against the Dubonnets, both of whom were soon back in the midst of Paris high society with only slightly damaged reputations.[39]

Not long after the ALU halted its investigation into Ruth Dubonnet, an innocent mix-up involving another American woman resulted in Fred Ayer meeting two very angry Army generals, one of whom was Supreme Allied Commander Dwight Eisenhower.

The episode began simply enough. The ALU routinely produced lists of American citizens suspected of having worked for the German propaganda ministry or any of its subordinate organizations. The lists were passed on to the CIC target teams with instructions to notify the ALU if the persons or any documents pertaining to them were located. One list included the name of a young woman who had reportedly done two broadcasts for Radio Vichy. Unfortunately, someone in CIC had sent out the list with the dramatic, if inaccurate, subject heading "Wanted by the FBI." As Fred later described it, the consequences

> were astonishing and immediate. One bitterly cold morning I was sitting in my Paris office, wearing two suits of long handled underwear, full uniform, a field coat with liner, and a knitted stocking cap. I was alternately pounding out sentences of report on the abominable portable, and feeding pieces of Prussian furniture into the stove, when I was interrupted by thunderous knocks on the door. What I admitted was a real, live, angry, two-star general, in the person of Everett Hughes, Eisenhower's Paris deputy. "What in the name of the imperishable so and so was the idea of putting the name of the daughter of one of our favorite generals on the FBI wanted list?"[40]

Fred hurriedly explained that the FBI was not "hunting" the young woman, only attempting to gather more information about her. He promised to send out the list again under a less inflammatory title, and Hughes left, apparently mollified.

A few days later, Fred was conversing with Gordon Sheen in the latter's office at the Trianon Palace hotel in Versailles when the telephone rang. The CI chief picked up the receiver and suddenly stiffened to attention. After tersely uttering "Yes, sir" several times, he hung up, turning to look accusingly at Fred. "Would it be too much to inquire what in Hell you've been up to now?" Sheen asked. "That was General Eisenhower, that's who that was. And he wants to see you *right now.*"

When Fred was ushered into the supreme commander's office minutes later, Eisenhower looked him up and down and then told him to take a seat. "Now what's this I hear about you hunting the daughter of one of my best generals?" he asked. Fred told him the same thing he'd told Hughes—that the FBI wasn't hunting the young woman. Eisenhower said he understood that labeling the CIC target list "Wanted by the FBI" had been a mix-up not of the ALU's making, but then added, "The trouble is that the girl is a receptionist at my headquarters, and what I want to know is this. Is she a proper person for me to have around?"

"I won't tell you that," Fred responded, "but I will finish a complete investigation and give you a full personal report. Whether or not she is then a proper person to have around will be up to the General to decide." Eisenhower glared at Fred, and for a moment the FBI agent was horrified that he might have gone too far. Just as the silence stretched almost to the breaking point, the supreme commander smiled, then laughed and said, "I don't blame you a bit, Ayer. You just go ahead and make a complete report. I admire your nerve."[41]

True to his word, Fred did undertake a full—if understandably hurried—investigation of the young woman. As he later wrote:

> In short order I submitted two exhaustive reports. The girl in question, at age 14, had been living with her mother in France at the outbreak of war. About two years later she had made two recordings describing the fashions of the younger ladies at the Longchamps [sic] race track. These had later been broadcast by Radio Vichy to show that all was still as before in the best of all possible Parisian worlds. All inquiries gave her otherwise a completely clean bill of health, and she was frank and truthful upon personal interview.[42]

Eisenhower thanked Fred for each of his reports, and for undertaking the investigation despite his already overwhelming case load. The young woman, for her part, went back to work with her security record unblemished.

The arrival of Bill Clark, Joe Dunn, and Dick Thompson in Paris, during the second week of January 1945, undoubtedly helped ease Fred Ayer and Don Daughters's crushing workload, but the ALU needed still more manpower in order to accomplish the increasing number of tasks assigned to it.

Moreover, senior SHAEF leaders had made it clear to Fred that they considered the FBI an absolutely essential part of the intelligence operations being planned during the subjugation and eventual Allied occupation of Nazi Germany. Fred had repeatedly emphasized the need for additional agents in successive messages to J. Edgar Hoover, beginning in November 1944, but it wasn't until April 1945 that his entreaties began to bear fruit.

On April 2, Fred wrote to the director regarding a series of meetings held between the existing members of the ALU and Gordon Sheen and Colonel

James Elder, the latter of the European Theater Provost Marshal's Office. The men thanked Fred and his team for the excellent work they'd been doing, both in dealing with American renegades and in undertaking a range of other tasks that supported SHAEF's intelligence, counterintelligence, and criminal-investigation operations. Sheen and Elder reiterated their desire—and that of both Brigadier General T. J. Betts, SHAEF's intelligence chief, and Eisenhower himself—to have FBI agents assigned to the U.S. Group within the Control Council for Germany. That organization would in effect be the Allies' initial military government in the newly vanquished Reich, and the Army intended the FBI agents to play a key role in it.[43]

Fred reported to Hoover that Betts would be sending a cable to the Bureau officially requesting that five additional agents and two male stenographers be assigned to the ALU. Three German-speaking agents—one of whom would be an expert in communist affairs—and one stenographer would join Bill Clark, Joe Dunn, and Dick Thompson in moving with American forces into Germany, while two French-speaking agents and the second stenographer would remain in Paris. Fred added that a follow-on request from SHAEF for a third French-speaking agent would likely reach Bureau headquarters within a week. The city of Wiesbaden, twenty miles west of Frankfurt and the capital of the German state of Hesse, had been designated as the headquarters of the American occupation zone, Fred reported. SHAEF's ultimate goal would be to have four FBI agents assigned there, with two others—including the expert on communist matters—to be assigned to the Control Council headquarters in Berlin following Germany's surrender. The other ALU members would operate from Paris. Moreover, Fred reminded Hoover, U.S. ambassador to France Jefferson Caffery had requested two agents to open and staff a legal attaché office in the embassy, though the matter was still pending.[44]

While Major General Clayton Bissell, the Army's overall intelligence chief, would have to grant permission for the requested additional agents to operate in the European theater under the G-2 umbrella, Fred said, the same wasn't true for two further agents that would be separately requested by SHAEF's Theater Provost Marshal, Major General Milton A. Reckord. He and Bissell had often butted heads on matters regarding the operations of their respective organizations, and Reckord made it quite clear that because he was not part of Bissell's Military Intelligence Division, he was not required to seek the latter's authorization or approval. Indeed, as Fred noted, Reckord was adamant that his request "should not be discussed with General Bissell in any way."[45]

SHAEF's request for additional agents did what Fred's repeated petitions had been unable to do. On April 17, the ALU chief was notified that the Bureau had received a memo from the War Department asking for the assignment in Europe of six additional agents and two male stenographers. The agents tapped for deployment to Europe were John Condon from the San Francisco field office, Erling Kloster and Bernard Rucks from New York, Roland L'Allier from Saint Paul, Boyd Sheets from Salt Lake City, and Howard Winter from New Orleans. The two stenographers were thirty-one-year-old Vincent Ascherl from Bureau headquarters in Washington and twenty-eight-year-old Robert Prather from the SIS office in Port-au-Prince, Haiti.[46] The six special agents had gone through the Army familiarization course, but the stenographers had not, because senior Bureau officials assumed they would work solely in an office environment. Information on the men's departure for Europe would be provided, Fred was told, as soon as details were finalized by Air Transport Command.

What had not yet been finalized at that point was the assignment of two Bureau agents to the Paris embassy. In an April 21 memo to Hoover, Assistant Director Daniel M. Ladd wrote that OSS chief William Donovan was holding up the dispatch of Horton Telford and Clement Rousseau, the two FBI agents tapped to open and staff the legat office.[47] Though the April 12 death of President Franklin Roosevelt had robbed Donovan of his most powerful ally in his ongoing turf war with the FBI, he had enough friends in the orbit of newly sworn-in President Harry Truman to delay the departure of the agents until Hoover agreed to put in writing exactly what the men would be doing in the French capital. Ladd pointed out in the memo that Donovan had already been told by the State Department that

> such an assignment would be for the purpose of securing information on various targets in France which would tie in with cases being investigated by the FBI in the United States; the securing of information on treason cases involving the radio broadcasters . . . and also as a liaison with other agencies in the French theater.[48]

Seeking to avoid another prolonged bureaucratic tug of war with the OSS director, Hoover authorized Ladd to send a letter to Donovan, through the State Department, reiterating the already stated purpose for having Telford and Rousseau at the embassy. That letter went out on April 26, and that same afternoon, the Bureau received a message forwarded by Bissell. The sender was

SHAEF commander Dwight Eisenhower, who asked for the soonest possible deployment by air of two French-speaking FBI agents, three German-speaking agents, one agent who was a specialist on communist matters, and two male stenographers. The supreme commander did not mention the embassy legat matter, since that was within Ambassador Caffery's purview.[49]

THE URGENT NEED FOR ADDITIONAL FBI AGENTS to support the occupation of Germany was underscored early on the morning of May 2, when Fred and Don were called to an emergency meeting at Gordon Sheen's office in Versailles. Almost as soon as they walked through the CI chief's door, he looked them each in the eye, smiled, and said simply, "Hitler's dead." The statement landed like a bomb, causing a few seconds of absolute silence before all three men simultaneously started laughing, whooping, and slapping each other on the back. When they'd all caught their breaths, Sheen explained that a British Broadcasting Corporation radio monitoring station near Reading, England, had picked up a Radio Berlin broadcast the previous evening. The German station had been playing solemn, funeral background music as an announcer somberly—if incorrectly—reported that the Führer had "fallen" the day before in a valiant, last-ditch fight against "Bolshevism."[50] Allied intelligence sources had verified that Hitler was dead, Sheen told the agents, though the exact circumstances of his passing were unclear.[51]

The three men agreed that Hitler's demise could only mean that Germany's surrender could happen at any moment. Soviet troops were already in Berlin, and American, British, and French forces held all of western Germany from the Baltics to northern Italy. There were still German holdouts, of course, and rumors were circulating that die-hard Nazis would retreat to an "alpine redoubt" somewhere in Bavaria or the Austrian Tyrol to continue the fight. But those fanciful tales of a mountain fortress that would be the cradle of a fourth German Reich were put eternally to rest when early on May 7 what was left of the Wehrmacht high command unconditionally surrendered all of its land, sea, and air forces to the Allies. Fred and Don were in Paris, and despite the fact that the surrender would not officially come into effect until May 9, Fred later wrote that

> as night approached, people began to pour from the buildings, from the offices, the cafes, the subways. They appeared to rise from the ground itself. All steps led to the Avenue of the Champs Élysées and

> then to its fountainhead, the Place de l'Étoile, where stands the Arc de Triomphe. Men, women and children converged on the place. Those who could not walk, those too young or too old, or too crippled by their wars, were carried. Some bore torches, others waved flags. Solid as the throng itself rose the roar of happy voices, far higher pitched and more carrying than the dull voice of anger and despair which had for too long been heard in the land.[52]

The two FBI agents were swept along by the crowds, their ears assaulted by the joyous shouts of the throng and the din of trumpets, drums, and likely even that signature sound of the City of Light, accordions. At one point, a B-17 Flying Fortress passed only a few hundred feet over the Arc and released a magnesium flare, a moment that Fred wrote "gave brightness of daylight to ten thousand joyous faces." The celebrations continued throughout the night, and on the morning of May 8—"Victory in Europe Day"—Fred and his companions took to the balcony of the avenue Mozart apartment to sing French and American anthems to the delight of crowds in the street below. Fred then delivered an oration in which he thanked the people of France for the "honor of having been able to participate in their brave fight for freedom." His impromptu speech was greeted with applause, he later said, like he had never received before or since. The next morning, when Fred went to a nearby kiosk to buy his morning paper, he was warmly greeted by the elderly World War I veteran who ran it. As Fred later remembered, "In one hand he carried a bottle, with the other he took a firm grip on my shoulder and, before I could stop him, he had kissed me on both cheeks. 'God bless you, *mon commandant,*' he said. 'By the words you spoke last night you have shown that you love and understand my country.' "[53]

While the German surrender marked the end of the greatest conflict Europe had ever endured, it by no means signaled an end to the work of the Army Liaison Unit. There were still American renegades and German war criminals to hunt down, and the beginning of a new—albeit cold—war for which to prepare. It would be a huge task and, fortunately, Fred Ayer and Don Daughters were about to receive reinforcements.

CHAPTER 10

New Blood, a Very Big Fish, and New Horizons

THE FIRST FEW MONTHS OF 1945 had been extremely busy ones for the members of the Paris-based Army Liaison Unit. In addition to wrapping up the cases involving Joseph Lincoln Luhan, Anthony Helfenstein, Max Stöcklin, the *Volksdeutschers*, Maurice Gagnon, Marvin Fritz, Florence Gould, and Ruth Dubonnet, the agents had also assisted in the Sigaba investigation. Moreover, in furtherance of the ALU's other assigned missions, by the end of March, Fred Ayer and his fellow agents had sent the Bureau some twenty reports concerning data uncovered in France pertaining to possible German espionage operations in the United States, and an additional dozen reports on communist subversive activities in the Free French forces and civil society.

One ALU report initially sent to Washington in late fall of 1944 had become increasingly relevant as Nazi Germany edged ever closer to defeat in the spring of 1945. The document concerned an interview Fred had conducted in October with Vicomtesse Gladys de Maublanc, a U.S. citizen and the sister of American cosmetics entrepreneur Elizabeth Arden. Arrested by the Gestapo in December 1943 for having helped downed Allied aviators evade capture by the Germans, de Maublanc had initially been incarcerated in Fresnes Prison, outside Paris. She was soon transferred to a special internee's compound at Ravensbrück, the women's concentration camp north of Berlin. In August 1944, she was moved again, this time to the internment camp at Vittel, from which she was liberated.

When Fred spoke with the woman following her return to Paris, she said that during her time in Ravensbrück, she had learned some potentially vital information. In conversation with other prisoners and with the camp's female SS guards, de Maublanc heard that a new course of instruction was being given at the large SS training facility located on the grounds of the sprawling camp. Trainees—both male and female—were being told of the attitude they should adopt toward advancing Allied forces. When the capitulation of local German units seemed imminent, the SS members were told to discard their uniforms and destroy any incriminating documents. The Allied troops were to be told by the now disguised SS members that they had always been opposed to the Nazi regime, they were ardent admirers of democracy, and they wanted to help in building a new, democratic Germany. As Fred wrote in his original report, the training at Ravensbrück demonstrated the "lengths to which the SS [is] apparently willing to go to preserve [itself] as a new underground in Germany."[1] A copy of the report was given to Gordon Sheen, and in March 1945, the SHAEF CI chief suggested that interrogating suspected "underground" SS members would be an ideal additional mission for the ALU, though Fred responded that such a task would require far more than the five agents that currently comprised the unit.

Fortunately, additional G-men were finally on the way.

IN RESPONSE TO THE WELCOME NEWS that additional agents would be coming to Europe, on May 8, Fred Ayer sent Hoover a message outlining a proposal for the unit's future organization and operations. In accordance with the wishes of both the Bureau and the Army, Fred wrote, the majority of the ALU's members should be moved forward into Germany with SHAEF. The command's CI Branch would be headquartered in Frankfurt, rather than Wiesbaden, as originally planned, and the ALU would share office space with Gordon Sheen's organization and the SHAEF CIC detachment. Fred noted that "the majority of operations of interest to the Bureau from now on, both from a counterintelligence point of view and with respect to the activities of traitors" would be centered in Germany.[2]

Fred added that as both the head of the ALU and a member of SHAEF's Counterintelligence Committee for Germany, he and one of the clerk-stenographers would—with the Bureau's permission—move to Frankfurt with all of the German-speaking agents (except Dick Thompson, who would remain with Twelfth USAG) and lead the ALU's activities in the former Reich. Should his proposal be accepted, Fred wrote, he would move the ALU's "German files"—those dealing with American renegades in Germany and Austria and key Nazi intelligence personalities—from Paris to Frankfurt. Fred pointed out that when SHAEF "dissolved" and became part of what would officially be designated the U.S. Group Control Council

(USGCC), that organization's counterintelligence efforts would be led by the same people who had comprised the U.S. element of SHAEF G-2's CI section—namely Gordon Sheen and his staff.

In closing, Fred said that since Germany would be the focus of the ALU's activities,

> it seems reasonable to me that I should conduct the center of our operations [there] with Paris acting more in a subsidiary capacity. I believe the job in Paris will become more and more one of liaison with the Embassy and the French police agencies, and a base for long-range political coverage. (Daughters has shown himself particularly adept in these matters, and it is my feeling that he would be the logical man to carry on with this work while my work would . . . be . . . directing the investigations in Germany and working closely with the officers with whom I have worked in the past.)[3]

When Fred did not receive a quick answer to his message, he assumed, rightly as it happened, that Hoover was coordinating with Bissell and other Army leaders in Washington before responding.

But other issues of concern to the ALU were moving forward. On May 15, a week after VE Day, Assistant Director Ladd sent a memo to his fellow assistant director, Edward A. Tamm, that OSS chief Donovan had belatedly agreed to the dispatch of Telford and Rousseau to Paris, though he told Ladd the Bureau "should stick to [its] own chores and not infringe" on what Donovan saw as the prerogatives of the OSS in Europe.[4]

On that same day, the six agents and both stenographers were in D.C., undergoing predeployment briefings. All eight men were given the necessary inoculations and provided with appropriate military apparel, travel orders, and identity cards issued by the Army's Adjutant General's Office (referred to, logically enough, as AGO cards). The front of each individual's card bore the man's photo, the date of issuance, and the job description "Administrative Assistant." On the reverse were his birth date, height, weight, eye and hair color, and images of his index fingers.

Suitably clothed and credentialed, five of the Bureau personnel—L'Allier, Kloster, Rucks, Sheets, and Ascherl—departed for France aboard an ATC flight on the morning of May 23. The three others—Condon, Winter, and Prather—flew out the following day. Finally, after months of pleading with Hoover for more men, Fred Ayer and Don Daughters were on the verge of having the resources they needed to conduct their own "two-front war" against America's enemies, both domestic and foreign, in liberated Europe and defeated Nazi Germany.

THAT ADDITIONAL MEN WERE ON THE WAY FROM THE STATES was indeed good news for Fred Ayer, because on May 17, the Paris ALU office had temporarily lost one of its four agents.

Early that morning, Fred received a phone call from Gordon Sheen announcing that Reichsmarschall Hermann Göring—who on May 7 had been captured in Austria by elements of the U.S. 36th Infantry Division—would be made available for questioning at the newly opened Seventh Army Interrogation Center (SAIC) in Augsburg. Because he had also been head of the Luftwaffe, Göring had been interviewed at length on May 10 by General Carl Spaatz, commander of U.S. Strategic Air Forces in Europe (USSTAF), Lieutenant General Hoyt Vandenberg, head of the U.S. Ninth Air Force, and members of their respective staffs.[5] Several American and Allied intelligence and counterintelligence organizations were now sending agents to take part in what would be several days of more expansive questioning of the portly Luftwaffe commander, Sheen said, and he asked if the FBI would like to participate. Fred's answer was a resounding yes, because as Hitler's longtime right-hand man, Göring would likely be able to provide important information on German espionage activities in the Western Hemisphere.

Tapped to undertake the trip, Joe Dunn managed to get to Le Bourget in time to grab a seat on the C-47 transport carrying interrogators to Augsburg. He and representatives of several other agencies—including Army intelligence, CIC, OSS's X-2, and MI6—were in a large room with the former *Reichsmarschall* by early afternoon. As Major Paul Kubala, the SAIC commander, noted after that first meeting:

> [Göring] is by no means the comical figure he has been depicted [as] so many times in newspaper reports. He is neither stupid nor a fool . . . but generally cool and calculating. He is able to grasp the fundamental issues under discussion immediately. He is certainly not a man to be underrated. Although he tried to soft-pedal many of the most outrageous crimes committed by Germany, he said enough to show that he is as much responsible for the policies within Germany and for the war itself, as anyone in Germany. . . .

> Goering [sic] is at all times an actor who does not disappoint his audience. His vanity extends into the field of the pathological, as is exemplified by the pearl-grey uniform, the heavy, solid gold epaulettes and an enormous diamond ring on his left hand, even though his medals were limited to two, including the Grand Cross of the Knight's Cross with Swords and Diamonds.[6]

The day following that first group interview with Göring, Joe Dunn was able to speak with the former *Reichsmarschall*, with Kubala as the only other person in the room. Over the course of several hours, Dunn questioned the prisoner about his knowledge of German espionage and sabotage operations in the Western Hemisphere, and about the current locations of former intelligence officers who might also be able to provide details of those activities.

As to the first topic, Dunn reported that Göring believed every Nazi espionage agent of any importance who went to the Western Hemisphere was detected by the FBI or by the police forces of the various Latin American countries—which were aided, Dunn pointed out in his report, by the FBI's SIS.[7] Regarding former German intelligence officers who might have pertinent knowledge of operations in North America, Göring mentioned Dr. Walter Schellenberg, the last chief of the Third Reich's foreign intelligence operations and a man of whom the Bureau was already well aware. The former *Reichsmarschall* then added two additional names that were new to Dunn—a Luftwaffe major named Friedrich Busch, and Wilhelm Ahlrichs, a *Kapitänleutnant* (lieutenant commander) who had apparently undertaken special operations for the Kriegsmarine. Göring said he didn't know the whereabouts of any of the men, and Dunn made a note to check whether the names were already on the SHAEF target list.

When, near the end of the interrogation, Göring was asked what he believed had been Germany's best sources of information from within the United States, he replied it was American newspapers, magazines, and radio programs. Göring stated that the greatest security mistake the United States had made during the war was allowing the publication or broadcast of vast amounts of information that, for the most part, had been only slightly restricted. Dunn's response to that and many of the prisoner's other statements weren't recorded, but his overall manner and his interrogation skills must have impressed Göring—at the end of the questioning the former *Reichsmarschall* removed his gold-braid rank epaulettes and presented them to the FBI agent.[8]

His questioning of Göring completed, Dunn stayed in Augsburg for a few days to gather documents before returning to Paris to brief Fred Ayer and write a report for Hoover. Göring, for his part, was transferred to "Camp Ashcan," a former luxury hotel in Mondorf-les-Bains, Luxembourg, that had been converted into a very-high-security holding facility for senior Nazis. The camp's commander, Colonel Burton C. Andrus, asked Fred Ayer to send samples of the dihydrocodeine tablets to which Göring was obviously addicted to the FBI Laboratory in Washington for analysis. Andrus, who went on to command the prison in which the German defendants were held during the Nuremberg Trials, later thanked the men of the ALU for "the clear and specific data" provided by the FBI lab, which he said had been "of immense value . . . in supervising the care and treatment of the individual addict."[9]

That addict was, of course, eventually tried at Nuremburg, found guilty, and sentenced to death. On October 14, 1946, the night before his scheduled hanging, Göring used a smuggled cyanide capsule to kill himself.

All six of the additional FBI agents and the two clerk-stenographers destined for the ALU were in Paris by May 27. They were not immediately able to begin work, however, for they first had to undergo the frustratingly bureaucratic procedure America's military services traditionally refer to—blandly and more than a little disingenuously—as "in-processing."

For the newly arrived Bureau men, the ordeal began calmly enough. They gathered at the Hôtel Trianon to meet with Gordon Sheen's executive officer, Major Thomas Nichol. He provided them with a SHAEF memorandum authorizing the use of military billets—likely a welcome development since all of the newcomers had spent their first nights in the French capital crammed into the avenue Mozart apartment with Fred Ayer, Don Daughters, Bill Clark, and Joe Dunn (Dick Thompson had already moved into Germany, attached to Twelfth USAG). Nichol's memo itself didn't get them places to stay—they had to present the document to the SHAEF billeting office in central Paris to actually secure rooms in one of the several hotels requisitioned for officer use.

Before they could check in with billeting, however, they first had to visit the office in the Hôtel Trianon annex belonging to the SHAEF personnel officer. After examining the men's AGO cards, the man issued them an additional form of identification, this one officially referred to as a Certificate of Identity of Non-Combatant but widely known as a "simulated rank" card (and often sarcastically as a "don't shoot me I'm not a spy" card). Almost identical to the AGO card, the document bore the man's photo, personal data, and military rank. The purpose of the card was to identify the bearer as a member of the Allied forces and ensure that in the event of capture by the enemy, the individual would be treated as a prisoner of war and afforded the privileges of an officer in the U.S. Army.[10] Why such a card was necessary now that hostilities had ended was never made clear to the bemused Bureau men.

There were additional necessary documents to come over the next few days. An Army Exchange ration card allowed the bearer to purchase cigarettes, sweets, fruit juices, and toiletries from the SHAEF post exchange in Versailles. A second Army Exchange card permitted the purchase of uniform items from the SHAEF officers clothing store, colocated with the post exchange. A third card granted the bearer access to any officers' club within the European Theater, though small print on the reverse stated that "any gambling debts incurred in such facilities are the bearer's sole responsibility." Only once the newly arrived Bureau men were in possession of all necessary SHAEF documents were they permitted to obtain the currency that was the recognized medium of exchange in all Allied military facilities in France—the franc. Upon the presentation of travelers' checks issued in Washington, the men were provided the French currency at an exchange rate of 50 francs to the U.S. dollar.[11]

The newly arrived agents had barely completed their in-processing when, on June 1, Hoover finally responded to Fred's May 8 message. In typically terse cable prose, the director's reply read:

> Bureau authority granted your removal to Germany with pertinent section of files. You will be in charge in Germany. Daughters to remain in charge in Paris for present. Advise date of departure of you and others and that additional communications arrangements are necessary.[12]

Having assumed that he would eventually receive official permission to split the ALU into two sections, Fred had been preparing for weeks for the move into Germany. He nonetheless felt as though he and his agents were playing catch-up, since many of SHAEF's staff sections had actually left Versailles in late February and established an interim headquarters in Reims, the French champagne center, ninety-three miles northeast of Paris. The command's G-2 office, including Gordon Sheen's counterintelligence group, had traveled directly to Frankfurt on May 26. Fred was eager to catch up, and after an all-day ALU staff meeting and farewell dinner, he and the German-speaking agents—Condon, Clark, Dunn, Kloster, O'Connor, Rucks, and Sheets—and stenographer Vince Ascherl (who also spoke passable German) departed for Frankfurt before dawn on June 5. Later that day, the three men remaining with Don Daughters in Paris—L'Allier, Winter, and Prather—all moved into the avenue Mozart apartment/office.

Traveling in a mini convoy consisting of a staff car and a deuce-and-a-half truck, the ALU men bound for Frankfurt made the 370-mile journey in two legs. The first day's travel took them to Strasbourg, in Alsace, where after an evening meal of C-rations, they all spent the night of June 6 in a single Model 1942 squad tent they'd carried with them from Paris.[13] The next morning, the group crossed the border into Germany and turned north, paralleling the east bank of the Rhine river as far as Karlsruhe. From there it was on to Mannheim, Darmstadt, and late in the afternoon, Frankfurt.

While the route of the ALU convoy had taken the men through some heavily damaged areas, they were not prepared for the devastation they found in Frankfurt. The major city of the German state of Hesse, Frankfurt had been relentlessly bombed by the American and British air forces beginning in 1941. The widespread damage caused by the Allied air raids was exacerbated by the three-day battle fought in late March 1945 between the city's defenders and General George Patton's Third Army. As Fred later described it, "The city itself was almost entirely flat. Over a stretch of at least a mile there was nothing left standing higher than a man's shoulder."[14] Fortunately, the administration building and housing area belonging to the IG Farben chemical cartel—one of whose companies had produced the Zyklon B gas used to murder millions during the Holocaust—were, as Fred wrote, "by some miracle, or else by precision missing on the part of our bombers . . . still standing and almost wholly intact. This complex was ideal for office space and billets, albeit we surrounded it with a barbed wire fence and forbade any fraternization with the Germans."[15]

The ALU team was able to quickly secure work areas and well-appointed sleeping quarters within the massive IG Farben headquarters building—a structure with some thousand rooms and ten thousand windows. Fred ended up sharing a two-bedroom apartment in what had been the complex's executive wing with two SHAEF friends, U.S. Navy Commander Dick Preston of the G-2 section and Army Colonel Ted Osborne of the Plans and Operations staff. Not only had the three men worked together in Paris, they were all originally from Topsfield, Massachusetts, and had known each other since childhood. They were fortunate in their choice of lodging, for their apartment was the closest to the wing's oil-fired heating system. This guaranteed the trio both abundant hot water and, as Fred later wrote, "an apparent popularity, less because of [our] great native charm than because officers senior to us had to remain in our good graces in order to enjoy the luxury of a hot bath."[16]

Less than a week after their arrival in Frankfurt, the ALU agents had their first "customers." The CIC section in the IG Farben building notified Fred that two suspected American renegades had been apprehended and were being held in a facility in Höchst, six miles west of central Frankfurt. Karl Scherzberg and Gertrude Hahn were not considered to be major figures in the Nazis' radio propaganda effort, but they would be the first U.S. citizens to be interrogated by the ALU in Germany proper. Fred assigned Erling Kloster to the task, and the agent spoke individually with each suspect on June 12 and 13.

Karl Herman Scherzberg Jr.

Born in Philadelphia, in 1921, to German immigrant parents Karl Sr. and Greta, Scherzberg grew up bilingual in English and German. His father had become wealthy in real estate, and was able to take his family on extended trips to Germany in 1913, 1932, 1936, and 1939. The purpose of the final visit was to enroll both his sons—Karl, eighteen, and Edmund, sixteen—in German vocational schools. Once the boys were settled, the parents returned to the United States.[17]

Karl Scherzberg Sr. had long been a member of German cultural societies in Pennsylvania and from 1932 onward was a vocal supporter of Hitler. During the family's summer 1939 visit to Germany, the elder Scherzberg spoke approvingly of the Nazis on a radio program broadcast from Berlin by the Reichs-Rundfunk-Gesellschaft (RRG), Nazi Germany's radio and television broadcast corporation.[18] Back in Philadelphia, he became so outspoken in his support for Hitler that, in 1940, the State Department refused to renew his passport for travel to Germany. His sons were still in Berlin when America entered the war in December 1941. As American nationals, they were briefly interned, but were soon released to the custody of German relatives.

In February 1944, Karl Jr. was summoned to the RRG's antenna complex in Königs Wusterhausen, eighteen miles southeast of Berlin, to which most broadcasting operations had been moved to escape Allied bombing of the capital. There the twenty-three-year-old was interviewed and given a voice test by Max Otto Koischwitz, one of the eight American broadcasters indicted for treason in 1943 and head of the North America Zone—that part of the network that concentrated on broadcasting in English to audiences in the United States and Canada. Scherzberg voiced news broadcasts on the RRG's overnight service until July 1944, when he left the organization.[19] In order to evade advancing Soviet forces, he and his brother Edmund moved steadily west, and when the war ended in May 1945, they were living in the vicinity of Kassel. There the brothers sought to register with U.S. forces as displaced persons, but Karl Scherzberg was arrested by CIC agents when his name showed up on a SHAEF watch list.

The young man that Erling Kloster met with in Höchst was more than ready to be as helpful and forthcoming as possible. He had been unaware that he was the subject of a treason investigation and told Koster that he had only gone to work for the RRG out of fear that he and Edmund would be sent to a concentration camp if he refused. He had only read the news, Scherzberg said, and had never done any political commentary or anti-American propaganda. Questioned about each of the forty-seven renegade broadcasters on the FBI's list, the young man said he had only worked directly with Koischwitz, whom he readily identified in a photo Kloster showed him. As Fred Ayer noted in the message he sent Hoover conveying Kloster's report, Scherzberg's knowledge of the operations and personnel involved in RRG broadcasts "was quite limited, because of the briefness of his employment as a news reader and because of the fact that he worked only during night hours at the Königs Wusterhausen studios."[20]

Scherzberg's very minor role in the overall Nazi radio propaganda effort, coupled with both his willingness to cooperate and the fact that witnesses to his acts would likely not be located, prompted the Department of Justice to decline to indict him. He was set free in the autumn of 1945, and both he and his brother had returned to the United States by 1947. Karl Scherzberg spent the rest of his life in Pennsylvania and died in 2010 at the age of eighty-nine.

Gertrude Hahn

While the case of the other alleged American renegade that Erling Kloster interrogated in Höchst was similar in some ways to that of Karl Scherzberg, there were also significant differences.

Born in Zweibrücken, Germany, in 1922, Gertrude Hahn immigrated to the United States with her parents the following year and gained U.S. citizenship through their naturalization.[21] Like Scherzberg, she was raised in Pennsylvania, though in Pittsburgh rather than Philadelphia, and also grew up fluent in English and German. An intelligent and popular student at Prospect Junior High and South Hills Senior High schools, Hahn eventually took art and clothing design classes at Carnegie Tech. In 1938, her father, an engineer, decided to take the family back to Germany where he believed he could get better jobs.[22]

Once in Germany, Hahn attended school for a time, but then secured a clerical job at the U.S. consulate in Frankfurt. She held that position until late 1939 or early 1940, when she was recruited by the RRG's North America Zone. After America entered the war in 1941, she was not interned. Unlike Scherzberg, she apparently took an active part in voicing propaganda programs, initially using the on-air name "Gertrude Williams." She would do a comical impersonation of "Gertie the Telephone Operator" who worked for the fictitious *Pittsburgh Tribune*, using the skit to spread the Nazi line. During Operation Torch—the Allied invasion of North Africa in November 1942—Hahn directed her programs at American GIs in that theater, taunting them that their wives or girlfriends back home were being unfaithful. The soldiers referred to her as "Gertie from Berlin," and famed war correspondent Ernie Pyle wrote that American soldiers thought her act was "pure ham" but were undecided whether to "kick her or kiss her" when they eventually got to Berlin.[23]

Over time, Hahn revealed snippets of her Pittsburgh background, and often ended her programs by saying "Goodnight, Madeline" or "Goodnight, Joyce"—high school friends who heard her and later identified her voice to the FBI.[24] By December 1942, the Bureau knew enough about Hahn to add her name to a list of American renegade radio broadcasters sent to Assistant Attorney General Wendell Berge. She also appeared on a March 3, 1943, internal FBI document that listed individuals who were to be investigated when agents were eventually dispatched to Europe.[25]

The publicity about Hahn in the United States and the revelation of her real name and Pittsburgh background apparently caused her to panic, for by February 1943, she had stopped doing her regular program. She did several special broadcasts from Cologne, where, according to Radio Berlin, she had volunteered for "war work." During her final broadcast, she announced that she had gotten married. After that program, Hahn disappeared until her arrest, in June 1945, by CIC agents, who located her not far from her birthplace in Zweibrücken.

By the time Hahn sat down across a table from Erling Kloster in Höchst, her legal status was unclear. In May 1945, in response to queries about her by American journalists, the War Department had unilaterally announced that her case would be handled by the United Nations Commission for the Investigation of War Crimes, and Hahn would likely be tried in Europe by an Allied military tribunal. The War Department had apparently not checked with the Department of Justice before releasing that statement, however, for DOJ continued to carry Hahn on its list of Americans potentially to be charged with treason and tried in the United States. When Kloster told the young woman that she could well spend the rest of her life in a U.S. prison, she broke down completely. She swore she had never spoken on the air after December 7, 1941, and said that any programs featuring "Gertie from Berlin" after that date—especially during the Allied campaign in North Africa—were voiced by someone else.[26]

Like Scherzberg, Hahn was eager to tell Kloster everything she knew about other American broadcasters who had worked for the Germans. Her cooperation, her apparently sincere regret for speaking on Radio Berlin before Pearl Harbor, her repeated protestations that the treason allegations against her were the result of "mistaken identity," and the unlikely possibility of locating eyewitnesses to her broadcasts convinced Kloster to recommend that she not be charged. As happened with Scherzberg, the DOJ concurred and Hahn was ultimately released from custody. She and her German husband traveled to the United States in 1947 and settled initially in New York. They eventually moved to Ohio, where "Gertie from Pittsburgh" died in 1977 at the age of fifty-five.

Just days after Erling Kloster completed his interrogations of Scherzberg and Hahn, Gordon Sheen told Fred Ayer that everyone in the SHAEF G-2 counterintelligence section had been directed to move from the IG Farben building to the CIC facility in Höchst. That compound had been selected as the assembly area for the various Army units that would form the nucleus of the USGCC. Since Fred and at least some of his agents would be assigned to that organization when it moved to Berlin, Sheen said he would like the ALU men to move to Höchst along with the CI section. Fred readily agreed, though it meant leaving the relative comfort of the IG Farben building. On June 19, the FBI men packed their gear, loaded their file cabinets into the back of a truck, and made the short drive to their new home. That turned out to be a relatively large and undamaged house that had been requisitioned by the Army. The wife of the former owner—an IG

Farben executive already in American custody for suspected war crimes—was required to serve as the agents' cook and housekeeper.

The ALU men had barely settled into their new home when Fred was notified that three more American renegades were available for interrogation: Herbert Burgman was at the CIC holding facility in Weisbaden, 20 miles to the west; Douglas Chandler was at the Seventh Army Interrogation Center in Augsburg, 160 miles to the southeast; and Edward Delaney was in the high-security Third Army Interrogation Center in Freising, 38 miles east of Augsburg. Fred immediately dispatched Walt Rucks and the recently returned Dick Thompson to Wiesbaden, Joe Dunn back to Augsburg, and Boyd Sheets to Freising.

Herbert John Burgman

Beginning the third week of March 1942, radio listeners across the central and eastern parts of the United States began hearing evening broadcasts from a station calling itself "Radio Debunk." It purported to be broadcasting from somewhere within America and said its purpose was to "wage a gallant struggle against the war-mongers of Washington."[27] Dozens of citizens wrote to the FBI to report the pro-German nature of the programs, prompting the Bureau to request transcripts from the Federal Communications Commission's Foreign Broadcast Monitoring Service (FBMS). As one publication noted, the Radio Debunk programs were quickly found to be "anti-British, anti-American, anti-communist, anti-Jewish, in fact, anti-everything except National Socialism."[28] The FBMS also determined that the broadcasts did not originate in North America but rather from a transmission site somewhere near Berlin.

The FBI was particularly interested in determining the identity of Radio Debunk's host, a man calling himself "Joe Scanlon" who had an upper Midwest U.S. accent and an easy familiarity with current American slang, entertainment figures, and sports teams. The name was obviously fictitious, since it did not appear in files held by the FBI or other federal and state agencies. However, "Scanlon" inadvertently provided certain clues to his identity during the course of his broadcasts. One was his characteristic accent, which several linguistic experts agreed was likely from Minnesota. Another was the man's repeated references to having served with the American Expeditionary Forces during World War I. "Scanlon" also mentioned that he had spent time in Germany immediately after the war, an indication that he might have been a member of the U.S. occupation forces.

The FBI's already keen interest in "Scanlon" and Radio Debunk was further heightened in mid-May 1942, when people across the Eastern Seaboard began receiving postcards promoting the station's broadcasts. Obviously mimeographed except for the recipient's typed-in address, the cards all had New York City postmarks and bore the same message:

> Want the Real Dope on the war news? Tune in every night American Station 7.2 Megacycles, Shortwave, 8:30 P.M. Eastern War Time.
>
> The Station's call letters are D-E-B-U-N-K.
>
> GET THE LOWDOWN ON WHAT'S GOING ON BEHIND THE SCENES! YOU CAN'T BE A WELL INFORMED AMERICAN UNLESS YOU HAVE THESE VITAL FACTS. IF YOU HAVE NO SHORTWAVE, ASK YOUR FRIEND TO LET YOU LISTEN IN ON HIS. YOU'LL BOTH PROFIT! DON'T MISS IT![29]

Four months later, the Bureau itself became the target of an on-air attack by "Scanlon."

> Do you know that the FBI . . . has already become the most powerful tool of FDR's Jewish brain trust? . . . That every job in the FBI paying 75 bucks a week, or more, is already in Jewish hands? That an American-Jew controlled and Jew-manned Gestapo is already a reality? It's no fairy tale. Yet it's enough to frighten more than just children.[30]

Despite the Bureau's best efforts, the real identity of "Joe Scanlon" remained a mystery until November 1944. While being interrogated in Paris by Don Daughters and Fred Ayer, the renegade Joseph Lincoln Luhan mentioned the names of twenty-one other Americans with whom he'd worked or whom he'd heard about. One of the names was "Brugman," [sic] an individual Luhan remembered as being a World War I veteran from somewhere in the upper Midwest. The name was on the list of suspected renegades that Fred provided to the Bureau on December 5, 1944, and though no first name was given, it was enough for agents in the United States to determine that "Joe Scanlon" was actually Herbert John Burgman.

Born to German immigrants in Hokah, Minnesota, in 1894, the suspect worked as a junior clerk at the State Department in Washington, D.C., before joining the U.S. Army in 1918.[31] He deployed to Europe that April as a warrant officer in the same unit as John E. Loskot, who himself would become a suspected American renegade in World War II (see chapter 8). In early 1919, Burgman joined the U.S. occupation forces in Germany. Following his discharge in August 1920, he remained in the defeated nation, and, based on his prewar Civil Service status, became a clerk and translator at the U.S. Military Mission in Berlin. He married a German woman and had a child, and after earning an advanced degree in economics at the University of Berlin, became a senior counselor at the U.S. embassy. Burgman only returned to the United States once during his residence in Germany, making a brief trip to Washington in 1937, accompanied by his wife and son.

One focus of Burgman's early work at the Berlin embassy was the economic policies of the nascent Nazi movement. Over time, he became a fervent admirer of Hitler, though he apparently kept his political beliefs—and his increasingly virulent anti-Semitism—largely to himself so as not to jeopardize his job. When America entered the war in December 1941, all embassy employees and their family members who had not already left Germany were ordered to report to Berlin's Potsdamer station to board a special train bound for Bad Nauheim. There the Americans were to be held in a requisitioned resort hotel until they could be exchanged for German diplomats interned in the United States. Burgman and his family did not show up at the station, having chosen to remain in Germany. Barely three months later, the future "Joe Scanlon" was already a paid staff member of the RRG's North America Zone.

By March 1945, many of the RRG's employees had been evacuated to Helmstedt, some hundred miles west of Berlin, in order to prevent their capture by the Soviets. Burgman was living in the town with his wife and son when, on May 14, members of the Army's 83rd CIC Detachment appeared at the family's small apartment. The American renegade was taken into custody based on the most recent SHAEF target list and was transported to the Ninth Army internment camp in Recklinghausen, northwest of Dortmund. The area was scheduled to become part of the British occupation zone, so within weeks of his arrest, Burgman was transferred to the CIC holding facility in Wiesbaden.[32]

During their first interrogation of the suspect, Rucks and Thompson found him to be extremely nervous and unfocused, and the agents thought he could be mentally ill. Concerned that any information they might be able to get from Burgman would later be thrown out of court were he to be found insane, the two agents took him to the Wiesbaden dispensary. There the suspect was examined by a U.S. Army doctor, who determined that the man was in a "mild depressive state" but was not mentally deficient and "could be considered responsible for his actions."

Over the next few days, Burgman calmed down and became quite talkative. He spoke in detail about the organization of the RRG's North America Zone and the personalities and actions of the other American broadcasters with whom he'd worked there—including Max Koischwitz, Robert Best, Fred Kaltenbach, Douglas Chandler, and Mildred Gillars. Burgman also gave a complete history of Radio Debunk and the key role he played in both developing its programs and presenting them as "Joe Scanlon." While he could shed no light on who had sent the postcards to random American listeners, he seemed to imply that the effort might have been undertaken by Abwehr agents operating in the United States.

Rucks and Thompson were justifiably proud of the breadth and depth of the information they'd been able to coax out of Burgman. The comprehensive report they presented to Fred Ayer upon their return to Frankfurt filled in a lot of blanks regarding the various American renegade broadcasters, especially those who had been indicted in 1943 (except for Ezra Pound, whom Burgman had never met). Moreover, "Joe Scanlon" had so incriminated himself as a willing spokesman for the Nazis that a treason conviction seemed a foregone conclusion.

It must therefore have infuriated Rucks, Thompson, and their ALU colleagues when, in December 1946, Burgman—after spending nineteen months in an Army stockade in Frankfurt—was released on orders of the Department of Justice owing to "a lack of sufficient evidence." He moved in with his wife and son in a Frankfurt suburb and actually took a job as an interpreter for a U.S. Army military police unit. His freedom was relatively short-lived, however, for in November 1948, he was rearrested. Flown back to the United States, he was indicted by a federal grand jury in Washington, D.C., on sixty-nine treason counts, thereby becoming the twenty-fifth American so charged for acts committed during World War II. In December 1949, Burgman was convicted on thirteen counts and sentenced to six to twenty years in federal prison. On December 16, 1953, he died of acute pulmonary edema at the Medical Center for Federal Prisoners in Springfield, Missouri, at the age of fifty-nine.

Douglas Arnold Chandler

On May 13, 1945, a U.S. Army sedan pulled up in front of a modest house in the small town of Durach, twelve miles north of the Austrian border, in the Oberallgäu district of Bavaria. The three members of the 206th CIC Detachment who emerged from the vehicle started toward the front door of the home, only to have it open before they'd had a chance to knock. A tall, slender, silver-haired man smiled politely at the trio and said, "I've been expecting you." The individual was U.S. expatriate and suspected traitor Douglas Chandler, but to the thousands of Americans who throughout the war heard his hatred-filled, treasonous broadcasts from Berlin, he was "Paul Revere."

Born in Chicago in 1899, Chandler was raised in Boston and Baltimore.[33] His father was both an academic who taught in exclusive private schools and a would-be entrepreneur whose business ventures generally ended in failure. Young Douglas attended a private boys' high school in Boston and, upon graduation, became a fledgling stockbroker in New York. He enjoyed no more success in financial affairs than his father had, and in July 1917—with America edging closer to full-scale participation in World War I—the twenty-eight-year-old Chandler enlisted in the Navy. He never left the United States, serving as a yeoman aboard the battleship/training vessel USS *Missouri* and at shore stations in Virginia.[34] His wide-ranging intellect and apparent disdain for anyone less well educated than himself made him understandably unpopular with his shipmates, who tended to ridicule his arrogance and affected aristocratic accent. Discharged from active duty in November 1918, he spent five months assigned to the Naval Reserve Force until released from service in April 1919.[35]

Chandler returned to New York, though he was no more successful as a stockbroker than he had been before the war. He began writing freelance newspaper and magazine articles to supplement his income, but it was not until his marriage in 1924 that his precarious financial situation changed decidedly for the better. His bride, Laura Jay Wurts, was the well-to-do and socially prominent great-granddaughter of John Jay, the first chief justice of the United States. Her father, Alexander Wurts, was a brilliant engineer and inventor who had become wealthy in his own right. Chandler saw it as his husbandly right to control his wife's money and quickly managed to significantly reduce their now mutual bank accounts through a series of spectacularly unsuccessful investments. The 1929 stock market crash further reduced the couple's wealth, and that year, Chandler moved his family—which by then included two young daughters—from New York to Maryland so that he could take a job as an assistant editor at *The Baltimore Sunday American*. That position was not quite as lucrative as the budding journalist had hoped it would be, and in 1931, Chandler uprooted his wife and children yet again, this time for Europe, where he believed what remained of their fortune would last longer.

Over the next several years, the Chandlers crisscrossed the Continent. First settling in France, they eventually lived or traveled for varying amounts of time in the Balkans, Greece, Austria, and Germany, with side trips as far afield as North Africa. Chandler was able to secure freelance writing and photography assignments from *National Geographic* and other American outlets, and by the time the family settled in the central German city of Göttingen in 1937, the failed New York stockbroker had morphed into something of an "international journalist." Joseph Goebbels's Propaganda Ministry had been courting Chandler since his first visit to Germany, giving him VIP access to Nazi Party rallies, senior leaders, and such "model penitentiaries" as Dachau. The fawning attention played into Chandler's inherent narcissism while also stoking his already pronounced anti-Semitism, his belief in the "inherent superiority" of the white race, and his growing fear of communism.

When World War II broke out in September 1939, the Chandlers were living on the island of Korcula, in the Adriatic Sea, off Yugoslavia's Dalmatian coast.[36] Forced to leave by what Chandler later claimed was "Jewish pressure," the family traveled to Florence. Long a strident opponent of what he saw as President Franklin Roosevelt's "socialist" policies and determination to "drag America into war," Chandler offered to serve as a radio commentator for Mussolini's Fascist government. When Rome rejected his services, he contacted friends in the Propaganda Ministry in Berlin, and by March 1941, Chandler and his family were settled into a house at Gustloffstrasse 45 in the German capital's Charlottenburg district, and he was on the staff of the RRG's North America Zone. His first broadcast, made on April 25, opened to the strains of "Yankee Doodle," the sounds of galloping hooves, and the announcement that "Paul Revere" was on the air.

Though laced with racist, anti-Semitic, and anti-Roosevelt bile, Chandler's first six months as an RRG propaganda broadcaster did not violate American law. It was only after returning to the air in January 1942, after a four-month break to renegotiate the financial terms of his contract, that he stepped firmly into traitorous territory. America had entered the war, and in his six weekly broadcasts—every evening but Saturday—Chandler was now consciously working to "provide aid and comfort" to his country's enemies. As one observer wrote, following Pearl Harbor, Chandler began

> pursuing his Nazi themes with increasing bitterness and incoherence. A typical venomous extract: "And for the winning of the war and the building of the new order, there is one outstanding figure, the genius of the 20th century, to thank. That is Adolf Hitler. . . . An alien mob dominated by Jewish-Masonic interests has taken a stranglehold on [America's] destiny. An imported alien mob, supported by your false leader, Franklin Delano Roosevelt.[37]

In the words of Dr. Albert A. Brandt, an exiled anti-Nazi German who knew Chandler, the broadcaster was "the most obnoxious American rogue in Naziland. Utterly insincere and mercenary, he broadcasts the lies of his masters back to his native country. He may be rated, weighing motive and not effectiveness, as America's traitor No. 1."[38]

While Chandler may have been one of Berlin's more effective American propagandists, as time passed, he undoubtedly also became one of its most eccentric. His affected blue-blood American accent increasingly veered toward British aristocratic, he raced around the Nazi capital in a maroon 1939 Mercedes Benz W153 cabriolet with American flags painted on its doors, and he routinely insulted and belittled his fellow American broadcasters—especially Edward Delaney—in front of other staffers. Chandler's behavior only worsened following his wife's death from tuberculosis in Berlin's Charité hospital on July 26, 1942. He took to drinking excessively before going on the air, and his outbursts against his colleagues, both German and American, became even more frequent and abusive. He openly contemplated suicide, asking coworkers which method they believed would be less painful—poison or gunshot.[39]

Chandler's downward spiral might have proven fatal, both professionally and literally, had it not been for a German coworker named Maria Moorgat. A radio script supervisor half Chandler's age, she gave the American a reason to live, and the two were married in December 1942. A few months later, increased Allied bombing raids on Berlin prompted the RRG to move most of its radio broadcasting operations to Königs Wusterhausen. Chandler, his two daughters, and his new wife moved to the new location, but in mid-1943, the American was transferred to Vienna. The family settled in the Austrian capital, with Chandler recording his programs at the local RRG studio for later transmission. In August, the now fifty-four-year-old Chandler and his twenty-eight-year-old wife welcomed their first child, a daughter.

By October 1944, the steady westward advance of Soviet troops prompted yet another relocation for Chandler and his family. Their new home was in

Durach, from where the American would make weekly sixty-five-mile rail forays to Munich to record his program at the RRG studios in the Bavarian capital. The Chandlers welcomed another daughter in March 1945. By that point, it was clear to the American renegade that the war was all but over, and he decided to lay low with his wife and four daughters to await whatever fate—and the Allies—had in store for him. When the CIC agents finally arrived on his doorstep, Chandler seemed almost relieved and offered no resistance when they handcuffed him and put him in the rear seat of the staff car.

A three-hour drive took the agents and their prisoner to the Seventh Army Interrogation Center. Chandler was first questioned by twenty-seven-year-old Captain Aldo E. Cesarini, an intelligence specialist with the Office of the U.S. Military Government. The young officer was on hand when, on June 22, Joe Dunn met with Chandler for the first time. That encounter lasted only an hour before ending abruptly, when the obviously agitated American renegade began complaining of a severe migraine. Despite the brevity of the initial interrogation, Dunn was able to glean several pieces of useful information. Among them were insights about the North America Zone's propaganda goals, the ways in which staff members were paid, and details about Chandler's fellow American broadcasters. Two particularly interesting bits of data concerned Max Koischwitz. First, according to Chandler, Koischwitz had conducted an intense love affair with fellow renegade broadcaster Mildred Gillars. Second, Chandler said that Koischwitz had died "sometime in 1944" from tuberculosis.

Dunn planned to return to SAIC the following day to continue his interrogation of Chandler, but was told by the facility's chief medical officer that the suspect was having a "severe mental crisis" and needed time to recover. Dunn therefore headed back to Höchst to provide Fred Ayer with an initial report; the information about Koischwitz's possible death was the subject of a message the ALU chief sent to Hoover on June 24.[40]

Various matters kept Dunn in the Frankfurt area for several weeks, though he received updates on Chandler from the CIC's German Intelligence Section at SAIC. In mid-July, two members of that unit—T/5s George Freimarck and Irving Rowe—sent Dunn a copy of the report they'd written after interrogating Chandler on the 12th.[41] The soldiers said the renegade

> claims complete ignorance of any of [the North America Zone's] inner workings. He is apparently unable to even grasp the implications of the question as to whether he could not see the facts that the regime rested on an absolute tyranny at home and was predicated

on successful wars of conquest abroad—much less answer such a question.[42]

When Dunn was finally able to schedule a return to SAIC to continue his interrogation of Chandler, he was told that the suspect—like Herbert Burgman—had been released from custody and allowed to return to his family. It wasn't until nearly eight months later that the Department of Justice finally decided it had enough evidence to indict "Paul Revere" for treason. On February 28, 1946, Dunn arrested Chandler at his home in Kempten, Bavaria. The FBI agent was finally able to interrogate the renegade at length; indeed, the now talkative Chandler provided statements that ultimately produced a forty-eight-page transcript.[43] That document proved a key piece of evidence when Chandler ultimately went on trial in Boston, in 1947. Indeed, so damning was the transcript that the accused tried to repudiate it by claiming that Dunn, whom he called the "Blond Beast," had "possessed hypnotic powers."[44] The bizarre defense didn't work, and Chandler was ultimately found guilty and sentenced to life imprisonment. That sentence was commuted in 1962 and the now seventy-four-year-old convicted traitor was released on the condition that he return to Germany and live with his eldest daughter. He initially did so, but eventually dropped from sight. He is rumored to have died in the Canary Islands in 1975 at the age of eighty-six.[45]

Edward Leopold Delaney

Late on the evening of May 18, 1945, two enlisted U.S. Army reporters for the military newspaper *Stars and Stripes* were fruitlessly searching the center of Prague, for a secure place to park their jeep overnight. The city was packed with the Soviet troops who had taken control of the Czech capital on May 9 following a popular uprising against German forces by local citizens and members of the resistance.[46] Initially greeted as liberators, the Russians quickly turned to arresting anyone thought to be anticommunist, looting private homes, and stealing any vehicle that caught their fancy. The two GI reporters, Staff Sergeant Howard Byrne and Corporal Klaus Mann, were in the city to document its occupation by the Soviets.[47] They'd signed for the jeep before leaving Nuremburg a few days earlier and had no desire to have to explain its subsequent theft—especially by supposed "allies." Moreover, the vehicle was packed with boxes of rations, two spare tires, jerry cans of gasoline, metal jugs of drinking water, sleeping bags and personal belongings, two portable typewriters, and several dozen rolls of film for Byrne's cameras.[48]

Byrne and Mann eventually found their way to the Hotel Šroubek on Wenceslas Square. They had just pulled up to the building and were discussing their next move when a well-dressed older man walked up to them and in American-accented English asked if they needed help. They explained their need for a secure place to park the jeep, and the man led Byrne to the hotel's front desk. The mysterious American rattled off a string of German to the clerk, who quickly handed Byrne two keys. One, the stranger explained, was for a deluxe room on the hotel's top floor, while the other would allow the GIs to park their jeep in the gated and guarded basement parking area. Byrne thanked the American profusely, and was only too happy to accept an invitation for himself and Mann to join the Good Samaritan for dinner in the hotel dining room the next evening. The Army reporter said that he'd also like to ask the man his impressions of the liberation of Prague.[49]

The following evening, Byrne and Mann knocked on the door of the American's room. After inviting them in for a predinner drink, he introduced himself as Edward Delaney, a name that immediately caught the reporters' attention. Seeing the surprise on their faces, the renegade broadcaster pulled out two scripts for shows he'd done for Czech radio during the battle for Prague. When Byrne asked if he could use information from the scripts in an article, Delaney readily agreed. He also provided the reporters with a copy of the letter he'd filed with the Swiss legation in Berlin protesting his 1943 treason indictment by the Department of Justice. Then, and later over dinner, Delaney insisted that he had never spoken against the United States and considered himself a patriotic American.[50] Indeed, he told his guests he wanted to go home and take legal action against the people who had called him a "shortwave traitor." Byrne and Mann were obviously not swayed by Delaney's self-serving and rather convoluted explanation of his wartime actions, because immediately after dinner, they reported him to the Czech police.

Delaney was taken into custody before dawn on May 20 and immediately driven to police headquarters. For the next thirty-seven days, he was held under harsh conditions in a Russian-run jail, where his fellow inmates were mostly Czech nationalists convicted of what were called "anti-Soviet" activities. Delaney was certain that he, like many of the other prisoners, would be summarily executed. But on June 26, he was taken from his cell, allowed to clean himself up, fed, and then driven to Pilsen. After spending the night in a much cleaner cell, he was picked up by two American military police soldiers and driven the 120 miles to the Third Army Interrogation Center in Freising. The following morning, he was led to a large interview room, where he found

Boyd Sheets waiting for him. Given that the FBI had been compiling a file on Delaney since before his 1943 indictment, the ALU agent knew quite a bit about the American renegade before he even entered the interrogation room.

Born the son of Irish immigrants in southeastern Illinois in 1885, Edward Delaney grew up in Glenview, a suburb of Chicago.[51] He was apparently orphaned at a relatively young age and was raised by relatives. At twenty-five, he moved to the West Coast to follow his dream of being a stage actor. After getting only bit parts in productions in San Francisco and Los Angeles, Delaney moved to New York, and spent the next several years touring North America with road show productions. Noticed by the representative of an Australian theater company, Delaney signed on to do plays Down Under and was in New Zealand when World War I broke out in 1914. The conflict quickly put an end to most theater work in Australia and New Zealand as both countries joined the British Commonwealth's war effort. Delaney returned to the United States, and after a pay dispute got him blacklisted in the emerging U.S. motion picture industry, he ended up touring South America, screening American silent movies with Spanish dialog cards.

When the United States entered the war in April 1917, Delaney—who had neglected to register for the draft—was on his way to Southeast Asia as a sales representative for a group of Australian film distributors. By 1920, he was in South Africa, working for a minor film production company in Johannesburg, but the following year moved on to Europe. He got parts in several road show theater companies in France and Britain, but a fortunate encounter with a member of the MGM film studio's promotion department brought him back to Chicago in 1924. He spent the next five years doing public relations work for MGM and its parent company, Loew's, Inc., being very well paid and developing a reputation as a glib but shallow charmer. Delaney's luck turned sour in 1929 when the stock market crash all but wiped him out financially, and when Loew's fired him in 1930, he used what remained of his money to sail back to Europe.

Delaney supported himself with a series of odd jobs, living cheaply while he wrote the first of two novels. *The Lady by Degrees* appeared in 1934, followed a year later by *The Charm Girl*. Light and breezy action romances, the books did well enough to support Delaney for a few years. He wasn't able to live in the way he would have preferred, however, claiming that his career had been "stifled" by Jews and communists. In 1937, Delaney took a job as an overseas agent for a small New York–based motion picture distribution company, and two years later, was working in Genoa. He moved on to Berlin, and just before the 1939 German invasion of Poland, his outspoken anti-Semitism and vociferous criticism of Franklin Roosevelt won him an audience with Karl Schotte, the German director of the RRG's North America Zone.

Having passed his "audition," Delaney was hired as a field correspondent. Using the pseudonym "E. D. Ward," he followed German troops into Denmark in April 1940, reporting that the invasion was in the best interests of the Danish people, because it prevented the nation's "occupation" by Britain and France. That would have turned Denmark into a "battlefield," he said, writing off the killing of Danish troops by German forces as merely "extremely unfortunate."[52] Having proved himself in Denmark, in May 1940, Delaney was tasked to follow German troops into Holland and Belgium. His reporting made him something of a celebrity in Berlin, though CBS journalist William L. Shirer wrote him off as

> a disappointed actor who used to have occasional employment with road companies in the United States. He has a diseased hatred for Jews, but otherwise is a mild fellow and broadcasts the cruder type of Nazi propaganda without questioning.[53]

Edward A. Harris of the *St. Louis Post-Dispatch* had even harsher words for Delaney, writing that Americans in Berlin before Pearl Harbor regarded him as an opportunist who had swung to Nazism "not from intellectual conviction, but from a yearning to achieve the recognition and publicity never accorded him by his own people. A failure [in America] he was, for a time, a big shot in Germany."[54]

On December 8, 1941, Delaney was offered the choice to be interned at Bad Nauheim and eventually returned to the United States or to remain in Germany. He chose the latter option, convincing himself that by staying in the Reich, he could "refute much fiction which other writers would produce about Central Europe from their vantage point—at great distances."[55] However, his resolve to report "the truth" from Germany eroded significantly as the war dragged on. Moreover, his increasingly erratic behavior caused his German superiors to severely reduce Delaney's air time. In April 1943, he decamped to Czechoslovakia, there to be encountered by Howard Byrne and Klaus Mann on May 18, 1945, outside the Hotel Šroubek.

When Delaney finally sat down across from Boyd Sheets in the Freising interrogation room, the accused renegade was more than ready to "explain" his wartime actions on behalf of Nazi Germany. He repeated his claim that he had never spoken against the United States, and when confronted with transcripts of broadcasts he'd made vilifying Roosevelt and the U.S. government as pawns of communists and "the international Jewish conspiracy," Delaney simply said he was exercising his free speech rights under the U.S. Constitution's 1st Amendment. He also argued that his move to Czechoslovakia and subsequent reporting on Soviet actions in that country "proved" that he was simply trying to alert the world to the dangers of Stalinism. That many of his reports from Prague were broadcast over Radio Berlin was simply coincidental, he said, though he admitted that he'd continued to receive payments from the RRG almost until the Soviets rolled into the Czech capital. At Sheets's urging Delaney provided

> a typewritten statement of several thousand words, covering all my activities, places of residence and data concerning persons with whom I had been in contact in the Axis countries, from the time of my last arrival in Europe early in the war, to the sudden incarceration in Prague.[56]

Despite the wealth of information Sheets obtained from Delaney, the accused renegade was released from custody and took up residence in a small hotel in Freising. But, as happened with both Herbert Burgman and Douglas Chandler, in March 1946, Delaney was rearrested by CIC agents. He was transported to the detention center at Camp King in Oberursel, near Frankfurt, where he was held for five months before again being released on the orders of the Department of Justice. Having obtained both a new passport and the sympathy of an aide to Robert Murphy, the senior political adviser to the military governor of the U.S. occupation zone General Lucius D. Clay, Delaney sailed for the United States. Taken into custody upon his arrival in New York, the former "E. D. Ward" pled his case in the court of public opinion, telling reporters that he was being persecuted for his anticommunist views while ignoring his pro-Nazi broadcasts from Berlin.

In those first few years following the end of World War II, American concerns about the threat posed by the Soviet Union had begun to coalesce into the Red Scare that would soon give rise to the excesses of McCarthyism. That may have been a factor in a federal grand jury's August 28, 1947, decision to dismiss the treason indictment against Delaney. Set free yet again, he not surprisingly became an ultraright-wing print journalist and radio broadcaster. Settling first in Arizona and later in southern California, he railed as loudly and virulently against "the communists who dominate our country" as he once had against the "international Jewish conspiracy." He threatened to sue anyone who brought up his wartime pro-Nazi broadcasts and carried on extensive correspondence with extreme right-wing organizations, both in the United States and abroad. Delaney was still working as a part-time print reporter and radio commentator when he was struck and killed by a car while crossing a street in Glendale, California, on July 1, 1972. He was eighty-six years old.

CHAPTER 11

Spymasters, Still More Renegades, and Legats

While Walt Rucks, Dick Thompson, Joe Dunn, and Boyd Sheets were interrogating suspected American traitors, Fred Ayer was about to question the individual widely considered by the Allies to be Nazi Germany's "Ace of Spies." That man was Walter Schellenberg.

Born in 1910 in Saarbrücken, the capital city of Germany's Saarland state hard on the French border, Schellenberg originally trained as a lawyer.[1] He joined the Nazi Party and SS in 1933, at least partly because doing so allowed him to obtain state subsidies he used to finance his further legal education. In the spring of 1935, Schellenberg took a temporary position in the administration section of the Berlin headquarters of the Sicherheitsdienst (SD), the intelligence service of the SS. After several months in private law practice, he returned to the SD, where he ultimately earned the patronage of both Reinhard Heydrich, chief of the Reich Security Main Office (RHSA), and of Heydrich's boss, Reichsführer-SS Heinrich Himmler.[2]

Schellenberg's intelligence, fluency in multiple languages, strong work ethic, and of course, his close relationships with Heydrich and Himmler fueled the young man's meteoric rise through the ranks of the SD. In April 1937, he was promoted to *Untersturmführer* (equivalent to a Wehrmacht lieutenant), and by September 1941, he was an *Obersturmbannführer* (lieutenant colonel) and second in command of the SD's Amt (bureau) VI. Responsible for intelligence activities outside the Reich, the department was referred to as Ausland (foreign)-SD. When the head of the bureau was fired for incompetence in March 1942, the thirty-two-year-old Schellenberg took over. His star rose further following Heydrich's June 1942 assassination in Prague and the failed assassination attempt against Hitler in July 1944. Because Abwehr chief Admiral Wilhelm Canaris was implicated in the latter plot, he was arrested and ultimately executed for treason, the Abwehr was abolished, and its foreign intelligence operations were transferred to Schellenberg's Amt VI.

Despite his widely acknowledged administrative skills, Schellenberg was no mere desk-bound bureaucrat. Over the course of his career in the SD, he took part in several field operations, among them Germany's 1938 annexation of Austria, the 1939 Venlo Incident,[3] negotiations with pro-Nazi groups in neutral Sweden, and the strengthening of ties with the intelligence and police forces of fascist Spain. He also spent time in Paris, where he was a key player in the Banque Charles affair that embroiled Jay and Florence Gould. On several occasions, he also apparently met with American renegades who were then broadcasting German propaganda from the occupied French capital.[4]

However, as the war ground on and Germany's dreams of victory started to fade, Schellenberg began to explore the possibilities of a negotiated peace between the Third Reich and its enemies. He sought to establish contacts with the Allies through both Swiss and Swedish intelligence and diplomatic channels—this despite the fact that by January 1945 he held two general officer–level ranks in the Nazi hierarchy—*SS-Brigadeführer* and *Generalmajor der Polizei*. When the war ended in May, Schellenberg was actually in Stockholm, staying at the home of Count Folke Bernadotte. The Swedish diplomat, who had played a key role in the efforts to achieve a negotiated peace with the Allies, was among those who urged Schellenberg to turn himself over to the Allies. Schellenberg spent just over a month writing a summary of the events immediately preceding Germany's surrender, and on June 17, flew to Frankfurt aboard a USAAF C-47 with Bernadotte and Colonel Charles E. Rayens, the U.S. military attaché in Stockholm.

Though senior U.S. counterintelligence officers were intensely interested in gaining control of Schellenberg, he was instead taken into custody by British personnel operating under the authority of Colonel Dick White of MI5. Rather than incarcerating the prisoner in the joint interrogation centers in Oberursel (Camp King) or Luxembourg ("Camp Ashcan"), White installed Schellenberg in a requisitioned private home in a Frankfurt suburb. There the former head of all Nazi foreign intelligence sat for over a week, awaiting the arrival of star British interrogator Jona von Ustinov. A German journalist and anti-Nazi who had taken United Kingdom citizenship in 1935, he had gone to work for MI5 before the outbreak of World War II. Though officially referred to by the code name U 35, Ustinov was widely known by the nickname Klop—the Russian word for bedbug.[5] However, when, on June 27,

Ustinov walked into the interrogation room for the first time, he introduced himself to those present as "Mr. Johnson."

Among the observers that first day was Fred Ayer. The ALU chief had been notified of the German prisoner's arrival in Frankfurt and had arranged through SHAEF's British liaison officers to attend at least the first few interrogations. Fred was, of course, extremely interested in anything Schellenberg might have to say about German espionage activities in the Western Hemisphere. But he was also interested in knowing what connection there might be between the chief of Amt VI and Maurice Gagnon—the American renegade the ALU had interrogated in Paris who had ended up killing himself while in custody. Fred's curiosity had been piqued by the fact that a few weeks earlier, CIC agents had discovered a vast trove of hugely important Sicherheitsdienst files that had been moved out of Berlin before the collapse and hidden in Bavaria. Among the documents were three in which Fred was particularly interested—a blank and apparently authentic U.S. passport, a second passport belonging to Gagnon issued in 1940 by the U.S. consulate in occupied Paris, and a third bearing the name William G. Bellmont and the same number as the Gagnon passport, but with a photo that was definitely Schellenberg.[6]

Klop Ustinov's approach to interrogating the former chief of Amt VI was decidedly not of the "bright lights and harsh treatment" variety. As Fred later wrote:

> The British officer who led off the questioning . . . extended his hand, and said "Doctor Schellenberg, I have had the opportunity of studying your career and activities for many years. They have been extremely interesting to me and I am delighted to meet you. There are many things which I think we will enjoy talking over together."[7]

Ustinov was not the only person in the room who found Schellenberg impressive. "The man who had been our major German opponent was extraordinary," Fred remembered. "His dynamic qualities were obvious. . . . He was fully the professional, with a fine analytical and unemotional mind. . . . He was very cooperative and truthful."[8]

Fred later had the chance to question Schellenberg one-on-one:

> It was a fascinating interview, much as if any professional, a cancer expert for instance, were querying a foreign colleague. It was not as if the representative of a conqueror were demanding answers of

> an enemy. He was completely frank, proud of techniques and mechanisms which had worked well and constructively critical of those which had not. I cannot today tell of the most interesting things he made known to me. Suffice it to say, he pointed up several glaring weaknesses in our own security practices and suggested various technical means of surveillance and espionage. . . . Also, at considerable length, he expounded his theory that the West had now even more to fear than before from Russia, and warned that we must never believe any [Soviet] expressions of friendly intent.[9]

Schellenberg also said that from the moment he took command of Amt VI, he was suspicious that the information being sent by radio from purported German spies in the United States was actually coming either from operatives who had been "doubled" by the FBI or directly from Bureau agents using captured German codes.[10] Schellenberg added that even if the agents in America were real, the problem was that they "belonged" to competing German intelligence organizations—the military services, the foreign ministry, and others—who refused to believe that their agents "had gone sour" and continued to forward the radio messages to "interested agencies" in order to keep themselves in favor with the Reich's senior leaders.

As Fred had suspected, Maurice Gagnon's passport had come into Schellenberg's possession in Paris. After Pearl Harbor, the Germans had confiscated the passports and other U.S. government–issued documents belonging to some of the American citizens who chose to stay in France, either to remain with family members or to collaborate with the Nazis. Those documents—as well as blank passports, rubber stamps, and other items taken from U.S. consulates and the offices of American-owned companies—were used as templates for forged papers provided to German agents sent to the Western Hemisphere. Some of the real documents were also heavily modified for use by senior Nazis, including Schellenberg, who might need to quickly escape Germany in the event of an Allied victory. As it turned out, the former chief of Amt VI was especially well-prepared—he handed over to Ustinov several doctored United Kingdom passports and an additional few forged U.S. documents to Fred.

Flown to England following the end of his questioning in Frankfurt, Schellenberg was incarcerated at Camp 020. In reality, a large, Victorian-era home in southwest London, the facility was used to house and interrogate high-value German agents and senior Nazis. While there, Schellenberg was questioned by representatives of several intelligence organizations—including Roderick "Rory" Cameron of the OSS's X-2 counterintelligence branch—before being sent back to Frankfurt on October 28, 1945. After comprehensive interrogations at Camp King in Oberursel, Schellenberg was transferred to Nuremburg. By giving evidence against other defendants, he managed to escape a harsh sentence himself. Sent to prison for just six years, he was released after only two owing to increasingly poor health. He ultimately settled in Turin, Italy, where he died of liver cancer in March 1952 at the age of forty-two.

JUST DAYS AFTER QUESTIONING WALTER SCHELLENBERG, Fred Ayer was asked by Gordon Sheen to take part in the apprehension of a wanted German war criminal. The man, Werner Rolf Mühler, was the former Gestapo chief in the French port city of Marseilles. He was said to be hiding on a farm on the northeastern shore of Lake Constance, the vast body of water bordered by Germany, Switzerland, and Austria. Fred would be accompanying two friends from the 307th CIC Detachment, Peter English and Victor Guinzbourg.

The CIC men were famous in Allied intelligence circles, both for their work before Germany's surrender and for several huge coups in the weeks since. Among the latter was their discovery of the trove of SD files that included Schellenberg's fake U.S. passports, and Guinzbourg's leadership of an Allied search party that recovered some twelve tons of Nazi gold hidden in Germany and Austria. The agent had also taken part in the capture and initial interrogation of Generalleutnant (Lieutenant General) Reinhard Gehlen, head of the Wehrmacht's anti-Soviet intelligence organization, and had been the first Allied interrogator of Waffen-SS special operations chief Otto Skorzeny. Guinzbourg was in charge of what Fred called the trio's "delightful hunting expedition" because he had worked undercover in German-occupied Marseilles and knew the Gestapo chief by sight.[11]

English and Guinzbourg had a good idea about the location of Mühler's bucolic hideout, and the three men found the place without difficulty. As Fred later wrote:

> We drove up to the farmhouse where he was supposed to live, and asked if he were around. A strapping great peasant woman told us that he was just then out chopping wood. We told her that we would go and collect him. She assured us this would not be necessary.

> Cupping her hands before her mouth, and seemingly using the full capacity of her 46-inch chest, she bellowed, "Komm sofort, come quickly. American officers are here. They come for you. They have come with guns."[12]

In response to the woman's call, the wanted man appeared from a nearby tree line, an axe over one shoulder. Apparently unfazed by the unannounced arrival of armed, uniformed Americans, Mühler said he would be ready to go to jail in a few minutes. He went into the house, followed by a cautious Fred with his hand on his holstered .45-caliber pistol, and began stuffing clothing and toilet articles into a small canvas bag.[13] The German then added a framed picture that he said was of his wife, though Fred noted that it was definitely not an image of the big-boned Brunhilde with whom Mühler had apparently been leading a "contemplative and rustic life."[14] After turning the former Gestapo man over to a nearby French military police unit, Fred and his companions spent two days exploring the border region and one morning managed to eat a delightful Swiss breakfast sitting at a table that literally straddled the border—an unusual but effective way to dine well without violating Switzerland's jealously guarded neutrality.

Though absent from Höchst for just three days, on his return, Fred found a stack of messages waiting on his desk. Among them were two from Hoover that dealt with personnel issues. The first said that the agents chosen to open the legal attaché office at the Paris embassy—Horton Telford and Clement Rousseau—would depart for France "on or about" July 1. The second message announced that two additional men would be joining the Army Liaison Unit. German-speaking agents Hans Wenthur and Joe Fellner had been selected to serve in Austria, the former at the headquarters of U.S. Occupation Forces Austria, in Salzburg, and the latter in Vienna, with the U.S. sector command.[15] The agents would travel via North Africa and Italy and, after checking in with Frank Amprim in Rome, should arrive in Austria during the first week of August. Wenthur and Fellner would be under Fred's operational control, the message said, though both would also respond to requests from U.S. Forces Austria commander General Mark Clark's counterintelligence chief.

A few days later, Fred got some long-awaited news from Gordon Sheen. The CI chief said that, with the German surrender and the cessation of combat operations, SHAEF was to be inactivated on July 14. The operational control of U.S. forces in Germany would then pass to U.S. Forces European Theater (USFET), commanded by General Joseph T. McNarney. Upon the inactivation of Twelfth USAG, its intelligence chief, Brigadier General Edwin L. Sibert, would take up the same position in USFET. But, Sheen added, his counterintelligence section and its attached ALU element would transfer as planned to Berlin as part of the USGCC.

Planning for operations in the former German capital had taken up much of Fred's time, even before he and the others had left Paris. It was in the battered environs of what was supposed to have been the center of Hitler's "Thousand Year Reich" that the ALU would likely find the remaining "most wanted" American renegades—the broadcasters who along with Edward Delaney, Douglas Chandler, and Ezra Pound had been indicted for treason in July 1943—or at least some indications of their whereabouts.

As Fred Ayer and his team in Höchst were preparing for the move to Berlin, Horton Telford and Bud Rousseau were setting up shop at the U.S. Embassy in Paris. The Bureau could not have chosen a better team to establish the first legal attaché office in France.

A thirty-six-year-old Idaho native, Telford had grown up there and in San Bernardino, California. A devout Mormon, he served as a missionary in France and Switzerland from 1930 to 1932, in the process becoming fluent in French. After graduating from Georgetown University in 1939, Telford joined the State Department. He was assigned to diplomatic courier work in Europe, first based in Rome and then in Berne, Switzerland. In October 1940, he set off on a trip to Rome, Venice, Belgrade, Salonika, Athens, and Istanbul. Unfortunately, he reached the Italian capital on the day Italy declared war on Greece. What should have been a routine ten-day journey turned into a three-week odyssey that required Telford to dodge strafing Italian aircraft in Salonika, artillery shelling, and at one point, the need to carry several pouches of secret diplomatic correspondence across a heavily guarded border at night. Through a combination of quick wits and courage, the young courier eventually made it back to Berne with all his documents secure.[16]

Following the attack on Pearl Harbor, Telford joined the FBI. After initial training, his language abilities and extensive experience abroad ensured that he was transferred into the SIS. In 1943, he was posted to the U.S. embassy in Havana, where he worked in the office of the Bureau's legal attaché. Rousseau was among his fellow SIS agents, and the two men formed a close friendship while investigating German espionage and propaganda activities on the island before Rousseau returned to Washington to take up a senior position at SIS.

When, in May 1945, the opening of the Paris legat office was finally cleared by both the State Department and Donovan of OSS, the Bureau's Crawford H. Carson, a senior aide to Hoover, recommended Telford for the job, writing:

> [He] speaks French fluently, has shown considerable administrative ability, and is rated a very good all-around Bureau agent. It is recognized that this assignment will call for a good deal of diplomacy and tact and it is my opinion that Telford would be the ideal man to be placed in charge in Paris. I feel confident that he would acquit himself creditably in such [a] position.[17]

Telford had requested Rousseau to be his deputy, and in his memo, Carson concurred. "Rousseau," he wrote, "is currently assigned . . . as a supervisor in the [SIS] and is rated as a good all-around Bureau agent. . . . It is my opinion that he can handle this assignment as Assistant Legal Attaché in Paris creditably."[18]

That thirty-three-year-old Clement Van Dyke Rousseau would be able to handle the deputy legat position would not have come as a surprise to anyone who knew or had worked with him. Born in Peoria, Illinois, "Bud" Rousseau grew up in Southern California. After graduating from Los Angeles High School—where he took four years of Spanish and two years of French—he went on to the University of California at Berkeley. While there, he was a broad jumper on the school's track and field team and a member of the Psi Upsilon fraternity. Rousseau graduated in May 1935 with a BS degree in commerce (an alternate name for business administration). At the time he registered for the draft in October 1940, he was living with his father in Beverly Hills and working as a credit manager for the General Motors Acceptance Corporation in Los Angeles. Rousseau joined the FBI in early 1942, and after initial agent training, he was tapped for SIS duty in Latin America. He spent some two years in Havana, where he worked closely with Telford. It was the men's excellent personal relationship, as well as Rousseau's language abilities and field experience, that led to his being chosen to for the Paris position.

Telford and Rousseau arrived in the French capital during the second week of July 1945, accompanied by London legat Joe Lynch. Ambassador Jefferson Caffery was happy to see the agents, though he emphasized his desire that Telford and his deputy not engage in any activities that might be construed as investigations into communist activities in France. As Lynch later reported to Hoover, during a meeting with Caffery at which Telford and

Rousseau were not present, the ambassador said that if communist-related investigations were necessary, they should be undertaken by Don Daughters and his team in such a manner that "they could not in any way be traced or connected to the embassy."[19] Lynch reported his conversation with Caffery to Hoover and asked for guidance on the subject of communist investigations. In a message to Daughters with Lynch in copy, the director stated that "the responsibility for the handling of Communist matters in Paris should primarily fall [on the ALU] . . . however, Mr. Telford should be kept fully informed concerning all developments."[20]

With the jurisdictional issues settled, Telford and Rousseau got to work. They were soon joined by Harry Jacobsen, an experienced Bureau clerk-stenographer who would be the team's secretary and code clerk. The three men then officially opened the Paris legal attaché office, a small two-room space on the mezzanine floor of the Embassy on the place de la Concorde. The two agents then spent several days in conferences with Daughters, Pete Winter, and Roland L'Allier. Telford and Rousseau were not officially part of the Army Liaison Unit and, as Hoover had stated, their tasks at the embassy would not include the sorts of investigations carried out by Daughters and his team. The legat and his deputy would, however, be required to interact with French intelligence and police organizations on a range of issues, and the relationships the ALU had already established with senior leaders in the French agencies would prove of immense value.

Telford, Rousseau, and Jacobsen had rented a three-story town house on the boulevard Victor Hugo, three miles from the Embassy. Telford noted in his diary that Paris was "quite different from the city I had known 13 years earlier." With the war in Europe over for barely two months, "there were no cars except military vehicles, the subway closed down at 10 p.m., [and] food, coal, electricity, gasoline, etc., were still rationed." Fortunately, the three men could use the U.S. forces commissary and post exchange, and had access to gasoline coupons and an embassy car.[21] There was no heat in their town house, however, so they had to rely on a fireplace for warmth.

The legat and his colleagues were tremendously busy from the time they landed in the French capital, both with their official duties and as hosts for a series of VIP guests. Some of the latter were personal friends of Hoover's while others included Justice Department officials such as Attorney General Tom C. Clark and Assistant AG Graham Morrison. But Telford, Rousseau, and Jacobsen also found time to relax, often in the company of well-to-do French friends.

One family frequently hosted the FBI men for golf, tennis, and swimming at an opulent summer home in Le Touquet, on the English Channel.[22]

The seaside excursions were a welcome break from a job that soon became both vitally important to the United States and increasingly challenging for the men of the Paris legat office. The months immediately following the end of the war in Europe were turbulent ones for France, as the nation came to grips with the divisiveness the conflict had caused. Millions of French people had not only welcomed the German invaders, many had actually enlisted in the virulently pro-Nazi Milice Française—the fascist paramilitary force of Vichy that helped round up Jews, Résistance members, and downed Allied aviators for imprisonment, torture, and execution. Thousands of French men willingly joined the Légion des volontaires français contre le bolchévisme (Legion of French Volunteers Against Bolshevism) to fight alongside the Wehrmacht in Russia. On the other side of the political coin, French communists—with Soviet help—were attempting to turn postwar France into a fascist state under Moscow's thumb. The men of the Paris legal attaché office would play an important role in keeping the United States informed about the many political, social, and legal challenges facing France in the late 1940s, and in ensuring that the law-enforcement agencies of both nations would continue to work together as the Cold War set in.

In the days leading up to SHAEF's inactivation, Fred Ayer had been considering the best way to allocate the members of the ALU in Germany.

As the former Nazi capital, Berlin was likely to be the most lucrative target area in terms of investigations of American renegades, research into wartime German espionage in Europe and the Western Hemisphere, and the postwar threat posed by communism and Soviet expansionism. But as home to the headquarters of U.S. Forces European Theater, Frankfurt would remain an important ALU "field office." Moreover, Fred believed that two other locations cried out for an FBI presence.

The first was Heidelberg, the famous university town on the Neckar River in Baden-Württemberg. It had escaped wartime destruction because it contained no valid military targets, and during the Allied advance, the Germans chose not to defend it. Soon after U.S. forces occupied the city on March 30, the 307th CIC Detachment—Pete English and Victor Guinzbourg's unit—began arresting university staffers suspected of membership in the SS and for other offenses. Fred believed there were three solid reasons to dispatch members of his team to Heidelberg. First, the ALU had been requested to aid in "denazification" investigations, and by assisting in the process in Heidelberg, the FBI agents could help get the medical school back up and running to ease Germany's dire shortage of physicians. Second, the university's archives were thought to contain potentially valuable files on the Nazis' rise to power and on horrific medical "experiments" conducted on concentration camp prisoners. Third, members of the 307th CIC Detachment still in Heidelberg were running counterintelligence operations throughout Baden-Württemberg and, based on Fred's earlier assistance to English and Guinzbourg, had offered to share information with the ALU.

The second location, Freising, was of interest for several reasons. Ten miles northeast of the city was the town of Moosburg, wartime home to Stalag VII-A. One of Nazi Germany's largest camps for Allied prisoners of war, after the surrender, it had been turned into a massive internment camp holding suspected German war criminals and former intelligence officials. In Freising itself was the Third Army Interrogation Center, the high-security holding facility where Edward Delaney was being held, and Fred hoped that other American renegades might also eventually show up there.

Ultimately, the ALU chief decided to split his group into four teams. He would take Jack Condon, Art O'Connor, and Dick Thompson with him to Berlin, plus either Hans Wenthur or Joe Fellner, if one of them eventually became available. Bill Clark and Vince Ascherl would remain in Frankfurt at USFET headquarters, Walt Rucks and Hal Kloster would move to Heidelberg, and Joe Dunn and Boyd Sheets would handle Freising since they were already familiar with the town and its interrogation center. As Fred told his agents, all but the Berlin assignment should be considered temporary—the men could be called to the former Nazi capital at any time if needed.

On July 13, Fred and the FBI men who had accompanied him from France gathered at the IG Farben building with the entire SHAEF staff to hear Eisenhower speak. "Ike" thanked the gathered troops for their service and lauded them for taking part in the "great crusade" to free Europe. In his last Order of the Day as SHAEF commander, issued on the morning of July 14 to mark the organization's inactivation and the activation of USFET, Eisenhower wrote, in part, "I pay tribute to every individual who gave so freely and unselfishly to the limit of his or her ability. Their achievements in the cause for which they fought will be indelibly inscribed in the pages of history and cherished in the hearts of all freedom-loving people."[23]

Three days later, Fred, Jack Condon, Art O'Connor, and Dick Thompson set off for Berlin before dawn. The agents traveled in an eight-vehicle caravan that included a total of fifteen intelligence officers from both the U.S. and British armies, as well as Dick Preston. Fred later noted that his friend was

> resplendent in full Navy uniform. He claimed that he gave much-needed dignity to the group. In view of the fact that he had been able to add a truck to our assortment of vehicles, and that we had loaded this truck with 40 cases of assorted spirits, we certainly agreed. After all, it was common knowledge that the Berlin water supply had become badly contaminated.[24]

The 270-mile journey to the former Nazi capital took the convoy of FBI agents and intelligence officers northeast, generally following the route of what had been a major railway line until repeated Allied air attacks had turned it into little more than twisted metal and bomb craters. After a brief stop in Fulda—a town that within a few years would become one of the most militarily important places in Europe—the caravan crossed into the Soviet occupation zone.[25] The remainder of the drive, as Fred later wrote,

> was a blow to any complacency we may have still felt [about postwar Soviet intentions]. It was a strange sensation being forced to tell our Red allies exactly how many men we were transporting in what vehicles across a country which we had jointly conquered. It was galling to have to adhere strictly to the limits of the very narrow corridor along which we were permitted to travel. It was worse than a slap in the face to be halted at gun point at Russian roadblocks, and submitted to the scrutiny given a suspicious line-crosser. And this was on the road to a city which we could have had for the taking. . . .[26]

The indignities foisted upon Fred and his fellow travelers by their erstwhile Russian allies finally ended when the caravan of vehicles crossed the Glienicker Brücke. The bridge over the Havel river marked the boundary between Potsdam, in the Soviet occupation zone, and the American Sector of Berlin.[27] While the men had seen much destruction on the drive from Frankfurt, nothing had prepared them for their first sight of the former Nazi capital. The nearly 75,000 tons of Allied bombs dropped on the city had ensured that vast swaths were nothing but rubble and the few buildings left standing were little more than fire-blackened shells. That damage had been hugely compounded by the vicious fight between advancing Soviet troops and German defenders. Nearly three months after the German surrender, the streets were still strewn with burned-out vehicles, both military and civilian, and throngs of gaunt Berliners lined up near Allied cargo trucks for food and water. Armed U.S. troops manned checkpoints on the main roads through the American Sector, and Fred caught glimpses of tanks and armored cars parked under trees on the east side of the city's Grunewald forest. The war in Europe might officially be over, but it was clear to Fred and his companions that the Allies were not yet ready to trust their former enemies.

Late in the afternoon, the caravan from Frankfurt pulled up in front of a complex of buildings on Kronprinzenallee in Zehlendorf, a neighborhood in the southwestern part of the American Sector. Until a few months earlier, the facility had housed the Luftwaffe's national air-defense coordination center, but on July 2, it had become the first headquarters of the U.S. Group Control Council.[28] Fred and his companions checked in at the billeting office, with the fifteen men subsequently being assigned to various requisitioned residences in the area. Fred, Dick Preston, and Jack Condon were given an address nearby and, keys in hand, drove to the house in the Army sedan in which they'd made the trip from Frankfurt. The men were pleased to find that their billet was what Fred later described as a "pleasant, middle-class house, equipped with the standard dormer windows, quarter acre of lawn, largely given over to a sick-looking vegetable garden, and just exactly three shade trees."[29] While the house was in relatively good shape except for what looked like a small shell hole in the roof, the surrounding neighborhood had obviously been ransacked by the Russians before they turned the area over to incoming American forces.

Fred and the others had been told that the owner of the house would greet them, but there didn't seem to be anyone around when they got there. As they were exploring the building, they discovered two women hiding in the basement, both weeping uncontrollably. When the Americans appeared the two backed away in fear. Using his few words of basic German, Fred

> convinced them that we had not come with intent of rape or murder, and both came out of their hiding place. They were a woman who might have been 40, and a girl of about 13, both gaunt, dirty, and in a state of terror that it is not good for anyone to look upon. We assured them that they had nothing to fear, that they could occupy the basement room and use the kitchen for their meals. All that we would ask was that they keep the house clean for us. The woman wept and tried

> to kiss our hands. . . . Later, in conversation, we learned that mother and daughter, the family of a fairly successful lawyer, had been caught in their home by Soviet troops and repeatedly raped.[30]

Over the next few days, all of the men who had driven in from Frankfurt to form the intelligence and counterintelligence sections of the USGCC settled into a requisitioned building a half-mile southwest of the Kronprinzenallee complex. The facility was on the grounds of the former Kaiser Wilhelm Institute for Physics, which had been founded in 1917 and was headed by Albert Einstein until he emigrated to the United States in 1933. Following Einstein's departure, the Nazis made the institute the center of German atomic bomb research and, under director Dr. Werner Heisenberg, the institute was on the verge of taking its small reactor critical when the war ended.[31] The Soviets seized the institute when they took Berlin in May 1945, and by the time Fred and the others moved in, all four floors and the basement of the building had been thoroughly looted. The Nazis' small reactor, all scientific equipment, cabinets full of files, and even toilets and water faucets were gone. The only traces that remained of the building's earlier, decidedly sinister use were unusually thick interior basement walls made of steel and concrete and pierced by tinted lead-glass windows. Fred, Jack Condon, Art O'Connor, Dick Thompson, and Vince Ascherl set up an office on the building's second floor.

During several briefings with Gordon Sheen and his staff, the FBI men were provided with a wealth of valuable background information. Allied-occupied Berlin was divided into four sectors—American, British, French, and Soviet. The American Sector, they learned, included six of the city's twenty historic prewar *Bezirke*, or boroughs. These areas (from west to east) were Zehlendorf, Steglitz, Schöneberg, Kreuzberg, Tempelhof, and Neukölln, and together they formed the roughly eighty-five-square-mile southwestern quadrant of the former Nazi capital. The American Sector was administered by the Berlin District headquarters, while the USGCC was part of the four-party Allied Control Council that upon its formal establishment in early August would govern occupied Germany. The ACC would be headquartered in the Schöneberg borough's ornate Kammergericht building, which had been the wartime venue for Nazi show trials.

The ALU's attachment to Sheen's USGCC counterintelligence section would theoretically allow Fred and his men to undertake investigations anywhere in occupied Germany, though gaining access to Russian-controlled areas would likely prove extremely difficult, if not impossible, given the

Soviets' already deeply uncooperative attitude toward the Western Allies. That intransigence aside, as part of the USGCC, the FBI agents could operate freely in the U.S., British, and French sectors of Berlin. They would also have access to two potentially valuable resources, the Berlin Document Center (BDC) and the Berlin District Interrogation Center (BDIC).

The BDC was established immediately after the Allied occupation as a central aggregation point for captured Third Reich records. Housed in a requisitioned mansion in Zehlendorf, the facility held millions of pages of Nazi documents, most of them recovered from a Munich suburb by CIC agents.[32] The trove included SS and Nazi Party membership documents, and among the latter were Auslands-Organisation records of U.S. citizens who were members of the Party and returned to Germany in 1937, 1938, and 1939.[33] Of special interest to Fred Ayer and his fellow agents were files on more than two million *Volksdeutscher* from around the world who had returned to the Reich either voluntarily or after being expelled from other countries between 1939 and late 1944.

The BDIC was a former civilian jail that had been turned into a holding center where captured Nazi civilian and military leaders could be questioned, primarily regarding war crimes. In addition, attachment to the USGCC gave the ALU agents in both Berlin and the larger American occupation zone access to other facilities holding senior Nazis outside the former capital. These included the Camp King detention center in Oberursel, which during the war had been a POW camp for downed Allied airman known as Dulag Luft, the Seventh Army Interrogation Center in Augsburg, and the large prison complex in Nuremberg that was soon to house Walter Schellenberg and other accused Nazis war criminals being tried by the International Military Tribunal.

In addition to the BDC and BDIC, there was a third Berlin resource in which the ALU agents were especially interested—the Haus des Rundfunks (Broadcasting House). The extensive complex on Masurenallee in the British-controlled Charlottenburg borough had, since 1933, been the headquarters of the aforementioned Reichs-Rundfunk-Gesellschaft. Completely controlled by Joseph Goebbels's Reichsministerium für Volksaufklärung und Propaganda (Reich Ministry for Enlightenment and Propaganda) from 1933 through May 1945, the RRG had produced programming for both German and foreign audiences. Broadcasts aimed at Britain, France, and other continental European nations were normally sent out over medium-wave transmitters under the Radio Berlin banner, while programming aimed at more distant audiences was transmitted by shortwave.[34] These were sent by an organization initially known, logically enough, as the Deutsche Kurzwellensender (German Short-Wave Station), usually abbreviated as KWS, which in 1943 was renamed the Deutschen Überseesender (German Overseas Stations) or DÜS.[35]

During the war years, the KWS/DÜS, while subordinate to the RRG, was headquartered in a separate building in Charlottenburg, with multiple transmitters, primarily in Bavaria and northwestern Germany. The programs were developed within individual RRG departments under the direction of the Propaganda Ministry's Broadcasting Division. The RRG production sections were focused on specific world regions, the "zones" mentioned earlier. These included Africa, Orient (Middle East and India), Empire (Far East and Australia), Brazil, Ibero-America, and North America (USA and Canada). Each zone comprised dependable German staffers and technicians—most of them Nazi Party members—and editors, commentators, and announcers who were either foreign nationals or repatriated Germans.[36]

While Germany had been broadcasting news, sports, and cultural programming to the United States since 1931, the RRG did not officially form the North America Zone until 1938. The initial programming was aimed at keeping the United States neutral in any new European war, primarily by extolling the "brotherly similarities" between Germany and America. Many broadcasts focused on the "great work" being done in the States by such pro-Nazi groups as the German-American Bund and, after the 1939 outbreak of war, attempted to exacerbate Americans' distrust of Britain and weaken the political and growing military ties between Washington and London. It was during the months before and just after Pearl Harbor that several Americans were first heard on the airwaves—including the seven suspected of broadcasting for the Nazis indicted for treason by the Justice Department in July 1943. For Fred Ayer and his FBI colleagues, the records of the RGG and KWS/DÜS were a key target in Berlin.

But they were not the only radio-related records in the former Nazi capital that were of keen interest to the ALU men. A second part of the Hitler government—Joachim von Ribbentrop's Foreign Ministry—had also operated a wartime foreign-broadcast department. Unlike Goebbels's heavy-handed and hardline approach to propaganda, the Foreign Office's Broadcasting Division sought to present Germany's views in a more refined and less confrontational way. Von Ribbentrop's radio operations were also organized by region, with the United States designated as Region VII and often referred to as the "USA Zone." It was the Foreign Office's Werner Plack who had recruited several American expatriates in Paris, and whether they had broadcast from France or Berlin their records, Fred believed, were still somewhere in the former Nazi capital.

Nor was it just files the ALU men would be searching for. Though Pound, Chandler, and Delaney were already in custody, the other renegade broadcasters indicted in 1943—Jane Anderson, Robert H. Best, Constance Drexel, Frederick W. Kaltenbach, and Max Koischwitz—were still at large and believed to be in Berlin or its environs. Moreover, Fred and his fellow agents had brought with them the names of two additional Americans thought to have broadcast for the Nazis, Fern Deussen and Gerhard Haase.

As it happened, the first names to be crossed off the ALU's Berlin list were the men Fred referred to as "the two Ks," Koischwitz and Kaltenbach.

Max Oscar Otto Koischwitz

While several of his fellow renegade broadcasters had backgrounds in journalism, Otto Koischwitz (as he preferred to be called) was a highly educated and, early in his career, well-respected academic. His metamorphosis from open-minded college professor to strident Nazi broadcaster stunned many of his students and colleagues, and ultimately led to his 1943 indictment.

Born in the then German village of Jauer in southwestern Silesia in 1902,[37] Koischwitz was the son of a doctor and grew up intellectually curious. He ultimately graduated with a PhD in medieval German literature from the University of Berlin, but was unable to find a suitable academic position in Germany, and in 1924, emigrated to the United States. He settled in New York, and eventually secured part-time teaching positions at New York University, Columbia University, and Hunter College. The latter institution granted him an assistant professorship in 1926, and he proved to be both an excellent and highly regarded classroom instructor. Indeed, in 1928, he was voted Hunter College's most popular teacher.[38] That same year, Koischwitz married Erna Keller, a Swiss immigrant, and the couple eventually had three daughters.

Koischwitz's originally moderate political views eventually began to change, at least in part because he felt that his career advancement was being inhibited by the fact that he was not a U.S. citizen. As a result, both he and his wife applied for—and in March 1935, received—naturalized citizenship, while their daughters were all citizens by birth.[39] Koischwitz's career position did not improve, however, and he began to lace his lectures with increasingly anti-Semitic comments while also insinuating that his advancement was being blocked by Jews in the college's hierarchy. By 1930, he was openly praising Hitler and Germany's burgeoning Nazi movement, an attitude that attracted the attention of New York's Anti-Nazi League. In August 1939, just weeks before the German invasion of Poland and the resultant outbreak of World War II, the League reported its findings to the New York City Board of Education. Told that he was under suspicion as an unfit teacher, Koischwitz requested a leave of absence from Hunter College. In mid-September, his request was granted, and he and his family decamped for Europe.[40]

After a brief stay in Denmark, the Koischwitz clan headed for Berlin, and by mid-January 1940, Otto was a member of the Foreign Ministry's USA Zone. Broadcasting initially as "Doctor Anders" and then as "O.K.," he towed the Nazi Party line in all respects. He frequently teamed up with Fred Kaltenbach for a show called "Fritz and Fred," during which the two men pretended to "debate" international issues—conversations which the pro-Nazi speaker always won. Koischwitz occasionally even brought his eldest daughter, Stella, on the air to portray a young American girl named "Little Margaret." She and "Doctor Anders" would chat about how wonderful life was in Hitler's Germany, where everyone was employed, well-fed, and blissfully content.[41]

Over time, Koischwitz rose to prominence not only as an on-air talent, but eventually as the head of the USA Zone. Beginning in 1942, he often partnered with Mildred Gillars, and the two soon became lovers despite the fact that Koischwitz's wife, Erna, was pregnant with the couple's fourth child. Whatever guilt Koischwitz may or may not have felt about his affair, he was reportedly heartbroken when his newborn lived only a week. That loss was compounded just days later when Erna died on August 24, 1943, in what was then the British Royal Air Force's largest bombing raid on the German capital. While still grieving, Koischwitz was forced by Joseph Goebbels to leave the Foreign Ministry's USA Zone and begin working for the RRG. Following the June 1944 Allied landings in Normandy, the propaganda minister sent the broadcaster into the field to do radio reports from the front lines in France and Holland. As American journalist William L. Shirer noted in a syndicated newspaper article on September 9:

> [Koischwitz's] . . . specialty was broadcasting eye-witness accounts from the various battle fronts on which the Americans were facing Germans. Since General [Omar] Bradley's Americans began their race across France I have not been able to catch any more

> broadcasts by [Koischwitz]. Presumably he began moving too fast to allow a pause at the microphone.[42]

It was true that Koischwitz had not been heard on the air since mid-August, and by digging around in the BDC, Fred Ayer and his colleagues were able to determine why. While reporting from the Netherlands, the renegade American had begun experiencing extreme symptoms of tuberculosis, an illness with which he'd first been diagnosed in 1929. Possibly exacerbated by the broadcaster's depression following the death of his wife and the difficult field conditions under which he'd been working, the disease came back in full force. Koischwitz was medically evacuated back to Berlin, where he died on August 31 of what his death certificate cited as tuberculosis and heart failure. When told of his death, his erstwhile lover and fellow radio traitor, Mildred Gillars, reportedly broke into hysterics and told everyone within earshot that he had been the love of her life. No one apparently gave much thought to Koischwitz's three daughters, now orphans in an increasingly war-ravaged city.[43]

The Department of Justice formally withdrew the renegade's treason indictment on October 27, 1947.

Frederick Wilhelm Kaltenbach

The other "K" that Fred Ayer and his team thought might still be in Berlin was Fred Kaltenbach—like Koischwitz, a highly intelligent former academic.

Born to German immigrant parents in Dubuque, Iowa, in 1895, Kaltenbach grew up in nearby Waterloo.[44] Though shy and introverted, he was an excellent student who, in high school, excelled in debate. Following his graduation, he and a younger brother, Gustave, went on a bicycle tour of Germany, where they were briefly interned following the 1914 outbreak of World War I. Despite that experience, Kaltenbach returned to the United States in December 1914 an admirer of all things German. He enrolled in Iowa's Grinnell College, but in June 1918, left school to enlist in the U.S. Army. After training at Fort Monroe, Virginia, he was commissioned a second lieutenant in the Coast Artillery Corps. He served only nine months on active duty before the end of the war led to his honorable discharge. His brother Gustave, on the other hand, was overseas for two years in the Army Medical Corps.

Instead of returning to finish a degree at Grinnell, Kaltenbach enrolled in the Iowa State Teachers College. He quickly became a star debater, winning several major tournaments and earning a statewide reputation as an orator. He nevertheless could not find a suitable teaching position following graduation, so he spent seven years as an appraiser for a Waterloo trust company. In 1927, Kaltenbach was hired to teach American history at a high school in Manchester, Iowa, but moved to Dubuque High School four years later to teach business law, economics, and history. During the summers, he worked on a master's degree in history at the University of Chicago, and in 1933, won a scholarship from the University of Berlin to pursue a doctorate. He took leave from Dubuque High School and spent two years in Germany. That experience convinced Kaltenbach that Adolf Hitler was the savior of Europe and the world's bulwark against communism, and what the young American called the "scourge of international Jewry."

A fanatical anti-Semite and virulently pro-Nazi by the time he returned to Iowa in 1935, Kaltenbach formed a coed high school group he named the Militant Order of Spartan Knights. Ostensibly a "hiking club," the organization was essentially a clone of Germany's Hitler Youth movement. Members wore brown shirts, carried walking sticks that looked more like clubs, and held secret rituals. Alarmed parents and school officials protested, and in June 1936, the Spartan Knights were shut down and Kaltenbach's teaching contract was terminated. He returned to Germany and began taking jobs as a freelance translator, and in 1936, was hired by the RRG and began making regular broadcasts to the United States. In February 1939, he married a German woman who worked for one of Luftwaffe chief and Reichsmarschall Hermann Göring's aviation propaganda magazines.

An excellent, persuasive speaker, as fluent in German as he was in English, Kaltenbach quickly became a key member of the RRG's stable of American broadcasters. Indeed, as William L. Shirer noted, the man from Iowa "is probably one of the best of the lot, actually believing in National Socialism with a sincere fanaticism. . . . He is not a bad radio speaker. . . . Most Nazis find him a bit 'too American' for their taste, but Kaltenbach would die for Nazism."[45] The Iowan's dedication to the Nazi cause kept him in Germany following America's entry into the war, and over the next two-and-a half years, he continued his assaults on Roosevelt, democracy, Jews, and communists. As Germany's military fortunes declined, however, his broadcasts grew less frequent and far less coherent. The American renegade's love affair with Nazism began to lose its luster, and he became increasingly withdrawn and depressive.

According to Fred Ayer's file on Kaltenbach, he was last heard on the air just days before Soviet troops entered Berlin. CIC soldiers had begun scouring the city soon after their own arrival, Fred read, and they eventually managed to locate Kaltenbach's wife. She told interrogators that agents of the NKVD—the Soviet secret police—had shown up at their apartment on May 18. The Russians had hustled Kaltenbach away, and his wife had received only one brief note from him since. The U.S. Group Control Council and U.S. Berlin District headquarters had both sought clarification about Kaltenbach's whereabouts, Fred learned, but the Soviets insisted they did not have the American renegade. Under the circumstances, the ALU suspended its search for Kaltenbach, and Fred notified Bureau headquarters that he would report on any new developments.

Almost a year later, in June 1946, the Berlin District headquarters learned that Fred Kaltenbach had died in Soviet captivity in October 1945. On the Department of Justice's recommendation, Judge David A. Pine of the U.S. District Court for the District of Columbia dismissed Kaltenbach's indictment on April 13, 1948.[46]

Fern Annemarie Deussen

In January 1945, while Fred Ayer was still based in Paris, he sent a message to Bureau headquarters regarding an American woman that French authorities believed was working for the German Foreign Ministry's USA Zone.[47] The DSM indicated that though the suspect had spent some time in the French capital, she had apparently left for Berlin before the June 1944 D-Day landings. Fred had therefore added her name to the list of individuals to be located once the ALU moved into Germany.

Fern Deussen was born in Stockton, in California's Central Valley, in February 1920.[48] Her father, Eduard, had emigrated from Germany in 1909, settling first in Chicago. There he met and married American-born Marie Kurens, the daughter of a German father and Danish mother. After World War I, Fern's parents relocated to California, where Eduard worked as a motion picture projectionist. Soon after Fern's birth, the family moved to Vallejo, north of San Francisco. Life in the Golden State apparently lost its allure, however, for in 1927, the Deussen clan moved again, this time to Warren Township, Illinois, just north of Chicago, on the shore of Lake Michigan. Fern's mother died there in 1929, after which Fern was sent to Germany to live with the family of her uncle, Friedrich Kaysel, near Düsseldorf.

Over the following nine years, Fern grew into a beautiful and well-educated young woman, fluent in German and French as well as English. Her time in Germany coincided with the rise of Nazism, which her father's relatives—and she—embraced wholeheartedly. Fern's father died in Chicago in 1937, and the following year, the eighteen-year-old returned to the country of her birth to settle his affairs. She didn't stay long, however, for she was back in Germany by the time war broke out in September 1939. After the French surrender in June 1940, Fern secured a job as a secretary and translator in the propaganda section of the German embassy in Paris. Her native fluency in English quickly caught the attention of ace radio talent recruiter Werner Plack, and by the time America entered the war in 1941, Fern was in Berlin working for the USA Zone.

The brief file on Deussen that Fred Ayer had carried from Paris did not indicate whether the young woman was at all troubled by her choice to remain in Germany after America's declaration of war. She was known to have voiced English-language radio programs, usually on innocuous social topics but also occasionally of a more pointed political nature, and occasionally spoke from the Foreign Ministry's alternate broadcasting studio in Luxembourg. There she worked with another American expatriate, Dr. Gerhard Haase. Deussen was not apparently considered a star, because her on-air appearances were irregular—at least as far as Allied monitoring stations could tell.

Despite diligent searching at the BDC, Fred and his fellow agents could find no further information on Deussen. Indeed, it was not until November 1945 that Joe Dunn was able to locate documents that shed light on the young woman's status. In January 1944, Fern married one Herbert Rudolf Kammerer, a German colleague from the USA Zone. The two had a daughter in April 1945, but the following November, Deussen died at age twenty-five of tuberculosis in St. Georgen in the Black Forest, which was then in the French occupation zone. Her daughter was ultimately adopted by an American Red Cross nurse who took the child to the United States in 1950.

Gerhard Hermann Haase

Fern Deussen's broadcasting colleague was born in Berlin in 1913, the son of the well-known artist Herman Alexander Haase. The family emigrated to the United States in 1922 and settled in Miami, where in addition to exhibiting his artwork in local galleries, the elder Haase established a high-end commercial painting business. His firm did the interiors for many of Miami's better known buildings, including the city's landmark Tower Theater.[49]

A naturalized U.S. citizen by virtue of his parents' naturalization, Gerhard Haase grew up fluent in both German and English. While he showed promise as an artist, he ultimately chose a different career path; after graduating from high school, he enrolled in the University of Florida's premed program. His grades were good enough to win him a place at the University of Berlin's renowned medical school, from which he graduated in 1937. After a brief trip back to Florida to visit his parents, the now Dr. Haase did two years of advanced surgical training at the University of Vienna. He was in the Austrian capital at the time of the March 1938 *Anschluss*, and according to information Fred Ayer had obtained from the DSM in Paris, soon after Austria's absorption into the Third Reich, the young bilingual physician was recruited for propaganda work by the ubiquitous Werner Plack.

Haase and Deussen were both working in Berlin by the time of Pearl Harbor. Like his female coworker, Haase spent less time in front of the microphone from early 1944 on. The Berlin-based ALU agents were able to determine from records unearthed at the BDC that in Haase's case, the reduction in air time was the result of the German capital's increasing need for skilled surgeons. Simply put, he was more valuable in one of Berlin's dwindling number of operating rooms than he was in a radio studio. And it was in a heavily bomb-damaged hospital in the American sector that CIC agents—acting on information provided by the ALU—found Haase during the last week of August 1945. He was taken into custody and lodged in the BDIC, where over a period of several weeks he was questioned by CIC agents and the ALU's Jack Condon.

Haase was able to provide useful information about the structure and operations of the Foreign Ministry's Broadcasting Division up through the time of his final departure from the organization just after D-Day. His truthfulness, willingness to assist his interrogators, and the fact that he successfully resisted intense pressure to join the Nazi Party earned him Condon's grudging respect. More important, Haase's sincere regret about being part of the propaganda effort aimed at America and his heartfelt apology for his broadcasts—coupled with the lack of the required two eyewitnesses—prompted Fred Ayer to suggest to Hoover that Haase not be charged as a traitor. The director apparently agreed, for though Haase's U.S. citizenship was revoked, the Justice Department declined to indict him for treason and he was freed from custody in November 1945.

Following his release, Haase went back to school. Undoubtedly burned out by the hundreds of surgeries he had performed under grueling conditions during the final months of the war and increasingly hampered by a finger damaged by bomb shrapnel, he chose a new medical path. When Berlin University reopened on January 29, 1946, Haase enrolled in a program that ultimately qualified him as a radiologist. He worked at various Berlin hospitals until December 1951, when he and his new bride, Johanna, emigrated to the

United States. He ultimately regained his American citizenship and worked in a Miami hospital until a few months before his death on July 25, 1971.

WHILE FRED AYER AND HIS FELLOW AGENTS were combing Berlin in search of information on the whereabouts of alleged U.S. renegades, a new member of the ALU was already questioning three American suspects in Austria. Two were accused of broadcasting propaganda for the Nazis, while the third had organized one of the largest German spy rings ever to operate in the United States.

CHAPTER 12

Suspects, Victory, and Storm Clouds

Hans Wenthur had arrived in Salzburg on August 2, 1945, having traveled solo by air from Washington, D.C., to Austria via North Africa and Italy. He cabled Fred Ayer four days later that he had already met and been briefed by the intelligence chief for U.S. Forces Austria, and that Joe Fellner was expected to arrive during the last week of August. The latter's assignment to the four-nation occupation force in Vienna had been delayed by bureaucratic wrangling between the U.S. and Soviet sector commanders.

On the positive side, during Wenthur's first three weeks in Austria, CIC agents arrested a trio of suspected American renegades. The first was an alleged propagandist who had not even been on the FBI's radar, the second was an unlikely spymaster, and the third was one of the eight broadcasters indicted in 1943. Perhaps more important, the latter was the first of the two women on that list to be apprehended.

Thornton Chapman Sinclair

The first suspect Hans Wenthur interrogated in Salzburg had been born the son of a prominent businessman in Fort Thomas, Kentucky, in 1904.[1] Like both Otto Koischwitz and Fred Kaltenbach, Thornton Sinclair was an academic—he received a BA from Miami University of Ohio in 1925, a Bachelor of Laws degree from Columbia University in 1931, and a PhD in history and political science from Harvard in 1935. While studying at Columbia, Sinclair secured a position teaching history and political science at New Jersey's Newark College of Rutgers University. It was a post he would hold for nearly ten years.

Sinclair had first gone to Germany in the summer of 1933, his announced intention being to study the political science aspects of the Nazi movement as part of the research for his doctorate. In July 1934, he married Cassandra

Taliaferro, who accompanied him to Berlin that summer and again in 1936 and 1937. During their sojourns in the German capital, the couple met and interacted with Nazi Party officials and members of the increasingly persecuted anti-Hitler movement. In his articles about Germany for American academic journals, Sinclair took a relatively neutral view of Nazism. He acknowledged Hitler's "excesses" but also said that the Führer had done much to unify a country that had been embroiled in civil war and political chaos for more than a decade after World War I. Sinclair's "open-mindedness" prompted the Nazis to give him special access to key events, including the massive party rallies held in Nuremburg each September.

Sinclair attended the 1936, 1937, and 1938 events, later writing about the structure, content, and conduct of the two earlier rallies in a journal article.[2] While the piece strove to maintain a dispassionate and academic tone, the author's grudging admiration for the pageantry, organization, and overall effect of the rallies on their participants seemed to leak into his prose. "For those present is reserved a close sight of the center of attraction, the *Führer.* His dramatic entry and exit make the opening [of the Party congress part of the rally] a stirring experience."[3] Apparently for the American observer as well, who continued, "Blasts of trumpets herald the arrival of the *Führer,* who, with his retinue, makes his triumphal entry, marching . . . to the stage to the strains of the 'Badenweiler March' and shouts and cries of 'Heil!'[4] Sinclair concluded his journal article by focusing even more closely on Hitler, writing:

> He is a dynamo of activity, making speech after speech, reviewing parades for hours, and holding his arm in continuous salute. All praise him and attribute all accomplishments to his will, inspiration, and genius. On proper occasion he is stern, yet he may be jovial and even paternal. He displays his versatility by the broad subject matter covered in his speeches. . . . The first question the returning visitor is asked is, "Did you see the *Führer?*"[5]

Whether Sinclair's breathless descriptions of the pomp and circumstance of the Nuremburg rallies and of Hitler's undoubted personal charisma were meant to be simply illustrative or were expressions of his own positive feelings about Nazism is unclear. However, upon his return to the United States following the 1938 rally, Sinclair began speaking more approvingly of the Nazis during his lectures at Newark College. In 1939, he divorced his wife, having begun a romantic relationship in Berlin with young

German surgeon, Dr. Margarete Hartman. Sinclair was back in Germany when World War II erupted, and he chose to remain in Berlin and went to work for the USA Zone as a translator and interpreter. Though he reportedly wrote some radio scripts, he apparently did not make any broadcasts, at least none that were monitored by the British or Americans. In 1940, he and Hartman had their first child, a daughter, and Sinclair quit his Foreign Ministry job sometime after Pearl Harbor. The pair had a second daughter in 1942, after which they moved to Bavaria, where Hartman became the family's sole breadwinner. On Valentine's Day, 1945, the couple married in Rosenheim, eleven miles north of the Austrian border.

On May 2, the 23rd Tank Battalion and other elements of the U.S. 12th Armored Division occupied Rosenheim as part of the American advance into Austria's Tyrol region.[6] Two days later, Sinclair was arrested by CIC agents at his home, and after initial interrogation in Rosenheim, he was transferred to the newly opened CIC holding facility in Salzburg. There, on August 8, he found himself staring into the eyes of Hans Wenthur. That first encounter lasted for forty minutes, during which Sinclair gave a general accounting of his time in Germany after the 1939 outbreak of war.[7]

He had gone to work for the USA Zone, he said, simply because he needed the money. His lecturer position at Newark College had been terminated following his return to Germany in 1939, and the Foreign Ministry offered him a decent salary to work as an interpreter and translator. While he "may have" contributed to "a few" radio scripts, he swore that he had never worked as an on-air broadcaster. Following America's 1941 entry into the war, he had immediately quit his job with the USA Zone, he told Wenthur, because he refused to work against his country on behalf of the Nazis. But hadn't he already done that? the FBI agent asked. By doing translations for the Foreign Ministry before 1941, hadn't he shown that he was at the very least a Nazi sympathizer? Sinclair vehemently denied ever being pro-Nazi and said that his physician wife had avoided ever being a member of the Nazi Party. The couple's move out of Berlin to the relative safety of Bavaria, Sinclair suggested, was partly because his wife was under Gestapo surveillance in the German capital.

Wenthur spoke again with Sinclair on August 9, by which point the FBI agent was coming to the conclusion that the suspect was telling the truth about the limited extent of his involvement with German propaganda broadcasts. Wenthur had thus far been unable to find any evidence that Sinclair had been anything more than an interpreter and translator for the

Foreign Ministry—no radio scripts to which the American had contributed had thus far been found—and he had resigned from both positions upon the United States' declaration of war. The fact that he had chosen to remain in Germany throughout the conflict could be explained by the fact that Sinclair did not want to abandon his partner and their children. However, before Wenthur made a final decision on whether to recommend treason charges against Sinclair, he wanted to explore some of the Nazi archives available in Frankfurt. He cabled Fred Ayer, who responded that they should meet at the IG Farben building so that Wenthur could touch base with the ALU team members serving in Germany.[8]

Wenthur arrived in Frankfurt on August 16, and over the following four days, held meetings with Fred, Joe Dunn, and Dick Thompson, as well as senior members of the USFET intelligence and counterintelligence staffs. Wenthur was also able to examine some records of the Foreign Ministry's Broadcasting Division that had been found in a small radio station near Frankfurt. The documents further convinced Wenthur that Thornton Sinclair did not warrant a treason indictment, a decision with which Fred concurred and that he relayed to the Bureau. The Department of Justice responded that no charges would be filed on the condition that Sinclair provide a detailed sworn statement regarding all of his activities in Germany between December 1941 and May 1945.

Wenthur's brief visit to Frankfurt was not just about finding more information on Sinclair. Fred asked the ex-policeman from Milwaukee to question a few high-ranking Germans who had resisted interrogations by other Allied intelligence officers. It was a stroke of genius on Fred's part, for as he later remembered:

> Many a captured German would remain sitting even if an American officer came into the room or cell. Not so with Hans. His whole demeanor and tone of voice could become so Prussian that his mere appearance caused Germans to jump to stiff and quivering attention.[9]

But Wenthur's short stay in Frankfurt was not all work. He lodged with Fred and the others at the house in Höchst, where the ALU men spent their evenings relaxing as Wenthur "played old Bavarian drinking songs on our piano . . . while a chorus of 190-pound char ladies sang."[10]

Wenthur returned to Salzburg on August 21. Four days later, Joe Fellner finally arrived in Austria, and the two agents spent a week going over files and cases, securing for Fellner the documents he would need to operate as part of the American sector command in Vienna. It wasn't until August 30 that Wenthur was able to get back to dealing with the Sinclair case. Having been unable to find any records in Frankfurt that disputed the American's story, the FBI agent told the suspect of the Department of Justice's decision not to indict him—on the condition that he provide a signed affidavit covering his stay in wartime Germany. Sinclair readily agreed, likely more than happy to have avoided legal jeopardy that would have prevented any meaningful postwar academic success in the United States.

Upon his release from the Salzburg CIC holding facility, Sinclair immediately returned to his home and family in Rosenheim. He, his wife, and their three daughters remained in Bavaria until the spring of 1947, when they relocated to an Allied-run displaced persons camp outside the northern German port city of Bremen. Sinclair departed for the United States on April 5 aboard the SS *Ernie Pyle*, a former troopship. He settled in Lexington, Kentucky, where he was offered a teaching position at Transylvania College. That appointment ignited a firestorm of controversy, largely because of a June 19 radio broadcast in which syndicated newspaper columnist Walter Winchell outlined Sinclair's work for the German Foreign Ministry between 1939 and 1941.[11] While Transylvania went on to hire Sinclair despite the adverse publicity, the academic—joined by his wife and daughters in December 1947—moved to the University of Houston in 1950. His wife took a position at the Texas Medical Center, then worked at the University of Texas's M.D. Anderson Cancer Center until shortly before her death in 1984. Sinclair, for his part, retired in 1973 and died in 1991.

When Hans Wenthur returned to Salzburg on August 21, he learned that during his absence, two additional American suspects had been apprehended by CIC agents in Vienna.

The first individual, a bespectacled middle-aged man, had walked into the headquarters of the U.S. zone on August 14. Shown into the office of Captain Hugh J. Downey, the visitor announced that he was an American citizen and wanted to go home. He had no passport, the man said, but he presented a certificate issued by the New York University Medical School that gave his name as Dr. Ignaz Theodore Griebl.[12] Downey recognized the name immediately, because it was on a combined U.S. Forces European Theater/U.S. Forces Austria watch list. The young officer quickly had

Griebl arrested by CIC agents. According to the watch list, the suspect was to be held until he could be interrogated by an ALU member, and since Joe Fellner had not yet arrived in the Austrian capital, Downey had Griebl confined in the CIC's Vienna holding facility.

Three days later, on August 17, the second suspect was hauled before Downey. In contrast to the rather mousy-looking Griebl, Constance Drexel was stylishly dressed. Her elegant appearance was significantly offset, however, by her foul mood. She was incensed by her arrest, which had occurred after she blurted out her identity to *Stars and Stripes* reporter Fred Wackernagel Jr. when the two accidentally met while walking in a Vienna park. Drexel screamed at Downey that she was innocent of the treason charge, that she had always been a good American and that her reputation had been impugned by "certain people" in the United States. She waved her U.S. passport around and repeatedly pointed to the American flag pin she wore on the lapel of her dress. Like Griebl, Drexel was to be held in custody so that she could be interrogated by an ALU member. When told she would be incarcerated until that time, she screamed, "I am to go to jail with common prostitutes and thieves?"[13]

When notified by Downey of the arrests of Griebl and Drexel, Hans Wenthur said he would get to Vienna as soon as possible. Owing to the agent's workload in Salzburg, he wasn't able to reach the Austrian capital until August 28, three days after Joe Fellner's long-delayed arrival there from the United States. The two agents agreed that it would be best to transfer both prisoners to Salzburg, since according to the four-power occupation agreement, if Griebl and Drexel were held in Vienna, the Soviets could demand access to them. NKVD operatives would be able to conduct their own interrogation, and in the process might learn details about German covert operations in America or anti-Western propaganda methods that could prove useful for Moscow. The two American renegades were duly packed off to Salzburg, where on August 30, Wenthur—after wrapping up his questioning of Thornton Sinclair—began separately interrogating them.[14]

Ignaz Griebl

There is an axiom in the world of espionage that a good spy should be so average-looking as to be essentially invisible in a crowd. Ignaz Griebl certainly fit the "average-looking" criterion. Short, plump, with a receding hairline, thin lips, and round, owlish glasses, he would not have stood out in any gathering. And yet, the essentially anonymous Dr. Griebl had gone out of his way to attract public attention while at the same time attempting to organize and operate what the FBI considered to be one of the most dangerous Nazi spy rings active in America before Pearl Harbor.

Born in 1898 to a prominent family in Straubing, a small city on the banks of the Danube river, in eastern Bavaria, Griebl was raised a Roman Catholic.[15] He served as an artillery officer in World War I and was wounded during fighting on the Italian front. While hospitalized, he met Maria "Mitzi" Glanz, an Austrian field nurse four years his senior. After the war, the pair stayed together, and Glanz helped put Griebl through medical school at the University of Munich. In 1922, she sailed for the United States and settled in New York, where Griebl joined her two years later. The couple married and lived on Mitzi's income as a nurse while her husband completed a year-long internship during the day and attended an intensive English-language course at Fordham University at night. After gaining his U.S. physician's certification, Griebl bought a small practice in Bangor, Maine, though after less than a year, he and his wife moved back to New York City. There Griebl established a thriving obstetrics and gynecology practice in Yorkville, a predominantly German enclave in Manhattan.[16] He also joined a variety of German social and cultural organizations, and was the official physician for several of them. The Griebls both became naturalized American citizens in 1929, and soon thereafter, Ignaz was commissioned a Medical Corps lieutenant in the U.S. Army Reserve.

By the early 1930s, Griebl was a well-known and generally well respected member of New York's German immigrant community, the latter despite having a much deserved reputation as a serial womanizer. He was also an outspoken anti-Semite and admirer of Adolf Hitler, and in 1933, he and Heinrich "Heinz" Spanknöbel cofounded an openly pro-Nazi organization called Friends of New Germany (FONG). The group included both immigrants and native-born Americans of German descent, and had been formed with the express permission of German deputy Führer Rudolf Hess. FONG's confrontational tactics and penchant for street violence soon began to produce an anti-Nazi backlash in the U.S. press and also attracted the attention of Congress. Spanknöbel fled to Germany and was replaced by Griebl as head of the organization.

On May 17, 1934, FONG held a mass rally at New York's Madison Square Garden. The cavernous venue was draped with American flags and swastikas, and more than fifteen thousand attendees listened as a parade of speakers extolled the purported virtues of Nazism. Among them was Griebl himself. In his native tongue, he shrieked that Germans in America would soon "demand adequate representation in city, county, state and federal governments" and threatened that "those who fight us must perish, socially as well as economically, because of our determination to destroy our enemies completely and without any consideration whatever!"[17]

Days after the Madison Square Garden event, a former senior member of FONG, Friedrich Karl Kruppa, testified before the U.S. House of Representatives' Special Committee on Un-American Activities. He said that German agents had been active in the United States for years, that Nazi propaganda was being smuggled into America in vast quantities, and that there were "Nazi cells" aboard all German-registered vessels calling at U.S. ports. Kruppa also told congressional investigators that Spanknöbel had not willingly fled to Germany, but had been kidnapped at gunpoint from a dinner being held at Griebl's home.

One would think that the philandering physician from Yorkville's widely reported and quite visible connection to FONG, the repeated mention of his name during the meetings of the Special Committee—and in a completely different context, the very public lawsuit brought against him by a woman whom he conned out of thousands of dollars on the pretext that the money would allow him to divorce his wife and marry the complainant—would have soured Germany's intelligence agencies on him. That was obviously not the case, for he'd became a paid agent in March 1934.

It was not the Abwehr that initially hired Griebl, however, but the Gestapo's Hamburg-based Maritime Bureau. The organization's chief, Inspector Paul Kraus, was in the process of enlarging the shipboard Nazi cells that Kruppa had told Congress about. The cell members not only moved pro-Nazi printed propaganda into the United States but acted as couriers—taking Berlin's instructions to agents in America and returning with the information the spies had gathered. Griebl's leadership in FONG gave him access to many German Americans who worked in such key American industries as aircraft production, shipbuilding, and electronics. Once on Kraus's payroll, the Yorkville physician showed a knack for recruiting valuable agents that likely surprised even himself. Griebl's unexpected success as a spymaster soon aroused the Abwehr's interest, and in late 1934, that agency's Bremen-based naval intelligence branch absorbed Kraus's Gestapo operation. Given the Abwehr code name Ilberg and the agency registration number A.2339, Griebl's primary assignments continued to be the recruitment of agents and the theft of U.S. military secrets.[18]

So successful was Griebl at his second profession that in June 1937, the head of the Abwehr's Bremen operation, Korvettenkapitän Erich Pfeiffer, invited the physician to visit Germany. The now thirty-nine-year-old Griebl did not make the transatlantic voyage accompanied by his long-suffering wife, but by statuesque thirty-one-year-old Katherina "Kate" Moog, a German-born nurse and U.S. citizen with whom the physician was conducting a torrid affair.[19] The two were feted by Pfeiffer as though they were visiting royalty and were ultimately taken by private train to Berlin to meet Abwehr chief Wilhelm Canaris. Germany's senior foreign intelligence officer thanked Griebl for his efforts in America and said the Abwehr would provide him with a home in Bavaria and the rank and salary of a captain in the Wehrmacht. The deed to the house and the accumulated military pay would be available whenever Griebl returned to the *Vaterland* for good.[20] Before leaving Berlin for the return to Bremen and the voyage back to America, Griebl and Moog were directed to set up a "honey trap" in Washington, D.C. Under Moog's supervision, the brothel's employees were to pump as much information as possible out of their military and government customers. Griebl's mistress ultimately declined, however, and the idea went nowhere.[21]

Upon his return to the United States, Griebl redoubled his efforts to recruit new agents and harvest the information of greatest interest to his Abwehr handlers. He and those working for him did well—that is, until a young and beautiful but somewhat careless hairdresser aboard the German transatlantic steamship *Europa* of the Norddeutscher Lloyd Line (NDL) was arrested by the FBI on February 4, 1938. The woman, Johanna "Jenni" Hofmann, was a low-level courier for the Abwehr who carried messages between German agents working in America and their handlers in Bremen and Berlin. She and a man named Karl Schlüter—a longtime Abwehr operative posing as a steward aboard *Europa*—had been working with two recently recruited agents. Günther Gustav "Gus" Rumrich and Erich Glaser were both onetime members of the U.S. Army, the former a native-born American citizen who had grown up in Austria-Hungary and the latter a German who'd become naturalized.[22]

Rumrich had deserted from the Army after embezzling funds, while Glaser had received an honorable discharge. The men had become friends while on active duty, and following Glaser's return to civilian life, they reestablished contact. Largely out of a need for funds to support his wife and two young sons, in January 1938, Rumrich had volunteered his services to the Abwehr. He eventually brought Glaser into the fold, and the two men planned various ways to obtain American military secrets. None of those plots came to fruition, and on February 15, 1938, Rumrich was arrested by the New York Police Department for attempting to obtain blank U.S. passports by masquerading as a State Department official. He was turned over to Special Agent Leon Turrou, at the time widely considered to be the best investigator and interrogator in the FBI.[23] Rumrich quickly spilled all he knew about Abwehr operations in America and gave the names of other covert operatives with whom he'd interacted, including Glaser, Schlüter, and Jenni Hofmann. When the latter was arrested, Turrou searched her room aboard *Europa* and found a cache of coded letters. He also discovered the key to the code, which the inept hairdresser was supposed to have memorized and then burned. Among the individuals to whom the letters were addressed were Miss Moog and one Dr. Ignaz T. Griebl of New York.

Within days of discovering and decoding the letters, Turrou accosted Griebl at his Yorkville office and took him in for questioning. After initially denying any connection to the Abwehr, the doctor turned on his erstwhile compatriots, just as Rumrich had. While minimizing his own activities, Griebl gave the FBI agent names, dates, places, and targets. Indeed, the physician provided so much information that at one point, he dramatically broke down in front of Turrou and sobbed that by being so cooperative with the FBI he had signed his own death warrant in Germany.[24] This episode—and the fact that a May 5 polygraph test had indicated that Griebl was being truthful about his professed limited involvement in espionage—convinced Turrou that the best way to gain more information from Griebl was to not arrest him. Instead, the doctor was released from custody on the condition that he testify before the federal grand jury that was being empaneled to investigate Nazi espionage in the United States. Griebl readily agreed but, true to form, had no intention of complying. On May 11, he abandoned both wife and current mistress, and stowed away on the Germany-bound NDL liner *Bremen*.

The spy's reception upon disembarking in his native land had not quite been what he'd expected. Griebl had fled the United States without his passport and with barely two hundred dollars in his pocket, and upon disembarking from *Bremen*, he'd been taken into custody by immigration police. He was briefly detained and had to pay a small fine for arriving without a passport, but was then released into the custody of the Abwehr's Erich Pfeiffer, who had received advance notice of the doctor's arrival. Griebl boasted that his loyalty to the Fatherland had never wavered, and that he had successfully weathered intense interrogation. Then, almost immediately, he began urgently demanding compensation for his services. Pfieffer decided to pawn Griebl off on

Abwehr headquarters in Berlin, and sent him to the agency's finance office. Later, from his temporary home in Würzberg, the doctor continued to badger Pfieffer for large sums of cash. Eventually Griebl was paid between 50,000 and 100,000 reichsmarks, after which he scuttled off to Vienna and disappeared from the Abwehr's radar.[25]

Griebl's escape from New York sent shock waves through the FBI. While the Bureau had been monitoring German propaganda activities in the United States and Berlin's support for groups such as the Friends of New Germany, Hoover and his senior staff had been largely unaware of the depth and breadth of actual Nazi espionage activities in America. Despite the ineptitude of many of those in Griebl's ring and affiliated groups, the potential threat that German agents posed to the U.S. military, the nation's industrial base, and its transportation networks was suddenly and dramatically made clear. Though, on June 20, the federal grand jury investigating German espionage in the United States indicted eighteen people, the majority of the defendants—including Griebl—were beyond the Justice Department's reach. Only four individuals were actually tried and convicted. Johanna Hofmann was sentenced to four years, Günther Rumrich, and Erich Glaser each got two years, and Otto Hermann Voss—a German-born employee of the Seversky Aircraft Company who had passed sensitive information to his Abwehr handlers—received a six-year sentence. Called as a witness during the trial, Kate Moog was not charged, despite her admission that she had met Abwehr chief Canaris during her visit to Germany with Griebl.

The handling of what came to be known as the Rumrich spy case—despite the minor role that particular individual played in the affair—was a public embarrassment for the Bureau. Hoover was incensed and blamed Turrou for Griebl's escape and everything else that had gone wrong with the investigation. After the agent sold his version of the story to the *New York Post* as a syndicated newspaper series, the director had Turrou "dismissed with prejudice" in June 1938. The articles were quickly published in book form as *Nazi Spies in America* and then made into a Warner Brothers motion picture titled *Confessions of a Nazi Spy*, starring Edward G. Robinson. Released in April 1939 (and rereleased, in 1940, with additional scenes), the story was a thinly veiled depiction of the Rumrich/Griebl case, though the names of the principal participants were fictionalized to avoid defamation suits.[26]

As humiliating as the case might have been for the FBI, it also prompted Hoover to completely revamp the Bureau's counterintelligence operations. Using improved methods of covert surveillance—including hidden cameras and microphones—as well as better investigative techniques, in June 1941, the FBI rounded up thirty-three members of a Nazi spy ring headed by South African–born Abwehr agent Fritz Duquesne. One of the latter's trusted operatives, German-born U.S. citizen William Sebold, was actually a double agent working for the Bureau. The arrests broke the back of Nazi espionage operations in the United States, and from that point on, virtually all information received by the Abwehr from "agents" in America was actually disinformation generated by the FBI.

The facts of the 1938 investigations of Ignaz Griebl and his associates were well known to Hans Wenthur, because after joining the FBI, the agent had been part of the Bureau task force that reviewed the entire affair as part of the continuing improvements made to the organization's counterintelligence operations. The FBI agent was thus very well prepared for his first hours-long meeting with Griebl, which took place in the Salzburg CIC facility's interrogation room on August 30, 1945. Then, and in a second exhaustive session on September 4, Wenthur was able to piece together Griebl's activities after he'd fled America aboard *Bremen*.[27]

After reaching Germany and eventually being debriefed and paid off by the Abwehr, by August 1938, Griebl had settled in Vienna. There he took over the lucrative medical practice of a Jewish physician who had been forced to flee to the United States. So profitable was the business that Griebl was able to purchase (at a vastly reduced price) the building at No. 7 Dionysius Andrassystrasse in which the clinic and seven apartments were located.[28] When Mitzi Griebl showed up in the Austrian capital after being released from custody in New York, she found her philandering husband living with a young Austrian woman named Helen Forster.[29] Having apparently finally reached her breaking point in terms of Griebl's infidelity, Mitzi left in disgust and returned to her native Graz. Her husband divorced her in May 1942 and subsequently married Forster, with whom he later had a child. The physician stayed in Vienna throughout the war and eventually ended up treating both military and civilian casualties of Allied bombing attacks.

Over the course of Wenthur's exhaustive interrogations of Griebl, the doctor spoke at length about his prewar activities in New York, though as with his earlier questioning by Turrou, he was careful to minimize his own activities. He denied playing any role in the Nazi war effort after returning to Germany in 1938 and spoke only of his work treating causalities brought into the 250-year-old Allgemeines Krankenhaus der Stadt Wien (Vienna General Hospital). Griebl insisted that he simply wished to return to the United

States, despite Wenthur's pointed observation that should the physician set foot in America, he would immediately be arrested as a fugitive, because of his sudden departure from New York while under a grand journey subpoena.

Upon the conclusion of Wenthur's final interrogation, Griebl—like Sinclair—wrote a lengthy statement giving his point of view on the activities that led him to be the subject of an FBI treason investigation. In his final report, Wenthur recommended that Griebl be held in custody until he could be returned to the United States to stand trial in accordance with the June 1938 indictment. Sometime in late 1945, however, Griebl vanished from the Salzburg holding facility under circumstances that remain unclear. He disappeared into the chaotic landscape of postwar Europe, never to be seen again. Auditors from the Property Control Subsection of the U.S. Military Government subsequently looked into Griebl's ownership of the Vienna apartment complex and medical clinic so that the former owner could eventually be compensated. They discovered that Griebl had taken out four bank loans on the property during the war, with the latter three all ostensibly to be used for property improvements.[30] None were made, and the philandering physician apparently used the funds to finance his last disappearance.

In March 1950, the espionage case against Ignaz T. Griebl was dropped.[31]

Constance Drexel

Born in November 1884 in Darmstadt, Germany, Constanze Louise Katherina Drexel was brought to the United States by her parents, Theodore and Zila, in 1895.[32] The family initially settled in Pennsylvania, where a second daughter, Norma, was born. Constance, as she was known in the family, became a U.S. citizen upon her parents' naturalization in 1899. By 1900, the Drexels were living in Massachusetts, where Theodore worked as a lithographer. Constance and her sister attended public schools, and family life was fairly normal until the parents divorced sometime around 1907. Theodore Drexel moved to Arizona, and by 1910, was confined to the mental institution where he would spend the rest of his life. His former wife took their daughters to Europe, and Constance attended school in Germany and France before graduating from the Sorbonne just before the 1914 outbreak of World War I.

It was that conflict that marked the start of Drexel's career as a journalist. She penned several pieces for American newspapers about her work with the French Red Cross early in the war, and after attending the 1915 International Congress of Women in the Netherlands, she increasingly wrote about "women's issues" and what she saw as a rising tide of militarism in

America. She worked tirelessly for the reelection of Woodrow Wilson in 1916, primarily because she believed he would keep the United States neutral. She ultimately joined the staff of the Philadelphia *Public Ledger*, and after America's 1917 entry into the war, she tried to go to Europe, intending, she said, to visit her ailing sister Norma in Switzerland. Public complaints that her openly pacifist writings were essentially pro-German led the State Department to suspend her passport.

After the armistice, Drexel did manage to get back to Europe, reporting on the Paris peace talks and various women's suffrage conferences. She also attended the funeral of her sister, who died in Geneva in 1920. Over the following fifteen years, Drexel gained a reputation as a keen observer of international events, reporting from Europe for outlets such as the North American Newspaper Alliance, *The New York Times*, and the *Chicago Tribune*. Beginning in the late 1920s, she began writing in increasingly positive terms about the Nazi movement, especially of the important role Hitler purported to envision for women in the "New Germany." Following the Nazis' takeover of the German government in January 1933, Drexel wrote so often and so approvingly of the Third Reich's social reform programs that Goebbels's Propaganda Ministry began offering her writing assignments.

In 1939, the newspaperwoman sailed for Germany, ostensibly to care for her mother, following the latter's "mental breakdown." Shortly after arriving in Berlin, Drexel began broadcasting for the RRG as part of the North America Zone. William L. Shirer, then still European bureau chief for CBS News, often ran into Drexel in the German capital and later wrote of her:

> The Nazis hire her, so far as I can find out, principally because she's the only woman in town who will sell her American accent to them. Bizarre: she constantly pesters me for a job. One American network hired her at the [1939] beginning of the war, but dropped her almost immediately.[33]

Drexel remained in Germany following Pearl Harbor, and thanks to her connections at the RRG, she was not interned. When, in November 1942, she applied to the U.S. State Department—through the Swiss embassy in Berlin—for an extension of her passport, she mentioned her mother's breakdown and added:

> She is now a mental patient in an institution near Wiesbaden . . . and in no condition to have traveled to the United States. I did not feel I could desert her and that is why I remained. In speaking on the German radio, I am following my own ideas; I am not [a] speaker about political or military matters but reporting cultural matters such as activities in the theater, music and on film.[34]

Drexel's rather disingenuous explanation of her continued presence in Nazi Germany did not sway the Department of Justice, and her inclusion in the July 1943 treason indictments ensured that U.S. forces would take her into custody at the earliest opportunity. She had spent much of the final three years of the war broadcasting intermittently from Vienna, and it was there that she was arrested by CIC agents on August 17, 1945. She was immediately transferred to the Salzburg holding facility, where Hans Wenthur first interrogated her on August 30.[35]

Drexel's initial statements to the FBI agent mirrored those she'd made in her 1942 passport renewal request. She had been "trapped" in Germany when war broke out in 1939, she said, and didn't want to abandon her mother. She had only taken the RRG job because she needed the money to live, since she couldn't get hired by any of the American radio or newspaper bureaus in Berlin. When American entered the war in 1941, the Germans refused to let her leave, Drexel told Wenthur, and she "had no choice" but to remain and continue broadcasting. She'd only spoken twice a week, she added, and had been shocked to learn that she'd been indicted for treason, since she was very careful to speak only of "lighthearted" social topics. Wenthur pointed out that what she said on the radio was not what got her indicted; it was the fact that she spoke at all. By doing broadcasts from Germany, she had most certainly given "aid and comfort" to the enemies of the United States in a time of war. It was a crime, Wenthur reminded her, that carried a possible death sentence.

Despite his dire predictions about the consequences of her actions, Wenthur's initial questioning of Drexel and a second session on September 4 convinced the seasoned FBI agent that trying her for treason would be a waste of time and resources. As far as could be determined, she had indeed confined her broadcasts to largely innocuous social topics, and those programs ended in July 1944. Moreover, most of the RRG technicians interviewed by the CIC or various members of the ALU professed not to remember her, and no two Germans would confirm seeing her doing the broadcasts.

In the end, Wenthur got Drexel to write and sign a lengthy account of her actions in Germany and Austria from 1939 to the day of her arrest. On September 15, he attached that document to the final report he sent to Fred Ayer in Berlin. After reading the document, Fred concurred with Wenthur's conclusion that Drexel should not be tried and so stated when he forwarded the final report to Bureau headquarters. The Department of Justice chose not to make an immediate decision, and Drexel was held in various internment camps for more than a year before being transported back to the United States aboard the *Ernie Pyle* in November 1946.

Drexel was confined on Ellis Island until April 13, 1948, when on the Department of Justice's recommendation, Judge David A. Pine dismissed the treason indictment (the same day he dismissed Fred Kaltenbach's). Drexel's American citizenship had never been revoked, and she went back to freelance writing. On August 28, 1956, the very day on which she was to leave for a new home in Switzerland, she died of a heart attack at the age of seventy-two.[36]

WHILE HANS WENTHUR WAS WRAPPING UP his investigations in Salzburg, ALU agents in Berlin and Frankfurt were looking into two other Abwehr operations that had taken place on American soil. One involved a Luftwaffe officer who participated in a pre–Pearl Harbor espionage campaign while possibly being a secret anti-Nazi, and the other, a Kriegsmarine lieutenant who'd helped put German saboteurs ashore in America, in what turned out to be one of Nazi Germany's largest intelligence failures.

MAJOR FRIEDRICH BUSCH

Following the 1938 breakup of the German spy ring of which Ignaz Griebl had been the de facto head, the Abwehr endeavored to establish a larger—and hopefully more productive—espionage group in the United States. The man chosen to head the effort was Frederick "Fritz" Duquesne, the South African-born naturalized American citizen who had been a German agent on and off since before World War I.[37] As Duquesne's primary lieutenant, the Abwehr chose William Sebold, a German-born engineer who had immigrated to the United States in 1922. Sebold had traveled to Germany in February 1939 to visit his mother and siblings, and though by then a U.S. citizen, he was detained by Gestapo agents upon arriving in Hamburg.[38] As a result of continued threats to his family members still in Germany, just after the outbreak of war in September, Sebold ultimately and very reluctantly agreed to become an Abwehr agent. Before being sent to Hamburg for several weeks of training, he asked if he could visit the U.S. consulate in Cologne to get a new passport, since his had been stolen. Given permission, he took the opportunity to tell a consular official about being forced to work for the Nazis. The individual was skeptical, but after Sebold's departure, the man sent a cable to the State Department outlining their conversation.

After being trained in how to send and receive secret radio messages and the methods used to reduce photos of secret documents to the size of postage stamps, Sebold was given a thousand dollars in cash, with which he was to buy a radio and a camera, and traveled by train to Genoa.[39] There, on January 29, 1940, he boarded the American Lines steamer *Washington*. Almost exactly a month later, on February 8, the ship hove to in New York's quarantine station, where health and customs officers boarded to do routine prechecks of the passengers and crew before the liner actually docked. Unnoticed among the officials were an FBI agent and a representative of the State Department. They quietly sought out Sebold, listened to his account of the events in Germany, and asked him to accompany them to the Bureau's office in downtown Manhattan. Once there, the anti-Nazi German American agreed to become the first counterspy in FBI history.[40]

Over the following months, Sebold ingratiated himself with Fritz Duquesne and members of his growing spy ring. Many of the meetings took place in a New York office suite the FBI had set up for "Harry Sawyer"—Sebold's cover name. Hidden cameras and microphones recorded each session, during which Duquesne and his agents spoke at length about the types of information they were trying to obtain and the methods they were using to do so. The Bureau subsequently established a covert radio station on the shores of Long Island Sound, from where FBI agents trained to mimic Sebold's "fist"—the unique way in which he tapped out code—transmitted erroneous information in messages the Nazis believed were coming from Duquesne and his agents via Sebold.[41] Over the course of nearly a year and a half, the FBI accumulated vast amounts of information about Nazi intelligence goals in the United States, and in June 1941, the Bureau arrested Duquesne and thirty-two members of his ring—including three women. All were ultimately sentenced to significant jail time, with Duquesne himself going to prison for eighteen years. Sebold, for his part, testified at the trials and then disappeared into what we now call "witness protection." He lived the remainder of his life in obscurity.[42]

The dismantling of the Duquesne spy ring caused jubilation across the United States and gave the American people confidence that, as the nation went into World War II, there was no major German espionage activity in the land. The Nazis, on the other hand, were horrified by the apparent ease with which the FBI had infiltrated and then rolled up the Duquesne network. But not everyone in Berlin's intelligence hierarchy was all that shocked by the Bureau's success. Though the Duquesne operation had belonged to the Abwehr, the SD's Walter Schellenberg, as mentioned earlier, had suspected that the information being received from the United States was being generated not by German agents but by the FBI. That remained true after the demise of the Duquesne network, since the Bureau continued to transmit fake messages from bogus German agents until the end of the war.

There were those within the top levels of the Abwehr itself who shared Schellenberg's suspicions. One of the first to become aware that the Duquesne ring was not what it seemed to be was Friedrich Busch, a forty-five-year-old Luftwaffe captain assigned to the Abwehr's Intelligenz-Luft section.[43] Abw I Luft, as it was referred to internally, was the group within Canaris's headquarters in Berlin tasked with air espionage. Busch had entered the Luftwaffe as an antiaircraft officer in the early summer of 1939, but the fact that he had attended school in Britain and spoke relatively fluent English led to his transfer to the Abwehr in late August. He was assigned to the section that dealt with operations in England, Abw I Luft/E, where he received regular abstracts of the messages presumed to be transmitted by William Sebold. In April 1941, Busch was transferred to Abw I Luft/A, the section that dealt with the United States, and eight months later, he was made chief of Abw I Luft-West, which combined both the British and American operations. In that position, he was privy to all radio traffic sent from supposed agents in the United States.

In March 1943, Busch was promoted to major and made the third assistant air attaché at the German embassy in neutral Sweden. The post was a cover for his continued Abwehr activities, including close cooperation with Walter Schellenberg. In July 1944, Busch was removed from the position in Stockholm because he had been found to be "politically unreliable." That determination stemmed from the fact that following World War I, he had been a prominent member of the liberal Deutsche Demokratische Partei (German Democratic Party). Even after Hitler came to power and abolished the DPP and other non-Nazi political organizations, Busch remained in contact with old friends, and even helped several escape to freedom before they could be arrested. Following his transfer to Sweden, he maintained social contacts with German political refugees, and helped several with living expenses and other aid. Perhaps most damning of all in the eyes of senior Nazis was the fact that Busch had never joined the Party. Given his background, it's something of a mystery as to how he ever made it into the Abwehr in the first place.

Following his removal from the Stockholm attaché position, Busch was granted a medical discharge and rejoined his family in the Bavarian town of Bad Hindelang. After Germany's surrender, he contacted the U.S. Army's 80th CIC Detachment in nearby Sonthofen, asking to be taken to Frankfurt so that he could provide information on wartime German espionage activities in the United Kingdom and United States. Taken into custody on July 25, 1945, he was held at the Third Army Interrogation Center in Freising until September 7, when he was transferred to U.S. Forces European Theater's Military Intelligence Center in Frankfurt. After questioning Busch, Captain Leroy Vogel of the USFET CI section wrote that the prisoner "appears to have been actively anti-Nazi as a civilian and as a member of the Abwehr. He often shut his eyes to the fact that agents working for him were also working for the Allied intelligence services."[44]

ALU member Bill Clark also interrogated Busch, and found that despite the officer's anti-Nazi beliefs, he attempted to do his duty in high-profile cases, apparently to avoid falling under suspicion himself. As the *History of the SIS Division* later summarized Clark's report:

> Busch [said] that he had been suspicious of William Siebold [sic], at the heart of the Duquesne spy case, believing the man to be controlled by the FBI. Busch said he was convinced that the United States had perfected powerful radio-direction finders that would make it impossible for Siebold to broadcast without being detected, so the messages being received in Germany must have been transmitted with the knowledge of the American law-enforcement and intelligence communities. Busch's warnings were "brushed aside," he said, because his superiors didn't believe the United States could have developed a system that Germany itself had been unable to produce. Busch added that the arrest of the Duquesne spy ring members caused a huge furor in Berlin, ultimately causing Foreign Minister Joachim von Ribbentrop to tell Abwehr chief Admiral Wilhelm Canaris that he would be held personally accountable if the incident prompted the United States to declare war on Germany.[45]

Had Busch's superiors taken his warnings about Sebold to heart, the outcome of the Duquesne espionage affair might well have been very different. As it was, Busch's comments to his various interrogators were, as one British MI5 officer wrote, "a powerful indictment of the German intelligence service as it functioned during the war and shows up its corruption and inefficiency to a marked degree."[46]

Friedrich Busch's testimony about the corruption of the German intelligence services was significantly reinforced and enlarged upon by the ALU's interrogation of one of Busch's Abwehr colleagues, the man who helped put German saboteurs ashore in America.

Kapitänleutnant Wilhelm Ahlrichs

Following America's entry into World War II in December 1941, Adolf Hitler directed Abwehr chief Canaris to plan and execute a sabotage campaign aimed at industrial and transportation infrastructure targets in the Eastern United States. Canaris assigned the task to the Abwehr's Abteilung II, which undertook sabotage, commando, and political and moral subversion operations. The man tapped to oversee the selection of the saboteurs was thirty-seven-year-old Oberleutnant (first lieutenant) Walter Kappe, who had lived in the United States for twelve years and, as press officer for the Friends of New Germany, had worked closely with Ignaz Griebl.[47]

Kappe believed that the men who were to be sent to the United States should have had spent considerable time there and should be at least reasonably fluent in English. To find such individuals, he scoured the rolls of the Ausland Institut, the agency that tracked all native Germans who had returned to the *Vaterland* after living abroad. Kappe eventually found twelve men who had lived and worked in the United States for varying amounts of time and spoke good English. Four of the candidates eventually dropped out, and in early April 1942, the eight remaining recruits were sent to an Abwehr training school outside Berlin to learn the skills of their new trade. These included the use of firearms, hand grenades, explosives, and detonators, as well as training in countersurveillance techniques and unarmed combat.

Because the saboteurs would be landed in America by submarine, a Kriegsmarine officer, Kapitänleutnant (lieutenant commander) Wilhelm Ahlrichs, helped supervise their training. Born in 1895 in northern Germany, he had served in the Imperial German Navy during World War I.[48] When the conflict ended, he became a merchant sailor, over time rising from young deck officer to experienced master of oceangoing vessels. He joined the fledgling

Abwehr in 1929, a covert position that allowed him to observe and report on harbors, shipping lines, and other key maritime intelligence issues. While he occasionally sailed to southern Europe and Scandinavia, the majority of his voyages were to America. Indeed, between 1931 and 1935, he made some thirty-one round trips between Bremen or Hamburg and such U.S. ports as New York, Boston, Philadelphia, Charleston, and Norfolk.

In 1933, Ahlrichs joined the Nazi Party, a move that undoubtedly helped his advancement both as a Kriegsmarine reservist and in the Abwehr. By the time war broke out in 1939, he was a senior officer in the former and a member of the latter's Abteilung II subgroup, which handled maritime operations. Ahlrichs helped plan naval commando raids that supported the Germans' 1940 invasion of Norway, and the following year, he became *Gruppenleiter* (chief) of section 2 of Abtielung II's Übersee (overseas) group. In that position, he was in charge of all Abwehr maritime operations aimed at the United States. As such, he was tasked with getting the eight Nazi saboteurs from Germany to France and then embarking them on the two U-boats that would take them across the Atlantic.

The submarines tapped for the covert mission were both Type VIIC boats, Kapitänleutnant Hans-Heinz Linder's *U-202* and Kapitänleutnant Joachim Deecke's *U-584*.[49] The plan that Ahlrichs helped develop called for *U-202* to drop four agents and their supplies on a beach on New York's Long Island, while *U-584* would land the other four saboteurs in Florida. Once ashore, the two groups were to sow terror across the U.S. Eastern Seaboard by attacking military installations, critical infrastructure, and random civilian targets. The destruction was intended to sap America's will to fight and exacerbate existing tensions between the nation's disparate ethnic, political, and religious groups. Operation Pastorius, as the planned assault was called, was to be a hammer blow that would knock the United States out of the war before the country could get itself completely into the fight.[50]

What actually happened, however, was considerably less dramatic.

Just after midnight on June 13, 1942, Linder brought *U-202* to the surface a few hundred yards off the shore of Amagansett, Long Island. Sailors quickly came on deck and deployed a large rubber boat, into which four men dressed in Kriegsmarine uniforms quickly climbed. After loading several waterproof crates of explosives, incendiaries, and detonators, the men—joined by a pair of *U-202*'s sailors armed with submachine guns—paddled the boat toward shore through swirling banks of thick fog. Once on the beach, the men hurriedly off-loaded their cargo and the two armed sailors paddled back to the submarine.

After burying the crates behind some sand dunes, the members of the landing party removed their naval uniforms to reveal civilian clothing.[51] At that moment, John Cullen, a young unarmed Coast Guardsman patrolling the shoreline, suddenly appeared out of the fog. When he accosted the strangers, the leader of the group—a German-born U.S. Army veteran turned Nazi saboteur named George Dasch—pressed a wad of cash into Cullen's hands and urged him to forget what he'd seen. Cullen immediately ran back to the nearby Coast Guard lookout station and reported his encounter with the Germans. By the time an armed search party returned to the landing site, the Germans were gone, having made their way to a nearby station and caught the early commuter train into New York. They may have escaped, but the search team recovered their discarded uniforms and retrieved the crates of explosives and other materiel.[52] Four nights later, Deecke's *U-584* surfaced off Ponte Vedra beach, just south of Jacksonville.[53] Edward John Kerling and his three compatriots made it ashore, changed into civilian clothes, and buried their explosives, all without being discovered. The men headed for the nearest railway station, where two bought tickets for Chicago and the other two for Cincinnati. All eight of the Operation Pastorius agents were to meet in New York City on July 4, prepared to begin their bombing campaign. Instead, by then, all were in FBI custody.

Soon after arriving in Manhattan, Dasch and Ernest Burger agreed that to continue the mission would be suicidal and instead decided to turn themselves in. On June 15, Dasch called the FBI's New York field office and told an agent of the sabotage mission, but was not taken seriously. Four days later, the German took to a train to Washington, D.C., and checked into a local hotel. He then called Bureau headquarters and repeated his story. This time, he was quickly taken into custody, and during interrogation, he revealed the names and locations of the other seven would-be saboteurs. All were arrested, questioned, and quickly tried before a military commission. Dasch and Burger were given lengthy prison terms, while the other six men were executed on August 8.

While the FBI's interrogations of the captured German saboteurs provided a wealth of information about their selection, training, and deployment, it wasn't until Wilhelm Ahlrichs was captured at the end of the war that the Bureau learned just how little confidence the Abwehr had had that the bombing campaign would succeed. Notified that Ahlrichs was being held in a British-run detention center near Hamburg, Fred Ayer dispatched Walt Rucks and Hal Kloster from Heidelberg to interview the former officer.

Ahlrichs told the agents that soon after meeting Dasch and his colleagues, he concluded that their mission would end in failure. The men were "only interested in getting to the United States with the huge sums of money entrusted to them and in having a good time," Ahlrichs said.[54] The saboteurs constantly argued among themselves, and Dasch had even threatened to turn Burger in to the FBI when they reached America. Moreover, while the men were in France awaiting their departure aboard the two U-boats, Dasch had been arrested by German military police because he did not have the proper identity cards. As he was being taken into custody, he blurted out details of the highly classified secret mission. When news reached Berlin of the saboteurs' arrests, Ahlrichs added, U-boat chief Admiral Karl Dönitz had forbidden further use of the Kriegsmarine's submarines.[55]

As with Friedrich Busch, the ALU's interrogation of Wilhelm Ahlrichs underscored the Abwehr's wartime propensity to overlook flawed plans, field inept agents, arbitrarily dismiss unpalatable facts, and court disaster, all in an attempt to respond to the whims of one man—Adolf Hitler.[56]

Late on August 14, Fred Ayer boarded a USAAF C-47 at Berlin's Tempelhof field for the three-hour flight to Paris. The ALU chief was on his way to the French capital to hold talks with Don Daughters and Horton Telford about the ways in which the Europe-based FBI agents could better organize their operations to deal with the rapidly changing intelligence situation on the Continent. The flight was late departing, and Fred didn't arrive at Le Bourget until nearly midnight. Once in the city, he chose not to disturb the men at the avenue Mozart apartment, instead checking into a hotel reserved for Allied officers.

The following morning, Fred arose somewhat later than he'd intended, and as he hurried toward the place de l'Opéra on his way to the U.S. Embassy, he noticed large crowds beginning to gather.[57] When he asked several of the milling people what was happening, one man responded, "Haven't you heard—don't you know? It's finished. It's all over. You, the Americans, have beaten Japan." As Fred later recalled:

> Soon we were unable to move, so great was the crowd. All faces were happy, some were expectant, most were curious. I asked what was going to happen. No one seemed to know, but all were sure that it would be something fine. I noticed that workmen had just

> finished erecting a sort of platform on the steps of the Opera House . . . . A tiny figure in glistening white satin moved from the building entrance down towards the platform. Cheering started near at hand, and finally swelled back to us. "It is your great singer, our friend Lily Pons," my neighbor told me. "Maybe she will sing to us."

A French-born soprano who gained American citizenship in 1940, Pons did indeed sing to the gathered crowds. "She sang," Fred wrote, "not in the voice of the concert hall, not in the tones of an aria, but in the triumphant trumpet call of a hymn of resurrection." Pons sang the national anthems of Britain, France, and America, with thousands of people joyously adding their voices. Looking around, Fred saw those around him singing with their faces turned to the sky, "voices raised in a hymn of love to their native land, eyes glistening with tears, happy tears after six terrible years of fear, death, slavery and dishonor. I felt that they were very beautiful faces indeed."

As wonderful as that day in the streets of Paris obviously was, Japan's agreement to stop fighting would have no real effect on the Army Liaison Unit's mission in Europe.[58] Indeed, Fred's meetings with Telford, Daughters, and others in the French capital were focused on the ways in which the ALU could "pivot" its activities toward the nation that was quickly proving itself to be America's primary postwar adversary, the Soviet Union. That same topic was foremost in Fred's discussions with Hoover when the ALU chief was called by back to Washington on August 28 for three intense days of discussions with the director and his senior subordinates.[59] But amid those talks, there were ominous signs that the ALU's future might not be as secure as Hoover might have hoped. As Fred recalled:

> The Department of State and the Army were at loggerheads. General "Wild Bill" Donovan and Hoover did not see eye to eye. Both of them together distrusted State. Everyone except the Army expressed the opinion that the Army should have a very small role in peacetime intelligence collecting. The Army felt, inasmuch as it had the responsibility for administering nearly all of the occupied areas, that it should have the direction of the entire effort. Each, alone, was partially right. All, together, turned out to be terribly wrong.[60]

Back in Germany after his whirlwind visit to D.C.—during which he was only able to spend a few precious hours with his family—Fred tried to forget the disturbing whispers about interagency bickering and its possible effect on the ALU's future. "Our time [in Berlin] was spent in doing our damnedest to set up a proper postwar network in one very important corner of the world," Fred recalled. "We ran into all of the expected local roadblocks, but were in a fair way to overcoming them."[61]

By that point, the end of September, the men of the ALU could feel justifiably proud of the job they'd done in the European theater, both before and after the final collapse of Nazi Germany. Frank Amprim's initial, pioneering work in North Africa, Sicily, and Italy; Fred Ayer and Don Daughters's establishment of the Paris office and their development of close personal and professional ties to Gordon Sheen's SHAEF counterintelligence group; the arrival of additional agents and the opening of offices in Allied-occupied Germany and Austria—all contributed immeasurably to the successful accomplishment of the missions they had been given by J. Edgar Hoover. The G.I. G-men had located and interrogated indicted American traitors and other alleged renegades, substantiating the guilt of many and helping to exonerate others; uncovered valuable information on German and Italian espionage, subversion, and sabotage operations in the Western Hemisphere; and begun to develop a comprehensive understanding of the threat posed by the Soviet Union in the postwar world. Moreover, the men of the ALU had managed to do their jobs under challenging conditions that included enemy action, widespread civil and political disruption, and open hostility on the part of both vanquished enemies and supposed allies.

Given the ALU's record of successes despite these obstacles, and in light of the strong and mutually respectful relationship the Bureau men had forged with their Army counterparts, Fred and his men believed they had laid the groundwork for a robust FBI counterintelligence presence in postwar Europe despite opposition from other agencies. It thus came as huge shock to all the members of the ALU when in early October 1945 they were suddenly and unexpectedly ordered to cease operations and return to the United States.

CHAPTER 13

Turf Wars . . . and a Legacy

TUESDAY, OCTOBER 2, 1945, BEGAN as just another workday for the widely scattered men of the FBI's Army Liaison Unit.

In Berlin, Fred Ayer, Jack Condon, Art O'Connor, and Dick Thompson were continuing to review captured German files, search for suspected American renegade broadcasters, and assist Gordon Sheen and his U.S. Group Control Council team. In Frankfurt, Bill Clark and Vince Ascherl maintained the Bureau's liaison with U.S. Forces European Theater's intelligence and counterintelligence staffs. Heidelberg-based Hal Kloster was aiding the Army's Counter Intelligence Corps in its continuing effort to "denazify" the fabled university town and following up leads throughout northern Germany (though without the help of Walt Rucks, who had returned to the United States five days earlier).[1] Joe Dunn and Boyd Sheets were plowing through seized documents in Freising and tracking persons of interest. Don Daughters, Roland L'Allier, Pete Winter, and Bob Prather in Paris were continuing to work closely with the French police and intelligence agencies. In Austria, Hans Wenthur and Joe Fellner were coordinating with both the CIC in Salzburg and the U.S. Sector Command in Vienna, while also pursuing suspected renegades. In Italy, despite his poor health, Frank Amprim continued to work on the Ezra Pound case, assisted by Jim Faziola and Jim Romano.[2]

That normal workday changed abruptly—at least for Fred and Don—in the early afternoon. The men had discussed the disconcerting rumors Fred had heard during his brief August trip to Washington but were nonetheless stunned to receive cables from FBI headquarters that began with the sentence: "Bureau desires that you and all members of your office in liaison with Army return to Washington immediately." After listing the names of the agents in each respective location, the cables added "you will not return or be replaced" and ordered Fred and Don to "transfer all files to Telford in embassy" and "advise Bureau approximate arrival date in Washington."

Then, by way of explanation for the extraordinary and unexpected directive, the cables read: "This action being taken as a result of General Sibert's recommendation that FBI operations [in Europe] be cut to two men. Impossible to operate under such conditions. Therefore, entire project of liaison with Army being discontinued."[3]

Don Daughters was the first to query the Bureau regarding USFET intelligence chief Brigadier General Edwin L. Sibert's unexpected decision to drastically reduce the number of FBI agents in France and Germany. The response—from Hoover himself—was short and to the point. "FBI and [Military Intelligence Division] in Washington as much surprised as you. Sibert's move not foreseen. Came out of clear sky here. When and if further clarification received you will be advised."[4]

Horton Telford received news of the ALU's unexpected dissolution at the same time as Fred and Don. The cable from Washington to the Paris legat read, in part:

> Bureau is advised via Army facilities all [FBI] personnel attached to Army liaison in France and Germany under Special Agents Daughters and Ayer of their immediate recall to Washington. They will not return nor be replaced. Files and equipment of both groups being forwarded to you in embassy for integration your files. Desire you confirm these instructions with both agent Daughters and Condon. . . . Desired both groups expedite return to Washington.[5]

Because they had been directed by Bureau headquarters to take responsibility for the ALU files, Telford and Bud Rousseau assumed—rightly—that the Paris legal attaché office would not be part of the withdrawal of FBI agents from Europe. Though relieved that they were to remain at work in the French capital, the two agents were understandably concerned that in addition to their existing duties, they might be required to perform at least some of the tasks undertaken thus far by the ALU men. Seeking clarification, on October 9, Telford sent an enciphered cable to Washington asking:

> In view of Bureau decision to withdraw all Army unit personnel from France and Germany please advise: 1. Whether pending leads [regarding American renegades still at large] Berlin office will be handled henceforth by Army through Bureau liaison in Washington or Paris. If latter, by what procedure. 2. Whether Bureau desires this

> office continue communist investigation now pending Paris Army Unit. 3. Whether agents and clerical personnel will be augmented here to properly handle this additional work. Recommend chief clerk Prather or O'Connor remain in Paris long enough to assist integration [Army Liaison] unit's files with ours.[6]

The Bureau's response, received in the Paris legat office on October 11, was unequivocal:

> Pending leads Berlin office canceled. Desire you continue communist investigations if possible with present personnel and if consistent with your liaison arrangement with embassy. Bureau contemplates sending no additional agent or clerical personnel Paris office at present time. Clerks Prather and O'Connor will return Washington immediately as ordered.[7]

Because the directive from Washington had not specifically mentioned the ALU agents working in Italy and Austria, Fred and Don initially hoped that the men in Rome, Salzburg, and Vienna might be exempt from the withdrawal order. That proved not to be the case, however. Frank Amprim, Jim Faziola, and Jim Romano received the withdrawal order on October 8, as did Hans Wenthur and Joe Fellner. The latter two were both in the Austrian capital when the cable arrived.[8] The next day, they mentioned the startling news to Brigadier General Edwin B. Howard, the intelligence chief for U.S. Forces Austria, whose response was equally unexpected. He urged them to ignore the Bureau's recall order and remain in Vienna, saying that the assistance the agents were providing to him and General Mark Clark was too important to be arbitrarily terminated.[9] On October 10, Howard's suggestion was seconded by his deputy, Colonel Charles C. Sloane Jr.[10] As tempted as Wenthur and Fellner may have been to follow the urgings of Howard and Sloane to stay in Austria, the two agents ultimately obeyed the orders of both Hoover and the man who had forced the director's hand regarding the ALU's presence in Europe—USFET's Edwin Sibert.

An Arkansas native and 1918 graduate of West Point, Edwin Luther Sibert was the son, grandson, and brother of generals. Originally commissioned as a field artillery officer, Sibert was first exposed to intelligence work while a member of the post–World War I U.S. occupation force in Germany's Rhineland. As one historian later put it, the young officer took to the new field "like a duck to water."[11] Sibert broadened his intelligence skills in 1940 and 1941 while serving as a military attaché in the U.S. embassy in Brazil, where he often briefed Ambassador Jefferson Caffery—the man with whom Fred Ayer and his Paris-based ALU agents would interact following Caffery's 1944 appointment as U.S. ambassador to France.

Following Japan's attack on Pearl Harbor and America's subsequent declaration of war against the Axis, Sibert became the senior artillery officer for the 99th Infantry Division. On October 5, 1943, he was handpicked by Lieutenant General Jacob L. Devers—commander of the aforementioned European Theater of Operations, United States Army—to become that organization's assistant chief of staff for intelligence. Sibert remained in that post until July 1944, when he became G-2 for Twelfth U.S. Army Group. As mentioned earlier in this volume, as G-2 of Twelfth USAG, Sibert met with Fred Ayer and gave the Army Liaison Unit permission to review German records captured by the command's subordinate units. Sibert also had allowed Dick Thompson to be attached to Twelfth USAG's counterintelligence section, and on several occasions, the general asked the FBI agent for updates on the status of the ALU's search for renegade Americans.

At no point in his various interactions with Fred Ayer or his fellow agents had Sibert voiced any dissatisfaction with the work the Bureau members were conducting in Europe. Even after becoming USFET G-2 in June 1945 (following the inactivation of Twelfth USAG), Sibert had continued to interact amiably with ALU members in Frankfurt and Berlin. So why did USFET's intelligence chief suddenly demand that the FBI's presence in Italy, France, Germany, and Austria be reduced to just two men? There are two possible reasons. The first was a simple personal grudge Sibert held against Major General Clayton Bissell, chief of the Army's Military Intelligence Division in Washington. The second was Sibert's firmly held belief that there should be only one dominant American intelligence organization in postwar Europe—the U.S. Army.

The source of Sibert's resentment toward Bissell was a person: Generalleutnant Reinhard Gustav Gehlen.[12] A professional soldier since 1923, in 1942, Gehlen became the head of Fremde Heere Ost (Foreign Armies East, FHO), the German general staff's intelligence branch dealing with the Eastern Front and the Soviet Union's military capabilities and intentions. An extremely effective intelligence officer and a supreme realist, Gehlen's reports to his superiors—and ultimately to Hitler himself—pulled no punches about how the so-called "Thousand Year Reich" would be crushed by the combined combat power of the British, Americans, and Soviets. Gehlen's clear-eyed analysis infuriated the Führer, who labeled the FHO chief a "defeatist" and had him removed from his position. But, as a postwar CIA report on Gehlen later noted, he

> did not leave Berlin emptyhanded. He knew that the FHO had some of the most important files in the Third Reich and that the possession of these records offered the best means of survival in the post-Hitler period. As the Soviets drew closer to Berlin, Gehlen dispersed his staff and transferred the FHO's intelligence files to secret locations in Bavaria. There, Gehlen and his handpicked officers waited to surrender to American forces. Gehlen believed the Western Allies and the Soviet Union, while wartime partners, would soon become peacetime rivals. With his knowledge about the Russians, combined with the FHO's collective resources, Gehlen felt he could influence relations between the East and West and help shape Germany's role in post-war Europe.[13]

Gehlen's instincts were correct, both in terms of the postwar relations between the Soviet Union and its former allies, and with regard to his personal value to the Americans. On May 22, 1945, the former FHO chief surrendered to a CIC team in the village of Fischhausen, at the southern end of Bavaria's Lake Schliersee. Gehlen revealed that fifty steel drums filled with FHO files were buried nearby, and he and the cache of records were initially sent to the Seventh Army Interrogation Center in Augsburg. On June 17, Sibert ordered Gehlen and the documents transferred to the facility for VIP prisoners in Wiesbaden. Seeking to use the former FHO chief and his valuable files as sources of intelligence on Soviet forces and intentions in Germany, Sibert initially neglected to mention Gehlen's capture to SHAEF commander Eisenhower, the OSS's X-2 Branch, the Counter Intelligence Corps, or Bissell in Washington.[14]

Gehlen's presence in Wiesbaden didn't remain a secret for long. On June 29, Bissell cabled both Eisenhower and Sibert that the German, any of his staffers who had also been captured, and the all-important FHO files should be sent to Washington. The directive didn't keep Sibert from making Gehlen and his records the core of a USFET intelligence effort aimed at the Soviets, an undertaking Sibert believed was of vastly more immediate importance than any operation MID might eventually embark upon. In the end, however, the MID director prevailed. On August 21—following coordination between Bissell and Eisenhower—Gehlen, five of his former subordinates, and the precious FHO files were flown to the United States. Sibert had not been told of the move in advance and was understandably livid that Bissell had apparently gone behind his back.

Though Gehlen was eventually returned to Germany to work with Sibert at USFET, Sibert never forgot what he believed to be an intentional slight by Bissell.[15] Because the MID chief had been a stalwart supporter of the Army Liaison Unit's presence and operations in the European theater, it is entirely possible that Sibert's decision to severely reduce the number of FBI agents in the region was simply a spur-of-the-moment decision intended to undercut Bissell's authority and prestige, as Sibert felt his had been diminished by the MID director. That could explain Hoover's statement to Don Daughters that Sibert's directive had "come out of a clear sky."

The second possible reason mentioned for Sibert's decision to so severely curtail the ALU's operations that Hoover would have no choice but to withdraw all of the agents is perhaps the more plausible: The USFET G-2 chief was known to favor the creation of a centralized American intelligence agency in Germany that would be solely under Army—meaning his—control. Sibert believed that bureaucratic rivalries and organizational duplications of effort among the various American agencies then undertaking intelligence and counterintelligence operations in the defeated nation—the FBI, OSS, and CIC—would only benefit the Soviets.[16]

Though Sibert's experiences dealing with the ALU had been generally positive, he believed—not without reason—that J. Edgar Hoover harbored dreams of massively expanding the FBI's operations outside the United States. Sibert had considered the ALU to be a useful adjunct to the Army's intelligence and counterintelligence activities in wartime Europe, and didn't particularly care whether the FBI's SIS became America's primary intelligence organization in Central and South America. But Sibert considered occupied Germany—and by extension, Western Europe—the Army's exclusive preserve. He was therefore loath to see the Bureau firmly establish itself in "his" territory and almost certainly saw the drastic reduction of ALU agents as the best way to force Hoover to throw in the towel. Sibert's intent was to ensure that the two agents allowed to remain in Europe would be unable to undertake any significant intelligence activities and would essentially just maintain a formal liaison at USFET.[17] Despite his own previous positive interactions with Fred Ayer, Eisenhower approved Sibert's plan for the reduction of the FBI presence in Europe[18]

Sibert had an unlikely ally in his quest to force the FBI out of Europe—"Wild Bill" Donovan. As Fred Ayer had no doubt heard during his August trip to Washington, the OSS director hoped his organization would become America's postwar global intelligence agency. That desire was born of necessity, because OSS had no other path to bureaucratic survival. It was, as one organizational history noted,

> a war agency with no statutory foundation for permanence. As such it had little strength—no sustaining traditions, no hallowed place in government, no core of influential alumni, no prestige in Congress, no deep and wide public support, nothing beyond temporary acceptance as an emergency mechanism in the war against Hitler and Tojo. Indeed, as a war agency it shared in that general unpopularity attaching to the swollen national government as being inefficient, wasteful and costly and, therefore, in need of dismantling as soon as military factors permitted it.... As a war agency OSS had no future.[19]

Simply put, if Donovan could not manage to find a secure niche for OSS in the broader world of postwar intelligence, his beloved organization would cease to exist. The possibility that the FBI would edge out OSS in the race to become America's sole postwar intelligence agency haunted Donovan. He believed that the Bureau not only had a postwar plan for achieving that goal but had been working toward it for some time. The OSS European Division under Lieutenant Colonel David K. E. Bruce had been carefully monitoring the growth of the ALU following its initial establishment in Paris, and saw no chance of limiting the Bureau's "definite extension" unless "steps [were] initiated in Washington."[20] Donovan was more than happy to lobby President Truman and other D.C. powerbrokers regarding what the OSS viewed as the FBI's inappropriate operations in Europe, motivated in part by the Bureau's unwavering opposition to any OSS activities in Latin America.

If Donovan believed that his support for the Bureau's ouster from Europe would win him Sibert's agreement for a larger postwar OSS presence on the Continent—or even the organization's continued existence—he was sadly mistaken. Even as Sibert was maneuvering to push the FBI out of Europe, forces in Washington were ensuring that OSS would itself be brought to heel. On October 1, 1945, President Truman signed an executive order that abolished the OSS and transferred its intelligence gathering and counterintelligence functions to a new organization called the Strategic Services Unit (SSU). Headed by Donovan's former deputy, Brigadier General John L. Magruder, and subordinate to the War Office, the SSU only enjoyed Sibert's support for a few months. In January 1946, the USFET chief ordered the SSU to hand over the majority of its counterintelligence operations in Europe to the Army's CIC, basing his decision on the SSU's shortage of personnel in the theater.[21] That same month, Truman signed a directive that established the Central Intelligence Group (CIG), which quickly absorbed the SSU. Ironically, in September 1946, Sibert—having seen the way the political winds were blowing in Washington with regard to the establishment of a civilian-run national intelligence agency—joined the CIG as assistant director of operations. Sibert remained in that post following the CIG's July 1947 transformation into the Central Intelligence Agency, but he was never really comfortable in the job. Both CIG and CIA were largely staffed by former OSS members, who saw Sibert as an "undeserving outsider." As one later history pointed out, he believed that neither organization "made full use of his talents, and in disappointment he rejoined the Army" in August 1948.[22]

J. Edgar Hoover's directive to withdraw the men of the ALU from Europe in response to what he called the "impossible" and "intolerable" conditions mandated by General Edwin Sibert did not result in the "immediate" action the director had hoped for. In addition to having to close the offices in Vienna, Salzburg, Berlin, Heidelberg, Frankfurt, and Freising and send hundreds of files to Telford and Rousseau at the Paris embassy, the ALU agents also had to contend with the Army's massively overloaded transportation system. Hundreds of thousands of U.S. servicemembers were being returned from Europe to the United States for demobilization. The ports bearing the brunt of the repatriation effort—Le Havre, Marseilles, Naples, and Bremerhaven among them—were clogged with people and materiel. The effort to return Stateside thus proved something of a challenge for some members of the ALU.

For the truly fortunate—or perhaps well-connected—agents, the most direct transportation was provided by the USAAF's Air Transport Command. On October 25, Don Daughters, Bill Clark, Jack Condon, and Roland L'Allier boarded an ATC C-54 at Le Bourget for the flight home.

The men found themselves in august company on the trip, sharing the plane with several senior military officers and a smattering of diplomats. After a brief refueling stop in Newfoundland, the C-54 shaped a course for National Airport in Washington, landing in the early afternoon. Don went to Bureau headquarters downtown to brief Hoover and his senior aides, while the other men hastily turned in their uniforms and other military gear before heading out on two weeks' home leave.[23]

For those not fortunate enough to secure an ATC seat, the first step in the journey Stateside was to obtain Army travel orders authorizing sea transportation and directing them to one of the embarkation ports. Whether by design or random chance, the majority of the ALU men destined to cross the Atlantic by ship were sent to Le Havre. The English Channel port on the right bank of the river Seine estuary had been heavily bombed, but within weeks after its capture by British and Canadian troops in September 1944, the city's vital harbor facilities had been put back into operation. The port became a key departure point for units being returned to the United States, and several large temporary camps were built in the region to house the tens of thousands of servicemembers awaiting transportation home. The various staging areas accommodated anywhere from three thousand to nearly sixty thousand people in seemingly endless rows of eight-man tents or small wooden huts, and bore the names of then popular brands of American cigarettes—Camp Lucky Strike, Camp Pall Mall, and so on.[24]

One facility, however, bucked the tobacco-oriented naming convention. Camp Home Run, in the Le Havre suburb of Sanvic, barely two miles north of the port, occupied the former fortress of Sainte-Adresse. One of three similar structures erected in the mid-nineteenth century to defend Le Havre, the hilltop fort had housed German garrison troops during the occupation. As a pre-embarkation staging area it accommodated some two thousand people, many of whom were "RAMPs" (Recovered American Military Personnel) freed from German prisoner of war camps. While not luxurious by any means, the conditions at Home Run were decidedly better than in the larger camps. The majority of the men lodged in the former fort slept indoors in casements and underground tunnel barracks rather than in tents, and meals prepared by Army cooks were served in shifts by young French women. As one American soldier later remembered, "Service deluxe was to be had at Camp Home Run . . . all the service one would want."[25]

The first ALU members to arrive at the camp were Boyd Sheets and Vince Ascherl. They'd flown from Frankfurt to Paris on October 27, and then taken the train to Le Havre the following day. They didn't have long to enjoy the services offered at Camp Home Run, because on the 31st they left France aboard SS *Howard Victory,* one of the many rapidly built *Victory*-class cargo vessels converted to carry passengers as part of the repatriation effort. The ship arrived in Boston on November 8, and both men immediately went home on leave.

Hans Wenthur and Joe Fellner were next to reach Le Havre. On October 25, they'd flown from Vienna to Frankfurt, where they were issued their USFET travel orders.[26] The agents flew to Paris on the 27th and met with Horton Telford, Dick Thompson, and Pete Winter. It wasn't all business for Wenthur and Fellner in the French capital, however, for before boarding the train to Le Havre on November 1, the two men managed to enjoy a little downtime. They took a walking tour of the city, shopped for gifts and souvenirs at the main American PX, and took in a midnight show at the Folies Bergère.[27] They left Paris by train at 7:45 on the morning of November 1 and arrived in Le Havre that afternoon. They spent the next two days dealing with paperwork—filling out customs declarations, obtaining special permits to carry their .38-caliber Police Special revolvers aboard ship, and ensuring that their shot records were up to date. On November 3, they were joined by Thompson, Winter, Art O'Connor, and Bob Prather. Wenthur and Fellner departed for New York the next day aboard the Navy troopship USS *Lejeune,* arriving eight days later. After completing their own predeparture paperwork, Thompson and the others left Le Havre on November 11 aboard SS *Marshall Victory* and arrived in Boston on the 17th. The last ALU member to transit through Camp Home Run was Erling Kloster. He, too, had traveled via Frankfurt and Paris, and left Le Havre on November 10 aboard SS *John S. Pillsbury,* arriving in New York on the 23rd.

The last three ALU men to leave Europe by sea—Frank Amprim, Jim Faziola, and Jim Romano—sailed from Naples on November 15 aboard SS *Sea Tiger.* It could not have been a pleasant voyage for Amprim, who had continued to suffer severe health problems following his return to Italy after initial treatment at Bethesda Naval Hospital for the *Entamoeba histolytica* parasite. His health deteriorated markedly in the days before he and his two fellow agents boarded ship, and by the time *Sea Tiger* reached New York on November 26, Amprim was suffering from the full-blown amoebic dysentery that would dog him for several months.

By early December 1945, only two members of the ALU remained in Europe—Joe Dunn and Fred Ayer.

Dunn had received special permission from Hoover to remain on the Continent as one of the two agents mentioned in USFET G-2 chief Edwin Sibert's decree. But rather than being essentially trapped in a do-nothing liaison position in Frankfurt as Sibert had intended, Dunn ranged throughout occupied Germany and the U.S. zone in Berlin. His goal was to wrap up the Bureau's investigation into the remaining American renegades indicted in 1943 but not yet apprehended—Jane Anderson and Robert Best. Both were ultimately arrested in Austria—Best, near the Yugoslav border, by British forces in January 1946 and Anderson, by Army CIC agents, in Salzburg in April 1947.[28] The other key person on Dunn's list of suspects to be located and apprehended—Mildred Gillars, Max Koischwitz's coworker and lover—was arrested in Berlin in March 1946 by CIC agents. She was convicted of treason in March 1949, released in 1961, and died in 1988. As mentioned earlier, Douglas Chandler had initially been arrested in May 1945 and was interrogated by Dunn before being inexplicably released. Dunn was able to take Chandler back into custody at his home in Kempton, Bavaria, in February 1946. The FBI agent finally returned to the United States in June.

Though there is some confusion over exactly when Fred Ayer flew back to the United States, he was apparently home with his wife and children by Christmas Day, 1945. There is no uncertainty, however, about his frame of mind following the dissolution of the ALU. As he later wrote:

> No doubt I greatly overrated my own importance at the time, as well as the size of the role that could be played by 20 or 30 men, no matter how well trained. Nevertheless, there was always sadness in seeing something destroyed for which one has labored hard, and these were highly emotional days. Of course I was personalizing, and perhaps over dramatizing the matter. But it is perfectly fair to say that even then I realized that no one else, no other organization or combination of services, was set up to do an intelligence job which had to be done.[29]

Fred returned to the Boston field office the first week of January 1946 feeling "heartsick and discouraged."[30] Bored with the types of cases assigned to him and seeing no future in the FBI, he resigned before the end of the month.

While Edwin Sibert's determination that the Army should be in sole control of American intelligence and counterintelligence operations in post-war Europe led to the ALU's dissolution, it did not result in the withdrawal of all FBI agents from the Continent. Indeed, two agents were dispatched to Germany even before Joe Dunn's final departure in the summer of 1946.

Special Agent Francis E. Crosby arrived in Berlin in February and spent a month going through captured German documents that were to be used as evidence in the upcoming International Military Tribunal in Nuremburg. When Crosby returned to the States in March, he was replaced by Special Agent Paul E. Ertzinger, who stayed until June. During that time, Ertzinger participated in the interrogations of Hermann Göring, Joachim von Ribbentrop, and Hans Fritzsche, Nazi Germany's best-known radio commentator and the last head of the RRG.[31]

While in Germany, Ertzinger worked with one of the FBI's most famous agents, Melvin Purvis. The man who had been involved in the pursuit and eventual killing of gangsters Charles "Pretty Boy" Floyd, Lester "Baby Face Nelson" Gillis, and John Dillinger had left the Bureau in 1935. In 1942, he'd joined the Army, serving as a military police officer and deputy provost marshal in North Africa, Italy, and during the Allied advance into Germany. After VE Day, Purvis and a fellow former FBI agent turned Army investigator—none other than Leon Turrou—tracked accused Nazi war criminals. By the time Ertzinger arrived in Germany, Purvis was the Nurenburg tribunal's chief American war crimes investigator.

In the end, Edwin Sibert's effort to totally banish the FBI from liberated Europe did not succeed. The Army Liaison Unit was gone, but the legal attaché office at the U.S. embassy in Paris not only survived—it flourished. Horton Telford and Bud Rousseau became the first of a long line of agents to staff that important office, which to this day remains a vital part of the FBI's international operations. More than two hundred Bureau agents and support personnel work in key cities around the world, seeking to protect the United States and its people by establishing and maintaining cooperative relationships with the law-enforcement and security services of our partner nations. It is a legacy of which Fred Ayer, Don Daughters, and the other men of the Army Liaison Unit would be justifiably proud.

Afterword

THE AMERICANS INVESTIGATED BY THE MEN of the Army Liaison Unit in newly liberated Europe were accused or suspected of committing one of the worst crimes a citizen of the United States can perpetrate—treason. Whether for money or power, out of self-loathing or hatred for the democratic, all-inclusive ideals this nation has long espoused (but admittedly, has often fallen short of embodying) many of those who were targets of the ALU decided to bet against America. To a greater or lesser extent, they gave aid and comfort to our enemies, choosing to pledge their allegiance to white supremacists, anti-Semites, self-aggrandizing dictators, and yes, mass murderers, and working for the ultimate victory of fascism at the expense of their fellow Americans.

That many U.S. citizens, whether native-born or naturalized, betrayed America in favor of Mussolini's Italy or Hitler's Germany should come as no surprise. As many historians and journalists have made clear, in the years before the outbreak of World War II, millions of people across our country fervently embraced the tenets of fascism—beliefs that were openly endorsed by such hugely popular and influential personalities as radio star Father Charles Coughlin and aviation hero Charles Lindbergh. Mass rallies at Madison Square Garden in 1934 and 1939 drew tens of thousands of actual and would-be Nazis, all screaming their support for a repugnant ideology whose self-aggrandizing, narcissistic, and sociopathic leader would ultimately lead his own nation, and much of Europe, to destruction.

The allure of fascism in 1930s America—and indeed, in our own time—is not difficult to understand. When people feel powerless in the face of global or national events, whether political, social, economic, or medical, or if they feel that their particular ethnic or religious group has been marginalized or its power or influence reduced, they often look for scapegoats. The need to find an "other" to blame for one's troubles is a universal human trait, and the advent of radio and more recent mass communication systems makes conspiracy theories, lies, baseless accusations, and threats of violence easy to disseminate and virtually impossible to counter. Once individuals come to believe that an authoritarian leader—like Mussolini, Hitler, or other, more recent fascist tyrants—is the answer to a nation's problems, wartime treason or peacetime sedition become all the more likely. It is then that people of goodwill who support democracy, justice, and human rights must work to halt the spread of the cancer that kills a nation's freedom.

The FBI of the 1940s was certainly not a perfect institution; its excesses and flaws both then and in later eras—especially during the Civil Rights movement and the Vietnam War—have been well documented. But the Bureau's intelligence and counterintelligence operations during World War II, both at home and abroad, were undoubtedly vital to the victory ultimately achieved by America and its allies. Likewise, the men of the Army Liaison Unit were imperfect. They were people of their time and undoubtedly shared many of the preconceptions and even the prejudices of 1930s and 1940s America. But they put aside their personal beliefs to help bring to justice those of their fellow citizens who were working to undermine our nation and, ultimately, who wished to see it devoured by fascist dictators. We who live in the United States of the twenty-first century, who cherish the ideals on which our nation was founded and the hard-won freedoms we have long enjoyed, must be just as willingly to come to America's defense.

Appendix: After the War

The Army Liaison Unit Members

Frank Amprim

The first FBI agent to go to Europe under Army cover in World War II resigned from the Bureau in 1946 and returned to his law practice in Wyandotte, Michigan, though still suffering health issues resulting from the dysentery he picked up in Italy. He eventually married, had a son, and became a lifelong member of the Society of Special Agents of the FBI. Amprim rarely spoke of his time in Italy during World War II, though he and former U.S. Army Counter Intelligence Corps agent Ramón Arrizabalaga kept up a friendly postwar correspondence until the latter's death. Amprim died on August 18, 1997, at the age of eighty-seven.

Vincent John Ascherl

After working as one of the Army Liaison Unit's three clerk-stenographers, Vince Ascherl ended up in the Bureau's New York field office while attending Fordham University at night. He graduated in 1949 with a law degree, and became an FBI special agent that year. His first posting was El Paso, where in August 1950, he married Mary Grace Margerum. They had four children, and the family lived in several states over the course of Ascherl's career. After his retirement from the Bureau, the couple moved back to El Paso, where Mary Grace died in January 1976. After her death, Ascherl studied for the Roman Catholic priesthood and was ordained in 1981. He died in El Paso on October 1, 2003, at the age of eighty-nine.

Arthur Avignone

Upon his return from Italy in March 1945, Art Avignone (sometimes spelled Avignon) was initially assigned to the New York field office. On November 18, 1950, he married Therese Crotta Tonissi in Idaho Falls, Idaho. Art left the FBI within a few years, and by 1960 was the CIA's deputy chief of station in Havana. He apparently used the cover name Wilmer Aretz when operating outside the U.S. embassy. When the Cuban government ordered the closure of the embassy on January 4, 1961, Art was one of the last people to leave the building. He later worked as an Agency liaison to the Brazilian federal police. Art died in Pompano Beach, Florida, on June 28, 1994, at the age of eighty-one.

Frederick Ayer Jr.

Following his resignation from the FBI in January 1946, Fred Ayer spent three months looking for a job in various parts of the nation's postwar intelligence apparatus. When he was not offered positions commensurate with his experience, he joined a commercial mining company as house counsel. He was quickly just as bored as he'd been when he'd returned to the Boston field office. In May 1947, Fred was offered the post of deputy legal adviser to the State Department's mission to civil war–torn Greece. The following year, he joined former OSS commander William Donovan in a congressionally mandated investigation of the murder in Greece of a CBS correspondent. Following two unsuccessful runs for attorney general of Massachusetts, Fred accepted a position as the secretary of the Air Force's special assistant for intelligence. He returned to private law practice in 1960, wrote *Yankee G-Man* and several other books, and died of a heart attack in 1974 while vacationing in Bermuda. He was fifty-nine years old.

Raymond James Bacigalupi

Upon his return from Italy, Ray Bacigalupi resigned from the FBI and worked as a certified public account for various San Francisco–based corporations. He eventually started his own firm in San Mateo, from which he retired in 1988 on his eightieth birthday. Ray died in Hillmar, California, on February 18, 2000, at the age of ninety-one.

William Harrington Clark

Like many of his former ALU colleagues, Bill Clark left the FBI soon after the end of World War II. He moved to New York State in late 1946 to join the faculty of the University of Rochester as an instructor in German. He ultimately became the school's associate dean of education and retired in 1983. Bill passed away at the age of seventy-eight on March 18, 1996, in Rochester.

John Irish Condon

Jack Condon remained an FBI agent after the war and participated in the Silvermaster case, the 1950s investigation of federal employees alleged to be covert agents of the Soviet Union. After leaving the Bureau, he practiced law in Pennsylvania. He died in Bryn Mawr on November 15, 2004, at ninety.

Donald Laurence Daughters

Though he worked briefly in the Boston field office following his return from Europe, Don Daughters soon left the Bureau to take a position with the American-owned United Shoe Company in Chile. He'd been very favorably impressed by the South American nation during his pre-ALU stint with the SIS, and the fact that his wife was Chilean made the move an easy choice. The couple and their four sons spent several years in Santiago, during which time Don worked as a part-time "cut-out" for the CIA's station chief. The man did not want prospective "assets" to be seen going in and out of the U.S. Embassy, so Don would interview them off-site. He eventually left United Shoe to work for RCA's South American branch, first in Chile and then in Brazil, and later worked for the Agency for International Development in Ecuador. Don retired in 1989 and died in Bethesda, Maryland, on September 2, 2006, at the age of eighty-nine.

John Eldon Dunn

Upon his eventual return from Europe, Joe Dunn testified at the treason trial of Douglas Chandler. He also helped investigate the treason case against Iva Ikuko Toguri D'Aquino, an American-born woman believed to have broadcast on behalf of the Japanese using the alias "Tokyo Rose." Joe retired from the FBI in 1965 and the following year became assistant professor of social sciences at Southern Oregon State College. He received a master's degree from the same institution in 1974 and was instrumental in establishing a law-enforcement degree program at Western Oregon State College. He died December 30, 1984, in Salem, Oregon, at the age of seventy-two.

James Daniel Faziola

Jim Faziola remained in the FBI after the war, working primarily on the West Coast. He took part in the Warren Commission investigation into the assassination of President John F. Kennedy. Jim died in Oxnard, California, on December 2, 1988, at seventy-eight.

Joseph George Fellner

After returning from Austria to the United States, Joe Fellner chose to remain in the FBI. He worked in the Seattle, New York, Chicago, Washington, and Milwaukee offices and upon retirement moved to Hawaii. He died in Honolulu in 1982 at the age of seventy-one.

Erling Harald Kloster

Hal Kloster stayed with the Bureau for two years after the end of the war, resigning in 1947. From then until 1994 he had a private law practice in Visalia, California, where he died in 1999.

Roland Octave L'Allier

Paris proved to be a continuing theme in Roland L'Allier's FBI career, because he was the legal attaché at the U.S. embassy in the French capital from 1951 to 1959. After retiring from the Bureau in 1962, he served as director of President Herbert Hoover's Presidential Library in Iowa. He died in Saint Paul, Minnesota, at the age of ninety-two, in June 2002.

Arthur Matthew O'Connor

The second of the clerk-stenographers to work with the Army Liaison Unit, Art O'Connor left the FBI following the end of the war. He spent twenty years as a Venezuela-based executive of the U.S.-owned Creole Petroleum Corporation, an affiliate of Exxon. After retiring from that position, he moved to Sarasota, Florida, where he passed away, in August 1994, at eighty.

Alfred Augustine Pease

After leaving the FBI, Al Pease worked as an instructor for International Police Services, Inc., a Washington, D.C.–based private company founded in 1952 to assist in the training of foreign police organizations. He later worked as a security consultant for International Intelligence, Inc. (also known as Intertel), originally a component of Resorts International and, in the 1970s, one of dozens of private intelligence networks offering confidential services to both individual and corporate clients. Al died in Arlington, Virginia, in October 1993, at the age of eighty-three.

Robert Eugene Prather

Bob Prather left the FBI after the war. He died in Churchville, New York, in November 2000, at the age of eighty-three.

James Romano

Upon his return from Italy in 1945, Jim Romano remained in the FBI for only a few months. In March 1946, he resigned and went back to work for the Pelham, New York, Police Department, which he'd left in 1942 to join the Bureau. Jim became chief of the department, retiring after twenty-one years in the position. He died in May 1973 at the age of fifty-one.

Bernard Walter Rucks

Walt Rucks left the FBI after his 1945 return from Europe. He went to work for IBM and spent several decades as the firm's special representative for federal programs. He died October 15, 1992, in Mission Viejo, California.

Boyd Verne Sheets

Another former ALU member who chose not to remain in the FBI after the end of World War II, in 1948, Boyd Sheets earned a doctorate in speech pathology from the University of Minnesota. He then spent eight years as director of the University of Utah's Speech and Hearing Clinic. In 1961, he was named the director of special education programs in the medical and scientific section of the United Cerebral Palsy Associations. He died in Nassau County, New York, on September 26, 1973, at the age of fifty-seven.

Richard Charles Thompson

Dick Thompson continued his FBI career after the war, ultimately spending twenty-five years in the Bureau. Following his retirement in 1965, he taught police science classes at Milwaukee Area Technical College. He retired from that position in 1977, and died in Wauwatosa, Wisconsin, in September 1997 at the age of eighty-seven.

Hans Wenthur

The former Milwaukee policeman remained in the FBI after his return from Austria and worked in the Milwaukee, San Antonio, and Los Angeles field offices. After retiring from the Bureau, he was a security consultant for Lockheed Aircraft and a private investigator. Hans Wenthur died in Los Angeles, in April 1968, at the age of sixty-three.

Howard Peter Winter

Pete Winter chose to stay with the FBI after the war. He worked in the legal attaché office in Santiago, Chile, and was Roland L'Allier's deputy in the Paris legat office in the early 1960s. He retired in 1966 with twenty-seven years' service and then spent eighteen years with the Florida Department of Transportation. He died in Tallahassee, in July 2003, at eighty-eight.

The Other Agents

Henry Gordon Sheen

The Army counterintelligence officer without whose friendship, guidance, and support Fred Ayer and Don Daughters could not have gotten the Army Liaison Unit up and running, stayed in the Army following the end of World War II. After service in Japan and Korea during the Korean War, Gordon Sheen was assigned to Fort Sam Houston, Texas. Following his retirement, he and his wife, Evelyn, settled in Bexar, Texas, and Gordon wrote several papers on Army counterintelligence operations. He died on June 22, 1958, at the age of fifty, and was buried next to his father at Arlington National Cemetery.

Ramón Arrizabalaga

The CIC agent who interrogated Ezra Pound in cooperation with the FBI's Frank Amprim left the Army in 1946 and returned to Nevada. He became a successful businessman in Fallon and served on the city's Chamber of Commerce. Upon the 1950 outbreak of the Korean War, Arrizabalaga reentered the Army, serving in military intelligence for two years. Following his discharge, he returned to Fallon, where he died, in 1984, at the age of seventy.

Myron Elmore Gurnea

After his 1944 inspection of Fred Ayer and Don Daughters's initial Army Liaison Unit operations in Paris, Bud Gurnea spent the following years as a senior FBI "troubleshooter." Sadly, while boating with friends on the Potomac River in August 1950, he fell overboard and drowned. He was forty-eight years old.

Clement Van Dyke Rousseau

Deputy Paris legal attaché Bud Rousseau remained in the FBI until 1947, at which time he became the New York–based director of Latin American operations for Dun & Bradstreet. He left the company in the early 1950s to join with several other former FBI agents in founding Investigators Inc., later known as Fidelifacts. The firm provided commercial firms with security screenings and background checks on prospective employees, and Bud owned and operated the Phoenix, Arizona, branch. He retired in 1985 and died in March 2003, at ninety-two.

Horton Rockwood Telford

Horton Telford remained the FBI's legal attaché in Paris until 1950. That same year, he married Chiyo Thomas, an American woman born in Japan to Mormon missionaries. In 1955, he was listed as a member of the State Department's Foreign Service Staff Corps. In 1961, Telford joined the Washington, D.C., law firm of Tyler and Stetter and opened the company's office in Leopoldville, Republic of the Congo. According to one former FBI agent, at some point Telford joined the CIA, though this has proven to be impossible to determine with any certainty. By the early 1970s, he was living in the affluent San Diego suburb of La Jolla, where he died in April 2000, at the age of ninety-one.

Arthur McCaslin Thurston

The Bureau's first legal attaché in London—and the man who helped pave the way for the Army Liaison Unit's operations in newly liberated Europe—left the FBI in January 1944. Commissioned a lieutenant in the Navy, he joined the OSS and spent the remainder of the war in China. Following the end of hostilities, Art joined General Douglas MacArthur's staff in Tokyo as an adviser on the modernization of the Japanese police. Art left the service in 1949, and from then until 1952, he was superintendent of the Indiana State Police. He then became president and chairman of the board of Farmers National Bank in his hometown of Shelbyville, Indiana. After his retirement from that position, Art was a consultant to the U.S. Agency for International Development, touring the world to lecture on the organization and operations of American law-enforcement agencies. Art died in December 2003, at the age of eighty-nine.

Acknowledgments

THE NECESSARY PREREQUISITE TO WRITING an accurate, compelling, and hopefully enjoyable work of history is deep and wide-ranging research. Locating and deciphering key documents, interviewing the colleagues or family members of the individuals who participated in the events at the core of the story, and, whenever possible, walking the ground on which the tale unfolded are all vital aspects of that research.

Fortunately, I am afflicted with a syndrome that affects many historians, journalists—and yes, intelligence professionals: research rapture. I love searching out those disparate and often contradictory bits of information that, if properly understood and merged, lead to a more comprehensive and enlightening grasp of the events and individuals I'm writing about. And an essential part of the rapture, for me at least, is the assistance I receive from others. In doing the research for this book, I was ably and generously aided by a variety of people both in the United States and abroad. I sincerely appreciate their advice, guidance, and support, without which *G.I. G-Men* could not have been written. Any errors or omissions in the book are, of course, mine alone.

First and foremost, I wish to thank my wife, Margaret Spragins Harding. This book, like those that came before it, would not have been possible without her love, patience, and wise counsel. Her French language skills were especially important on this project, as were her considerable talents as proofreader and fact-checker. I am truly blessed to have her in my life.

I would also like to thank my agent, Scott Mendel. A dear friend of many years, he has managed to guide me on the best literary course despite my occasional drifts into narrative backwaters. I also greatly appreciate the efforts of my Kensington editor, James Abbate, and ace photo researcher Satu Haase-Webb.

Heartfelt thanks are also due to Ellen Hampton, an American-born journalist, educator, and author, as well as a longtime resident in France. As with my previous book, *Escape from Paris*, Ellen was absolutely indispensable when it came to locating, evaluating, and in several cases translating key records held in various French archives.

Another individual who was absolutely instrumental in making this book possible was a man I never met—Frederick Ayer. FBI agent, raconteur, intelligence official, and author, Fred's book *Yankee G-Man* was an indispensable resource. Filled with essential information about the personnel and operations of the Army Liaison Unit, the book is also suffused with humor and wry observations about the agents and soldiers with whom Fred worked. He was by all accounts a fine human being, and he died far too young.

I am also indebted to the following:

In the United States

Raymond J. Batvinis, former FBI special agent and longtime author on the Bureau and its history. Ray's books *Hoover's Secret War Against Axis Spies* and *The Origins of FBI Counterintelligence* were essential reading during my research and writing of *G.I. G-Men*, and Ray gave unstintingly of his time, knowledge, and advice.

Dr. John Fox, FBI historian, who helped me locate photos of some of the key individuals who took part in the events chronicled in this book.

Dave Daughters and his brothers provided wonderful photos of their father, Don, and of Fred Ayer, as well as helping me obtain a copy of the oral history of Don and his wife, Yvonne, compiled by Anton Daughters.

Wenthy Wenthur Marcy, who allowed me to use excerpts from her father Hans Wenthur's wartime diary and provided photos of Hans and other ALU agents.

Tony Pease and his siblings, for providing information about their father's work in Italy with Frank Amprim, as well as allowing me to use a photo of their dad in Army uniform.

John and Karina Rousseau, son and daughter-in-law of Clement "Bud" Rousseau, and John's sisters, Kathie and Suzy, who shared Bud's stories of his time in Paris, photos of him taken while he was stationed in Cuba early in his SIS career, and excerpts from Horton Telford's diary that pertain to the period when he and Bud worked together in the Paris legal attaché office.

Joan Arrizabalaga, daughter of CIC agent Ramón Arrizabalaga, for sharing with me her memories of her father and her advice on locating the photos of Ramón, Frank Amprim, and Ezra Pound taken during the latter's interrogation following his arrest in Italy.

Willa Jacob and Christian Goodwillie of Hamilton College's Burke Library for providing me with the images of Ramón Arrizabalaga, Frank Amprim, and Ezra Pound.

Mark Heater, for providing photos of Horton Telford.

Mike Constanty of Westmoreland Research, who doggedly hunted down key documents for me at the National Archives.

Thomas Houghton, Jermaine Scott, Brittanie Sadler, Jacquelyn Beasley, Michael Heichelbech, and other archivists and staffers in the Special Access and Freedom of Information Act office at the National Archives, for their help in obtaining archived FBI, OSS, and U.S. Army documents. My thanks also to the staffs of the Departments of State and Justice FOIA offices for their assistance.

Howard Zar, executive director of Lyndhurst Mansion—Jay Gould's estate in Tarrytown, New York.

Sarah Lauderdale of Hamilton-Wenham Public Library in Massachusetts for her assistance in researching the history of the Ayer family.

Arthur Braswell of Duke University's David M. Rubenstein Rare Book and Manuscript Library for guidance on obtaining photos of Warrington Dawson.

The staff of the Air Force Historical Research Agency at Maxwell AFB, Alabama, for help in locating records of the various Air Transport Command units flying into and out of newly liberated France in 1944.

In Canada

Kened Sadiku in the Media Relations office of the Canadian department of National Defence, for assistance in tracking down photos of Sir William Stephenson of British Security Coordination. Thanks also to Gary Solar, formerly of the Intrepid Society, for providing images and background information on Sir William. Richard Provencher, chief of media relations for Library and Archives Canada, also provided valuable guidance regarding holdings pertaining to Sir William.

In the United Kingdom

The research staff at the U.K. National Archives in Kew, who helped me locate pertinent MI5 and MI6 files and photos of key individuals. Staffers at the Imperial War Museums were also helpful in locating and obtaining useful materials.

Bevan Price and other members of U.K. Rail Forums, for educating me on the details of train travel in Britain during World War II and providing actual 1942–44 timetables for key rail lines.

In France

The staff of the American Library in Paris, for assistance in tracking down details on Frank O'Neill and other Americans resident in France before and during the German occupation.

The staff of the Musée national de la Légion d'honneur et des ordres de chevalerie, for their help in locating the documents pertaining to Warrington Dawson.

Sylvie Zaidman of the Musée de la Libération de Paris for her guidance on researching the tumultuous days just before and just after Paris's liberation.

In Germany

The Bundesarchiv-Abteilung Militärarchiv in Freiburg, for help in locating records for the Abwehr office in occupied Paris.

The Bundesarchiv Koblenz, for help in researching the records of the SS, SD, and Kripo offices in occupied Paris.

Notes

Prologue

1. Officially known as the Monuments, Fine Arts and Archives Program, the organization comprised several hundred art historians, curators, and similar experts from the United States and other Allied nations. Most of its members had no prior military experience, and their sometimes eclectic approach to uniforms and military protocol often was a source of confusion or humor for frontline troops.
2. In the 1930s, the slang term "G-man" came into widespread use in America to denote any agent of the United States government, though the most used connotation was for special agents of the FBI.

Chapter 1: Hoover Casts a Net

1. According to Central Intelligence Agency historian Thomas F. Troy, in his comprehensive volume *Donovan and the CIA*, the nickname "Wild Bill" was bestowed on Donovan when he commanded Troop I ["eye"] of the 1st New York Cavalry, a National Guard unit called up for service on the U.S.–Mexico border in 1916. Though in his mid-thirties, Donovan was in excellent physical condition and routinely outperformed his younger troops during training. When he chided them for what he considered their premature exhaustion on an endurance march, one soldier is said to have responded, "We ain't as wild as you are, Bill." Donovan went on to command the 1st Battalion, 165th Infantry, in France in World War I, and in 1923, he was awarded the Medal of Honor for his actions at the October 1918 battle for the Ardennes village of Landres-et-St. Georges.
2. Hoover's dislike for Donovan stemmed from the latter's 1924–25 tenure as head of the Justice Department's Criminal Division, a period during which the two men clashed repeatedly. *Donovan and the CIA*, p. 25.

3. Beverly Gage's Pulitzer Prize–winning volume, *G-Man: J. Edgar Hoover and the Making of the American Century*, is a fascinating overview of Hoover's early life, his eventual rise to power as head of the FBI, and his preoccupation with the fight against communism.
4. For a comprehensive overview of pro-Nazi groups and their activities in pre–Pearl Harbor America, see Bradley W. Hart's excellent *Hitler's American Friends: The Third Reich's Supporters in the United States*.
5. Minnesota Republican Sen. Ernest Lundeen was among the most vocal anti-Roosevelt and pro-Germany legislators in Washington until his August 1940 death in a still-mysterious airplane crash. His story, and that of the larger pro-Nazi, antidemocratic movement at work in America before Pearl Harbor is brilliantly told in journalist Rachel Maddow's *Prequel: An American Fight Against Fascism*.
6. Gage, *G-Man*, p. 205.
7. An excellent source on the FBI's war against Axis espionage efforts in the United States both before and after Pearl Harbor is Raymond J. Batvinis's *Hoover's Secret War Against Axis Spies: FBI Counterespionage During World War II*. And, as noted earlier, Hart, *Hitler's American Friends* is a comprehensive history of the rise and fall of the would-be American Reich.
8. "Intelligence Liaison Between the FBI and State, 1940–44," in *Studies in Intelligence*, Vol. 49, No. 3 (2005).
9. Berle was undoubtedly one of the most interesting members of Roosevelt's "Brain Trust," the president's group of informal advisers. Berle entered Harvard at fourteen and went on to complete both BA and MA degrees in history by 1914, at the age of nineteen. He received his LLB degree from Harvard Law School in 1916 at the age of twenty-one. Berle enlisted in the Army following America's entry into World War I and was commissioned a second lieutenant, serving as an intelligence officer at the U.S. Army War College and in the U.S.-occupied Dominican Republic. He stayed in the Army after the 1918 Armistice and was assigned to the American Commission to Negotiate the Peace at Paris as an adviser on Russian, Polish, and Baltic affairs. His disagreement with the details of the final 1919 Versailles Treaty prompted him to resign his commission and go into private law practice. It was his experience as a military intelligence officer, as well as his earlier legal and diplomatic

experiences, that led to him acting as the State Department's liaison for intelligence matters.

10. Details of the creation, organization, and initial operations of the SIS in Latin America are drawn from the first volume of the five-volume *History of the SIS Division*, pp. 2–11 and 46–49 (hereafter *SIS History*).

    An internal FBI study completed in 1947, the *History* is a truly exhaustive study of every aspect of the SIS and is surprisingly candid in its conclusions regarding the organization's weaknesses as well as its strengths. Interestingly, on February 12, 1946, the Central Intelligence Group (which on September 18, 1947, became the Central Intelligence Agency) released its own, considerably more concise, overview of the history of SIS, *Special Intelligence Service of the Federal Bureau of Investigation*. The five-page document is a straightforward and objective review of SIS's creation and general operating procedures up through the date of publication.
11. *SIS History*, op cit.
12. Ibid.
13. Indeed, jurisdictional squabbles among the FBI, Navy, and Army regarding the SIS and its activities continued following the agency's creation and initial operations, necessitating a series of additional interdepartmental conferences and several "delineation agreements" to further specify each department's responsibilities and areas of operation.
14. *SIS History*, Volume I, p. 2.
15. Ibid.
16. Ibid., p. 3.
17. Former Special Agent William T. Baker, quoted in an August 26, 2004, interview by Brian Hollstein, in the collection *SIS Oral Histories*.
18. Ibid., p. 6.
19. Ibid., p. 98.
20. Ibid., p. 5.
21. Ibid., p. 6.
22. Ibid., p. 4
23. Ibid., p. 11.
24. Ibid., p. 97.

25. Ibid., p. 99.
26. Ibid., p. 97.
27. Ibid., p. 16.
28. Ibid., p. 16.
29. *Studies in Intelligence*, op cit.
30. *The American Foreign Service Journal*, Vol. 18, No. 6, June 1941, p. 312.
31. *SIS History*, p. 30.
32 Ibid.
33. Ibid. The Bedaux case—including the suspect's suicide while in custody in the United States—is also covered extensively in Charles Glass's excellent *Americans in Paris*.

Chapter 2: Our Man in London

1. Some sources mention that Thurston arrived at London's Victoria Station, though that facility primarily handled departures to and arrivals from the southeast of England. Since the young FBI agent is known to have traveled from Foynes to Prestwick by air, he would have boarded a train to London either in Kilmarnock, some twelve miles from Prestwick or, having taken a commuter line to Glasgow, from there to the British capital. Either way, he would have traveled south aboard a train operated by the London, Midland and Scottish Railway. The majority of that firm's trains operating between London and Scotland used St Pancras as their southern terminal.
2. In response to growing German militarism, in July 1909, Britain's Committee of Imperial Defence formed the Secret Service Bureau, jointly headed by Army officer Vernon Kell and the Royal Navy's Mansfield Smith-Cumming. In 1911, the bureau was divided into two entities, a domestic security section headed by Kell and a foreign intelligence section led by Smith-Cumming. During World War I, the organizations were renamed as, respectively, Military Intelligence Sections 5 (MI5) and 6 (MI6). Both designations were ultimately officially replaced, with MI5 becoming the Security Service and MI6 the Secret Intelligence Service, though both are still widely referred to by their MI monikers. In this volume, I will use MI6 to refer to the Secret Intelligence Service to avoid confusion with the FBI's Special Intelligence Service, which was also known as SIS.

3. Randolph Churchill's recollections, February 13, 1963, quoted in Martin Gilbert's masterful *Winston S. Churchill: Finest Hour, 1939–1941*, p. 358.
4. The total number was 1,949—1,161 written messages and telegrams from Churchill to Roosevelt, and 788 from Roosevelt to Churchill, according to the 1987 three-volume work *Churchill and Roosevelt: The Complete Correspondence*, edited by Warren F. Kimball, then professor of history at Newark College of Rutgers University.
5. For reasons that were unclear even to his contemporaries, Menzies pronounced his family name as "Mingess."

   The tradition of referring to the director of MI6 as "C" originated with the agency's first head, Royal Navy Captain Mansfield Smith-Cumming, who assumed the post in 1911 and often signed documents with the letter C. Vernon Kell, first head of MI5, was widely referred to as "K." Ian Fleming's popular James Bond novels and the movies spawned from them gave the erroneous impression that the head of MI5 is code-named "M," though during and since World War II, the agency's director general has been referred to simply as "DG."
6. Born in Winnipeg, Manitoba, in January 1897, as William Samuel Clouston Stanger, to a Scottish father and Icelandic mother but raised by Icelandic Canadian relatives, Stephenson had a difficult childhood. A loner for most of his early life, he left school after the sixth grade and went to work at a series of odd jobs. After returning from World War I and eventually attaining increasing wealth, the young man began purposely obfuscating various aspects of his personal history, a fact that has subsequently caused much confusion among his various biographers. His penchant for reinventing himself and various aspects of his life continued until his death. For what is thought to be one of the most accurate biographies, see Bill Macdonald's *The True Intrepid: Sir William Stephenson and the Unknown Agents*.
7. Stephenson's wife, the former Mary French Simmons, was born in Springfield, Tennessee, in 1901. She and Stephenson were married in London in July 1924.
8. Hyde, *Room 3603*, pp. 20–21.
9. Stephenson had earlier in life been an amateur lightweight world champion and boxed in interservice bouts during World War I. He met Tun-

ney, then a Marine and the American Expeditionary Forces champion, at several matches—though they never fought each other, given the wide disparity in their weight classes. Their friendship lasted until Tunney's death in November 1979.

10. The April 15, 1940, arrival date for Stephenson and his wife aboard *Manhattan* is drawn from the vessel's official "Manifest of Alien Passengers" filed with the U.S. Immigration and Naturalization Service upon arrival at the port of New York. Several earlier writers have confused this date with the couple's later June 21 arrival aboard *Britannic.*

    Tunney gave his account of his role in facilitating the Stephenson–Hoover meeting during a 1968 CBC radio program called *The Great Canadian Spy.* A transcript of the interview is held by the University of Regina, and is quoted in Macdonald, *The True Intrepid.* The April 16 date for the Stephenson–Hoover meeting is from Batvinis, *Hoover's Secret War Against Axis Spies*, p. 25.

11. The general outlines of the Hoover–Stephenson meeting and its outcome are drawn from Hyde, *Room 3603*, pp. 48–49, and Batvinis, *Hoover's Secret War*, pp. 25–26.

12. H. Montgomery Hyde's *The Quiet Canadian*, p. 26.

13. Ibid., p. 28.

14. This quote, which appears in Macdonald, *The True Intrepid*, first appeared in the forward to H. Montgomery Hyde's 1983 book *Secret Intelligence Agent: British Espionage in America and the Creation of the OSS.* In his introduction to *British Security Coordination: The Secret History of British Intelligence in the Americas, 1940–1945* (the collected "official" history of BSC amassed by William Stephenson, H. Montgomery Hyde, and others immediately after the war but not published in full until 1998), military historian Nigel West implies that Churchill's stirring exhortation likely never happened.

15. Some accounts suggest Stephenson and Donovan first met, in 1916, when the latter was on a fact-finding mission to England for the Rockefeller Foundation's War Relief Commission (before America entered the war) and spoke with Stephenson while the young Canadian was recovering from being gassed. In 1944, Donovan said he didn't remember meeting Stephenson during World War I, though in latter years, he agreed that he might have encountered the younger man but didn't learn

his name at the time. It may also have been that Stephenson first met Donovan when the latter's New York law firm handled some legal affairs for one of Stephenson's companies. However the men initially met, by the late 1930s, they were widely known in Washington circles as good friends. Indeed, those who knew both men referred to them as "Little Bill" (the diminutive Stephenson) and "Big Bill" (Donovan).

16. Cave Brown, *Wild Bill Donovan: The Last Hero*, p. 148. Also quoted in Macdonald, *The True Intrepid*.
17. Drawn from "Security Coordination Circular No. 9," April 19, 1941.
18. Batvinis, *Hoover's Secret War*, p. 25.
19. Hyde, *Room 3603*, p. 18.
20. Ibid., pp. 91–92.
21. "Functions of Security Coordination," October 1, 1941.
22. Hyde, *Room 3603*, p. 236.
23. The less savory of BSC's activities in the United States are well-documented in, among other volumes, the excellent Mahl, *Desperate Deception: British Covert Operations in the United States, 1939–1944*.
24. Memo, Berle to Welles, dated March 31, 1941. The original document is held in Record Group 59, "General Records of the Department of State" at the U.S. National Archives. Berle's comments are also quoted in Macdonald, *The True Intrepid*.
25. Troy, *Donovan and the CIA*, p. 83. Formed in July 1940, the Special Operations Executive was tasked with undertaking covert military operations in Axis-held territory. Its brief included espionage, sabotage, assassination, and aid to local resistance movements, among other "ungentlemanly" pursuits. SOE was instrumental in teaching those vital wartime skills to operatives of the fledgling U.S. Office of Strategic Services.
26. Berle's diary entry for March 5, 1942, is quoted in Macdonald, *The True Intrepid*.
27. Hart, *Hitler's American Friends*, p. 13.
28. Troy, *Donovan and the CIA*, p. 32.
29. The fact that Donovan set up COI's New York offices on the same 36th floor of Rockefeller Center that was home to Stephenson's BSC head office was seen by Hoover as proof that Donovan and Stephenson were in

flagrant and intentional violation of the terms of the original U.S.–U.K. intelligence-sharing agreement.

30. Troy, *Donovan and the CIA*, p. 32.

31. Liddell Diary, entry for June 5, 1942, p. 593. Liddell was a prolific—some might say obsessive—diary keeper throughout his time at MI5. Typing his entries neatly into small lined notebooks, he recorded extensive details of virtually all his professional interactions with British and foreign individuals. The diaries are held in record group KV-4/190 at the U.K. National Archives.

32. Liddell Diary, entry for June 6, 1942, p. 597. KV-4-190.

33. Ibid., entry for June 16, 1942, p. 614.

34. Ibid., entries for November 15 and 19, 1942, pp. 931, 943.

35. While some sources have indicated that Thurston's flight departed from Pan American's seaplane base at Port Washington, near Glen Cove, Long Island, Pan Am had left that base in March 1940 to shift operations to the Marine Air Terminal. The Port Washington facility was turned into a Grumman Aircraft production plant in April 1942, and operated there until the end of the war.

36. Drawn from a November 22, 1942, letter from Thurston to his parents. The letter is quoted in Batvinis, *Hoover's Secret War*, p. 70.

37. As a result of the expansion, the Embassy's address was technically Nos. 1–3 Grosvenor Square.

38. By the time of Thurston's arrival in London more than two thousand people worked at the Embassy and in the surrounding U.S. military offices. Indeed, the number of Americans present around Grosvenor Square prompted local British residents to refer to the area as "Little America" and, in a waggish reference to the ETO commander's German ancestry, as "Eisenhower Platz."

39. Winant—known to his close friends as Gil—described what he called his "apartment and workshop" on pp. 2–3 of his 1947 memoir, *Letter from Grosvenor Square: An Account of a Stewardship*.

    As a decorated U.S. Army Air Service pilot in World War I, Winant had commanded an observation squadron that saw action over the Western Front. After the war, he went into politics, serving successively as a New Hampshire state legislator, governor of New Hampshire, chairman of the U.S. Social Security Board, and head of the International Labor Organization. Though a Republican, he was tapped by President Franklin Roosevelt to replace Joseph P. Kennedy Sr. as ambassador in London after Kennedy publicly and frequently opined that Britain couldn't win against the Nazis and that American should come to some sort of "understanding" with Hitler. The married Winant is widely believed to have had a long running affair with Prime Minister Winston Churchill's second daughter, Sarah Churchill, while stationed in London. The relationship reportedly ended badly, and its end is thought to have contributed significantly to Winant's problems with depression and, ultimately, to his decision to commit suicide. He took his own life on November 3, 1947, the same day *Letter from Grosvenor Square* was published.

40. Drawn from Raymond Batvinis's article "A Thoroughly Competent Operator: Former SA Arthur Thurston," in the October/November 2017 edition of *The Grapevine*, newsletter of the Society of Former Special Agents of the FBI.
41. Ibid.
42. *Hoover's Secret War Against Axis Spies*, p. 76. In a letter quoted by author Batvinis, Thurston assured his parents that he was "reasonably comfortable and not suffering any undue hardships." He even noted that a maid did his laundry and that he was served breakfast every morning in the flat's small dining room.
43. Liddell Diary, entry for November 30, 1942, p. 952. KV-4/190.
44. Confidential letter from Winant to Petrie, dated December 3, 1942. KV-4/395, p. 124.
45. Liddell Diary, entry for December 3, 1942, pp. 5–6. KV-4/190.
46. Ibid., entry for December 4, 1942, pp. 8–9. KV-4/190.
47. Batvinis, *Hoover's Secret War Against Axis Spies*, p. 79.
48. Telegram, from C.S.S. for Stephenson Personal, December 9, 1942. KV-4/395.
49. Telegram, from Director, Security Coordination, New York, to C.S.S., December 14, 1942. KV-4/395.
50. Liddell Diary, entry for December 22, 1942, p. 37. KV-4/191.
51. Established by Churchill on May 27, 1940, as the Home Defence (Security) Executive, or HD(S)E, the organization comprised representatives

of the Home Office, the Commander in Chief of Home Forces, MI5, and MI6. Renamed the Security Executive (SE) in October 1941, the organization was empowered to supervise all matters pertaining to the nation's internal security and initiate action through the appropriate departments.

52. KV-4/447.

53. Raymond Batvinis gives a fascinating and in-depth account of the Ostrich program and its importance to the Bureau in *Hoover's Secret War*, pp. 81-89.

54. Liddell Diary, entry for April 2, 1943, pp. 196–97. KV-4/191.

55. Ibid., entry for August 16, 1943, p. 142. KV-4/192.

56. Quoted in *Desperate Deception*. Author Thomas Mahl found the statement in the Ernest Cuneo Papers, held at the Franklin D. Roosevelt Library in Hyde Park, New York.

57. The XX (for double cross) system was devised by MI5 early in the war as a way to turn captured Axis agents to British use by having them transmit disinformation back to their controllers. Thanks in large part to Ultra intercepts, by mid-1941, virtually all covert agents sent to the United Kingdom by Germany and Italy—as well as homegrown turncoats operating as espionage agents in Britain—had been captured and turned.

58. Charles Bedaux was eventually transported to the United States and incarcerated in the Immigration Detention Center in Miami while the status of his U.S. citizenship was being determined. On February 18, 1944, while still in custody, he apparently killed himself with an overdose of Luminal, an antiseizure medication he had been provided with to help control his chronic insomnia. Glass, *Americans in Paris*, pp. 338–40.

59. One of the three autonomous components into which the Army was organized at that point in the war, the Army Ground Forces comprised those units and organizations that undertook or directly supported ground combat operations. The Army Service Forces handled logistics, supplies, engineering, medical activities, and related services, and the U.S. Army Air Forces handled all aviation matters.

60. Liddell Diary, entry for January 26, 1944, pp. 123–24. KV-4/193.

Chapter 3: A Pound of Flesh

1. Details on Pound's relationship with Fascist Italy's propaganda organs is drawn largely from Dr. Robert A. Corrigan's pioneering 1972 study, *Ezra Pound and the Italian Ministry for Popular Culture*. Corrigan's dogged and exhaustive research at the Library of Congress, the National Archives, and the Department of Justice turned up a trove of largely forgotten Pound-related documents, including the original typescripts of all of the poet's radio broadcasts——and many of the documents bear marginal notes handwritten by Pound himself. His comprehensive study of Pound's wartime propaganda activities led Corrigan to believe that the poet was not, as many of his supporters believed, either an "innocent dupe" of the Italian Fascists nor a psychologically impaired eccentric who let his extreme anti-Semitism and bizarre economic theories lead him into foolishly rooting against his native land.
2. Corrigan, *Ezra Pound and the Italian Ministry for Popular Culture*, p. 31.
3. Pound had actually been working as a print propagandist for Fascist Italy since the mid-1930s, primarily contributing articles to British fascist journals. His propaganda and interactions with Sir Oswald Mosley's British Union of Fascists attracted the attention of MI5, which began intercepting Pound's mail and tracking his movements. Nor was that the first time Britain's intelligence services had taken an interest in the American poet. During World War I, Pound's apparent support for Irish and Indian nationalists had prompted the British government to start a file on him, which included extracts from intercepted mail and telegrams. See *Ezra Pound Files,* (MI5), 1918-1949. KV-2/875. UKNA.
4. Following America's entry into World War II, the Foreign Broadcast Monitoring Service was renamed the Federal Broadcast Intelligence Service. After the war, the agency was again renamed, becoming the Foreign Broadcast Information Service. In 1947, it became part of the Central Intelligence Agency.
5. The memo, dated October 11, 1941, was reproduced in Pound scholar Emily Mitchell Wallace's paper, "The Last Diplomatic Train From Rome in 1942: Ezra Pound's Passport and His Kafkaesque Nostos," presented on July 3, 2009, at the 23rd Ezra Pound International Conference in Rome. The memo has subsequently been cited by several

authors, including A. David Moody in Volume 3 (*The Tragic Years, 1929–1972*) of his masterful Pound biography.

6. FBI Pound file.
7. Ibid.
8. Ibid.
9. The other individuals—Fred W. Kaltenbach, Constance Drexel, Robert H. Best, Edward Leo Delaney, Jane Anderson, and Douglas Chandler—are dealt with in later chapters of this volume.
10. FBI Pound file, op cit.
11. The states were Alabama, California, Colorado, Connecticut, Idaho, Illinois, Louisiana, Maryland, Massachusetts, Minnesota, Montana, Nevada, New Jersey, New York, Pennsylvania, and Utah.
12. By the time two FBI agents were dispatched to North Africa to investigate Charles Bedaux following the January 1943 deaths of Percy Foxworth and Harold Haberfeld, the region was no longer an active combat zone and the agents operated "in the open" rather than under military cover.
13. The agent's last name has often been incorrectly rendered as Ampirin, Amprin, and even Ampirini.
14. Having the head of a family travel to America ahead of spouse and children was a common occurrence because it allowed the first arriving family member to find work and housing before the others landed.
15. Details on Frank Amprim's application, background investigation, hiring, initial training, and first assignments are drawn from his FBI personnel file.
16. Agents directly assigned to SIS were given three- or four-digit identification numbers, with the former belonging to men who had joined SIS earlier and the latter to those brought on later in the organization's history. While Amprim's personnel file does not mention an SIS number, it may be among the redactions.
17. In U.S. military practice, a brevet rank gives the holder certain authorities and privileges for a specified period or while serving in a specific position. Amprim and the other FBI agents who would later work under Army cover were given brevet officer ranks to provide them with a

certain status within the military rank structure, as well as to authorize their access to military facilities and transportation.

During World War II, the term Army of the United States (AUS) generally referred to officers and enlisted personnel who had been drafted or had enlisted for the duration of the conflict, as opposed to members of the Regular Army (RA), who were generally long-service professionals. This can be a confusing distinction, in that RA personnel could be given higher, temporary ranks in the AUS for specific periods or reasons, and then revert to their original RA ranks upon completion of the specified duty. The AUS was inactivated in 1973 when the United States suspended the draft and transitioned to an all-volunteer military.

18. *SIS History*, pp. 464–65.
19. Renovated and significantly enlarged after the war, the Saint-George still exists as the Hotel El-Djazaïr.
20. *History of Allied Forces Headquarters and Headquarters NATOUSA, Part 2: December 1942-December 1943.*
21. Communication No. 6, Amprim to Hoover, November 9, 1943. FBI, Pound file.
22. An almost mythical figure in OSS history, William Eddy was born in Lebanon of American missionary parents and grew up speaking fluent Arabic and French in addition to English. He served in combat in France with the Marines in World War I, after the war becoming a professor of English literature. He returned to the Marines in 1940 and worked for the Office of Naval Intelligence before being attached to OSS. For a fascinating and thorough look at Eddy's life and accomplishments both in and outside military intelligence, see *Arabian Knight: Colonel Bill Eddy USMC and the Rise of American Power in the Middle East* by Thomas W. Lippman, former Middle East bureau chief for *The Washington Post.*
23. Corvo enlisted in the Army before Pearl Harbor, and despite being a lowly private, his ideas for ways in which to conduct anti-German and anti-Fascist operations in Italy caught the attention of the OSS and won him a commission. His exploits behind enemy lines are legendary within special operations circles, and his memoir *Max Corvo: OSS Italy 1942–1945, A Personal Memoir of the Fight for Freedom* is a must-read for students of unconventional warfare.

24. Chief, SI(I) to Commander, OSS Algiers, December 2, 1943. Scamporino's reference to the FBI agent as "Ampirin" throughout the memo is the likely origin of various authors' misspelling of Amprim's last name.
25. Ibid.
26. Several Allied units sent small, vehicle-mounted reconnaissance groups toward Rome, each hoping to be the first to enter the city. While elements of the U.S. 3rd, 85th, and 88th infantry divisions all entered the capital early on June 4, most historians—including those at the U.S. Army Center of Military History in Washington—credit the FSSF detachment with actually being first into the capital. See the chapter "Special Operations in the Mediterranean" in Hogan, *U.S. Army Special Operations in World War I* and "First Special Service Force: Patrol to Rome."
27. The opulent building is now home to RAI (Radiotelevisione Italiana), Italy's postwar public national broadcaster.
28. Thirty-year-old Art Avignone was born and raised in Washington, D.C., where his family owned and operated the popular Avignone Frères restaurant. A Catholic University law graduate, he joined the FBI in 1940 and carried the SIS number 250. Avignone returned to the United States from Italy in February 1945, where he was assigned to the SIS's Army Liaison Office at Bureau headquarters.

    Thirty-six-year-old Ray Bacigalupi was born and raised in San Francisco and graduated from the University of California, Berkeley in May 1930. He worked as an accountant for the Crown Zellerbach Company until entering the FBI in 1941. He returned to the United States from Italy in August 1945.

    Two other members of SIS, special agents William P. Camusi and James Romano, also worked with Frank Amprim in Rome. Both agents arrived in early 1945 and were officially assigned to the FBI office in the newly reopened U.S. Embassy. Neither agent operated under Army cover, and both returned to the United States in October 1945—Camusi from Casablanca and Romano from Naples.
29. Why Amprim—ostensibly an Army officer—was sent to Bethesda rather than to Walter Reed Army Hospital in the District is unclear. It may simply have been that there were more beds available at the former.

30. Pound married Dorothy Shakespear in London in 1914 and, as her *New York Times* obituary put it following her death in 1973 at the age of eighty-seven, "For the better part of 50 years, Mrs. Pound was the poet's uncomplaining companion through his lean years of struggle in London, days of literary glory in Paris, a decade of illness and pro-fascist activity in Rome, and 12 years of incarceration as insane at St. Elizabeth's Hospital in Washington." Ezra Pound met Rudge, an American-born concert violinist, in the early 1920s. They soon became both lovers and artistic collaborators, the pair doing much to popularize the music of Antonio Vivaldi. Pound and Rudge had a daughter, Mary, in 1925, though the child spent most of her early life with a German-speaking family in the Italian Tyrol paid to look after her. Dorothy Pound gave birth to a son, Omar, in Paris in 1926, and Ezra Pound gave the boy his last name, though the poet was not his biological father.
31. Cornell, *The Trial of Ezra Pound: A Documented Account of the Treason Case by the Defendant's Lawyer*, p. 52. The majority of the 92nd Infantry Division's senior officers were white, while some three hundred second lieutenants, first lieutenants, and a few captains were Black, as were virtually all of the division's enlisted soldiers.
32. The basic details of Pound's last few days in Sant'Ambrogio and his first day in Allied hands are drawn primarily from Pound and Spoo (eds.), *Ezra and Dorothy Pound: Letters in Captivity, 1945–1946*; Schloss, *Let the Wind Speak: Mary de Rachewiltz and Ezra Pound*; Carson, *Olga Rudge and Ezra Pound*; and Moody's *Ezra Pound: Poet*, Volume 3: *The Tragic Years 1939–1972*.
33. Details on the 92nd Division CIC Detachment's organization and operations are drawn from the unit's June 1945 "Detachment History." Details on the role Arrizabalaga played in Frank Amprim's interviews of Pound and in the FBI agent's searches of the Casa 60 cottage and interactions with Olga Rudge, Dorothy Pound, and Mary Pound are drawn from Arrizabalaga's 1956 "Memoir."
34. The CIC detachment chief's full name, in the Spanish manner, was Ramón Arrizabalaga Erquiaga, though he went by his father's surname. Born in 1914 in Lander, Nevada, to Basque immigrant parents, Arrizabalaga had enlisted in the Army in January 1942. His fluency in Euskara (Basque) and Spanish, and competence in French and Italian, led to his selection for CIC training. Sent to North Africa in 1943 as part of

the Fifth Army CIC Detachment, in October 1944 Arrizabalaga was promoted from T5 (technician fifth grade) to first lieutenant and given command of the newly organized 92nd Division CIC Detachment.

35. Olga Rudge's quote is drawn from Pound and Spoo (eds.), *Ezra and Dorothy Pound, Letters in Captivity, 1945–1946*, p. 6. The *carabinieri* are Italy's paramilitary gendarmerie and can be deployed both for civil policing and duty in war zones.
36. FBI Pound file.
37. The Salo Republic was a Nazi puppet state established in northern Italy following Italy's 1943 surrender to the Allies. On May 12, 1945, the Fifth Army CIC Detachment captured Pound's personnel file from the Ministry of Popular Culture at Salo, proving that he had made and been paid for broadcasts on behalf of the Fascist rump state.
38. Ramón Arrizabalaga Collection of Ezra Pound, YCAL MSS 161.
39. FBI Pound file.
40. Ibid. One has to wonder how Olga felt about the search and Dorothy's apparent eagerness to assist Amprim and Arrizabalaga. As the renter of record, Olga was the sole legal occupant of the Casa 60 rooms while the Pounds were essentially just long-term guests.
41. Pound's FBI case file includes Amprim's complete notes on the typewriter. The FBI agent confiscated the machine on August 9, 1945, and tracked down the dealer from whom Pound had purchased it. The dealer provided complete records, including the serial number (27780) and the date of initial sale (February 25, 1938). Amprim took several "specimens" of the type produced by the machine, which had a distinctively misaligned letter "t."
42. Quoted in Pound and Spoo (eds.), *Ezra Pound: Poet*, Volume 3: *The Tragic Years, 1939–1972*.
43. Ezra Pound to Shakespear and Parkyn, Dorothy Shakespear Pound's family solicitors in London, October 5, 1945. Quoted in *Ezra and Dorothy Pound: Letters in Captivity, 1945–1946*, p. 107.
44. Quoted in ibid., p. 47.
45. Arrizabalaga's 1956 "Memoir."

46. These conditions were essentially replicated for "high risk" detainees at the U.S. military detention center at Guantánamo Bay Naval Base, Cuba during the United States' War on Terror.
47. Quoted in Carpenter, *A Serious Character: The Life of Ezra Pound*, p. 663.
48. FBI Pound file.
49. Details drawn from Holder's "Record, with Affidavit, of the Trip from Rome to Bolling Field D.C. With Ezra Pound," found in National Archives Record Group 153 and quoted in its entirety in Pound and Spoo (eds,), *Ezra and Dorothy Pound: Letters in Captivity, 1945–1946*, pp. 195–201. Air Transport Command flights into the D.C. area normally landed at National Airport, just across the Potomac River in Virginia. However, since Pound legally had to be delivered to the jurisdiction in which he had been indicted, the aircraft instead diverted to the USAAF's Bolling Field in D.C.
50. Avignone returned to the United States in March 1945, and Bacigalupi followed in September. Two agents then dispatched to assist Amprim—Alfred A. Pease (SIS No. 546) in March and April and James D. Faziola (SIS No. 7265) from July to November. Both worked out of the U.S. Embassy.

    Born in New York in 1912 of Italian immigrant parents, Rita Zucca was schooled in Italy and began doing Axis propaganda broadcasts from Rome in 1943. Accusations of treason were dropped when it was discovered she had renounced her U.S. citizenship in 1943. She was convicted of collaboration by the Italian government but served less than a year in prison.

Chapter 4: Agents to Officers

1. The direct quotes and key details used in this and following chapters are drawn from Fred Ayer's wonderful 1957 memoir *Yankee G-Man*. The quotation cited here is from p. 103 of that volume. Ayer was a fine writer and insightful observer of the world around him, and he kept meticulous notes throughout his FBI career and his subsequent positions within the U.S. government. *Yankee G-Man* is by turns enlightening, poignant, self-deprecating, painfully honest, and delightfully cynical, and it is the best first-person account we have regarding the FBI agents sent to Europe and their operations in the newly liberated countries.

2. Frederick was a *very* popular first name for males through many generations of Ayers, a fact that can cause more than a little confusion when trying to wade through the family's genealogy. For many years, our Fred Ayer's father styled himself Frederick Ayer Jr., which would imply that his middle name was Charles. For several years after his birth, our Fred Ayer was referred to as Frederick Ayer III, which would imply that his middle name was the same as both his father's and grandfather's. However, our Fred Ayer never used a middle name, even on official records, and when he was about ten years old, his father dropped the "Jr." and our Fred Ayer picked it up. For clarity, the Frederick Ayer Jr. in this volume is the FBI agent born in 1915.
3. As Fred Ayer later wrote: "Grandfather Ayer was the first New England businessman to give female employees a monthly day off with pay at a time of their own choosing. Fellow manufacturers told him that he was insane and would ruin business. He was told the same thing when he helped finance Alexander Graham Bell and the New York subway system." Ayer, *Before the Colors Fade: Portrait of a Soldier*, p. 39.
4. The five-bedroom, five-bath house at 59 Walnut Road still exists, and at the time of writing was on the market for $4,399,000.
5. Ayer, *Yankee G-Man*, p. 4.
6. Ibid., p. 1.
7. Fred Ayer and Jack Kennedy had known each other at Harvard, but were not close friends. Kennedy entered the Navy in October 1941 and due to the influence of his father—former U.S. ambassador to the United Kingdom Joseph P. Kennedy Sr.—was initially assigned to ONI as a way to keep him out of harm's way. JFK was introduced to Inga Arvad by his sister Kathleen, who worked with the Danish-born reporter at the *Washington Times-Herald*. Following the revelation of his affair with Arvad, Kennedy was transferred out of ONI and ultimately ended up in command of *PT-109* in the Pacific. Arvad was never charged with any crime and eventually married cowboy movie star Tim McCoy. She died in Nogales, Arizona, in 1973 at the age of 60. For the fascinating story of Arvad's life, see *Inga: Kennedy's Great Love, Hitler's Perfect Beauty, and J. Edgar Hoover's Prime Suspect* by Scott Farris.

   Kennedy was grand marshal at Harvard's 1963 commencement. Fred Ayer was also in attendance, and when the president walked past Fred loudly whispered, "How's Inga?" Kennedy spun around and responded, "You son of a bitch!" This exchange is quoted in Farris's *Inga*.

8. Ayer, *Yankee G-Man*, p. 14.
9. Ibid., p. 10.
10. Frederick Ayer III, known within the family as Rick, also attended the Hill School and Harvard. He then graduated from Duke University Medical School and was doing a residency in Baltimore, Maryland, where he died on May 27, 1972, from burns resulting from a flash fire in his apartment. Fred and Anne Ayer had two other children, a second son and a daughter.
11. Ayer, *Yankee G-Man*, p. 106.
12. Ibid., pp. 106–107.
13. Over the course of World War II, approximately twenty thousand military intelligence specialists—both enlisted men and officers—were trained at Camp Ritchie. Among them were some two thousand German Jewish refugees who were trained primarily in prisoner of war minterrogation techniques. The Counter Intelligence Corps trained hundreds of agents at Camp Ritchie, including many of Japanese descent who later played an important role in the postwar occupation of Japan.
14. The two agents who joined Frank Amprim in Italy in the late summer of 1944, Art Avignone and Ray Bacigalupi, were not part of the Camp Ritchie group. They were drawn directly from the SIS and underwent very basic military training at Fort Belvoir, Virginia, as had Amprim. The four other agents sent to assist Amprim after the departure of Avignone and Bacigalupi—Alfred A. Pease, James D. Faziola, William P. Camusi, and James Romano—all worked out of the U.S. Embassy in Rome, and though they were not under Army cover and did not receive any military training, they did occasionally operate in Army uniforms.
15. Now Honolulu International Airport.
16. In *Yankee G-Man*, Fred Ayer refers to four former Mormon missionaries as being part of the FBI's Army Liaison Unit in Europe, but at the time of writing, only two of the agents had been identified as former missionaries.
17. Lief Kloster was among some 1,600 Allied POWs being transported from the Philippines to Japan aboard the transport vessel *Oryoku Maru*

when the ship was attacked and sunk by aircraft from the U.S. carriers *Hornet* and *Cabot* on December 14, 1944. Kloster was among those killed during the attack.

18. The school is now known as St. Lawrence Seminary High School.
19. The official names of German organizations can be long and unwieldy, even for German speakers, so the entities are often referred to by acronyms or abbreviated titles. For example, during the Nazi years, the initials SS stood for Schutzstaffel, or "protection unit," Gestapo was an acronym of Geheime Staatspolizei (Secret State Police) and Kripo was an acronym of Kriminalpolizei (the civilian Criminal Police).
20. Details on the training of the ALU agents at Camp Ritchie are drawn from Ayer, *Yankee G-Man* and from syllabi from the intelligence and counterintelligence courses offered during 1944.
21. Ayer, *Yankee G-Man*, p. 109.
22. Order of battle intelligence seeks to establish the identity, location, purpose, and movements of enemy units based on information drawn from captured documents, communication intercepts, direct observation, the interrogation of enemy prisoners, and data provided by friendly civilians.
23. Ayer, *Yankee G-Man*, p. 110.
24. Details on Don Daughters's early life are drawn from "Donald L. Daughters, Yvonne A. Fath," an extensive 225-page 1998 oral history compiled by Anton Daughters, Don's nephew. It is a wonderful account of the lives of Don and his Chilean-born wife, and was kindly provided to the author by the Daughters family.
25. Ayer, *Yankee G-Man*, pp. 110–11.

Chapter 5: City of Light

1. Bissell's official title was assistant chief of staff, intelligence, on the War Department General Staff. He assumed the position in January 1944 and held it until May 1946.
2. Ayer, *Yankee G-Man*, p. 111.
3. Unlike the ramjet-powered, subsonic V-1 flying bomb, the supersonic V-2 could not be shot down or knocked off course. The official designation given to the missile by the German military was *Aggregat-4*, meaning it was the fourth in an aggregate series of liquid-fueled rockets intended for offensive military use.

4. Ayer, *Yankee G-Man*, p. 112.
5. Ibid., p. 113.
6. On April 4, 1945, Lynch abruptly returned to the United States because of a family crisis, a "brief visit" Guy Liddell noted in his diary (KV4-196, p. 209). Though some writers have contended that Lynch remained in the United States and was replaced at that time as the London legat by Jack Cimperman, messages sent from C.H. Carson to D.M. Ladd (on August 2, 1945) and from Hoover to Don Daughters in Paris (on August 3, 1945) prove that Lynch had returned to Britain and was still the London legat at that point. Upon Lynch's ultimate departure, Jack Cimperman did step in as legal attaché, a role that became permanent following the end of the war.
7. Ayer, *Yankee G-Man*, p. 111.
8. Built in 1910 and long the hotel of choice for diplomats, celebrities, and the very well-to-do, it is now known as the Waldorf Astoria Versailles-Trianon Palace.
9. Formed during World War I as the Corps of Intelligence Police (CIP), part of the Army's Military Intelligence Division, CIC was reorganized, enlarged, and renamed in 1942.
10. Copeland, *The Game Player: Confessions of the CIA's Original Political Operator*, p. 15.
11. Ayer, *Yankee G-Man*, p. 121.
12. Cable, Ayer to Hoover, September 30, 1944. Subject: Arrival of Special Agents Ayer and Daughters in Paris.
13. Ayer, *Yankee G-Man*, p. 113. Though happy to be freed from the German yoke, many Parisians were—as a *New York Times* story noted—so irked by the requisitioning of so many Paris hotels by the U.S. Army that they found an alternate meaning for SHAEF. According to the French, it stood for Société des Hôtelières Americains en France, or the Society of American Hotel Keepers in France.
14. It is likely that the apartment was confiscated from Jewish owners, though this has been impossible to determine for certain.
15. As recently as 2023, a smaller apartment in the 15, avenue Mozart building were selling for €800,000, roughly $865,000.
16. Ayer, *Yankee G-Man*, p. 114.

17. Ibid., p. 182.

18. Ibid.

19. Until they were eventually authorized to transmit classified information via secure Army cable links, Fred Ayer and Don Daughters dispatched their reports to FBI headquarters by secure mail. They deposited their letters and reports in one of SHAEF's many secure mail pouches, large canvas and leather satchels with belt-like top closures that could be fitted with padlocks. The pouch would then be routed to the nearest Army Post Office (APO), where mail destined for the United States would be loaded aboard a military transport aircraft. The secure pouches were officially designated JQMD (for Indiana's Jeffersonville Quartermaster Depot) Postal Security Letter Mail Bags. On average, letters dispatched from Paris reached Washington within five days.

20. Letter, Ayer to Hoover, October 1, 1944. Subject: Communist Infiltration of the FFI.

21. Fred Ayer and Don Daughters both wrote reports, but until the latter took over the Paris office following Ayer's 1945 move to Berlin, all ALU reports originating in the Paris office went out over Ayer's signature.

22. Ayer to Hoover, October 29, 1944. Subject: M. le Commissaire Badin, Source of Information.

23. While the TR—and later the SSM—focused on neutralizing German agents, they also worked against other foreign intelligence services operating in Vichy, including those of Belgium, Poland, Great Britain, de Gaulle's Free French, and various communist organizations. In postwar memoirs, former TR and SSM operatives insisted such actions against Allied intelligence services, and also against French Résistance groups, were necessary to prevent the Germans from taking operations into their own hands. Paillole himself provided vital information to the British even while ostensibly operating against them. One of the best overall examinations of Vichy's intelligence services—and of the role Paillole played in them—is Simon Kitson's excellent *The Hunt for Nazi Spies: Fighting Espionage in Vichy France*.

24. Ayer to Hoover, October 16, 1944. Subject: Liaison with DSM.

25. Ibid.

26. Ibid.

27. The name of the street is also sometimes rendered as Souchet.
28. Fred set out his proposed itinerary in an October 13, 1944, cable to Hoover, titled "Travel of SA Ayer to Forward G-2 Headquarters."
29. At the time of Fred Ayer's visit, Twelfth Army Group comprised the First, Third, and Ninth U.S. armies. Twelfth AG later also controlled the Fifteenth U.S. Army.
30. The account of Fred Ayer's visit with Patton is drawn from *Before the Colors Fade: Portrait of a Soldier,* Fred's 1964 biography of his famous uncle, and from his *Yankee G-Man.*
31. Ayer, *Before the Colors Fade,* pp. 161–62.
32. Ayer, *Yankee G-Man,* p. 170.
33. Ibid., p. 171.
34. Ayer, *Before the Colors Fade,* p. 166.
35. Ayer to Hoover, October 23, 1944. Subject: Marlene Dietrich, Bureau Contact.

    It's interesting that Dietrich expressed her admiration for the Bureau, given that Hoover had long been convinced she was a German agent and had had her under surveillance for some time both before and during the war. No evidence was ever found that the actress was a spy for the Nazis, and following the war, she was awarded both the U.S. Medal of Freedom and French Légion d'honneur for her wartime efforts in support of the Allied cause.
36. While the partition of defeated Germany into zones occupied by the four Allied powers was not officially adopted as policy until the February 1945 Yalta Conference, the broad outlines of the occupation zones had been discussed at the 1943 Tehran Conference. Senior U.S. military intelligence leaders started planning for the challenges the occupation would present long before Germany was actually defeated, and Sands's comments to Fred Ayer about wanting FBI agents as part of the U.S. occupation forces indicated how far ahead the Twelfth Army Group counterintelligence chief was thinking.
37. Ayer to Hoover, October 21, 1944. Subject: Dispatch of German-Speaking Agents to Europe.
38. Ibid.
39. Ayer, *Yankee G-Man,* p. 114.

40. Ayer to Hoover, October 24, 1944. Subject: Assignment to SHAEF of Bureau Representative Specially Briefed on Communist Matters.
41. Ibid.
42. The first senior British official with whom Gurnea and Naughten met was none other than Guy Liddell. Accompanied by Joe Lynch, the two agents visited Liddell's London office on December 6 to—as the MI5 official later recorded—"find out whether G2 are anxious to have any FBI representatives in Germany and if so, what their assignment would be. Hoover is anxious not to go into the field except at the request of G2." Liddell Diary, entry for December 6, 1944, p. 312. KV4-195, 14 October 1944-15 December 1944.
43. Ayer, *Yankee G-Man*, p. 114.
44. Inspector Myron Gurnea, Inspection Report, Paris Office, December 21, 1944. Gurnea also noted that at the time of the report, Fred Ayer's annual salary was $4,600, roughly equivalent to $81,000 in 2024 dollars, adjusted for inflation.
45. Ibid. Gurnea noted that Don Daughter's annual salary at the time was $3,000, or roughly $67,000 in 2024 dollars.
46. Ayer, *Yankee G-Man*, p. 114.

Chapter 6: The Curious Case of W. Dawson

1. Although his origins are unclear, it is likely that Peter Widlöcher—also sometimes rendered Widloecher—was either born in Alsace or came from an Alsatian background. Both versions of his name are common in the region, and he is mentioned as having been fluent in French from a young age. What he did between the time he fled Paris and the end of the war is unclear. Beginning in 1949, he was noted as being an assistant professor and then professor of French and French studies at Goethe University, his alma mater, and he was teaching there as late as the early 1980s. However, the author has been unable to locate any information pertaining to his later life and death.
2. Dr. Thomas McDow, the prominent Charleston physician who killed Frank Dawson, first met Hélène Burdayron when he was called to the Dawson's home to treat the sick child of one of the household servants. McDow was immediately smitten and began following the young

governess whenever she left the Dawson house. He proposed marriage, despite the fact that he already had both a wife and a mistress. The young woman complained to Frank Dawson about the doctor's unwanted attentions, which led to the confrontation that resulted in Dawson's death. After a widely publicized court case dubbed "The Trial of the Century," McDow was acquitted of murder by reason of self-defense, but he ultimately committed suicide following revelations that he had been named a suspect in an insurance scandal and that he had told his mistress that he intended to murder his wife. Novelist and biographer Roxanna Robinson, Frank Dawson's great-granddaughter, provided the author with details on Dawson's life and death.

3. There has long been speculation among literary scholars and historians about Warrington Dawson's sexuality. Whether he was gay is not relevant to the subject of this book—we are only concerned with his patriotism.

4. In 1958, United Press Associations became United Press International, better known as UPI.

5. Both books were generally well received, though one review of *The Scar* said, "It is a rather depressing book, and its execution falls far short of its artistic intention."

6. Dawson's time as director-general of the Foreign Press Association is discussed in both Dale B. J. Randall's 1968 book *Joseph Conrad and Warrington Dawson: The Record of a Friendship* and in Dr. Arnold T. Schwab's review of the book in the May 1971 issue of the journal *Modern Philology*. Schwab, a renowned professor of English (University of Michigan, the University of California at Los Angeles, and California State University at Long Beach) had himself carried on a long correspondence with Dawson beginning in the 1950s and took exception to many parts of Randall's volume.

7. Present-day Kenya, the Republic of Congo, Sudan, and South Sudan.

8. Dawson's recollections of his time with Roosevelt in Africa are drawn from *Opportunity and Theodore Roosevelt*, a memoir that Dawson had privately printed in 1910. The cited quote appears on p. 27.

9. Renowned historian Edmund Morris deals in depth with Roosevelt's African expedition in *Colonel Roosevelt*, the third and final volume in Morris's Roosevelt trilogy. The cited quote appears on p. 571.

10. *Colonel Roosevelt*, p. 18.
11. Dawson, *Opportunity and Theodore Roosevelt*, p. 29.
12. Sanderson stayed in Nairobi until 1910, when he and his wife and their two daughters returned to England. Sanderson became assistant headmaster at Elstree, an elite preparatory school founded by the Sanderson family and at that time located in Hertfordshire. Ted Sanderson remained at the school for the rest of his life and was headmaster at the time of his death in 1939.
13. Some sources indicate that Dawson did not begin lecturing about Conrad until 1912, well after their first meeting. However, in letters to Arnold Schwab in 1954, Dawson said that he'd begun his lectures on Conrad in 1910.
14. Schwab, in his review of Randall, *Joseph Conrad and Warrington Dawson: The Record of a Friendship*.
15. Dawson made the employment claims cited here in a September 17, 1944, document titled "Personal Record." The information was included as an attachment to a letter Dawson addressed to the Assistant Chief of Staff, G-2, Communications Zone, U.S. Army, Paris. His reason for writing this letter and the veracity of his claims—is dealt with later in this chapter.
16. Letter, Warrington Dawson to Franklin D. Roosevelt, March 13, 1933.
17. Letter, Franklin D. Roosevelt to Warrington Dawson, March 28, 1933.
18. Memo, Franklin Roosevelt to Sumner Welles, June 1, 1937.
19. Memo, Franklin Roosevelt to Eleanor Roosevelt, June 11, 1937.
20. Dawson lived for many years in a large and lavishly furnished apartment at 19, rue du Maréchal Joffre in Versailles. By 1942, his declining financial situation—his government retirement payments and book royalties had been interrupted by the war—forced him to move to a somewhat smaller but no less garishly appointed apartment at 2, rue de la Paroisse, a mile to the north.
21. Letter, Brigadier General R. W. Hasbrouck to Warrington Dawson, September 15, 1944.
22. Letter, Warrington Dawson to Assistant Chief of Staff, G-2, Communications Zone, U.S. Army, Paris, September 17, 1944.

23. Details of the DSM search of Dawson's apartment are drawn from an account he gave two American officers from Gordon Sheen's CI office on October 23. Captain W. Tait's report of the encounter—aptly titled "Search of Mr. J. [sic] Warrington Dawson's Apartment"—was submitted to Sheen on October 24.
24. Robins's first name and the organization to which he was assigned were redacted in most copies of the U.S. documents dealing with Dawson. However, the author was able to locate unredacted copies of several of the items, which indicate that the man was Brooklyn-born 1st Lieutenant William Eugene Robins. British author and former military intelligence officer Keith Ellison's excellent volume *Special Counterintelligence in WWII Europe* identifies Robins as a member of the Division of Counter-Espionage Intelligence of the X-2 (counterintelligence) branch of the OSS's Paris office at 18–20, rue Petrarque. That Dawson thought Robins looked "extremely young" is understandable—the twenty-two-year-old OSS agent stood only 5 feet 5 inches and weighed barely 130 pounds. How the Paris X-2 office learned about Widlöcher's file on Dawson before SHAEF CI did remains unclear.
25. Ibid.
26. CIC Special Agent Donald Cannon to Captain Tait, CIC Paris Field Security Officer. Subject: Warrington Dawson. October 26, 1944. As noted earlier in this volume, CIC special agents generally wore civilian clothes and did not reveal their military ranks. Cannon was, in fact, a staff sergeant.
27. The agent's first name is unclear, though we know that he was a sergeant assigned to the same SHAEF-attached CIC Field Security Office as Tait, Morrison, and Cannon.
28. Report, Sergeant West to SHAEF Field Security Office. Subject: Impressions from Conversation with Mr. Warrington Dawson on October 24, 1944. October 26, 1944.
29. From 1885 to 1946, the top U.S. diplomat in Sweden was officially referred to as "envoy extraordinary and minister plenipotentiary" rather than ambassador. The latter term is used here for clarity.
30. Transmittal letter, Widlöcher to Bergmann, June 26, 1942. All quotes drawn from the captured Widlöcher files are based on the translation done by Fred Ayer and Don Daughters.

31. Letter, Bergmann to Widlöcher, July 1, 1942.

32. Memorandum, Widlöcher to Schlottman, December 3, 1942.

33. Memorandum, Widlöcher to Schmidt, January 20, 1943.

34. Details on Werner Plack's early life and his time in Hollywood are drawn largely from a 1940 FBI report on his activities provided to MI5 by London-based FBI legal attaché John Cimperman. That report was included in MI5's extensive file outlining Plack's wartime recruitment of such British renegades as John Amery and of author P. G. Wodehouse.

35. The screenwriter was Sydney "Sy" Bartlett. After Pearl Harbor, Bartlett joined the U.S. Army Air Forces and was assigned as an intelligence officer to the Britain-based U.S. Eighth Bomber Command. In that capacity, he flew as an observer on an RAF night bombing mission over Berlin and, as he later told the story, he was allowed to "pickle" the aircraft's payload over the target and thus became the first USAAF officer to bomb Berlin. In an Associated Press newspaper story that ran across the United States on March 29, 1943, by then Major Bartlett said he was glad he hadn't had to bail out over Berlin. "I declared war on the Axis all by myself when I socked [Werner] Plack. . . . I imagine he would have liked to meet me on his home grounds." Later, Bartlett ran into his old friend Bernie Lay Jr., an Army pilot between the wars who had made a name for himself as a screenwriter in 1930s Hollywood. Lay had rejoined the USAAF on the outbreak of war and was in England as the commander of the B-24-equipped 487th Bombardment Group. After the war, Lay and Bartlett cowrote *12 O'Clock High*, a fictionalized account of the Eighth Air Force's birth and early operations. The novel was turned into a 1949 motion picture starring Gregory Peck and also served as the basis for a popular 1960s American television series.

36. Memorandum, Widlöcher to Schlottman, March 11, 1943.

37. Memorandum, Widlöcher to Schleier, April 9, 1943.

38. The account of Fred Ayer's initial interrogation of Warrington Dawson is drawn from "Re: Francis Warrington Dawson—Treason," the October 29, 1944, report Ayer sent to J. Edgar Hoover via the SIS European Desk.

39. Ibid., p. 2.

40. Ayer, *Yankee G-Man*, p. 125.

41. Cable, Ayer to Hoover, October 31, 1944. Subject: Francis Warrington Dawson–Treason, p. 1. Dawson and Caffery had known each other since the latter was a first secretary at the Paris embassy in 1919.
42. Ibid., p. 2.
43. Cable, Caffery to Hull, October 31, 1944. Subject: Case of Francis Warrington-Dawson [sic].
44. Cable, Ayer to Hoover, November 19, 1944. Subject: Francis Warrington Dawson—Treason.
45. Cable, Caffery to Hull, December 4, 1944. Subject: Case of Warrington-Dawson [sic].
46. The physician reports were found in a DSM file on Dawson held in the archives of the Service Historique de la Défense in Vincennes. They were located and translated by journalist and historian Ellen Hampton at the author's request.
47. Fred Ayer wrote that after several months of investigation, he was able "with ill-concealed pleasure" to place on the desk of Dawson's unnamed but high-ranking "social acquaintance" not only the original scripts Dawson wrote for the Germans, but also the "old propagandist's" German pay vouchers. *Yankee G-Man*, p. 125.
48. The 1948 statute that governs current treason prosecutions—18 U.S. Code §2381—expands on the constitutional definition: "Whoever, owing allegiance to the United States, levies war against them or adheres to their enemies, giving them aid and comfort within the United States or elsewhere, is guilty of treason and shall suffer death, or imprisoned and fined, and incapable of holding any U.S. office." It retains the requirement for two witnesses.
49. Letters, FCC Chairman E.K. Jett to J. Edgar Hoover, December 5 and 10, 1944.
50. Ayer, *Yankee G-Man*, p. 124.

Chapter 7: Renegades and Monuments Men

1. This number is based on a SHAEF G-2 record card.
2. Details on Frank O'Neill's early life and move to Europe are drawn from the article "From Post-Dispatch Newsboy to World's Greatest Jockey" by Paris-based American writer Lincoln Eyre, in the August 13, 1922, edition of the *St. Louis Post-Dispatch.*

3. Fred Burlew returned to the United States in 1916 and became a very successful trainer. He died in 1927 at the age of fifty-six.
4. That $25,000 was roughly equal to $440,000 in 2024 dollars.
5. Michael Reynolds, *Hemingway: The Paris Years* (New York: W.W. Norton, 1999), p. 58.
6. The owner of Chez Elle, famed French singer Lucienne Boyer, directed that a placard reading NO JEWS ALLOWED be posted at the entrance to the cabaret. The sign was one of several ways in which Boyer attempted to prevent the deportation of her Jewish husband to a concentration camp.
7. The younger O'Neill is often referred to as Frank Jr., though that is inaccurate, given that his middle name was different from his father's. Though not a gifted equestrian, the younger man was a talented fencer, who, in his younger years, had been a challenger for the youth championship of France.
8. As far as can be determined from existing sources, Mary O'Neill and her daughters did not work at the bar. It is possible that the three women had left Paris for Vichy before America's 1941 entry into the war or perhaps even afterward. The United States and Vichy were not at war, and Americans were not interned there until after the Germans occupied Vichy in November 1942. It is possible that Mary and her daughters were able to travel from there to the United States, though that, too, is unclear. We know that all three were living in America as of 1948, and that at the time of their deaths, both sisters were living in San Diego, California.
9. Details of Joseph Luhan's early life are based on genealogical records.
10. Details on Luhan's life in France between the wars—including his marriage, children, and employment—and during World War II are drawn from a series of three reports compiled by the Paris Prefecture of Police (1941, 1942, and 1944). These reports are held by *Les archives de la préfecture de Police* in the Le Pré Saint-Gervais area of Paris. Luhan's wife's maiden name is sometimes rendered as Jouin.
11. The Hotel Bristol was Werner Plack's preferred lodging in Paris, and he stayed there at least twenty-six times between April 1942 and June 1944. The list of Plack's visits to the hotel—complete with room numbers and the names of guests he received (including Joseph Lincoln

Luhan)—was compiled in March 1945 by British Major William James Skardon of MI5 based on the guest cards kept by the hotel and provided to Skardon by the manager, a Monsieur Vidal. In December 1949, it was Skardon to whom atomic scientist Klaus Fuchs first admitted spying for the Soviet Union during and just after World War II. Fuchs's admission to Skardon sparked the investigation of atomic espionage that ultimately led to the arrest, trial, conviction, and execution of Americans Julius and Ethel Rosenberg.

12. All of the reports Fred Ayer and Don Daughters sent back to FBI headquarters carried a subject line that gave a suspect's name followed by the crime(s) they were believed to have committed. The federal violations—treason, sedition, espionage, trading with the enemy, etc.—were listed for administrative and tracking purposes and did not indicate that a suspect had been either charged with or convicted of the named offense.
13. Fred Ayer reported on the details of Luhan's apprehension and initial interrogation in a November 29, 1944, report to Hoover titled "Joseph Lincoln Luhan—Treason." Ayer also wrote about Luhan in *Yankee G-Man*, pp. 126–29. The account in this volume is based on information from both sources.
14. Interview of Donald and Yvonne Daughters by Anton Daughters, December 1988, p. 93.
15. Ayer, *Yankee G-Man*, p. 128.
16. Ibid.
17. Joseph Lincoln Luhan—Treason, op cit.
18. Message, Lt. Col. F.A. Calvert to Assistant Chief of Staff, G-2, SHAEF. Subject: Frank O'Neil [sic] (Suspect American Citizen). November 25, 1944.
19. Ayer to Hoover, December 17, 1944. Subject: Changed: Frank J. O'Neill, was Frank O'Neal, Frank O'Neil Sr.—Treason.
20. Another member of Luhan's extended family is at the center of a larger and as yet unsolved mystery. His sister, wealthy Los Angeles socialite Mrs. Emily "Mimi" Boomhower, was the widow of millionaire and big-game hunter Novice E. Boomhower. She was a popular and outgoing woman who loved giving parties at her lavish mansion in Bel Air almost as much as she liked younger men, nightclubs, and appearing in the society columns of the *Los Angeles Times*. On August

18, 1949—the day after the tenth anniversary of Novice Boomhower's death—friends expecting to meet Mimi for a prearranged social event could not get in touch with her. When they went to her home, they found all the lights on, but no one answered the door. Two LAPD detectives who entered the home the following day found everything in order but no sign of Mimi. Her disappearance made headlines across the country, but despite a vigorous investigation by both local police and the FBI, no trace of Mimi was ever found and her fate remains a mystery to this day. In December 1956, she was declared legally dead, and her handwritten 1946 will leaving her estate in equal parts to her brother Joseph and her sisters indicates that she likely never knew of her brother's treason. Boomhower's will was likely the reason Luhan was able to live so well in Paris.

21. The creation and operations of the Monuments, Fine Arts and Archives Section Unit (MFAA) are detailed in several excellent books, including Robert M. Edsel's *The Monuments Men: Allied Heroes, Nazi Thieves, and the Greatest Treasure Hunt in History*; and James J. Rorimer's autobiographical *Monuments Man: The Mission to Save Vermeers, Rembrandts, and Da Vincis from the Nazis' Grasp*.
22. Rorimer recounts the tank episode in *Monuments Man*.
23. Details of Anthony Helfenstein's early life and World War I Army service are drawn from genealogical records.
24. Ayer to Hoover, November 4, 1944. Subject: Anthony G. Helfenstein—Treason. According to French police records, Helfenstein also used a variety of other aliases including "Haribel," "Gérard," and "Tony Gérard."
25. The establishment and operations of the *bureaux d'achats* are well-documented in such works as Christopher Othen's *The King of Nazi Paris: Henri Lafont and the Gangsters of the French Gestapo; Paris at War: 1939–1944* by David Drake; and *Priscilla: The Hidden Life of an Englishwoman in Wartime France*, Nicholas Shakespeare's fascinating exploration of his late aunt's World War II experiences.
26. The name is sometimes rendered as Stoecklin, and even as Stoocklin.
27. Stöcklin's name appears frequently in official OSS, MFAA, and Roberts Commission reports dealing with German art looting in occupied Europe. The Roberts Commission "Card File on Art Looting Suspects, 1943-1946," specifically mentions Stöcklin's role regarding *The Open*

Window, Étretat, and says he was involved in several other "exchanges" with the Einsatzstab Reichsleiter Rosenberg.

28. Ayer to Hoover, December 6, 1944. Subject: Anthony G. Helfenstein, et .al.—Treason.
29. Ibid. Van Houten's hope for a commuted sentence was in vain. He was convicted of espionage by the French in late November 1945 and executed on April 11, 1946.
30. The details of Fred Ayer's interview with Max Stöcklin at Fresnes Prison are drawn from Ayer's December 21 report to Hoover and from the signed statement by Stöcklin that accompanied the report. Additional details on Stöcklin and Odette Poirier are drawn from a dossier (Cour de Justice de la Seine Z/6/152) on the two held by the Archives Nationales de France.
31. Jeanne Karpeles was born in 1912 in San Marcello Pistoiese, Italy, to a Jewish family. False papers, supplied by Brandl, identifying her as Roman Catholic, allowed her to escape deportation to a concentration camp.
32. That American citizen Helfenstein was allowed to travel across occupied France and into the heart of Nazi Germany on his own at the height of the war strongly implies that he did so under Abwehr protection. He did not make the journey as Anton Krammer—as a foreigner, he was required to register with the local police in Prien am Chiemsee, and he did so under his own name and with his actual birthplace and birth date.
33. Details drawn from a November 2, 1946, French police report on Anthony Helfenstein held by Les Archives de la Préfecture de Police.
34. AGWAR to SHAEF Main for Personal Attention Ayer, December 31, 1944. Subject: Treason—Anthony G. Helfenstein.
35. Article 43 of U.S. Code §843(a) states, in part, that "a person charged with desertion . . . in time of war . . . may be tried and punished at any time without limitation."
36. Report of the Death of an American Citizen, U.S. Embassy, Paris, France, December 3, 1954.
37. Stöcklin's mistress, Odette Poirier, was sentenced to four years in prison for acting as an accomplice to Stöcklin's crimes. In addition, Poirier's property was confiscated and she was subjected to "*la dégradation natio-*

nale," which included revocation of such rights of citizenship as voting or working for government institutions.

38. Ayer to Hoover, November 19, 1944. Subject: Dispatch of Additional Agents to European Theater.

Chapter 8: *Volksdeutschers,* Renegades Redux, and the Lost Sigaba

1. Many Americans first became aware that U.S. citizens served in the World War II German armed forces because of the hit 2001 HBO miniseries *Band of Brothers.* Based on historian Stephen Ambrose's nonfiction book chronicling the wartime operations of the 101st Airborne Division's Company E, 2nd Battalion, 506th Parachute Infantry Regiment, the series dealt with the *Volksdeutscher* issue in episode 2, "Day of Days." Sgt. Donald Malarky is stunned to discover that a German POW is, like Malarky himself, a native of Oregon. When asked how he ended up "in a Kraut uniform," the POW answers that his ethnic German family answered the call for "all true Aryans to return to the Fatherland." The actual number of U.S. citizens who served in the German military during World War II has never been established.
2. Berquist to Commanding General, European Theater of Operations (Through Commanding General, Twelfth Army Group), October 19, 1944. Subject: Alleged Treason of Walter Windisch, United States Citizen.
3. Ayer to Hoover, November 19, 1944. Subject: Walter Windisch—Treason.

    Thanks to genealogical and other records not available at the time, we now know that several of Walter Windisch's statements to both the 94th CIC officers and to Fred Ayer were not accurate. Windisch was born in 1923, not 1925, and though he and his family may have visited France in 1933, he was still attending high school in Illinois in early 1940. He did apparently take some sort of technical training after arriving in France and, at some point, lost his left thumb in an industrial accident.
4. Ibid.
5. Ibid.
6. SHAEF Main (G-2) to Twelfth Army Group Rear (G-2), December 13, 1944. Subject: Mohr.

7. Headquarters, Twelfth Army Group, Bradley, to Supreme Commander, AEF Main, December 30, 1944.
8. The liner was temporarily detained and searched by U.S. Customs officers but was allowed to depart for home on the evening of August 31. Following the September 1 declaration of war, *Bremen* sailed a roundabout course to Murmansk, Russia, where most of her crew members—including Franz Mohr—were sent back to Germany by train. The liner ultimately returned to Bremerhaven, where, in March 1941, she was gutted by a fire started by a disgruntled young crewman. *Bremen* was scrapped for steel to be used in other vessels, and her hulk was destroyed by explosives in 1946. For the full story of the famous ship—and other notable passenger vessels that saw duty in wartime—see the author's book *Great Liners at War.*
9. Sheen to Twelfth Army Group G-2, January 11, 1945. Subject: Fritz Mohr.
10. Ayer to Hoover, February 6, 1945. Subject: William [sic] Augustin—Treason.
11. *Oberfeldwebel* in the World War II Luftwaffe was a senior enlisted rank roughly equivalent to a master sergeant in the U.S. Army Air Forces. *Obergefreiter* was roughly equal to a USAAF private first class. The Luftwaffe used enlisted pilots to fly second-line aircraft, such as transports, target tugs, etc. The aircraft flown by Heinz-Jakob Murk apparently belonged to Transportfliegerstaffel (Air Transport Squadron) 2 based in Hommelvik, Norway.
12. Murk's account of his meeting with Charles Reininghaus is contained in the German aviator's interrogation statement. That document is part of an eleven-page file on Reininghaus (designated X8370013) held at the U.S. National Archives and Records Administration (NARA) in College Park, Maryland.
13. During World War II Nazi Germany's combat parachutists, known as *Fallschirmjäger,* were part of the Luftwaffe.
14. Charles Reininghaus's POW interrogation report is included in his file, X8370013, at NARA College Park.
15. Ayer to Hoover, February 18, 1945. Subject: Charles Reininghaus—Treason.

16. Lewis's letter is also included in Reininghaus's file, X8370013, at NARA College Park.
17. Genealogical records that were not available to investigators in the 1940s have revealed several discrepancies in Charles Reininghaus's interrogation statements. No documents that have yet come to light prove that he was born in the United States. Indeed, in his 1933 naturalization petition, Kurt Reininghaus stated that Charles (whom he referred to as Karl) was born in Germany. That same form gives the son's birth date as May 16, 1925, not 1922, as Charles told the POW interrogators. Moreover, the family's 1950 census information also gives 1925 as the year of Charles's birth. How and when Charles Reininghaus became an American citizen thus remains unclear at the time of writing.
18. Details of Maurice Gagnon's early life are drawn from genealogical records.
19. Ayer to Hoover, November 29, 1944. Subject: Joseph Lincoln Luhan—Treason.
20. Ayer to Hoover, January 13, 1945. Subject: Maurice S. Gagnon—Treason.
21. Though Gagnon did not know it during his initial interrogation, Fred already knew about his first trip to the German capital. During an earlier interrogation by MI5, captured British renegade Gerald Percy Hewitt had spoken about meeting Gagnon at the Adlon in 1940. Hewitt quoted the American as saying then that he would "speak for the German radio" but didn't want to produce written articles. The British renegade also described Gagnon as "boastful and aggressive." This information was provided to Fred Ayer in a December 22, 1944, message from the SHAEF MI5 Liaison Section.
22. Ayer to Hoover, January 13, 1945. Subject: Maurice S. Gagnon—Treason.
23. Ibid.
24. U.S. Embassy, Paris. Report of the Death of an American Citizen, March 6, 1946. FBI.
25. Königs Wusterhausen had long been a center of German radio broadcasting. The country's first transmission antennas were erected there before World War I. By the early 1930s, several shortwave and longwave towers broadcast programs throughout Western Europe and as far as

North America. The radio facilities were taken over by the Nazis following Hitler's rise to power, and after the end of World War II, the site was used by the East German government.

26. Ayer to Hoover, November 27, 1944. Subject: Marvin H. Fritz—Treason.
27. It is possible that Marvin Fritz actually first met Werner Plack in Los Angeles in the mid-1930s. Fritz's German immigrant parents, August and Gertrude (Geissler) Fritz, were rumored to have been members of a social organization to which Plack also belonged. Moreover, Plack's status as a decent amateur-league tennis player may have brought him into contact with Marvin Fritz, a champion junior player in Southern California.
28. Bodenplatte was the Luftwaffe's final attempt to gain air superiority over Holland, Belgium, and western Germany, as part of the endgame of the Battle of the Bulge. More than a thousand German fighters attacked Allied airfields, in the process destroying some five hundred Allied aircraft, most on the ground. The operation ultimately failed, in large part because the Allies were able to quickly replace lost aircraft, something the Luftwaffe was no longer capable of doing.
29. The term Communications Zone (abbreviated Com Z) referred to the area of the European Theater of Operations that was directly behind the combat front and through which were funneled all materiel and supplies required to support and maintain the frontline forces. In early 1945, Com Z ETO was headquartered in Paris and commanded by Major General John C. H. Lee.
30. Ayer to Hoover, March 10, 1945. Subject: Administrative—Trip to Southern France by S.A. Donald L. Daughters. Details of Don Daughters visit to southern France used in this section are drawn entirely from that message.
31. The airfield designated Y-14 by the USAAF is now Marseille Provence Airport.
32. Ayer to Hoover, March 10, 1945. Subject: Administrative—Trip to Southern France by S.A. Donald L. Daughters.
33. Unfortunately, the content of Loskot's various letters, and of William Joyce's responses, is unknown at the time of writing. The original letters

and the copies Gordon Sheen provided to Fred Ayer and Don Daughters were apparently destroyed at some point after the war.

34. Ayer to Hoover, February 3, 1945. Subject: John E. Loskot with Aliases Ino Loskot, Ino E. Losket—Treason.

35. The name Sigaba was neither an abbreviation nor an acronym. According to the National Security Agency's Center for Cryptologic History, Army cryptographic devices of the World War II period were given code names that began with "SIG" for "signals" followed by randomly chosen letters. The NSA's National Cryptologic Museum says the Sigaba "was the only machine system used during World War II to remain completely unbroken by an enemy. The Germans referred to [it] as the 'Big' machine. It utilized the same principle of rotating, removable, wired rotor wheels that the German Enigma [cryptographic machine] employed. However, unlike the stepping motion of the Enigma, the SIGABA's motion appeared to be random. It wasn't, but it was so complicated the German's never broke it and the Japanese gave up trying."

    Details on the theft of the Sigaba are drawn primarily from a formerly secret NSA report titled "The Colmar Incident: A Cryptographic Device Lost in World War II Operations," which was declassified and released online by the agency in 2008; "Search for the Stolen SIGABA"; and *The SIGABA/ECM II Cypher Machine: "A Beautiful Idea."*

36. Oddly enough, given the Sigaba's importance, until June 1945, there was no Army regulation requiring that the machine be under twenty-four-hour armed guard as long as it was secured within a protected code room or being kept in a purpose-designed safe. That said, most units that used the device normally kept it under armed guard when it was being transported, which always entailed the use of a safe. There are conflicting explanations about why the truck in Colmar was left unattended. Most official Army sources cite "exhaustion" on the part of the vehicle's operators, while several unofficial sources say the driver and codriver were being "entertained" by very friendly local women.

37. Ayer to Hoover, March 14, 1945. Subject: Special Mission of Special Agents Ayer and Thompson to Sixth Army Group.

38. Ayer, *Yankee G-Man*, p. 147.

39. Ibid.

40. Ibid., p. 149.

41. Ayer to Hoover, March 14, 1945. Subject: Special Mission of Special Agents Ayer and Thompson to Sixth Army Group.

Chapter 9: "Horizontal Collaborators," Angry Generals, and a Momentous Day

1. Lynch to Hoover, September 11, 1944. Subject: Mrs. J. Gould.
2. Hoover to Lynch, November 4, 1944. Subject: Mrs. J. Gould—Treason. Also Hoover to Ayer, same date, same subject.
3. Susan Ronald's *A Dangerous Woman: American Beauty, Noted Philanthropist, Nazi Collaborator: The Life of Florence Gould* is an excellent and very thorough examination of Gould's life and the source of much of the information in this chapter regarding her childhood.
4. Belvedere is in Marin County, four miles north of San Francisco. Maximin Lacaze commuted across the Bay by ferry to his newspaper job in the city.
5. The legislation was intended, in part, to prevent the foreign-born, non-U.S. citizen wives of American citizens from absconding back to their home countries with funds that should rightfully be passed on to the deceased husband's relatives in the United States.
6. Henry Heynemann and his mother, and possibly Henry's brother James, had left Paris before the outbreak of war to travel in Switzerland and Germany.
7. Many period newspapers incorrectly reported that the marriage took place in Madrid. As Susan Ronald points out in *A Dangerous Woman*, Henry and Florence initially intended to marry in the Spanish capital. When various legal issues arose over Florence's age and the requirement under French law that her mother publish the marriage bans at least ten days before the ceremony, the young couple decided to marry in Paris.
8. Florence Lacaze was a U.S. citizen by birth. The uncertainty over whether she lost that initial citizenship status when taken to France by her mother would cause much confusion during the Army Liaison Unit's investigation of her.
9. Some sources still use the affected last name La Caze when referring to Florence. She never legally changed the spelling, so it remains Lacaze in this volume.

10. Frank O'Neill not only rode for Jay Gould but the two were occasional neighbors—Gould owned a villa at 5, avenue Picard in Maisons-Laffitte, less than a mile from O'Neill's.
11. Gould's second wife, the English-born former musical comedy actress Edith Kelly Gould, fought the French divorce in American courts and countersued Gould in a battle that lasted some four years before she eventually gave up.
12. Among those reputed to be Florence Gould's pre–World War II lovers were Maurice Chevalier, Charlie Chaplin, and Joseph P. Kennedy Sr.
13. Though Jay Gould was known to frequently use the derogatory French term *Boche* when referring to Germans, his wife did not—perhaps because of her intimate relations with several members of the so-called "master race."
14. In what would prove to be one of those strange coincidences of war, Florence Gould's apartment at 2, boulevard Suchet was barely 250 yards northeast of 18, boulevard Suchet, which would become the DSM interrogation center used by the agents of the Army Liaison Unit to interview, among others, Florence Gould.
15. A highly decorated World War I veteran and author of one of the most celebrated memoirs of that conflict, *Storm of Steel*, Jünger was a conservative but abhorred the Nazis. Both Knochen and Oberg were involved in deporting French Jews to concentration camps, and Oberg is widely known as the "Butcher of Paris."
16. Essentially a high-class prostitution ring, the "gray mice" network in which Florence Gould was involved should not be confused with the female German service members who served in occupied France. They were known as "gray mice" because of the drab color of their uniforms and their retiring and unassuming affect in public.
17. Both during and immediately after the war, the term "horizontal collaborator" was applied to any woman (and occasionally to men) who during the occupation had sex with a German, whether out of love, for protection, or simply as a business transaction. As France was liberated, many of these women (but few men) were publicly humiliated by having their heads shaved, many were beaten, and an unknown number were killed outright. Given her affairs with German officers and officials, Florence Gould was, by definition, a horizontal collaborator.

18. Despite Prince Louis II of Monaco's early declaration of neutrality, Fascist Italy occupied the principality in November 1942. Following Italy's September 1943 surrender to the Allies, German troops moved in and remained until the September 1944 Allied invasion of southern France prompted their withdrawal.
19. Beevor and Cooper, *Paris After the Liberation, 1944–1949*, p. 205.
20. Born in New York in 1910, Charles Cushman Michaelis's father was a very successful advertising executive who, in 1912, moved to Paris, with his family, to head his company's operations in France. Charles grew up in a nonobservant Jewish family and, from an early age, was completely bilingual in English and French. From 1929 to 1933, he played semiprofessional ice hockey for the teams CSH Paris and Stade Français, after which he became a well-known sports promoter in the French capital. In 1935, he met and married the German alpine ski champion Hildegard Sturm, whose refusal to ski for Nazi Germany at the 1936 Winter Olympics resulted in her being jailed as a political prisoner. When war broke out in September 1939, Charles Michaelis was in the United States, and in March 1942, he enlisted in the U.S. Army. His language skills and experience living and working in Europe quickly brought him to the attention of the OSS. Initially posted to the X-2 office in London, he and the other members of SCU 105 came ashore at Normandy on June 10, 1944. Following the German surrender, he and his wife reunited. Michaelis spent the remainder of his life as a Paris-based sports promoter. He died in the French capital in 1984, and he and Hildegard are buried next to each other at Bagneux cemetery.
21. Details of Don Daughters's interrogation of Florence Gould are drawn from his April 6, 1945 report titled Florence Juliette Lacaze Gould—Treason, File No. 61-34. Hereafter cited as Daughters Report of Gould Interrogation.

    Hector O'Connor's deal for leniency in return for his cooperation was apparently honored. He was not prosecuted for treason by the United States, and currently available records indicate that other than his brief initial incarceration in Nice, the alleged collaborator was not tried or punished by the French. He went on to operate an art dealership in Dublin, Ireland, where he died sometime in the 1990s.
22. Letter, Henry R. Labouisse Jr. (Counselor for Economic Affairs) to Secretary of State Joseph Grew, March 26, 1945. Subject: Participation of

Mrs. Florence Gould in the Banque Charles; Transmittal of Testimonial Letters.

23. Daughters Report of Gould Interrogation, op cit.
24. Ibid.
25. Ibid.
26. Guy Hottel, SAC, Washington Field Office to J. Edgar Hoover, April 25, 1945. Subject: Mrs. Frank J. Gould—Treason.
27. Caudle to Hoover, November 2, 1945. Subject: Mrs. Florence Gould—Treason.
28. Details on Ruth Obre's early life are drawn from genealogical records.
29. American hostess, gossip columnist, and radio personality Elsa Maxwell was present at the Paris dinner party and overheard Ruth Dubonnet's remark. Maxwell wrote about the incident in her syndicated newspaper column "Elsa Maxwell's Party Line" on February 19, 1945.
30. Drue Leyton's birth name was Dorothy Blackman. As an actor, Jacques Tartière went by the stage name Jacques Terrane, though his wife always used the surname Tartière.
31. Quoted in "Elsa Maxwell's Party Line" on January 15, 1945.
32. Details of Drue Tartière's life in Barbizon and her early Résistance activities are drawn from her 1946 book *The House Near Paris: An American Woman's Story of Traffic in Patriots*. Hereafter cited as *The House Near Paris*.
33. Tartière, *House Near Paris*, p. 108.
34. Ibid., p. 306.
35. "Elsa Maxwell's Party Line," January 15, 1945.
36. Douglas's syndicated article about the visit to Drancy and encounter with Ruth Dubonnet appeared in the October 23, 1944, edition of the *St. Louis Star-Times* and other American newspapers.
37. Ayer to Hoover, October 6, 1944. Subject: Madame André Dubonnet—Information Concerning.
38. Ibid.
39. The only real legal difficulty Ruth Dubonnet encountered as a result of her wartime activities concerned her U.S. citizenship. She claimed to have taken French citizenship in 1943 solely to avoid suspicion by the

Gestapo, despite the fact that her status as an American was well known throughout all levels of the German occupation apparatus. Following the end of the war, she went through a protracted effort to have her U.S. citizenship reinstated, even going so far to have special legislation introduced in Congress to do so. That legislation was passed out of Congress, but was then vetoed by President Harry Truman. Ruth and André Dubonnet separated in the late 1940s and ultimately divorced. André married yet again, and died in 1980 at the age of eighty-two. Ruth finally regained her U.S. citizenship in the early 1960s and died in France in 1992 at the age of ninety-two.

40. Ayer, *Yankee G-Man*, pp. 175–76.
41. Ibid., pp. 176–77.
42. Ibid., p. 177.
43. Ayer to Hoover, April 2, 1945. Subject: Assignment of Additional Personnel to European Theater—Administrative.
44. Ibid.
45. Ibid.
46. Communications Section, FBI Headquarters, to Ayer via SHAEF Mission to France. April 17, 1945. No Subject.
47. D.M. Ladd to J. Edgar Hoover, April 21, 1945. Subject: Assignment of Agents to Embassy in Paris.
48. Ibid.
49. Deputy Chief, Military Intelligence Division, to Reynolds, FBI, April 26, 1945. Subject: Message from Eisenhower.
50. According to the BBC, the first person in England—and likely in the entire Allied world—to learn of Hitler's death was twenty-four-year-old Karl Lehmann. A German Jew, the young man had fled to England in 1936 and eventually found work at the BBC monitoring station.
51. It ultimately became clear, of course, that Hitler and Eva Braun, the longtime companion whom he'd married just hours earlier, had killed themselves as their massive underground bunker was about to be taken by Soviet troops.
52. Ayer, *Yankee G-Man*, p. 150.
53. Ibid., p. 152.

Chapter 10: New Blood, a Very Big Fish, and New Horizons

1. Ayer to Hoover, October 29, 1944. Subject: SS School at Ravensbruck [sic], Germany.
2. Ayer to Hoover, May 8, 1945. Subject: FBI Coverage in Continental Europe—Administrative.
3. Ibid.
4. D.M. Ladd to E.A. Tamm, May 15, 1945. No subject.
5. "Interrogation of Reich Marshal [sic] Herman Goering." Ritter Schule, Augsburg, May 10, 1945.
6. "Herman Goering Talking." Seventh Army Interrogation Center, May 19, 1945. Thirty-eight years old at the time he led the interrogation of Hermann Göring, Paul Kubala had been born in Berlin in 1907 and emigrated to the United States at the age of seventeen. Fluent in German, English, French, and two other languages, he enlisted in the Army at the age of twenty-one. As commander of the Seventh Army Interrogation Center, he interviewed or supervised the interviewing of some 2,500 Nazi and Italian Fascist prisoners. He transferred to the Air Force following that service's creation, ultimately retiring as a lieutenant colonel. He died in 1967 at the age of sixty.
7. The information Hermann Göring provided to Dunn is summarized in Volume II of the *SIS History*, pp. 434–35.
8. *Yankee G-Man*, p. 183.
9. Andrus to Ayer, July 12, 1945. No Subject. Dihydrocodeine (also known by the brand name paracodeine) is an opioid analgesic developed in Germany before World War I. Göring was known to have been abusing the drug since at least the early 1930s.
10. The simulated rank card was not solely a World War II phenomenon. The author carried one while working as a civilian Army journalist in then West Germany in the mid-1980s. Given what seemed at the time the very real possibility of a Soviet attack across the inner German border, the card was never out of his possession.
11. Details of the SHAEF in-processing procedure are drawn from Fred Ayer's February 19, 1945 message to Hoover titled Paris Office Administrative Matters.

12. Hoover to Ayer, via SHAEF Mission to France, June 1, 1945. No Subject.
13. A forerunner of the post–World War II General Purpose (GP) Medium tent familiar to Korea- and Vietnam-era U.S. military personnel, the M-1942 tent was intended to shelter an entire twelve-man infantry squad. The tent could be erected by four people in less than fifteen minutes—under optimal conditions.
14. Ayer, *Yankee G-Man*, p. 157.
15. Ibid. The IG Farben Building remained under U.S. military control until 1995, when it was turned over to the German government. At the time of writing, the building houses the Westend campus of the University of Frankfurt.
16. Ibid., p. 158.
17. Details of Karl Herman Scherzberg Jr.'s early life are drawn from genealogical records. Information regarding his father's Nazi sympathies and the family's pre-1940 visits to Germany are drawn from the transcript of a lawsuit (*Scherzberg v. Maderia, Lt. Col., Cavalry, U.S. Army, et al.*) filed in July 1944 in the U.S. District Court for the Eastern District of Pennsylvania. The suit was in opposition to an earlier individual exclusion order against the elder Scherzberg by the U.S. Army's Eastern Military Area. Citing his frequent and vocal support for Nazi Germany after December 1941, the Army order sought to prevent Scherzberg Sr. from residing anywhere on the East Coast of the United States. The ban was ultimately set aside by the federal judge hearing the case.
18. Contrary to popular belief, television was not a post–World War II invention. America's RCA Corporation had demonstrated an all-electronic TV in 1936, and by 1938, the technology allowed Germany to televise the 1938 Olympics, albeit to a fairly limited worldwide audience. The American Federal Communications Commission authorized commercial television broadcasting in the United States on July 1, 1941. Five months later, motion pictures of the Japanese attack on Pearl Harbor were the first war images to be broadcast on TV in the United States.
19. Signed Statement by Karl Herman Scherzberg given to SA Erling Kloster, June 13, 1945. Included in Ayer to Hoover, June 15, 1945. Subject: Karl Herman Scherzberg—Treason.
20. Ayer to Hoover, op cit.

21. Details on Gertrude Hahn's early life are drawn from genealogical records.
22. Details on Gertrude Hahn's life in Germany are drawn from multiple newspaper stories that ran after she was publicly identified as a renegade broadcaster and following her arrest in 1945. These include the *St. Louis Post-Dispatch* (August 24, 1943), the *Pittsburgh Press* (October 17, 1943), the *Pittsburgh Sun-Telegraph* (May 20, 1945), the *Pittsburgh Post-Gazette* (July 2, 1945), and others.
23. *Pittsburgh Press,* October 17, 1943.
24. *Pittsburgh Post-Gazette,* August 24, 1943.
25. Memo, J. Edgar Hoover to Assistant Attorney General Wendell Berge, December 2, 1942. Also, Assistant Director Edmund P. Coffey Sr. to Hoover, et al., March 3, 1943.
26. In their excellent book *Hitler's Airwaves,* authors Horst J. P. Bergmeier and Rainer E. Lotz state that at least some of the programs attributed to the Gertrude Hahn from Pittsburgh were actually voiced by a German actress named Gertude Hahn, who was better known by her maiden name, Gertrude Seitz. Born in Stuttgart in 1905, Seitz had lived in the United States for a few years and could do a convincing American accent.
27. *Washington Star,* March 31, 1942.
28. *Movie and Radio Guide,* April 1942.
29. The postcards' message was included in a May 25, 1942, message sent to Hoover and the Bureau's Technical Library by the FBI field office in Buffalo, New York.
30. Text included in message from D.M. Ladd to Hoover, September 29, 1942. Subject: Radio Propaganda Allegation that FBI is Jewish Controlled.
31. Details on Herbert J. Burgman's early life and Army service are drawn from genealogical and military records. There has long been confusion over Burgman's birth date. While most sources list it as 1894, he himself often gave it as 1896. Several official U.S. government documents, including his passport applications, use the latter date.
32. Details of Herbert Burgman's capture and interrogation by Army Liaison Unit members Rucks and Thompson are drawn from their report,

which was sent as an attachment to Fred Ayer's June 21, 1945, message to Hoover.

33. Details of Douglas Chandler's early life are drawn from genealogical records.
34. The *Missouri* (BB-11) to which Chandler was assigned during World War I was a *Maine*-class battleship that was scrapped in the early 1920s. The more famous *Missouri* (BB-63) upon which the instrument of Japan's unconditional World War II surrender was signed in September 1945 was launched in January 1944.
35. Chandler left active duty as an enlisted chief yeoman, though there are indications he was commissioned an ensign following his transfer to the Naval Reserve Force.
36. Now Korčula, Croatia.
37. "How Does a Traitor Get That Way?" by Edward A. Harris, in the *St. Louis Post-Dispatch*, August 8, 1943.
38. After leaving Germany in the late 1930s because of rising anti-Semitism, Dr. Alfred Brandt became a professor of philosophy at Dana College in Nebraska and a vocal critic of the Nazis. His comments about Douglas Chandler—whom Brandt had known in both the United States and Germany—first appeared in an article Brandt wrote for the December 1943 issue of *Read* magazine. His remarks were quoted by columnist Nell Battle Lewis in the May 27, 1945, edition of the Raleigh, North Carolina, *News & Observer.*
39. Schofield, *Treason Trail*, p.71.
40. Ayer to Hoover, June 24, 1945. Subject: Max Otto Koischwitz, was Treason.
41. T/5 stood for Technician, Fifth Grade, a specialist enlisted rank denoting soldiers with special technical (or language) skills who were not trained to be combat leaders.
42. German Intelligence Section Special Interrogation Series No. 20, July 12, 1945.
43. Schofield, *Treason Trail*, p. 41.
44. Edwards, *Berlin Calling*, p. 145.
45. Bergmeier and Lotz, *Hitler's Airwaves*, p. 63.

46. Although the Germans had unconditionally surrendered to the Allies early on the morning of May 7, SS units in Prague had continued trying to put down the rebellion with the aid of Luftwaffe bombing attacks. Soviet forces entered the city on May 9 and, with the help of Czech resistance fighters and armed civilians, cleared the remaining German forces from the city. Soon afterward, NKVD agents attached to the Soviet maneuver units began arresting any Czech deemed to be a threat to Soviet rule, including many of the same resistance members who had helped liberate Prague.
47. Klaus Mann, the son of the famous German writer Thomas Mann, had fled Germany in the late 1930s and ultimately settled in the United States. He became a U.S. citizen in 1943, the same year he enlisted in the U.S. Army. He was trained at Camp Ritchie, Maryland, and initially served as a translator for the Counter Intelligence Corps before transferring to *Stars and Stripes*.
48. News of Edward Delaney's encounter in Prague with Howard Byrne and Klaus Mann ran in newspapers throughout the United States on June 19 and 20. All of those accounts were based on a *Stars and Stripes* release sent out early on the 19th. Byrne's firsthand (but non-bylined) account of the incident ran in *Stripes*' London and Paris editions on June 20, 1945.
49. Details on Delaney's interactions with Howard Byrne and Klaus Mann are drawn from the various newspaper articles written about the encounter, and from Delaney's account in his 1969 book *Five Decades Before Dawn*. While essentially a supremely self-aggrandizing and self-exculpatory volume that ignores virtually all the facts concerning his work for the Germans, the book (oddly enough) seems to get most dates pertaining to his war years right.
50. Delaney, *Five Decades Before Dawn*, p. 155.
51. Details of Edward Delaney's childhood and early adult life are drawn from genealogical records and from his FBI file.
52. Edwards, *Berlin Calling*, pp. 24–25.
53. Shirer, *Berlin Diary*, p. 543.
54. "How Does a Traitor Get That Way?" August 8, 1943.
55. Delaney, *Five Decades Before Dawn*, p. 115.

56. Ibid., p. 162.

Chapter 11: Spymasters, Still More Renegades, and Legats

1. Details on Walter Schellenberg's life and career are drawn from several sources, including his FBI and MI6 files, and the books Doerries, *Hitler's Last Chief of Foreign Intelligence*; Schellenberg, *The Labyrinth*; Blandford, *SS Intelligence*; and Doerries, *Hitler's Intelligence Chief*.
2. Established by Reichsführer-SS (head of the *SS*) Heinrich Himmler in September 1939, the RHSA (Reichssicherheitshauptamt) was subordinate to Himmler in his dual role as head of the SS and all of Germany's police forces. The RHSA thus controlled the Sicherheitsdienst (SD) and the Sicherheitspolizei (security police), which itself comprised the Gestapo and Kripo.
3. On November 9, 1939, the SD lured two British agents to Venlo, a Dutch city on the German border, ostensibly to meet members of the anti-Hitler resistance within the German armed forces. On Himmler's orders, Schellenberg organized the kidnapping of the British agents from a café just yards from the German border. Their capture severely disrupted British intelligence activities on the Continent and further enhanced Schellenberg's reputation within the Reich. Though imprisoned in various concentration camps, the British agents both survived and were liberated by American forces in May 1945. For an excellent account of the events at Venlo and their aftermath by one of the captured British agents, see Captain S. Payne Best's *The Venlo Incident: A True Story of Double-Dealing, Captivity, and a Murderous Nazi Plot* (New York: Hutchinson, 1950; reprint: Barnsley, UK: Pen and Sword Books, 2010).
4, Schellenberg's visits to Paris were not solely for official business. He is thought to have been one of fashion designer Coco Chanel's many German lovers and may also have been on intimate terms with Florence Gould during the establishment of Banque Charles.
5. In his fascinating and deeply researched book *The Bedbug: Klop Ustinov, Britain's Most Ingenious Spy*, author Peter Day says the nickname was bestowed on Ustinov by "a very understanding wife on account of his extraordinary capacity to hop from one woman's bed to another in the King's service." Klop Ustinov was the father of famed British actor Sir Peter Ustinov.

6. Ayer to Hoover, 8 June 1945. Subject: Walter Schellenberg—Interrogation of.
7. Ayer, *Yankee G-Man*, p. 186.
8. Ibid.
9. Ibid., p. 187.
10. *SIS History*, Volume II, p. 436. Schellenberg's suspicions were well founded. From 1942 to 1945, the FBI operated a covert radio monitoring and transmitting station in Wading River, New York, on the shores of Long Island Sound. FBI technicians and agents lived and worked in Benson House, a former family home, sending erroneous information in coded messages the Nazis believed were coming from their U.S.-based operatives.
11. Victor Samuel de Guinzbourg is literally a counterintelligence legend. Born in Russia to a Jewish family in 1906, he and his two siblings were taken by their parents to France a few years after the failed 1905 Revolution. In 1910, the family emigrated to the United States, settling in Brooklyn. Both of de Guinzbourg's parents became naturalized U.S. citizens but spent much of the boy's youth in Paris. De Guinzbourg was highly intelligent, and by his early twenties, he was completely fluent in French, Russian, English, German, and at least six other languages. He was living in New York when the United States entered the war in 1941 and very quickly enlisted in the Army. His amazing language skills soon got him transferred to CIC, and his first overseas assignment was to North Africa (where he met and worked with Frank Amprim). He went on to serve in both German-occupied and liberated France, Belgium, Italy, Austria, and Germany, in the process winning numerous awards from several nations. After the war, he left the Army as a colonel and ultimately became the director of the National Counter Intelligence Corps Association and the executive officer of the United Nations' Military Staff Committee. He died in New York on April 17, 1976, at the age of seventy.
12. Ayer, *Yankee G-Man*, p. 163.
13. On the advice of his CIC colleagues, Fred Ayer had temporarily given up his FBI-issued .38-caliber revolver for the harder-hitting Model 1911 semiautomatic pistol.
14. Ibid.

15, As with defeated Germany, Austria was divided into four occupation zones—American, British, French, and Soviet. The Austrian capital, Vienna, like the former German capital, was divided into four zones and was deep inside the Soviet occupation zone, as Berlin was in Germany.

16. The account of Horton Telford's adventurous 1940 diplomatic courier trip is drawn from the article "Via Diplomatic Courier" in the June 1941 issue of the *American Foreign Service Journal*.

17. C.H. Carson to D.M. Ladd, May 15, 1945. Subject: Assignment of Bureau Agents to the American Embassy, Paris, France.

18. Ibid.

19. The substance of Joe Lynch's discussion with Ambassador Caffery was included in an August 2, 1945, summary provided by Crawford Carson to D.M. Ladd with Subject: FBI Coverage in Continental Europe.

20. Hoover to Daughters, August 3, 1945. Subject: Planning for the Study of the Communist Party in France.

21. Horton Telford's personal journal deals in detail with his time in both Havana and Paris. Key pages of the document were provided to the author by the family of Clement "Bud" Rousseau.

22. Not only did the jaunts to the seaside afford the Bureau men some much needed downtime, it also brought together Bud Rousseau and his future wife, Jacqueline Nyala Hawkins. The couple married on March 21, 1947, in Paris and were ultimately together for fifty-six years.

23. The quote is drawn from the complete text of Eisenhower's final SHAEF order of the day as found on p. 515 of Pogue, *The Supreme Command*, in the series *The United States Army in World War II: European Theater of Operations*.

24. Ayer, *Yankee G-Man*, p. 165.

25. The town of Fulda lies at the foot of two relatively level passes through otherwise hilly and heavily forested terrain. Those passes have long been a favored route for armies moving between the eastern and western parts of Germany, and during the Cold War were considered a primary attack route for Soviet armies seeking to conquer what was then West Germany and advance all the way to the English Channel. The U.S. Army and the Soviets massed huge forces on their respective sides of the border between East and West Germany, with the opposing forces often less

than a mile apart. The author clearly remembers the eerie sensation of standing atop an American watchtower, using binoculars to look across that narrow strip of heavily mined earth only to discover a Russian soldier in his own watchtower staring back.

26. Ayer, *Yankee G-Man*, p. 165.
27. During the Cold War, the Soviets and the NATO nations often exchanged captured espionage agents across the Glienicker Brücke, leading to it being widely referred to during that period as "The Bridge of Spies."
28. The complex would ultimately become the headquarters of the U.S. military government and, during the Cold War, of the U.S. Army's Berlin Brigade.
29. Ayer, *Yankee G-Man*, p. 166.
30. Ibid., p. 167.
31. Heisenberg and his planned assassination by baseball player turned OSS agent Moe Berg are the subject of Nicolas Dawidoff's excellent 1994 book *The Catcher Was a Spy: The Mysterious Life of Moe Berg* (New York: Pantheon) and the 2005 film starring Paul Rudd as Berg and Mark Strong as Heisenberg.
32. The majority of the documents were discovered in May 1945 in a paper mill in Freimann, some six miles northeast of central Munich, where the Nazis had intended to have them destroyed.
33. Officially titled the Nationalsozialistische Deutsche Arbeiterpartei/Auslands-Organisation (Nazi Party/Foreign Organization) and generally referred to the AO, the organization was considered a "region" of the Party. It included all German citizen Party members living outside Germany. The AO documents are specifically mentioned in the FBI's *SIS History, Volume II, p. 436.*
34. Shortwave uses high frequencies that are able to reach greater distances by "bouncing" transmissions off the earth's ionosphere. Medium wave is generally used for shorter distances and local broadcasts.
35. Details on the KWS/DÜS are drawn largely from Bergmeier and Lotz, *Hitler's Airwaves.*
36. Ibid., p. 40.
37. Originally part of Poland, the region of Silesia that incorporates the town of Max Otto Koischwitz's birth changed hands many times over

the centuries. Ruled at various times by Poland, Bohemia, Sweden, Prussia, and Austria-Hungary, in 1871, the region became part of Germany and remained so until 1945. Once again part of Poland, Jauer is now known by its original Polish name, Jawor.

38. Details on Koischwitz's early life and academic career in the United States are drawn from genealogical records, his FBI file, and other sources as noted.
39. The eldest daughter, Stella, was born in New York in 1928. Her sisters, twins Renate and Helen, were born in the city in 1930.
40. Bergmeier and Lotz, *Hitler's Airwaves*, pp. 55–56.
41. Stella Koischwitz spoke about the program at length, in January 1946, during a series of interviews with Berlin CIC Detachment agent William Klufa. She also provided Klufa with several bound volumes of her father's scripts. In a March 6, 1949, letter to the editor of the Minneapolis *Star Tribune*, Klufa described each of the volumes as being "as thick or thicker than a Minneapolis telephone directory."
42. *Pittsburgh Post-Gazette*, September 9, 1944.
43. The three Koischwitz sisters—Stella, Renate, and Helen—all eventually emigrated to the United States.
44. Details of Fred Kaltenbach's early life are drawn from genealogical records; from the articles "Goebbels's Iowan: Frederick W. Kaltenbach and Nazi Short-Wave Radio Broadcasts to America, 1939–1945" and "Kaltenbachs: A Solid American Family With a Shadow"; and from Kaltenbach's FBI file.
45. Shirer, *Berlin Diary*, p. 322.
46. *New York Times*, April 13, 1948, p. 8.
47. Ayer to Hoover, January 7, 1945. Subject: Fern A. Deussen—Treason.
48. Details of Fern Deussen's early life are drawn from genealogical records and from her FBI file.
49. Details of Gerhard Haase's early life are drawn from genealogical records and from his FBI file.

Chapter 12: Suspects, Victory, and Storm Clouds

1. Details of Thornton Chapman Sinclair's early life are drawn from genealogical records.

2. *The Public Opinion Quarterly*, October 1938, pp. 570–83.
3. Ibid., p. 572.
4. Ibid.
5, Ibid., p. 583.
6. The advance of the 23rd Tank Battalion into Austria and the role some of the unit's members played in the Battle of Castle Itter—one of the last combat actions in the European theater and the only time American and German soldiers joined forces to defend a medieval castle against SS troops—is the subject of the author's 2014 *New York Times* bestseller *The Last Battle*.
7. Hans Wenthur's diary, August 8, 1945.
8. Ibid.
9. Ayer, *Yankee G-Man*, p. 183.
10. Ibid.
11. Walter Winchell's statements about Thornton Sinclair's work for the Nazis were repeated nationwide in the journalist's syndicated newspaper column on June 20, 1947.
12. Details of Griebl's interactions with Downey of U.S. Forces Austria's counterintelligence section are taken from Special Agent Joseph Fellner's October 12, 1945, summation of Griebl's interrogations by both Hans Wenthur and Fellner himself. That summation was included in Fellner's October 15 message to Hoover, titled Re: Dr. Ignaz Theodor Griebl. The report uses the correct version of the suspect's first name, which many newspapers of the day incorrectly spelled "Ignatz." The name is spelled Ignaz on the suspect's birth certificate, his World War I German army documents, his naturalization papers, and his New York state medical license, among other official documents. Moreover, when writing his signature Griebl always used Ignaz, not Ignatz. The later version apparently was widely used by his New York patients of Eastern European background, who would have found it more familiar.
13. The Drexel quote appears in the article "Bay State Captain Arrests Girl Traitor" in the August 20 edition of the *Boston Globe* under Otto Zausmer's byline.
14. Wenthur diary, August 30, 1945.

15. Details on Griebl's early life are drawn from genealogical records and from Fellner to Hoover, October 15, 1945. Subject: Dr. Ignaz Theodor Griebl—Espionage.
16. Details on the Griebl's early years in the United States are based largely on Fellner to Hoover, October 15, 1945. Subject: Dr. Ignaz Theodor Griebl—Espionage; on former FBI agent Leon G. Turrou's syndicated newspaper account of his investigation of Griebl's espionage activities; and on Rhodri Jeffreys-Jones's deeply researched 2020 book *The Nazi Spy Ring in America: Hitler's Agents, the FBI and the Case That Stirred the Nation* (Washington, DC: Georgetown University Press).
17. Quoted by former FBI agent Leon G. Turrou in his syndicated December 15, 1938, newspaper article "Super-patriot Pose of Wealthy Doctor Proved Deception." Turrou had attended the 1934 rally while still an FBI special agent.
18. *The Game of the Foxes* (New York: David McKay), p. 30. While not a major character in Ladislas Farago's monumental 1971 history of World War II German espionage in the United States and United Kingdom, Ignaz Griebl does rate several mentions.
19. Kate Moog had briefly been married to a man named Emil Busch (sometimes rendered as Bush). He filed for divorce in Mexico in June 1934 on the grounds that his wife had deserted him. She traveled to Germany using a passport issued under the name Katherina Busch, though she generally insisted on being called Kate Moog. She owned and ran a nursing home, and originally met Griebl when he transferred patients there.
20. *Hitler's Undercover War*, p. 36. William Breuer's 1989 volume covers much of the same ground as *The Game of the Foxes*, but benefits from the addition of information not available to Farago.
21. While being interrogated by the British after the war, Erich Pfeiffer said that the "honey trap" story was complete nonsense and "could only have originated in the mind of Griebl." See Appendix III, p. 28, of *Camp 020 Interim Report on the Case of Erich Pheiffer* [sic], KV2/267 (hereafter Pfieffer Interim Report).
22. Details on the early lives of Rumrich and Glaser are drawn from genealogical records.
23, For the fascinating, complete story of Leon Turrou's life and his investigation of Nazi spy rings in pre–Pearl Harbor America, see Jeffrys-Jones,

The Nazi Spy Ring in America, and Batvinis, *Hoover's Secret War Against Axis Spies*.

24. Turrou, *The Nazi Spy Conspiracy in America*, p. 130.
25. Pfieffer Interim Report, Part II, p. 10.
26. The use of fictitious names in *Confessions of a Nazi Spy* did not prevent Kate Moog from suing Warner Brothers for $75,000. Called "Erika Wolf" in the film, Moog was depicted by German-born actress Lya Lys, whose looks, clothing style, and mannerisms Moog claimed were identical to her own. The syndicated United Press article "Movie Star's Height Wins Suit for Warner Brothers," which ran nationwide, reported that during the February 10, 1941, hearing of the case in a New York courtroom, the judge had Moog and Lys stand next to each other in front of the jury. At 6 feet tall, the brunette Moog towered over the 5 foot, 3 inch, blonde Lys. Moog's suit was summarily dismissed.

    In May 1939, Moog had sent Erich Pfieffer a copy of the American edition of *The Nazi Spy Conspiracy in America*, which the Abwehr handler thought was largely a work of fiction created by Leon Turrou to enhance his own reputation. Later, another German agent in New York sent Pfieffer a complete set of reels of *Confessions of a Nazi Spy*, which was frequently shown for the amusement of Pfieffer's Abwehr colleagues. Pfieffer Interim Report, Part II, p. 11.
27. Wenthur diaries, August 30 and September 4, 1945.
28. Until 1938, the entire building—including the medical clinic on the ground floor—had been owned by Otto Fischer, a Jewish developer who fled to the United States after the *Anschluss*. He rented the rooms that formed the medical practice to his cousin, the physician who also fled Austria.
29. Fellner to Hoover, October 15, 1945. Subject: Dr. Ignaz Theodor Griebl—Espionage. Maria Griebl had been taken into custody as a material witness after her husband fled to Germany. She testified to the New York grand jury that she's known nothing about her husband's espionage activities.
30. *Cases and Reports Relating to Property and Equipment Released by Vienna Area Command (VAC) to the Austrian Government*. V1.1529/XIX, Ignatz Theodor Griebl.

31. Despite Griebl's mysterious disappearance from the Salzburg CIC facility, the information Hans Wenthur was able to draw from him was, according to the *SIS History,* Volume II, "One of the most outstanding examples of the value of having Bureau representatives with the American occupation forces."
32. Details of Constance Drexel's early life are drawn from genealogical records.
33. Shirer, *Berlin Diary,* p. 322.
34. Constance Drexel's statement was quoted in a June 14, 1946, memo from Nathan T. Elliff, assistant chief of the Justice Department's National Defense Section, to Theron L. Caudle, assistant chief of DOJ's Criminal Division, with the subject line Treason Cases.
35. Wenthur diary, August 30, 1945.
36. Scholars have long debated Constance Drexel's age at the time of her death, because she often gave differing dates for her birth. John Carver Edwards, author of the excellent *Berlin Calling,* states that she was born on November 28, 1894. I have chosen to accept the FBI's statement that she was born a decade earlier, on November 28, 1884, primarily because her *younger* sister Norma was born in Pennsylvania in November 1885.
37. For the complete and utterly fascinating story of Duquesne's life as soldier, big-game hunter, reporter, and German spy, see Art Ronnie's *Counterfeit Hero: Fritz Duquesne, Adventurer and Spy* (Annapolis, MD: Naval Institute Press, 1995).
38. One of the earliest accounts of Sebold's forced career as a double agent is included in *Passport to Treason: The Inside Story of Spies in America* by Alan Hynd. For a more recent recounting of Sebold and the Duquesne ring, see Peter Duffy's excellent *Double Agent: The First Hero of World War II and How the FBI Outwitted and Destroyed a Nazi Spy Ring.* Details on Sebold's role as a double agent are drawn largely from the latter source.
39. The funds provided to Sebold in 1940 would equal roughly $22,000 in 2024.
40. Duffy, *Double Agent,* p. 141.
41. See n. 456.

42. Fritz Duquesne was released after fourteen years due to ill health and died in 1956 in New York City. William Sebold suffered from increasingly serious manic depression and was ultimately committed to California's Napa State Hospital. He died there of a heart attack in 1970 at the age of seventy.
43. Details of Friedrich Busch's early life and World War II service with the Abwehr are drawn from several sources, including an interrogation conducted by British Captain J. C. Hales at the U.S. Third Army Interrogation Center at Freising on August 7, 1945; two U.S. Forces European Theater interrogation reports—one done in October 1945 and the other in January 1946; Busch's MI5 file, *Busch, Friedrich* (KV-2/529); and the *SIS History*, Volume II.
44. Preliminary Interrogation Report No. 73, USFET-MIS, October 2, 1945.
45. *SIS History*, Volume II, p. 435. While Friedrich Busch may indeed have been an anti-Nazi whose actions helped damage German intelligence operations, he nonetheless had to take responsibility for his wartime actions. After his many interrogations, he was turned over to the French, who imprisoned him for 10 years. After his release, he returned to his family's commercial fish business and died in Bremen in the late 1970s.
46. Captain J. C. Hales, Interrogation of Major Friedrich Busch, August 13, 1945.
47. Details on Walter Kappe and the selection of the Operation Pastorious saboteurs are drawn primarily from Rachlis, *They Came to Kill: The Story of Eight Nazi Saboteurs in America.*
48. Details of Wilhelm Ahlrichs's early life and voyages are drawn from genealogical records.
49. First commissioned into the Kriegsmarine in 1938, the Type VIIC was the most common U-boat in service throughout World War II. More than 560 variants of the VIIC served during the conflict, and they comprised the majority of German submarines lost to enemy action, accidents, and unspecified causes.
50. Walter Kappe gave the German sabotage campaign the code name Fall Pastorius (Operation Pastorious) as an ironic homage to Franz Daniel Pastorius, who, in 1683, led several Mennonite and Quaker families to Pennsylvania.

51. The German saboteurs came ashore wearing Kriegsmarine uniforms so that should they be captured immediately upon landing, they would be incarcerated as prisoners of war rather than executed as spies.
52. The submarine that delivered Dasch and his compatriots to Long Island had its own narrow escape. After putting the saboteurs ashore, *U-202* had grounded on a sandbar and was unable to move until the morning tide came in. Still under the cloak of thick fog, the U-boat managed to make it back to sea and returned to its base in Brest, France. The submarine's luck ran out on June 2, 1943, when it was sunk 260 miles southeast of Cape Farewell, Greenland, by the British sloop HMS *Starling*. Thirty of the U-boat's crewmembers survived; eighteen did not.
53. After putting the Operation Pastorius saboteurs ashore in Florida, *U-584* made it safely back to France and resumed normal war patrols. On October 31, 1943, the submarine was in the North Atlantic, some 815 miles northwest of the Azores, when it was caught on the surface by three U.S. Navy TBM Avengers launched from the escort carrier USS *Card*. The U-boat dived and was attempting to slip away when it was hit by a Mark 24 acoustic homing torpedo dropped by one of the Avengers. Joachim Deecke and all fifty-two members of his crew were lost.
54. Ahlrichs's opinions about Operation Pastorius and the men assigned to carry it out are drawn from a summation of Rucks and Klosters's interrogation of the former Abwehr officer in *SIS History*, Volume II, p. 435.
55. In one of war's sad ironies, Wilhelm Ahlrichs's son Harry, an enlisted radio operator, died on June 30, 1944, when *U-441* was sunk by depth charges in the English Channel with the loss of all hands.
56. Operation Pastorius was not Wilhelm Ahlrichs's last foray into covert maritime operations. After World War II, he joined West Germany's federal intelligence service, the Bundesnachrichtendienst (BND), and posed as a civilian mariner to spy on Soviet Bloc ports and naval activities. His luck ran out in December 1959, when he was arrested in Danzig, Poland, while photographing military barracks and naval vessels. In early 1960, he was sentenced to fifteen years in prison, and upon being pardoned in 1965, he returned to Hamburg, where he died sometime in the 1970s.
57. Fred Ayer's account of VJ Day in Paris is drawn from *Yankee G-Man*, pp. 152–53.

58. August 15, 1945, was the date on which Tokyo agreed to cease hostilities. The actual capitulation was not official until September 2, when Japanese officials signed the instrument of surrender aboard the USS *Missouri* anchored in Tokyo Bay. Most Americans are not aware that fighting between U.S. and Japanese forces actually continued for three days after August 15. As recounted in the author's 2015 book *Last to Die: A Defeated Empire, a Forgotten Mission, and the Last American Killed in World War II*, renegade Japanese fighter pilots who did not obey Emperor Hirohito's command to stop fighting attacked American reconnaissance aircraft over Tokyo for three days after the ceasefire went into effect. On August 18, Sgt. Anthony Marchione, a twenty-one-year-old native of Pottstown, Pennsylvania, was killed by enemy fire while aboard a B-32 Dominator, thus gaining the dubious distinction of being the last American servicemember killed in combat in World War II.
59. According to a USAAF manifest, Fred Ayer flew from Paris to the United States (via Stephenville, Newfoundland) aboard an ATC C-54 that landed at Washington National Airport on August 28. Among his fellow passengers on the trip was Russian-American aviation pioneer—and USAAF consultant—Alexander De Seversky.
60. Ayer, *Yankee G-Man*, p. 200.
61. Ibid., p. 197.

Chapter 13: Turf Wars . . . and a Legacy

1. The Bureau paid for Walt Rucks to fly from Paris to Washington, D.C., on an Air Transport Command C-54 that arrived at National Airport on September 27. While the reasons for Rucks's early return from Europe remain unclear, he may have been acting as a courier for sensitive information being sent to Hoover by Paris-based legal attaché Horton Telford. Whatever the purpose of Rucks's journey, he did not return to ALU duty in France.
2. James Daniel Faziola and James Romano traveled to Italy together in July 1945 as replacements for Arthur Avignone and Alfred Pease, who returned to the United States in, respectively, March and April 1945. Faziola and Romano were both fluent Italian speakers. While they wore Army uniforms, they had not undergone special military-related training before deploying to Europe. Both men worked closely with Amprim

and Special Agent Ray Bacigalupi, the latter of whom returned to the United States in September 1945.

3. Headquarters FBI to U.S. Group Control Council, Office of the Director of Intelligence, for SA Frederick Ayer. No Subject. October 2, 1945; and Headquarters FBI to Headquarters, U.S. Forces European Theater (Rear), for SA Donald Daughters. No Subject. Oct. 2, 1945.
4. Hoover to Daughters via Legal Attaché Office, Paris, France. No Subject. October 11, 1945.
5. Headquarters FBI, to Telford, Legal Attaché, U.S. Embassy, Paris, France. No Subject. October 2, 1945.
6. Telford to Headquarters FBI via State Department. No Subject. October 9, 1945.
7. Headquarters FBI to Telford, Legal Attaché, U.S. Embassy, Paris, France. No Subject. October 11, 1945.
8. In his diary, Hans Wenthur noted that on October 2, he'd been summoned to Vienna by Joe Fellner so that the two agents could discuss their current cases and map out a strategy for supporting U.S. Forces Austria's future counterintelligence operations.
9. Wenthur diary, October 9, 1945.
10. Ibid., October 10, 1945.
11. Boghardt, *Covert Legions*, p. 25.
12. Details on Gehlen's initial military career, the wartime activities of Fremde Heere Ost, and Gehlen's postwar career as the first head of West Germany's federal intelligence agency, the BND, are drawn from his voluminous CIA file.
13. See the monograph *Forging an Intelligence Partnership: CIA and the Origins of the BND, 1945–1949*, Volume I, p. xiv.
14. Boghardt, *Covert Legions*, pp. 267-268.
15. The U.S. government—specifically the Central Intelligence Agency—saw Reinhard Gehlen as an essential tool in the post–World War II struggle against Soviet expansionism. Indeed, with the CIA's political and financial support, the former FHO chief and his subordinates ultimately became the core of West Germany's postwar intelligence agency, known as the Gehlen Organization. In 1956, that de facto group was absorbed into the nation's official intelligence service, the BND. Gehlen

headed the organization until his retirement in 1968. He died in 1979 at the age of seventy-seven.

16. Boghardt, *Covert Legions*, p. 141.
17. *SIS History*, Vol I., p. 146.
18. Ibid.
19. Troy, *Donovan and the CIA*, p. 276.
20. Ibid., p. 275.
21. Ruffner, *Eagle and Swastika: CIA and Nazi War Criminals and Collaborators*, p. 18.
22. Boghardt, *Covert Legions*, p. 103. Following his departure from CIA, Edwin L. Sibert held several additional senior Army positions, including commanding general of the western (Pacific) section of the Panama Canal Zone. Sibert retired from the Army in 1954 and died in 1977 at the age of eighty.
23. Passenger Manifest, ATC Flight 2314, October 25, 1945.
24. The camps were established before the end of hostilities in Europe and were initially used to house replacement personnel being brought into the theater to participate in the final battles against Nazi Germany. The use of cigarette names for the camps was intended to prevent the Germans from discovering the camps' existence and locations.
25. Former POW Bernard McKenzie, quoted by his son in the blog *Past Present Future*, February 12, 2017.
26. Details on the journey of Hans Wenthur and Joe Fellner from Austria to Camp Home Run and their embarkation in Le Havre are drawn from Wenthur's diary entries for the period October 24–November 5, 1945.
27. After the Folies Bergère performance, Hans Wenthur scribbled a one-word entry in his diary—"nudity." Whether he approved or not is unclear.
28. Handed over to U.S. forces, Robert H. Best was returned to the United States for trial. He was convicted on twelvecounts of treason and sentenced to life in prison, but died in custody in 1952. Anderson was not sent back to the United States, because the charges against her were dropped for lack of evidence and because she had held dual U.S.-Spanish citizenship through marriage since the early 1930s. Anderson died in Spain in 1972 at the age of eighty-four.

29. Ayer, *Yankee G-Man*, p. 200.
30. Ibid.
31. Göring and Ribbentrop were both convicted and sentenced to death, but Fritzsche was acquitted largely because he had not taken part in or supported the Nazis' anti-Jewish policies.

Bibliography

Archives and Abbreviations

Documents were obtained from the following sources, which are attributed as cited.

United States

AHEC: U.S. Army Heritage and Education Center, Carlisle, Pennsylvania.

BRBML: Beinecke Rare Book and Manuscript Library, Yale University, New Haven, Connecticut.

CIA: Central Intelligence Agency, Langley, Virginia.

CMH: U.S. Army Center of Military History, Fort McNair, Washington, D.C.

DSCUA-UOT: Department of Special Collections and University Archives, McFarlin Library, University of Tulsa, Tulsa, Oklahoma.

DTIC: Defense Technical Information Center, Fort Belvoir, Virginia.

FBI: Federal Bureau of Investigation, Washington, D.C.

FDRPLM: Franklin D. Roosevelt Presidential Library and Museum, Hyde Park, New York.

NARA-MMRC: National Archives and Records Administration, Modern Military Records Center, College Park, Maryland.

NARA-NPRC: National Personnel Records Center, Saint Louis, Missouri.

OH-USDS: Office of the Historian, U.S. Department of State, Washington, D.C.

United Kingdom

IWM: Imperial War Museums, London.

UKMOD: Ministry of Defence, London.

UKNA: National Archives, Kew, Richmond, Surrey.

France

AN: Archives Nationales de France, Pierrefitte-sur-Seine.

APP: Archives de la Préfecture de Police, Le Pré-Saint-Gervais.

BDIC: Bibliothèque de Documentation Internationale Contemporaine, Nanterre.

SHD: Service Historique de la Défense, Vincennes.

Germany

BA-B: Bundesarchiv, Berlin.

BA-F: Bundesarchiv-Militärarchiv, Freiburg.

Official Documents

Affaire sur les agents de services secrets Américaine. 1943-1945. 2ème Bureau. SHD.

Amprim, Frank L. Personnel File. FBI.

Anthony Helfenstein File. 1946. APP.

Axel Wenner-Gren Files. 1939–1941. FBI.

Blum, Hans Karl Albrecht (PF603145/V1). 1945. KV-2/3163. UKNA.

British and U.S. Suspected Traitors. Five folders, War Office 219/5293-5297. UKMOD.

British Embassy Circular No. 165: "Functions of Security Coordination in Protecting British Interests." November 18, 1941. KV-4/446. UKNA.

Busch, Friedrich, alias Bergman or Berkman. 1945. KV-2/529. UKNA.

Camp 020 Interim Report on the Case of Erich Pheiffer [sic]. 1945. KV-2/267. UKNA.

Cases and Reports Relating to Property and Equipment Released by Vienna Area Command (VAC) to the Austrian Government, 1945-1950. V1.1529/XIX, Ignatz Theodor Griebl. NARA-MMRC.

Charles H. Reininghaus File (X8370013). 1944–1945. NARA-MMRC.

Consolidated Interrogation Report, Personalities of German Foreign Language News and Propaganda Broadcasts. Berlin District Interrogation

Center, G-2 Division, U.S. Headquarters, Berlin District, 1945. NARA-MMRC.

Constance Drexel Files. 1941–1945. FBI.

Counter Intelligence Corps History and Mission in World War II. NARA-MMRC.

Chronologie de l'activité du 5e bureau de l'armée (1940-1944). SHD.

Dannhaeuser, Wilhem (PF 603188). 1945. KV-2/2866. UKNA.

Detachment History, Counter Intelligence Corps, 92nd Infantry Division, 24 June 1945. Ramon Arrizabalaga Collection of Ezra Pound, BRBML.

Donald S. Day Files. 1942–1946. FBI.

Douglas Chandler Files. 1942–1946. FBI.

Edward L. Delaney Files. 1941–1946. FBI.

Ezra Pound (American Traitor): Capture and Disposal. U.K. War Office 204/12602. UKNA.

Ezra Pound Files, U.K. Security Service (MI5), 1918-1949. KV-2/875. UKNA.

Ezra Pound Case File, 100-HQ-34099, 1942-1945. Boxes 1815-1816 (FBI). Record Group 65. NARA-MMRC.

Fern A. Deussen File, 1945–1946. FBI.

First Special Service Force: Patrol to Rome. N.D., CMH.

Florence Lacaze Gould Files. 1944–1960. FBI.

Francis Warrington Dawson Files, 1944–1945. 2ème Bureau. SHD.

Fred W. Kaltenbach Files. 1940–1946. FBI.

Friedrich Wilhelm Grimm Files, 1945. 2ème Bureau. SHD.

Functions of Security Coordination, October 1, 1941. KV-4/446. UKNA.

Functions of Security Coordination in Protecting British Interests, British Embassy Circular No. 165, November 18, 1942. UKNA.

Gehlen, Reinhard von. 1945. KV-2/2862. UKNA.

Gerhard Herman Haase File. 1942–1947. FBI.

German Intelligence Activities in China During World War II. Strategic Services Unit, March 1, 1946. CIA.

The German Intelligence Service and the War. Office of Strategic Services, Washington, D.C. N.D. CIA.

Guy Liddell Diaries, 1942–1943. KV-4/190-191. UKNA.

Handling Allied Nationals Who Have Collaborated or Served With the Enemy. Supreme Headquarters Allied Expeditionary Force, December 2, 1944. NARA-MMRC.

Herbert J. Burgman Files. 1942–1946. FBI.

History of Allied Forces Headquarters and Headquarters NATOUSA, Part 2: December 1942-December 1943. NARA-MMRC.

History of the Office of the Theater Provost Marshal, ETOUSA, 1 October 1944-8 May 1945. NARA-MMRC.

History of the Special Intelligence Service, Vols. 1–8. FBI, 1947.

Holdings and Opinions, Board of Review, Branch Office of the Judge Advocate General, European Theater of Operations, Vol. 12. Office of the Judge Advocate General, Washington, D.C., 1946. NARA-MMRC.

INTERPOL (International Police) Files, Part 3. 1945–1950. FBI.

Interrogation of Major Friedrich Busch. August 13, 1945. KV-2/529. UKNA.

"*Interrogation of Reich Marshal* [sic] *Hermann Goering*." Ritter Schule, Augsburg, May 10, 1945. NARA-MMRC.

Interrogation Report, "Herman Goering Talking." Seventh Army Interrogation Center, May 19, 1945. NARA-MMRC.

Jane Anderson Files. 1941–1946. FBI.

Liaison and Exchange With the Federal Bureau of Investigation, Jan. 1938-Dec. 1942. U.K. Security Service (MI5), KV 4/394. UKNA.

Liaison and Exchange With the Federal Bureau of Investigation, Jan. 1942-Dec. 1945. U.K. Security Service (MI5), KV 4/395. UKNA.

London Mission. Office of Strategic Services, Washington, D.C., 1945. NARA-MMRC.

Max O. Koischwitz Files. 1941–1946. FBI.

Max Stoecklin [sic] *File*. 1945. Dossier de Cour de Justice de la Seine Z/6/152. AN.

Military Intelligence Service in the European Theater of Operations. HQs., U.S. Forces European Theater, N.D. CIA.

Organisation and Functions of Security Coordination. ND. KV-4/446, UKNA.

Organisation of and Liaison with British Security Coordination USA, 1941-1946, Volume 1: U.K. Security Service (MI5), KV 4/446. UKNA.

Organisation of and Liaison with British Security Coordination USA, 1941-1946, Volume 1: U.K. Security Service (MI5), KV 4/447. UKNA.

Organization and Operation of the Theater Intelligence Services in the European Theater of Operations. Report of the General Board, United States Forces European Theater, 1945. NARA-MMRC.

OSS Art Looting Investigation Unit Final Reports, 1943-1946. NARA-MMRC.

Passenger Manifest, Air Transport Command Flight 2314, October 25, 1945. NARA-MMRC.

Recommendation for Award of Officer of the Most Excellent Order of the British Empire to Colonel Henry Gordon Sheen, U.S. Army, N.D. War Office 373/152/505, UKNA.

Records of the American Commission for the Protection and Salvage of Artistic and Historic Monuments in War Areas (The Roberts Commission); *Card File on Art-Looting Suspects, 1943–1946.*

Report on OSS Activities for the Month of January, 1944. CIA.

Résumé de l'Action des Services de Contre-espionage Militaire français de juillet 1940 à novembre 1944. Vol. 1, 1946. SHD.

Robert H. Best Files. 1941-1946. FBI.

Schellenberg, Walter Friedrich. Various dates. KV-2/94, 2/95, 2/96, 2/98, 2/99. UKNA.

Security Coordination Bulletin No. 1, ND. KV-4/446, UKNA.

Security Coordination Circular No. 5, April 19, 1941. KV-4/446, UKNA.

Sir William Stephenson File. N.D., FBI.

Special Intelligence Service of the Federal Bureau of Investigation. Central Intelligence Group, Washington, D.C., 1946. CIA.

Statement of Ezra Pound to Ramon Arrizabalaga and Frank Amprim, May 7, 1945. Ramon Arrizabalaga Collection of Ezra Pound, BRBML.

U.S. Forces Paris Telephone Directory. United States Forces European Theater, 1944. NARA-MMRC.

Walter Schellenberg File. 1945. FBI.

Walter Schellenberg Files. U.K. Security Service (MI5), KV-2/94, KV-2/95. UKNA.

Welcome to Paris. United States Army Air Forces Air Transport Command, European Division, 1944. NARA-MMRC.

Werner Plack File. U.K. Security Service (MI5), KV-2/3550. UKNA.

Interviews

Condon, John Irish Jr. Audio-recorded by the author, December 4, 2021.

Daughters, David. Audio-recorded by the author, January 14, 2022.

Daughters, Donald and Yvonne. Audio-recorded by Anton Daughters, December 1988.

Marcy, Wenthy Wenthur. Audio-recorded by the author, December 3, 2021.

Correspondence

AGWAR [Adjutant General, War Department] to SHAEF Main for Personal Attention Ayer. Subject: Treason—Anthony G. Helfenstein. December 31, 1944.

Alden, S.S., to D.M. Ladd. Subject: Francis Warrington Dawson—Treason. November 30, 1944. FBI.

———, to D.M. Ladd. Subject: REDACTED. December 4, 1944. FBI.

Amprim, Frank L., to Ramon Arrizabalaga Jr. No Subject. November 29, 1948. DSCUA-UOT.

———, to Prof. John Edwards. Subject: Ezra Pound Arrest. January 3, 1956. DSCUA-UOT.

———, to Prof. John Edwards. Subject: Ezra Pound Arrest. May 8, 1956. DSCUA-UOT.

Andrus, Colonel Burton C., to Ayer. No Subject. July 12, 1945. NARA-MMRC.

Arrizabalaga, Ramon Jr., to Prof. John Edwards. Subject: Ezra Pound Arrest. December 19, 1955. DSCUA-UOT.

———, to Prof. John Edwards. Subject: Ezra Pound Arrest. January 31, 1956. DSCUA-UOT.

———, to Prof. John Edwards. Subject: Ezra Pound Arrest. March 13, 1956. DSCUA-UOT.

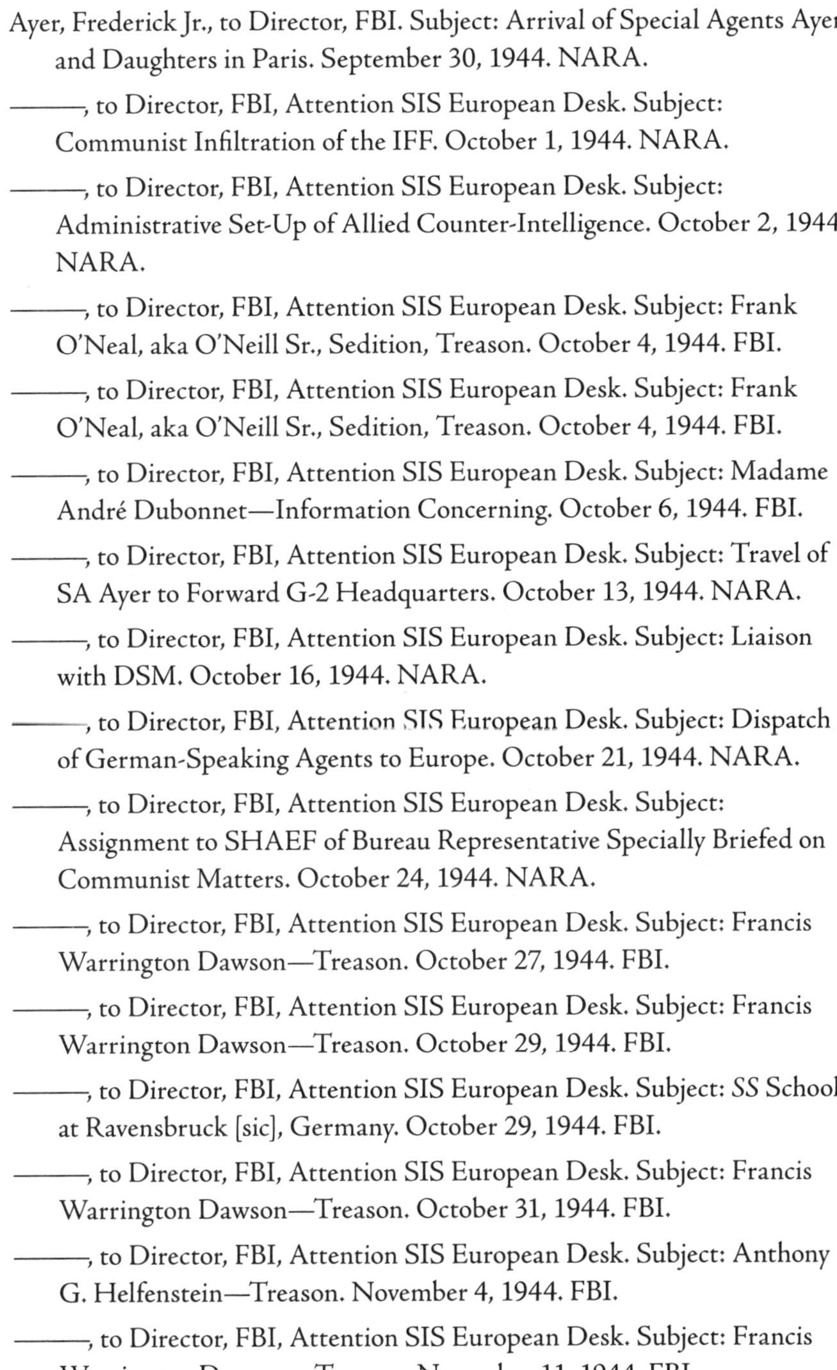

Ayer, Frederick Jr., to Director, FBI. Subject: Arrival of Special Agents Ayer and Daughters in Paris. September 30, 1944. NARA.

———, to Director, FBI, Attention SIS European Desk. Subject: Communist Infiltration of the IFF. October 1, 1944. NARA.

———, to Director, FBI, Attention SIS European Desk. Subject: Administrative Set-Up of Allied Counter-Intelligence. October 2, 1944. NARA.

———, to Director, FBI, Attention SIS European Desk. Subject: Frank O'Neal, aka O'Neill Sr., Sedition, Treason. October 4, 1944. FBI.

———, to Director, FBI, Attention SIS European Desk. Subject: Frank O'Neal, aka O'Neill Sr., Sedition, Treason. October 4, 1944. FBI.

———, to Director, FBI, Attention SIS European Desk. Subject: Madame André Dubonnet—Information Concerning. October 6, 1944. FBI.

———, to Director, FBI, Attention SIS European Desk. Subject: Travel of SA Ayer to Forward G-2 Headquarters. October 13, 1944. NARA.

———, to Director, FBI, Attention SIS European Desk. Subject: Liaison with DSM. October 16, 1944. NARA.

———, to Director, FBI, Attention SIS European Desk. Subject: Dispatch of German-Speaking Agents to Europe. October 21, 1944. NARA.

———, to Director, FBI, Attention SIS European Desk. Subject: Assignment to SHAEF of Bureau Representative Specially Briefed on Communist Matters. October 24, 1944. NARA.

———, to Director, FBI, Attention SIS European Desk. Subject: Francis Warrington Dawson—Treason. October 27, 1944. FBI.

———, to Director, FBI, Attention SIS European Desk. Subject: Francis Warrington Dawson—Treason. October 29, 1944. FBI.

———, to Director, FBI, Attention SIS European Desk. Subject: *SS* School at Ravensbruck [sic], Germany. October 29, 1944. FBI.

———, to Director, FBI, Attention SIS European Desk. Subject: Francis Warrington Dawson—Treason. October 31, 1944. FBI.

———, to Director, FBI, Attention SIS European Desk. Subject: Anthony G. Helfenstein—Treason. November 4, 1944. FBI.

———, to Director, FBI, Attention SIS European Desk. Subject: Francis Warrington Dawson—Treason. November 11, 1944. FBI.

———, to Director, FBI, Attention SIS European Desk. Subject: Francis Warrington Dawson—Treason. November 11, 1944. FBI.

———, to Director, FBI, Attention SIS European Desk. Subject: Anthony G. Helfenstein—Treason. November 14, 1944. FBI.

———, to Director, FBI, Attention SIS European Desk. Subject: Francis Warrington Dawson—Treason. November 19, 1944. FBI.

———, to Director, FBI, Attention SIS European Desk. Subject: Walter Windisch—Treason. November 19, 1944. FBI.

———, to Director, FBI, Attention SIS European Desk. Subject: Marvin H. Fritz—Treason. November 27, 1944. FBI.

———, to Director, FBI, Attention SIS European Desk. Subject: Anthony G. Helfenstein—Treason. November 28, 1944. FBI.

———, to Director, FBI, Attention SIS European Desk. Subject: Joseph Lincoln Luhan—Treason. December 5, 1944. FBI.

———, to Director, FBI, Attention SIS European Desk. Subject: Anthony G. Helfenstein—Treason. December 6, 1944. FBI.

———, to Director, FBI, Attention SIS European Desk. Subject: Changed: Frank J. O'Neill, was Frank O'Neal, Frank O'Neil Sr.—Treason. December 17, 1944. FBI.

———, to Director, FBI, Attention SIS European Desk. Subject: Anthony G. Helfenstein, et al.—Treason. December 21, 1944. FBI.

———, to Director, FBI, Attention SIS European Desk. Subject: Organization and Operations of Free-French Intelligence Services. December 28, 1944. FBI.

———, to Director, FBI, Attention SIS European Desk. Subject: Francis Warrington Dawson—Treason. December 28, 1944. FBI.

———, to Director, FBI, Attention SIS European Desk. Subject: Fern A. Deussen—Treason. January 7, 1945. FBI.

———, to Director, FBI, Attention SIS European Desk. Subject: John E. Loskot with Aliases Ino Loskot, Ino E. Losket—Treason. February 3, 1945. FBI.

———, to Director, FBI, Attention SIS European Desk. Subject: William [sic] Augustin—Treason. February 6, 1945. FBI.

———, to Director, FBI, Attention SIS European Desk. Subject: Charles Reininghaus—Treason. February 18, 1945. FBI.

———, to Director, FBI, Attention SIS European Desk. Subject: Paris Office Administrative Matters. February 19, 1945. FBI.

———, to Director, FBI, Attention SIS European Desk. Subject: Administrative—Trip to Southern France by S.A. Donald L. Daughters. March 10, 1945. FBI.

———, to Director, FBI, Attention SIS European Desk. Subject: Special Mission of Special Agents Ayer and Thompson to Sixth Army Group. March 14, 1945. FBI.

———, to Director, FBI, Attention SIS European Desk. Subject: Francis Warrington Dawson—Treason. March 18, 1945. FBI.

———, to Director, FBI, Attention SIS European Desk. Subject: Assignment of Additional Personnel to European Theater—Administrative. April 2, 1945. FBI.

———, to Director, FBI, Attention SIS European Desk. Subject: Role of FBI in Counterintelligence Plans for Occupied Germany. April 20, 1945. FBI.

———, to Director, FBI, Attention SIS European Desk. Subject: United States Counterintelligence Planning Committee for Germany. May 16, 1945. FBI.

———, to Director, FBI, Attention SIS European Desk. Subject: Karl Herman Scherzberg—Treason. June 15, 1945. FBI.

———, to Director, FBI, Attention SIS European Desk. Subject: Max Otto Koischwitz, was Treason. June 24, 1945. FBI.

Barker, Sgt. J., SHAEF CIC, to Field Security Officer, SHAEF CIC. Subject: Impressions of October 25 Discussions With Mr. Warrington Dawson. October 26, 1944. FBI.

Berge, Wendell, Assistant Attorney General, to Director, FBI. Subject: Subjects for Further Investigation [Pertaining to alleged treason]. November 25, 1942. FBI.

———, to Attorney General Francis Biddle. Subject: Proposed Indictments for Treason of the Following American Citizens Broadcasting Enemy Propaganda from Axis Countries to the United States. January 15, 1943. NARA-MMRC.

———, to L.M.C. Smith, Chief, Special War Policies Unit, War Division, Department of Justice. Subject: American Citizens Broadcasting From Enemy-Controlled Radio Stations. May 6, 1943. NARA-MMRC.

Bergmann, Hauptman, German Censorship Office, Paris, to Herr P. Widlöcher, German Radio Service, Paris. Subject: Dawson Letters to U.S. Ambassadors. June 26, 1942 [FBI translation]. FBI.

——— to Herr P. Widlöcher, German Radio Service, Paris. Subject: Dawson Letters Free of Secret Writing. July 1, 1942 [FBI translation]. FBI.

Berquist, Colonel E.C., to Commanding General, European Theater of Operations (Through Commanding General, Twelfth Army Group), October 19, 1944. Subject: Alleged Treason of Walter Windisch, United States Citizen. FBI.

Blake, Col. F.A.A., G-2 Division, SHAEF, to Direction de la Sécurité Militaire. Subject: Warrington Dawson. November 13, 1944. SHD.

Caffery, Jefferson, Office of the Representative of the United States, Paris, to The Secretary of State, Washington. Subject: Case of Francis Warrington-Dawson [sic]. October 31, 1944. FBI.

Calvé, Dr. Jacques, to Police d'Etat de Siene-et-Oise. Subject: Warrington Dawson. November 25, 1944. SHD.

Calvert, Lt. Col. F.A. Jr., to Assistant Chief of Staff, G-2, Supreme Headquarters, AEF (Forward), APO 757, U.S. Army, ATTN: CID. Subject: Warrington Dawson. September 26, 1944. FBI.

Cannon, Special Agent Donald, CIC, to Captain Tait, Field Security Officer, CIC, FS Section. Subject: Warrington Dawson. October 26, 1944. FBI.

Carson, C.H., to D.M. Ladd. Subject: Francis Warrington Dawson—Treason. November 22, 1944. FBI.

———, to D.M. Ladd. Subject: Assignment of Bureau Agents to the American Embassy, Paris France. May 15, 1945. FBI.

———, to D.M. Ladd. Subject: FBI Coverage in Continental Europe. August 2, 1945. FBI.

———, to D.M. Ladd. Subject: Closing Bureau's Army Liaison Units In France and Germany. October 4, 1945. FBI.

———, to D.M. Ladd. Subject: Closing Bureau's Army Liaison Units In France and Germany. October 11, 1945. FBI.

———, to D.M. Ladd. Subject: Return of Personnel from France and Germany. October 30, 1945. FBI.

Caudle, Assistant Attorney General Theron L., to Director, FBI. Subject: Ezra Pound—Treason. October 19, 1945. FBI.

———, to Director, FBI. Subject: Mrs. Florence Gould—Treason. November 2, 1945. FBI.

———, to Director, FBI. Subject: Treason Investigations in Europe. February 12, 1946. NARA-MMRC.

Cerillet (?), 2ème Bureau, 5ème Section, to Mr. Chamberlain and FBI. Subject: Warrington Dawson. October 19, 1944. SHD.

Cimperman, J.A., to Director, FBI, Attention: SIS European Desk. Subject: Frederick Wilhelm Kaltenbach. September 4, 1944. FBI.

Clark, Assistant Attorney General Tom C., to J. Edgar Hoover. Subject: Francis Warrington-Dawson [sic]—Treason. December 15, 1944. FBI.

———, to Director, FBI. Subject: Francis Warrington-Dawson [sic] December 26, 1944. FBI.

———, to Director, FBI. Subject: Francis Warrington-Dawson [sic] June 9, 1945. FBI.

Communications Section, FBI Headquarters, to Fred Ayer via SHAEF Mission to France. April 17, 1945. No Subject. FBI.

Daughters, Donald, to Director, FBI. Subject: Additional Personnel for the Paris Office. September 7, 1945. FBI.

Dawson, Warrington, to Secretary of State Henry L. Stimson. Subject: Report by the Special Assistant of the Embassy in France [Regarding Japan's Intentions in the Pacific]. February 7, 1933. OH-USDS.

———, to President Franklin D. Roosevelt. Subject: Forwarding of *Chicago Tribune* (Paris) Article. March 13, 1933. FDRPLM.

———, to President Franklin D. Roosevelt. Subject: Forwarding of Photograph of Society of the American Friends of Lafayette Reception. May 24, 1934. FDRPLM.

———, to Marguerite Le Hand. Subject: Thanks for Autographed Photograph of President Roosevelt. September 19, 1934. FDRPLM.

———, to President Franklin D. Roosevelt (via telegram). Subject: Condolences on Death of Assistant Secretary of the Navy Henry Roosevelt. February 24, 1936. FDRPLM.

———, to Assistant Chief of Staff, G-2, Communications Zone, U.S. Army, Paris. Subject: Personal Record. September 17, 1944. FBI.

Department of State, U.S., to Mr. Roads, FBI. Subject: Francis Warrington Dawson. November 18, 1944. FBI.

———, to FBI. Subject: Francis Warrington Dawson. January 2, 1945. FBI.

Deputy Chief, Military Intelligence Division, to S.W. Reynolds, FBI. Subject: Message from Eisenhower. April 26, 1945. FBI.

Edwards, Prof. John, to Frank L. Amprim. Subject: Ezra Pound Arrest. December 9, 1955. DSCUA-UOT.

———, to Ramon Arrizabalaga Jr. Subject: Ezra Pound Arrest. December 9, 1955. DSCUA-UOT.

———, to Ramon Arrizabalaga Jr. Subject: Ezra Pound Arrest. January 19, 1956. DSCUA-UOT.

———, to Frank L. Amprim. Subject: Ezra Pound Arrest. January 20, 1956. DSCUA-UOT.

———, to Ramon Arrizabalaga Jr. Subject: Ezra Pound Arrest. February 16, 1956. DSCUA-UOT.

Elliff, Nathan T., to Theron L. Caudle. Subject: Treason Cases. June 14, 1946. FBI.

Ely, Samuel C., to Nathan T. Eliff. Subject: American Renegades in Europe. August 10, 1945. FBI.

Fellner, Joseph G., to J. Edgar Hoover. Subject: Dr. Ignaz Theodor Griebl—Espionage. October 15, 1945. NARA-MMRC.

Headquarters FBI, to Headquarters, U.S. Forces European Theater (Rear), for SA Donald Daughters. No Subject. October 2, 1945. FBI.

Headquarters FBI, to Telford, Legal Attaché, U.S. Embassy, Paris, France. No Subject. October 2, 1945. FBI.

Headquarters FBI, to U.S. Group Control Council, Office of the Director of Intelligence, for SA Frederick Ayer. No Subject. October 2, 1945. FBI.

Flinn, Dennis A., to J. Edgar Hoover. Subject: Suggestions on Intelligence Operations in Europe. November 23, 1944. FBI.

Foley, Edward S., Memo for Files. Subject: Ezra Pound. April 23, 1952. FBI.

Gurnea, Myron, to J. Edgar Hoover. Subject: Inspection Report, Paris, France. February 13, 1945. FBI.

Hanratty, J.P., to Director, FBI. Subject: Francis Warrington Dawson. November 17, 1944. FBI.

Hasbrouck, Brig. Gen. Robert W., to Warrington Dawson. No Subject. September 15, 1944. FBI.

Headquarters FBI to Legal Attaché, U.S. Embassy, London. No Subject. October 11, 1945. FBI.

Hoover, J. Edgar, to Assistant Attorney General Wendell Berge. Subject: Individuals to be Further Investigated (Treason). December 2, 1942. FBI.

———, to Brigadier Sir David Petrie, Director, MI5. Subject: Arthur M. Thurston. February 2, 1943. FBI.

———, to Legal Attaché, U.S. Embassy, London. Subject: Mrs. J. Gould—Treason. November 4, 1944. FBI.

———, to Special Agent Frederick Ayer Jr. Subject: Mrs. J. Gould—Treason. November 4, 1944. FBI.

———, to Chairman, Federal Communications Commission. Subject: Francis Warrington Dawson. November 17, 1944. FBI.

———, to Chairman, Federal Communications Commission. Subject: Francis Warrington Dawson. November 24, 1944. FBI.

———, to Special Agent Frederick Ayer Jr. Subject: Francis Warrington Dawson—Treason. December 6, 1944. FBI.

———, to Special Agent Frederick Ayer Jr. Subject: Francis Warrington Dawson—Treason. December 14, 1944. FBI.

———, to Special Agent Frederick Ayer Jr. Subject: Francis Warrington Dawson—Treason. December 16, 1944. FBI.

———, to Special Agent Frederick Ayer Jr. Via cable. No Subject. December 29,1944. FBI.

———, to Special Agent Frederick Ayer Jr. Via cable. No Subject. June 1, 1945. FBI.

———, to Special Agent Frederick Ayer Jr. Subject: Francis Warrington Dawson—Treason. June 21, 1945. FBI.

———, to Special Agent Donald Daughters. Subject: Planning for the Study of the Communist Party in France. August 3, 1945. FBI.

———, to Special Agent Donald Daughters. Subject: FBI Army Liaison Units in the European Theater. September 12, 1945. FBI.

Hottel, Guy, SAC, Washington Field Office, to J. Edgar Hoover. Subject: Mrs. Florence Gould—Treason. April 26, 1945. FBI.

Humbert, Dr. E., and Dr. A. Ducamp, to Police d'Etat de Siene-et-Oise. Subject: Warrington Dawson. June 30, 1941. SHD.

Humbert, Dr. E., to Police d'Etat de Siene-et-Oise. Subject: Warrington Dawson. November 24, 1944. SHD.

Jett, E.K., Federal Communications Commission, to J. Edgar Hoover. Subject: Francis Warrington-Dawson [sic]. December 5, 1944. FBI.

———, Federal Communications Commission, to J. Edgar Hoover. Subject: Ivan Starold, aka Francis Warrington-Dawson [sic]. December 22, 1944. FBI.

Jewell, D.A., SHAEF CIC, to Officer Commanding, CIC/FS Section, HQs. SHAEF. Subject: Information Provided by Warrington Dawson. October 26, 1944. FBI.

Labouisse, Henry R. Jr., to Secretary of State Joseph Grew. Subject: Participation of Mrs. Florence Gould in the Banque Charles; Transmittal of Testimonial Letters. March 26, 1945. FBI.

Ladd, D.M., to J. Edgar Hoover. September 29, 1942. Subject: Radio Propaganda Allegation That FBI is Jewish-Controlled. FBI.

Ladd, D.M., Assistant Director, to J. Edgar Hoover. Subject: Assignment of Agents to Embassy in Paris. April 21, 1945. FBI.

———, to E.A. Tamm. No Subject. May 15, 1945.

Larson, C.H., to D.M. Ladd. Subject: Memorandum for Mr. Ladd, Francis Warrington Dawson—Treason. November 23, 1944. FBI.

Le Hand, Marguerite A., to Warrington Dawson. Subject: Transmittal of Autographed Photograph of President Roosevelt. August 28, 1934. FDRPLM.

———, to Department of State (Attention: Mr. Dunn). Subject: Preparation of Response to Warrington Dawson Regarding Gift to President Roosevelt of the Book *Washington Nous Voici* by French Naval Lieutenant Robert de Loture. December 17, 1934. FDRPLM.

Luessy (?), 2ème Bureau, to unknown recipient. Subject: Warrington Dawson. N.D. SHD.

Lynch, Joseph L., Legal Attaché, London, to Director, FBI, Attention SIS European Desk. Subject: Mrs. J. Gould. September 11, 1944. FBI.

McGranery, Assistant to the Attorney General, to U.S. Marshal W. Bruce Matthews. Subject: Italian Citizens to Appear as Witnesses in Trial of Ezra Pound. October 29, 1945. NARA-MMRC.

Menzies, Stewart, Chief, S.I.S., to William Stephenson, BSC. Subject: Reference Your Telegram 153 of 6th December 1942. KV-4/395, UKNA.

MI-5 Liaison Section, SHAEF, to FBI Liaison Section, SHAEF, Message SLB3/NEW/28. Subject: Maurice Gagnon. December 22, 1944. UKNA.

Paillole, Direction de la Sécurité Militaire, to Col. Blake, SHAEF, and M. Bloom. Subject: Warrington Dawson. November 9, 1944. SHD.

Pound, Omar S., to Joan Arrizabalaga. Subject: Location of Ezra Pound photograph. March 7, 1996. Ramon Arrizabalaga Collection of Ezra Pound, BRBML.

Roosevelt, Franklin D., to Warrington Dawson. Subject: Thanks for Clipping from *Chicago Tribune* (Paris). March 25, 1933. FDRPLM.

———, to Warrington Dawson. Subject: Thanks for Condolences on the Death of Assistant Secretary of the Navy Henry Roosevelt. February 25, 1936. FDRPLM.

———, to Sumner Welles. Subject: Retention of Warrington Dawson on Staff of U.S. Embassy, Paris. June 1, 1937. FRDPLM.

———, to Mrs. Roosevelt. Subject: Desire of Warrington Dawson to Be Retained at Paris Embassy, Health Has Failed. June 11, 1937. FDRPLM.

———, to Attorney General Francis Biddle. Subject: Treason Indictments for U.S. Citizens Aiding Hitler on the Radio. October 1, 1942. NARA-MMRC.

Rouart, Dr. Julien, to Police d'Etat de Siene-et-Oise. Subject: Warrington Dawson. November 26, 1944. SHD.

Rudge, Olga, to Ramon Arrizabalaga. Subject: Gift of Ezra Pound Book *Confucio: Ta S'EU Dai Gaku Studio Integrale*. May 31, 1945. Ramon Arrizabalaga Collection of Ezra Pound, BRBML.

SHAEF Main (G-2) to Twelfth Army Group Rear (G-2). Subject: Mohr. December 13, 1944. NARA-MMRC.

——— to Twelfth Army Group (G-2). Subject: Mohr. January 11, 1945. NARA-MMRC.

Stephenson, Major J.F.E., MI-5 Liaison, SHAEF, to F.B.I. Liaison Section, SHAEF. Subject: Louis Harl, Georges de Mauduit, Gagnon. December 22, 1944. UKNA.

Strickland, J.C., to D.M. Ladd. Subject: Francis Warrington Dawson, Treason. November 17, 1944. FBI.

———, to D.M. Ladd. Subject: REDACTED. December 12, 1944. FBI.

Tait, Captain W., CIC Section, G-2, SHAEF, to Head, CI Sub Division, G-2, SHAEF. Subject: Search of Mr. J. [sic] Warrington Dawson's Apartment. October 24, 1944. FBI.

———. CIC Section, G-2, SHAEF, to Head, CI Sub Division, G-2, SHAEF. Subject: Mr. Warrington Dawson. October 26, 1944. FBI.

Telford, Special Agent Horton R., Legal Attaché Office, Paris, France, to Headquarters FBI. No Subject. October 9, 1945. FBI.

———, to Director, FBI. Subject: Francis Warrington-Dawson [sic]. December 21, 1945. FBI.

Thomas, Chef de 2ème Bureau, to Direction de la Sécurité Militaire (unknown recipient). Subject: Warrington Dawson. Handwritten, undated. SHD.

———, to Direction de la Sécurité Militaire (unknown recipient). Subject: Warrington Dawson. October 30, 1944. SHD

———, to Direction de la Sécuritè Militaire. Subject: Warrington Dawson. November 18, 1944. SHD.

———, to Capitaine Desormeau, Services de Documentation. Subject: *Affaire* Warrington Dawson. March 23, 1945. SHD

———, to Lieutenant Avot, Services de Documentation. Subject: Warigton [sic] Dawson. May 15, 1945. SHD.

Thurston, Arthur M., to J. Edgar Hoover. Subject: OSS Access to Ostrich Source Material. April 3, 1943. FBI.

Tully, Grace, to Warrington Dawson. Subject: Thanks for Photograph Sent to President Roosevelt. July 10, 1934. FDRPLM.

Unknown, to SHAEF Field Security Officer. Subject: Summary of Discussions with Warrington Dawson. October 26, 1944. FBI.

Unknown, to Director, FBI. Subject: Paraphrase of Telegram Received Re: Francis Warrington Dawson. October 31, 1944. FBI.

West, Sgt., to SHAEF Field Security Office. Subject: Impressions from Conversation with Mr. Warrington Dawson on October 24, 1944. October 26, 1944. NARA-MMRC.

Widlöcher, Dr. Peter, German Radio Service Paris, to Hauptman Bergmann, German Censorship Office, Paris. Subject: Dawson Letters to U.S. Ambassadors [FBI translation]. June 26, 1942. FBI.

———, to Rudolf Schleier, German Embassy, Paris. Subject: Warrington Dawson [FBI translation]. March 3, 1942. FBI.

———, to Herr Schlottman. Subject: American Informant Report [FBI translation]. December 3, 1942. FBI.

———, to Paul Karl Schmidt, Foreign Ministry Press Office, Berlin. Subject: Warrington Dawson [FBI translation]. January 20,1943. FBI.

———, to Herr Schlottman. Subject: Radio for Warrington Dawson [FBI translation]. March 11, 1943.

———, to Rudolf Schleier, German Embassy, Paris. Subject: Missing English-Language Periodicals [FBI translation]. April 9, 1943. FBI.

———, to Rudolf Schleier and Herr Gerlach, German Embassy, Paris. Subject: Missing English-Language Periodicals [FBI translation]. July 20, 1943. FBI.

Oral Histories

Baker, William T. Conducted August 26, 2004, by Brian Hollstein for the compilation *SIS Oral Histories* by the Society of Former Special Agents of the FBI, Inc.

McKim, Edward D. Conducted February 19, 1964, by James R. Fuchs.

Winter, Howard P. Self-conducted, 1970.

Secondary Sources

Books

Abetz, Otto Friedrich. *Histoire d'une politique franco-allemande*. Paris: Stock, 1953.

Alford, Kenneth D. *American Crimes and the Liberation of Paris: Robbery, Rape and Murder by Renegade GIs, 1944–1947*. Jefferson, NC: McFarland, 2016.

Aron, Robert. *France Reborn, The History of the Liberation*. Trans. Humphrey Hare. New York: Scribner, 1964.

Ayer, Frederick Jr. *Yankee G-Man*. Chicago: Henry Regnery, 1957.

———. *Before the Colors Fade: Portrait of a Soldier, George S. Patton Jr.* Boston: Houghton Mifflin, 1964.

Balfour, Michael. *Propaganda in War, 1939–1945: Organizations, Policies and Publics in Britain and Germany*. London: Routledge and Kegan Paul, 1979.

Batvinis, Raymond. *The Origins of FBI Counterintelligence*. Lawrence, KS: University Press of Kansas, 2007.

———. *Hoover's Secret War Against Axis Spies: FBI Counterintelligence During World War II*. Lawrence, KS: University Press of Kansas, 2014.

Becker, Marc. *The FBI in Latin America: The Ecuador Files*. Durham, NC: Duke University Press, 2017.

Beevor, Anthony, and Artemis Cooper. *Paris After the Liberation, 1944–1949*. New York: Doubleday, 1994.

Bergmeier, Horst J. P., and Rainer E. Lotz. *Hitler's Airwaves: The Inside Story of Nazi Radio Broadcasting and Propaganda Swing*. New Haven and London: Yale University Press, 1997.

Blandford, Edmund L. *SS Intelligence: The Nazi Secret Service*. Shrewsbury, UK: Airlife, 2000.

Boghardt, Thomas. *Covert Legions: U.S. Army Intelligence in Germany, 1944–1949*. Washington, DC: U.S. Government Printing Office, 2022.

Boveri, Margaret. *Treason in the Twentieth Century*. London: MacDonald, 1956.

Breuer, William. *Hitler's Undercover War: The Nazi Espionage Invasion of the USA*. New York: St. Martin's Press, 1989.

Carpenter, Humphrey. *A Serious Character: The Life of Ezra Pound.* Boston: Houghton Mifflin, 1988.

Cave Brown, Anthony. *Wild Bill Donovan: The Last Hero.* New York: Times Books, 1984.

———."C": *The Secret Life of Sir Stewart Graham Menzies, Spymaster to Winston Churchill.* London: Macmillan, 1987.

Carson, Anne Conover. *Olga Rudge and Ezra Pound.* New Haven, CT, and London: Yale University Press, 2001.

Copeland, Miles. *The Game Player: Confessions of the CIA's Original Political Operative.* London: Aurum Press, 1989.

Cornell, Julien. *The Trial of Ezra Pound: A Documented Account of the Treason Case by the Defendant's Lawyer.* London: Faber and Faber, 1966.

Cornut-Gentille, Gilles, and Philippe Michel-Thiriet. *Florence Gould: Une Américaine à Paris.* Paris: Mercure de France, 1989.

Dawson, Warrington. *Opportunity and Theodore Roosevelt.* Privately published, 1924.

Day, Peter. *The Bedbug: Klop Ustinov, Britain's Most Ingenious Spy.* Hull, UK: Biteback, 2015.

Defrasne, Jean. *Histoire de la Collaboration.* Paris: Presses Universitaires de France, 1982.

Delaney, Edward L. *Five Decades Before Dawn.* Pasadena, CA: Deljon , 1969.

Delarue, Jacques. *Histoire de la Gestapo.* Paris: Librarie Arthème Fayard, 1962.

Doerries, Reinhard R. *Hitler's Intelligence Chief: Walter Schellenberg.* New York: Enigma Books, 2009.

Drake, David. *Paris at War, 1939–1944.* Cambridge, MA: Harvard University Press, 2015.

Duffy, Peter. *Double Agent: The First Hero of World War II and How the FBI Outwitted and Destroyed a Nazi Spy Ring.* New York: Scribner, 2014.

Edsel, Robert M. *The Monuments Men: Allied Heroes, Nazi Thieves, and the Greatest Treasure Hunt in History.* New York: Center Street Books, 2009.

Edwards, John Carver. *Berlin Calling: American Broadcasters in Service to the Third Reich.* New York: Praeger, 1991.

Ettlinger, Harold. *The Axis on the Air.* New York: Bobbs-Merrill, 1943.

Farago, Ladislas. *The Game of Foxes: The Untold Story of German Espionage in the United States and Great Britain During World War II.* New York: David McKay, 1971.

Farris, Scott. *Inga: Kennedy's Great Love, Hitler's Perfect Beauty, and J. Edgar Hoover's Prime Suspect.* Guilford, CT: Globe Pequot Press, 2016.

Flannery, Harry W. *Assignment to Berlin.* New York: Alfred A. Knopf, 1942.

Gage, Beverly. *G-Man: J. Edgar Hoover and the Making of the American Century.* New York: Viking Books, 2022.

Garder, Michel. *La Guerre Secrète des Services Spéciaux Français, 1935–1945.* Paris: Cercle du nouveau livre, 1967.

Geddes, Gary. *Conrad's Later Novels.* Montreal: McGill-Queen's University Press, 1980.

Gentry, Curt. *J. Edgar Hoover: The Man and His Secrets.* New York: W.W. Norton, 1991.

Gilbert, James L., et al. *In the Shadow of the Sphinx: A History of Army Counterintelligence.* Washington, DC: U.S. Government Printing Office, 2005.

Gilbert, Sir Martin. *Winston S. Churchill,* Volume VI: *Finest Hour, 1939–1941.* London: William Heinemann, 1983.

Gildea, Robert. *Marianne in Chains: Daily Life in the Heart of France During the German Occupation.* New York: Metropolitan Books, 2003.

Glass, Charles. *Americans in Paris: Life and Death Under Nazi Occupation.* New York: Penguin Group, 2009.

———. *The Deserters: A Hidden History of World War II.* New York: Penguin Press, 2013.

Gordon, Bertram M. (Editor). *Historical Dictionary of World War II France: The Occupation, Vichy, and the Resistance, 1938–1946.* Westport, CT: Greenwood Press, 1998.

Grimm, Friedrich. *Mit offenem Visier: aus den Lebenserinnerungen eines deutschen Rechtsanwalt.* Berg am Starnberger See, Germany: Druffel Verlag, 1961.

Harding, Stephen. *Escape from Paris: A True Story of Love and Resistance in Wartime France.* New York: Da Capo Press/Hachette, 2019.

Hart, Bradley W. *Hitler's American Friends: The Third Reich's Supporters in the United States*. New York: St. Martin's Press, 2018.

Hogan, David W. Jr. U.S. *Army Special Operations in World War II*. Washington, DC: U.S. Army Center of Military History, 1992.

Hyde, H. Montgomery. *The Quiet Canadian: The Secret Service Story of Sir William Stephenson*. London: Hamish Hamilton, 1962.

———. *Room 3603: The Story of the British Intelligence Center in New York During World War II*. New York: Farrar, Straus, 1963.

Hynd, Alan. *Passport to Treason: The Inside Story of Spies in America*. New York: Robert M. McBride, 1943.

Jeffreys-Jones, Rhodri. *The Nazi Spy Ring in America: Hitler's Agents, the FBI and the Case That Stirred the Nation*. Washington, DC: Georgetown University Press, 2020.

Kershaw, Alex. *Avenue of Spies*. New York: Crown Books, 2015.

Kitson, Simon. *The Hunt for Nazi Spies: Fighting Espionage in Vichy France*. Chicago and London: University of Chicago Press, 2008.

Kimball, Warren F. *Churchill and Roosevelt: The Complete Correspondence*. Princeton, NJ: Princeton University Press, 1987.

Kloman, Erasmus H. *Assignment Algiers*. Annapolis, MD: Naval Institute Press, 2005.

Lashmar, Paul. *Spies, Spin and the Fourth Estate: British Intelligence and the Media*. Edinburgh, Scotland: Edinburgh University Press, 2020.

Little, Marie-Noëlle. *The Knight and the Troubadour: Dag Hammarskjöld and Ezra Pound*. Uppsala, Sweden: Dag Hammarskjöld Foundation, 2011.

Macdonald, Bill. *The True Intrepid: Sir William Stephenson and the Unknown Agents*. Vancouver, Canada: Timberholme Books, 1998.

MacDonnell, Francis. *Insidious Foes: The Axis Fifth Column and the American Home Front*. New York: Oxford University Press, 1995.

MacPherson, Nelson. *American Intelligence in Wartime London*. London: Frank Cass, 2003.

Maddow, Rachel. *Prequel: An American Fight Against Fascism*. New York: Crown Books, 2023.

Mahl, Thomas E. *Desperate Deception: British Covert Operations in the United States, 1939–1944*. Washington, DC, and London: Brassey's, 1998.

McDowell, Warren F. *Churchill and Roosevelt: The Complete Correspondence.* Princeton, NJ: Princeton University Press, 1987.

Miannay, Patrice. *Dictionnaire des agents doubles dans la Résistance.* Paris: Le Cherche Midi, 2005.

Mitchell, Alan. *Nazi Paris: The History of an Occupation, 1940-1944.* Oxford, UK: Berghahn Books, 2008.

Moats, Alice-Leone. *No Passport for Paris.* New York: G.P. Putnam's Sons, 1945.

Morris, Edmund. *Colonel Roosevelt.* New York: Random House, 2010.

Mucklow, Timothy J. *The SIGABA/ECM II Cypher Machine: "A Beautiful Idea."* Fort Meade, MD: National Security Agency Center for Cryptologic History, 2015.

Othen, Christopher. *The King of Nazi Paris: Henri Lafont and the Gangsters of the French Gestapo.* Hull, UK: Biteback, 2020.

Paillole, Paul. *Services Spéciaux (1935–1945),* Paris: Éditions Robert Laffont, 1975.

———. *L'homme des services secrets: Entretiens avec Alain-Gilles Minella,* Paris: Éditions Julliard, 1995.

Pierre, Willis J. *A Tablet on a Wall.* Kearney, NE: Morris, 2012.

Pogue, Forrest C. *The Supreme Command.* In the series *The United States Army in World War II: European Theater of Operations.* Washington, DC: U.S. Government Printing Office, 1954.

Porter, Ray. *Uncensored France: An Eyewitness Account of France Under the German Occupation.* New York: Dial Press, 1942.

Pound, Omar, and Robert Spoo (Editors). *Ezra and Dorothy Pound: Letters in Captivity, 1945–1946.* London: Oxford University Press, 1999.

Rachlis, Eugene. *They Came to Kill: The Story of Eight Nazi Saboteurs in America.* New York: Random House, 1961.

Randall, Dale B. J. *Joseph Conrad and Warrington Dawson: The Record of a Friendship.* Durham, NC: Duke University Press, 1968.

Rist, Charles. *Une saison gâtée: Journal de la Guerre et de l'occupation (1939–1945).* Paris: Fayard, 1983.

Ronald, Susan. *A Dangerous Woman: American Beauty, Noted Philanthropist, Nazi Collaborator: The Life of Florence Gould*. New York: St. Martin's Press, 2018.

Rorimer, James J. *Monuments Man: The Mission to Save Vermeers, Rembrandts, and Da Vincis from the Nazis' Grasp*. New York: Rizzoli Electa, 2022.

Schellenberg, Walter. *The Labyrinth: Memoirs of Walter Schellenberg, Hitler's Chief of Counterintelligence*. New York: Da Capo Press, 2000.

Schloss, Carol Loeb. *Let the Wind Speak: Mary de Rachewiltz and Ezra Pound*. Philadelphia: University of Pennsylvania Press, 2023.

Schofield, William G. *Treason Trail*. New York: Rand McNally, 1964.

Shakespeare, Nicholas. *Priscilla: The Hidden Life of an Englishwoman in Wartime France*. New York: Harper, 2014.

Shirer, William L. *Berlin Diary: The Journal of a Foreign Correspondent, 1934–1941*. New York: Alfred A. Knopf, 1941.

Stephenson, William, et al. (Editors). *British Security Coordination: The Secret History of British Intelligence in the Americas, 1940–1945*. New York: Fromm International, 1998.

Stevenson, William. *A Man Called Intrepid: The Incredible World War II Narrative of the Hero Whose Spy Network and Secret Diplomacy Changed the Course of History*. Reprint: Guilford, CT: Lyons Press, 2000.

Stivers, William, and Donald A. Carter. *The City Becomes a Symbol: The U.S. Army in the Occupation of Berlin, 1945–1949*. Washington, DC: U.S. Government Printing Office, 2017.

Swift, Daniel. *The Bughouse: The Poetry, Politics, and Madness of Ezra Pound*. New York: Farrar, Straus and Giroux, 2017.

Tartiére, Drue, and M. R. Werner. *The House Near Paris: An American Woman's Story of Traffic in Patriots*. New York: Simon & Schuster, 1946.

Theoharis, Athan G. *The FBI: A Comprehensive Reference Guide*. Phoenix, AZ: Oryx Press, 1999.

Tromblay, Darren E. *The FBI Abroad: Bridging the Gap Between Domestic and Foreign Intelligence*. London and Boulder, CO: Lynne Rienner, 2020.

Troy, Thomas F. *Donovan and the CIA: A History of the Establishment of the Central Intelligence Agency*. Arlington, VA: University Publications of America, 1984.

———. *Wild Bill and Intrepid: Donovan, Stephenson and the Origins of CIA*. New Haven, CT: Yale University Press, 1996.

Turrou, Leon G., as told to David G. Wittels. *The Nazi Spy Conspiracy in America*. London: George G. Harrup, 1939; reprint: *Spying on America: Leon G. Turrou's The Nazi Spy Conspiracy in America*. Edited and with an introduction by Paul Rich. Washington, DC: Westphalia Press, 2013.

Winant, John G. *Letter from Grosvenor Square: An Account of a Stewardship*. Cambridge, MA: Riverside Press, 1947.

Zaloga, Steven J. *Liberation of Paris, 1944*. Oxford, UK: Osprey, 2008.

Newspaper Articles

Berkshire Eagle (Pittsfield, MA). "The Fascist Mr. Pound Relies on Democratic Justice." May 16, 1945.

Boston Globe. "Bay State Captain Arrests Girl Traitor." August 20, 1945.

Charleston News and Courier (Charleston, SC). "Warrington Dawson Dies at Versailles." September 24, 1962.

Chicago Sun. "Poet-Prisoner Pound Calls Hitler Saint." May 8, 1945.

Chicago Tribune (Paris). "Today in Society" (Dawson Recital). March 13, 1933.

Daily Express (London). "New Secret Service Link-up." April 9, 1943.

Free Press (Mankato, MT). "American Treason Suspects." May 21, 1945.

Gazette-Journal (Reno, NV) "Fallon Officer Reviews Efforts to Get Traitor." March 29, 1946.

Herald Tribune (New York). "Army Is Asked to Send Pound Back for Trial." May 30, 1945.

Los Angeles Times. "Hollywood Man First U.S. Flyer to Bomb Berlin." March 29, 1943.

News and Observer (Raleigh, NC) "Local Angle on a Traitor." May 27, 1945.

New York Times. "American Writer Wins French Academy Prize." December 24, 1928.

———. "Versailles Hails Dawson." March 20, 1932.

———. "2 U.S. Citizens Held in Austrian Jail." August 21, 1945.

———. "Warrington Dawson, 85, Dead; Former Newsman Was Author." September 27, 1962.

———. "Frederick Ayer, U.S. Aide Abroad: Author and Ex-F.B.I. Agent in Europe is Dead at 57, Declined Senate Job." January 5, 1974.

Observer-Dispatch (Utica, NY). "Ezra Pound to Face Treason Charge." May 13, 1945.

Pittsburgh Post-Gazette (Pittsburgh, PA). " 'Gertie' on Berlin Radio Is Former Local Resident." August 24, 1943.

———. "American Radio Traitors Cease Berlin Broadcasts" (in the syndicated column "The Propaganda Front"). September 9, 1944.

———. "The Barbizon School" (in the syndicated column "Elsa Maxwell's Party Line"). January 15, 1945.

———. "Stirrup Cup" (in the syndicated column "Elsa Maxwell's Party Line"). February 19, 1945.

———. "Post-Gazette Picture Identifies Berlin Gertie." July 2, 1945.

———. "Ex-Pittsburgh Girl Asks to Forget Berlin Radio." January 13, 1947.

Pittsburgh Press (Pittsburgh, PA). "Berlin's Gertie Does Not Talk Much Any More [sic]." October 17, 1943.

———. "Pittsburgh's Berlin Gertie Faces War Criminal Trial." May 20, 1945.

———. "Gertrude Hahn Home, Married and Free of 'Berlin Gertie' Charge." January 12, 1947.

Pontiac Press (Pontiac, MI). "Ezra Pound: An Unregenerate Traitor." May 16, 1945.

South Bend Tribune (South Bend, IN.). "Ex-City Writer Called Traitor." July 20, 1944.

Star Tribune (Minneapolis, MN). "Axis Sally Radio Scripts Reported Found in Berlin." March 6, 1949.

St. Louis Post-Dispatch (St. Louis, MO). "From Post-Dispatch Newsboy to World's Greatest Jockey." August 13, 1922.

———. "How Does a Traitor Get That Way?" August 8, 1943.

St. Louis Star-Times (St. Louis, MO). "Berlin Gertie Said to Be From Pittsburgh." August 23, 1943.

———. "Two American-Born Women Held by French as Collaborators." October 23, 1944.

St. Petersburg Evening Independent (St. Petersburg, FL). "Army Reporters Capture Traitor." June 20, 1945.

Washington News (Washington, DC). "Four Accused Traitors to Be Sent Here Soon." June 6, 1946.

———. "U.S. May Not Press 26 Sedition Charges, Is Hint." August 25, 1946.

Washington Post. "The Propaganda Front." February 14, 1943.

———. "Fighting Words." May 3, 1997.

Monographs

The Grapevine, official publication of the Society of Former Special Agents of the Federal Bureau of Investigation, Inc. January 1949.

Forging an Intelligence Partnership: CIA and the Origins of the BND, 1945–1949: A Documentary History, Volume I (Kevin Ruffner, ed.). Center for the Study of Intelligence, 1999.

Oral Histories

SIS Oral Histories. Society of Former Special Agents of the FBI, Heritage Oral History Program, National Law Enforcement Officers Memorial Foundation Museum. N.D.

Howard Winter. Self-recorded oral history, 1970. Courtesy of the Winter Family.

Magazine/Journal Articles

The American Weekly. "The Gould Jinx Never Sleeps." July 2, 1944.

Boghardt, Thomas. "America's Secret Vanguard: U.S. Army Intelligence Operations in Germany, 1944–1947," *Studies in Intelligence*, Vol. 57, No. 2. June 2013.

Corrigan, Robert A. "Ezra Pound and the Italian Ministry of Popular Culture," *The Journal of Popular Culture*, Vol. 4, Issue 4. March 1972.

D'Abzac-Epezy, Claude. "Armée et Secrets, 1940–1942," *Bulletin de L'Institute Pierre Renouvin*, No. 36. February 2012.

Dawson, Francis Warrington. "Hunting With Roosevelt in East Africa," *Hampton's Magazine*. November 1909.

Enderle-Ristori, Michaela. "Un Tourant Pour *L'Aktion Übersetzung?* Otto Abetz et L'Organisation des Traductions de L'Allemand," *Atlantide* (Université de Nantes), No. 8. 2018.

Flick-Steger, Carl (Charles Flicksteger). "The Adlon Bar Gang," *XXth Century Magazine* (Shanghai). 1943.

Freyeisen, Astrid. "XGRS—Shanghai Calling: Deutsche Rundfunkpropaganda in Ostasien Während des Zweiten Weltkrieg," *Rundfunk und Geschichte*. January/April 2003.

Graham, Elyse. "The P Source: How Humanities Scholars Changed Modern Spycraft," *Princeton Alumni Weekly*. December 2020.

Grandin, Thomas. "Brief Account of an Investigation of Radio in its Political Aspects and Projection for a Listening Center," *Geneva Studies* (Geneva Research Center), VIII. December 31, 1938.

———. "The Political Use of the Radio," *Geneva Studies* (Geneva Research Center), Vol. 3, No. 10. August 1939.

Hammond, Emily C. "U.S. Reporter of the Air," *The American Foreign Service Journal*, Vol. 19, No. 9. September 1942.

Höhne, Heinz. "Pullach Internal," *Der Spiegel*. February 5, 1971.

Johnson, Thomas M. "Search for the Stolen Sigaba," *Army Magazine*. February 1962.

Kagan, Jérôme. "Florence Gould: The Secrets of a Billionaire," *France-Amérique*. August 25, 2022.

Laurie, Clayton D. "Goebbels's Iowan: Frederick W. Kaltenbach and Nazi Short-Wave Radio Broadcasts to America, 1939–1945," *Annals of Iowa*. Summer, 1994.

Movie and Radio Guide. " 'Bunk' from Station Debunk." April 1942.

Province, Charles M. "Patton and His Guns," *Guns Magazine*. December 1986.

Schwab, Arnold T. "*Joseph Conrad and Warrington Dawson*, a Review." *Modern Philology*, May 1971.

Seabrook, William. "The Sad Plight of the Cinderella Countess," *The American Weekly*. December 10, 1944.

Seldon, Zachary. "Special Intelligence Service of the Federal Bureau of Investigation: Forgotten Forerunner of the Central Intelligence Agency," *International Journal of Intelligence and Counterintelligence*, Vol. 36, Issue 4. 2022.

Sheen, H. Gordon. "The Disintegration of the German Intelligence Services," *Military Review*. June 1949.

Sinclair, Thornton Chapman. "The Nazi Party Rally at Nuremburg," *The Public Opinion Quarterly*. October 1938.

Der Spiegel. "Erschießen oder erhängen?" April 5, 1998.

St. Johns, Adela Rogers. "Lt. Gen. and Mrs. George S. Patton Jr.," *Cosmopolitan*. November 1943.

Teale, Edwin. "America Listens In," *Popular Science*. June 1941.

Webb, G. Gregg. "Intelligence Liaison Between the FBI and State, 1940–1944," *Studies in Intelligence*, Vol. 49, No. 3. 2005.

Wilson, Jane. "Via Diplomatic Courier," *The American Foreign Service Journal*, Vol. 18, No. 6. June 1941.

Film/TV

Interview with Frederick Ayer. *The Merv Griffin Show*, Season 1, Episode 1. September 2, 1965.

Miscellaneous

Beer, Dr. Siegfried. *Target Central Europe: American Intelligence Efforts Regarding Nazi and Early Postwar Austria*. Working Paper 97-1. Karl-Franzens Universität, Graz, Austria, August 1997.

Dallas, William B., Major, U.S. Army. *The Role of Counterintelligence in the European Theater of Operations During World War II*. MA Thesis, U.S. Army Command and General Staff College, Fort Leavenworth, Kansas, 1993.

Hershey, Gregory C. *Over the Line: John Edward Lawler and the FBI*. MA Thesis, Virginia Commonwealth University, 2008.

Nelson, David Conley. *The Mormons in Nazi Germany: History and Memory*. PhD Dissertation, Texas A&M University, 2012.

Ruffner, Kevin Conley. *Eagle and Swastika: CIA and Nazi War Criminals and Collaborators*. Draft Working Paper, CIA History Staff, 2003.

Wenthur, Hans. "Diary, 1945." Courtesy of Wenthy Wenthur Marcy.

Index